You're Reading in the Wrong Direction!!

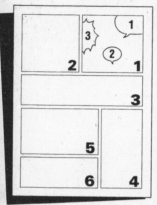

Whoops! Guess what? You're starting at the wrong end of the comic! ...It's true! In keeping with the original Japanese format, **Slam Dunk** is meant to be read from right to left, starting in the upper-right corner.

Unlike English, which is read from left to right, Japanese is read from right to left, meaning that action, sound effects and word-balloon order are completely reversed... something which can make readers unfamiliar with Japanese feel pretty backwards themselves. For this reason, manga or Japanese comics published in the U.S. in English have sometimes been published "flopped"–that is, printed in exact reverse order, as though seen from the other side of a mirror.

By flopping pages, U.S. publishers can avoid confusing readers, but the compromise is not without its downside. For one thing, a character in a flopped manga series who once wore in the original Japanese version a T-shirt emblazoned with "M A Y" (as in "the merry month of") now wears one which reads "Y A M"! Additionally, many manga creators in Japan are themselves unhappy with the process, as some feel the mirror-imaging of their art alters their original intentions.

We are proud to bring you Takehiko Inoue's **Slam Dunk** in the original unflopped format. For now, though, turn to the other side of the book and let the quest begin...!

–Editor

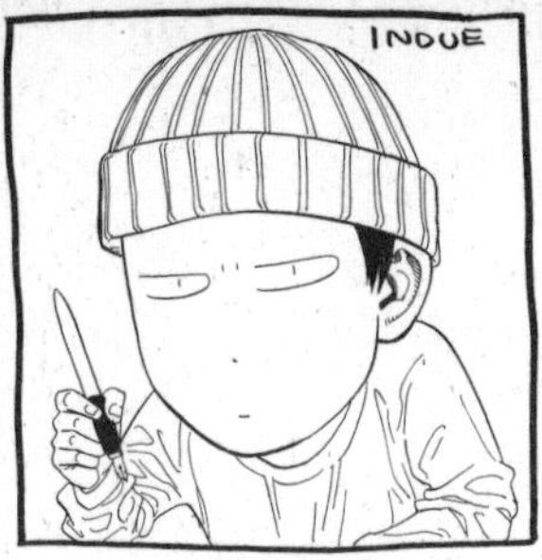
INOUE

井上雄彦

Takehiko Inoue

1. OUR PLANS TO START A RECREATIONAL BASKETBALL LEAGUE FINALLY MIGHT BECOME A REALITY.

2. WHETHER IT'S THE HOUSING LOAN ISSUE OR HIV INFECTIONS CAUSED BY UNHEATED BLOOD PRODUCTS, I FEEL THE ROOT OF JAPAN'S PROBLEMS IS THE SAME. IF WE DON'T CHANGE OUR BAD HABITS, PROBLEMS WILL ARISE IN DIFFERENT FORMS.

3. I DISCOVERED THAT I LOVE CURRY RICE. ESPECIALLY WATERY CURRY THAT SOAKS INTO THE RICE.

Takehiko Inoue's *Slam Dunk* is one of the most popular manga of all time, having sold over 100 million copies worldwide. He followed that series up with two titles lauded by critics and fans alike—*Vagabond*, a fictional account of the life of Miyamoto Musashi, and *Real*, a manga about wheelchair basketball.

SLAM DUNK
Vol. 28: Two Years

SHONEN JUMP Manga Edition

STORY AND ART BY TAKEHIKO INOUE

English Adaptation/Stan!
Translation/Joe Yamazaki
Touch-up Art & Lettering/James Gaubatz
Cover & Graphic Design/Matt Hinrichs
Editor/Mike Montesa

© 1990 - 2013 Takehiko Inoue and I.T. Planning, Inc.
Originally published in Japan in 1995 by Shueisha
Inc., Tokyo. English translation rights arranged with
I.T. Planning, Inc. All rights reserved.

The SLAM DUNK U.S. trademark is used with
permission from NBA Properties, Inc.

Some scenes have been modified from the original
Japanese edition.

The stories, characters and incidents mentioned in this
publication are entirely fictional.

Printed in Canada

Published by VIZ Media, LLC
P.O. Box 77010
San Francisco, CA 94107

10 9 8 7 6 5 4 3 2 1
First printing, June 2013

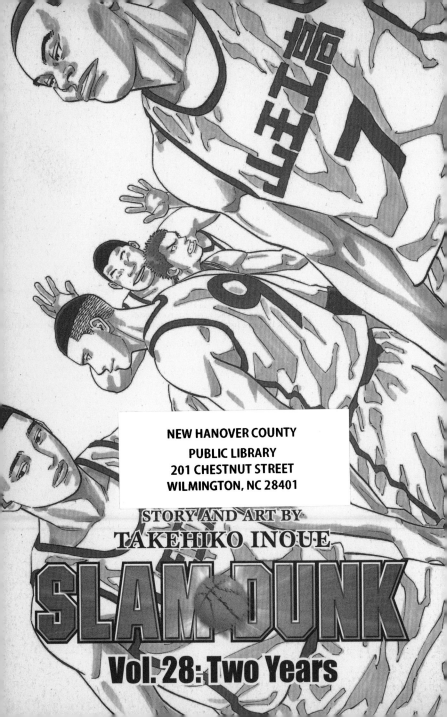

STORY AND ART BY
TAKEHIKO INOUE

SLAM DUNK

Vol. 28: Two Years

Character Introduction

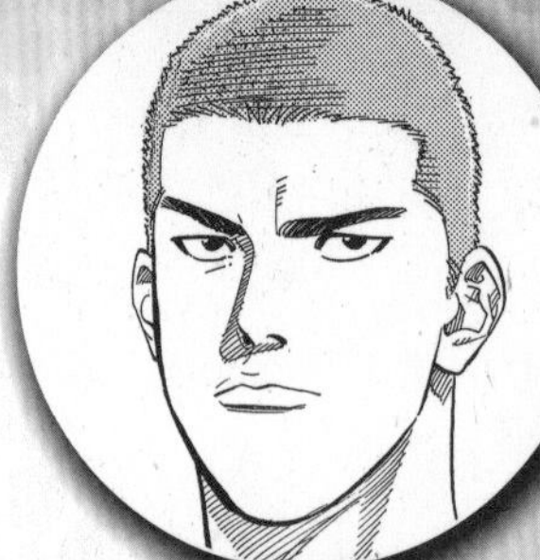

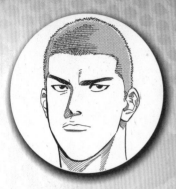

Hanamichi Sakuragi
A first-year at Shohoku High School, Sakuragi is in love with Haruko Akagi.

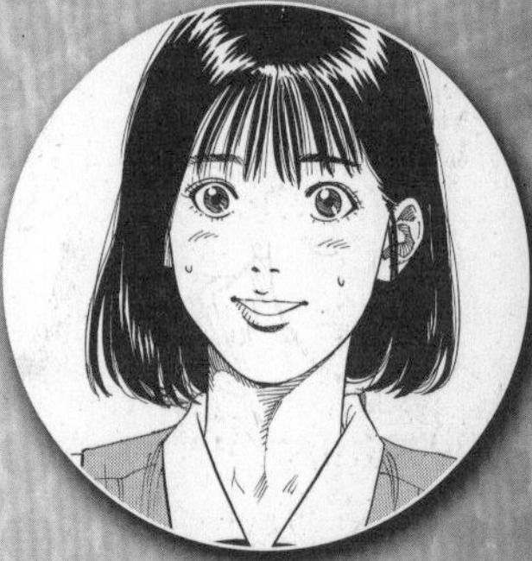

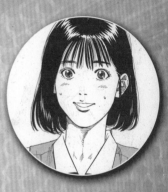

Haruko Akagi
Also a first-year at Shohoku, Takenori Akagi's little sister has a crush on Kaede Rukawa.

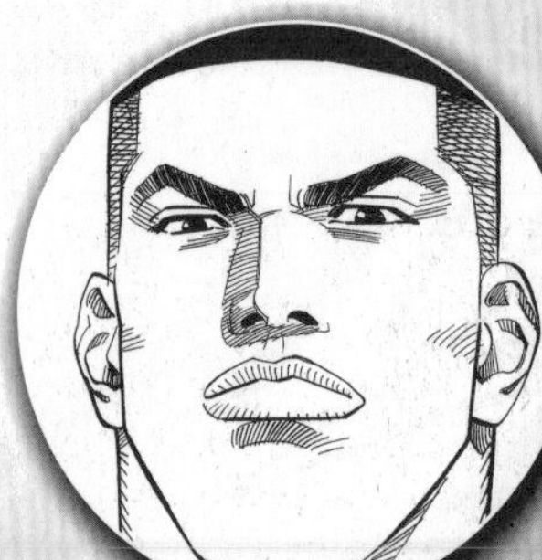

Takenori Akagi
A third-year and the basketball team's captain, Akagi has an intense passion for his sport.

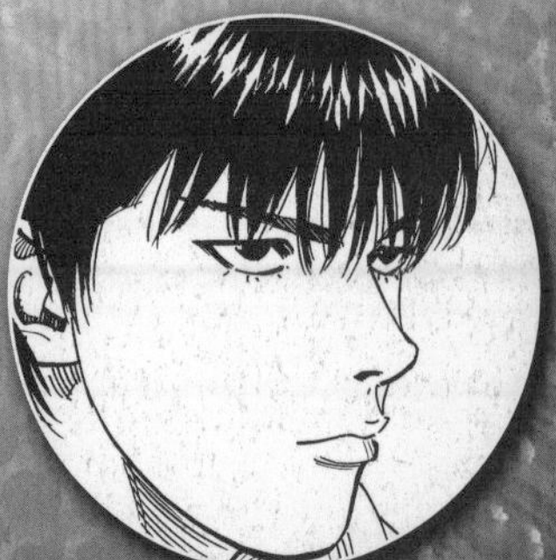

Kaede Rukawa
The object of Haruko's affection (and that of many of Shohoku's female students!), this first-year has been a star player since junior high.

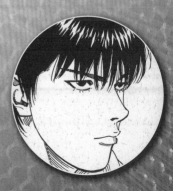

Sawakita

Fukatsu

Kawata

Ryota Miyagi
A problem child with
a thing for Ayako.

Ayako
Basketball Team
Manager

Hisashi Mitsui
An MVP during
junior high.

Our Story Thus Far

Hanamichi Sakuragi is rejected by close to 50 girls during his three years in junior high. He joins the basketball team to be closer to Haruko Akagi, but his frustration mounts when all he does is practice day after day.

Shohoku advances through the Prefectural Tournament and earns a spot in the Nationals.

Shohoku makes it to the second round to face Sannoh Kogyo, last year's national champions and considered by most to be the best team in the country.

Shohoku gets on a roll and finishes the first half with a two-point lead over Sannoh. However, Sannoh quickly turns things around in the second half and builds a seemingly insurmountable twenty-point lead.

Vol. 28:
Two Years

Table of Contents

O.R.

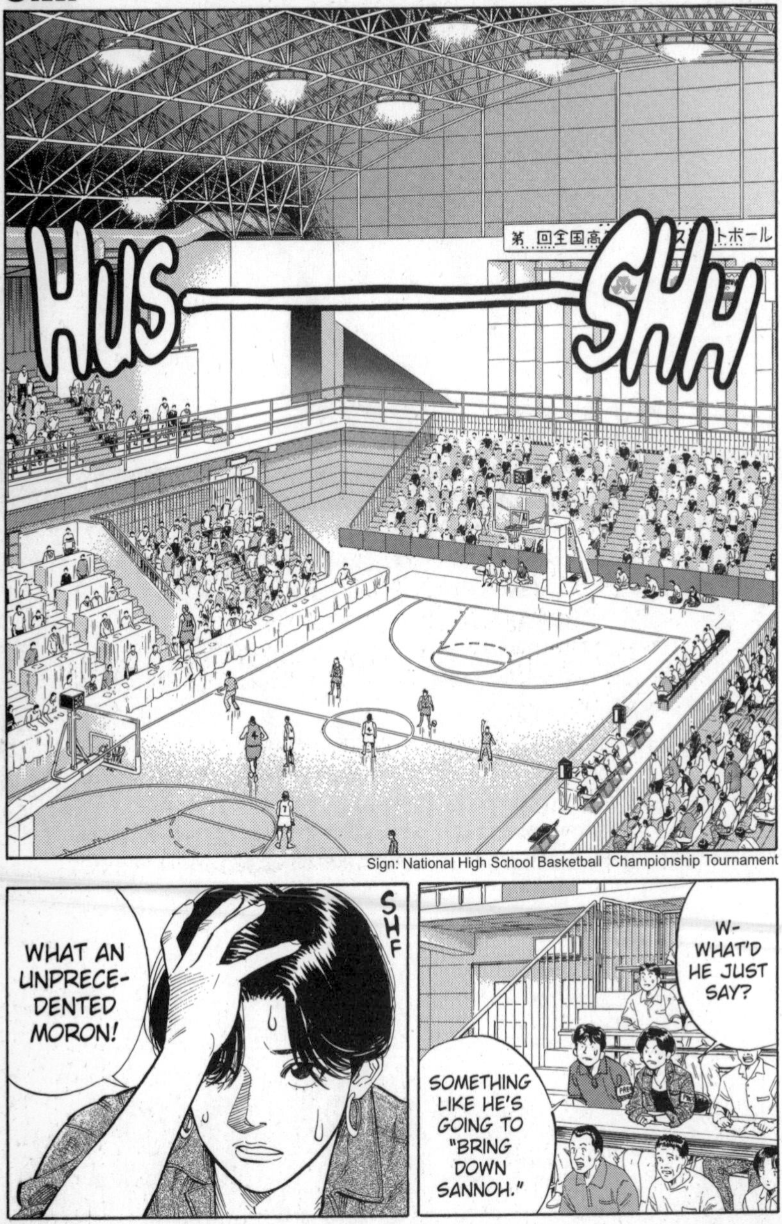
HUSSHH
W-WHAT'D HE JUST SAY?
SOMETHING LIKE HE'S GOING TO "BRING DOWN SANNOH."
SHF
WHAT AN UNPRECEDENTED MORON!
Sign: National High School Basketball Championship Tournament

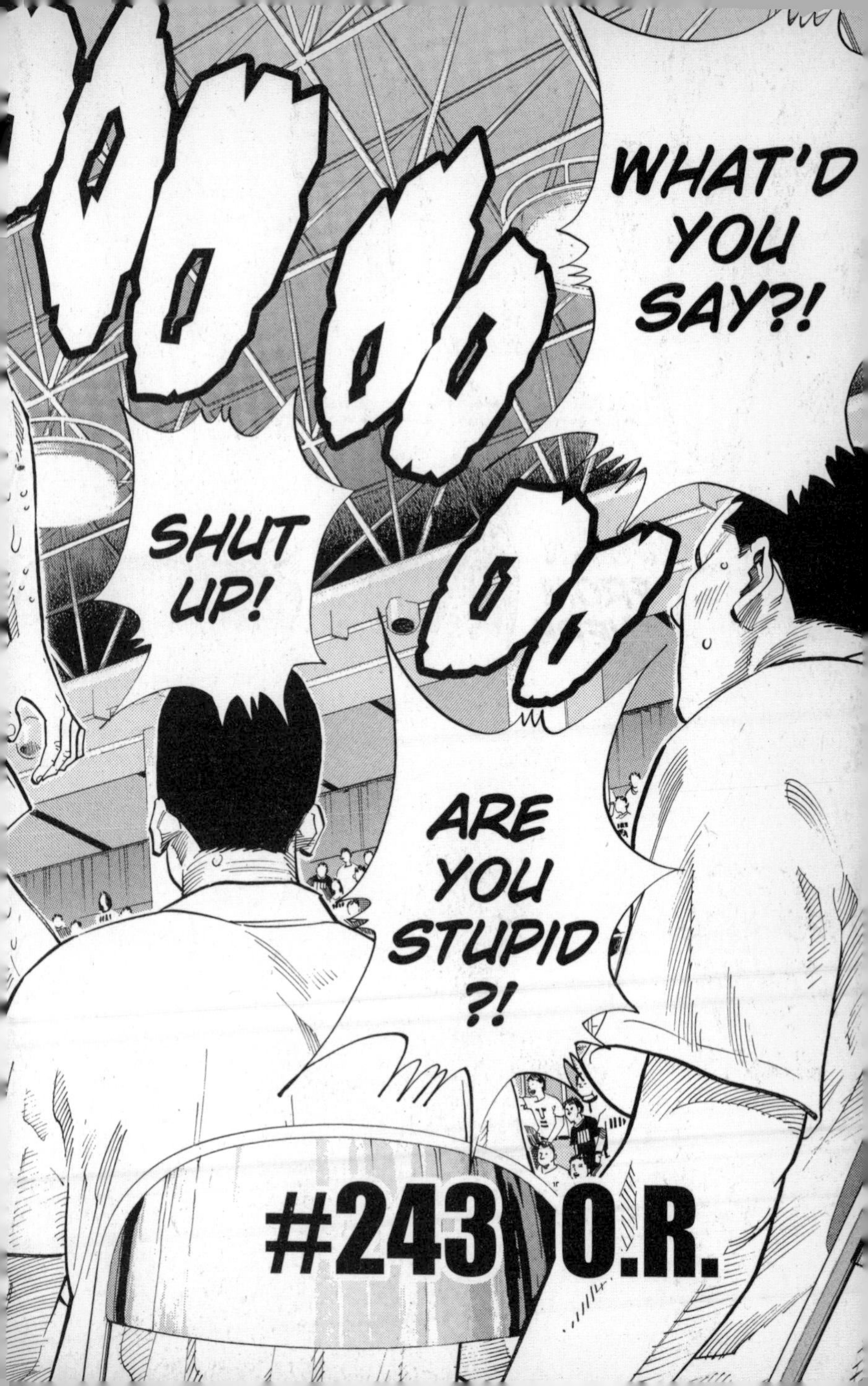
WHAT'D YOU SAY?!
SHUT UP!
ARE YOU STUPID ?!

#243 O.R.

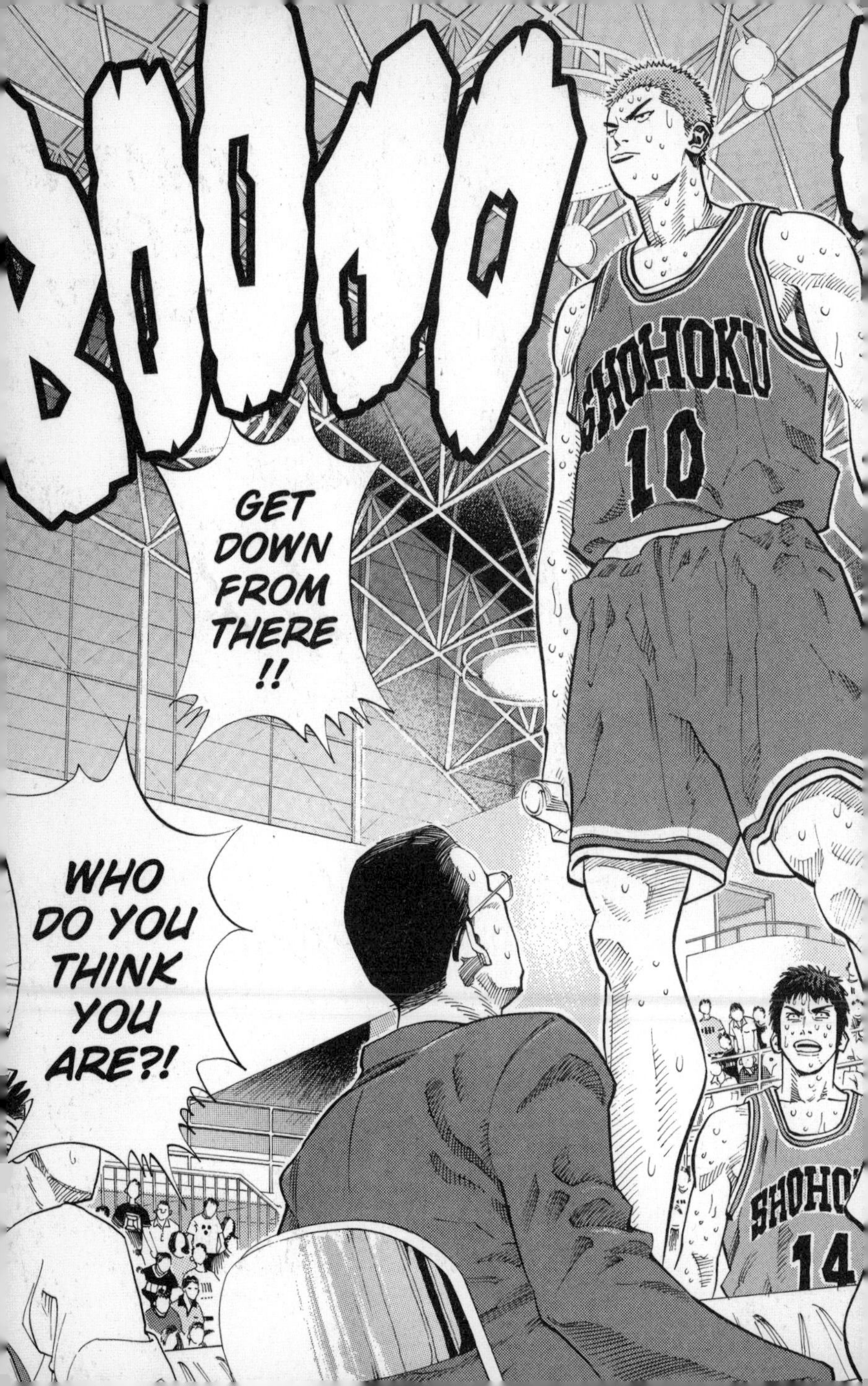
GET DOWN FROM THERE!!
WHO DO YOU THINK YOU ARE?!
SHOHOKU
10

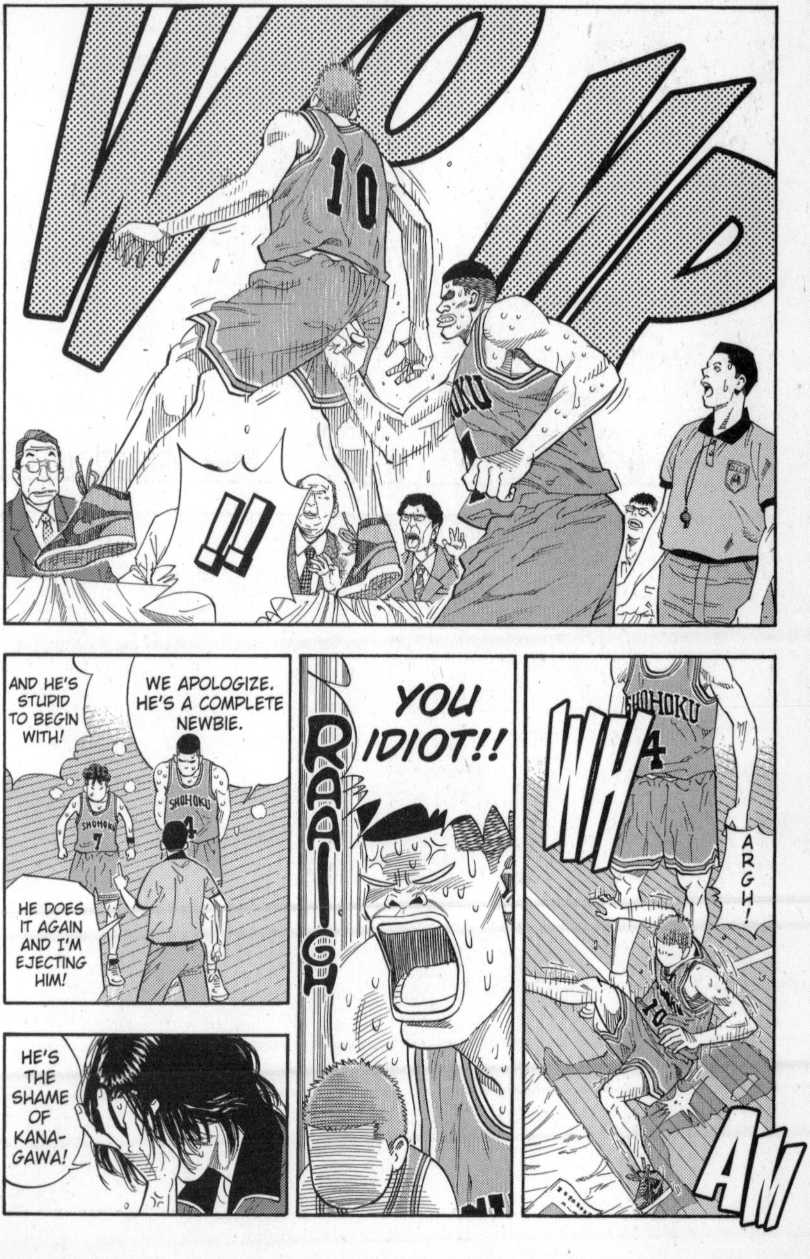
WOMP
!!
WH
AM
ARGH!
YOU IDIOT!!
RAAIGH
WE APOLOGIZE. HE'S A COMPLETE NEWBIE.
AND HE'S STUPID TO BEGIN WITH!
HE DOES IT AGAIN AND I'M EJECTING HIM!
HE'S THE SHAME OF KANA-GAWA!

READ THIS WAY

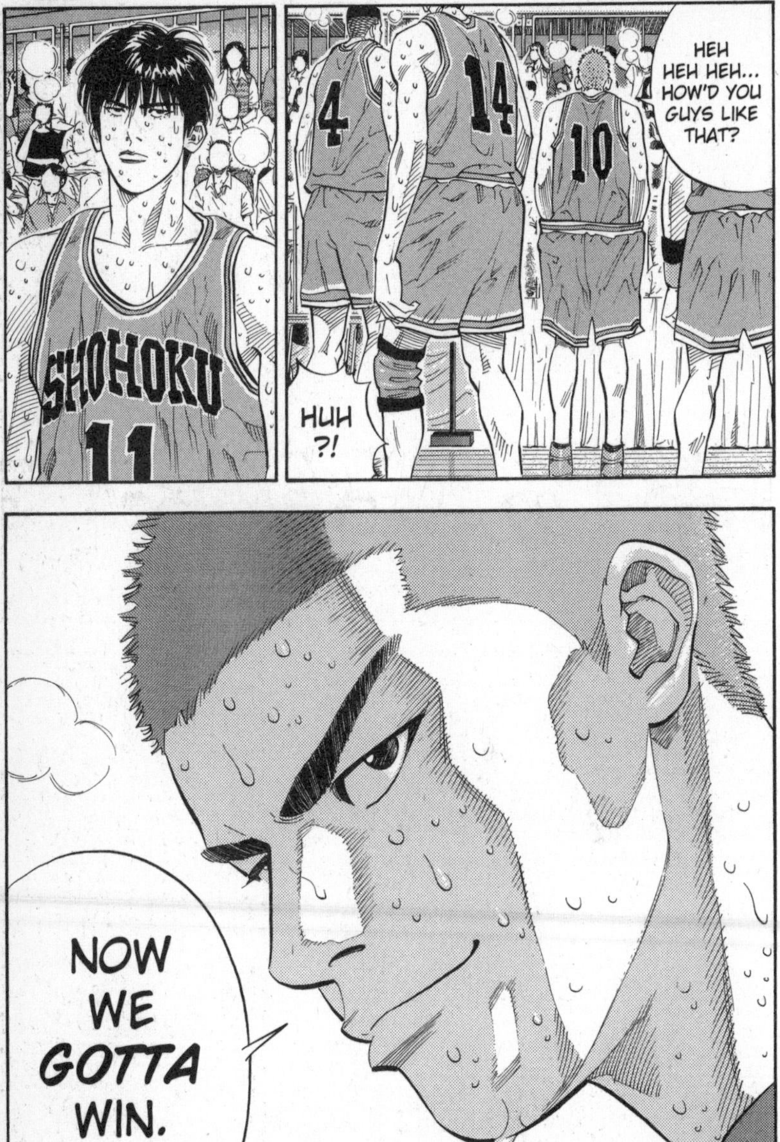
HEH HEH HEH... HOW'D YOU GUYS LIKE THAT?
HUH ?!
SHOHOKU 11
NOW WE *GOTTA* WIN.

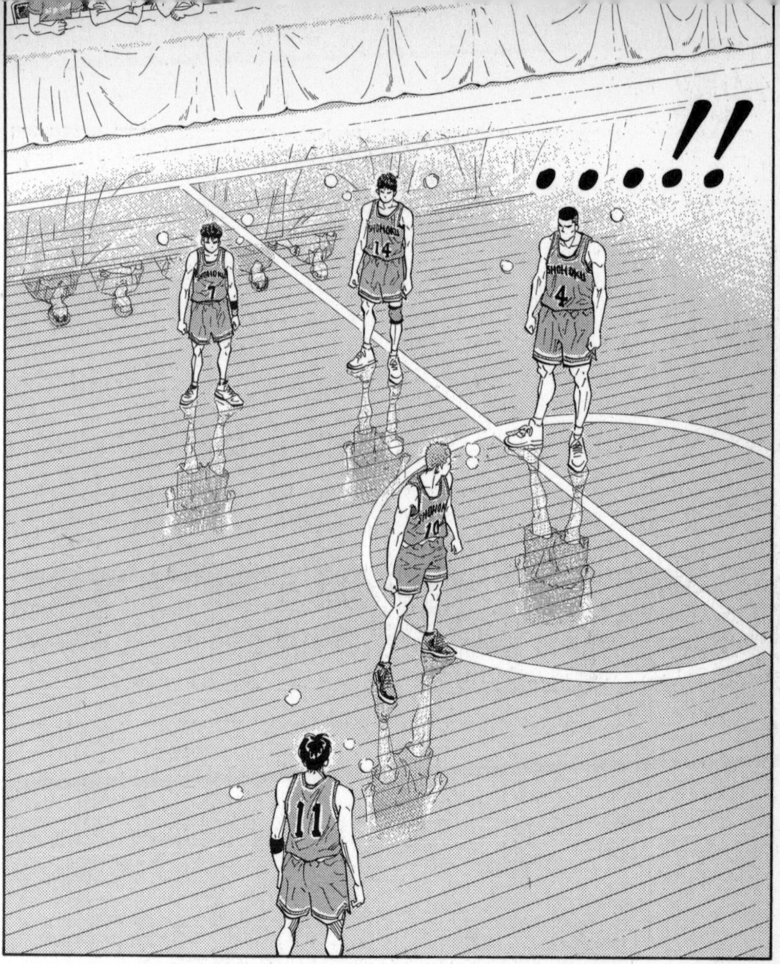
....!!

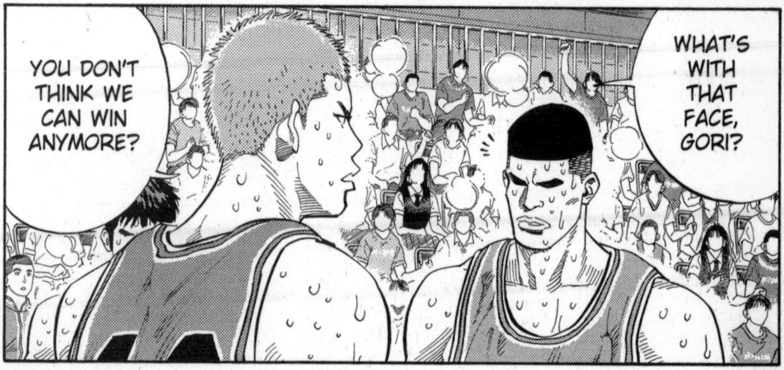
WHAT'S WITH THAT FACE, GORI?
YOU DON'T THINK WE CAN WIN ANYMORE?

READ THIS WAY

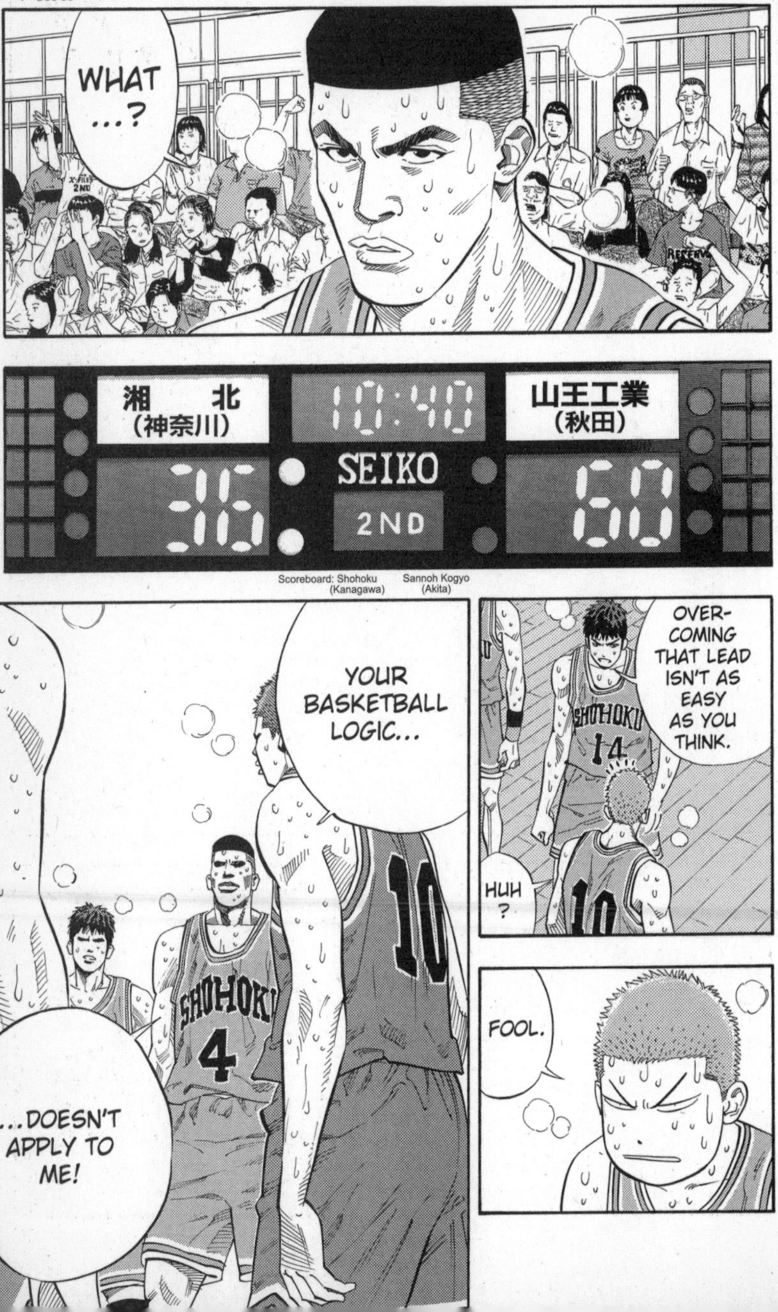
WHAT ...?
湘北
(神奈川)
10:40
山王工業
(秋田)
SEIKO
36
2ND
60
OVER-COMING THAT LEAD ISN'T AS EASY AS YOU THINK.
HUH?
FOOL.
YOUR BASKETBALL LOGIC...
...DOESN'T APPLY TO ME!

Scoreboard: Shohoku (Kanagawa) Sannoh Kogyo (Akita)

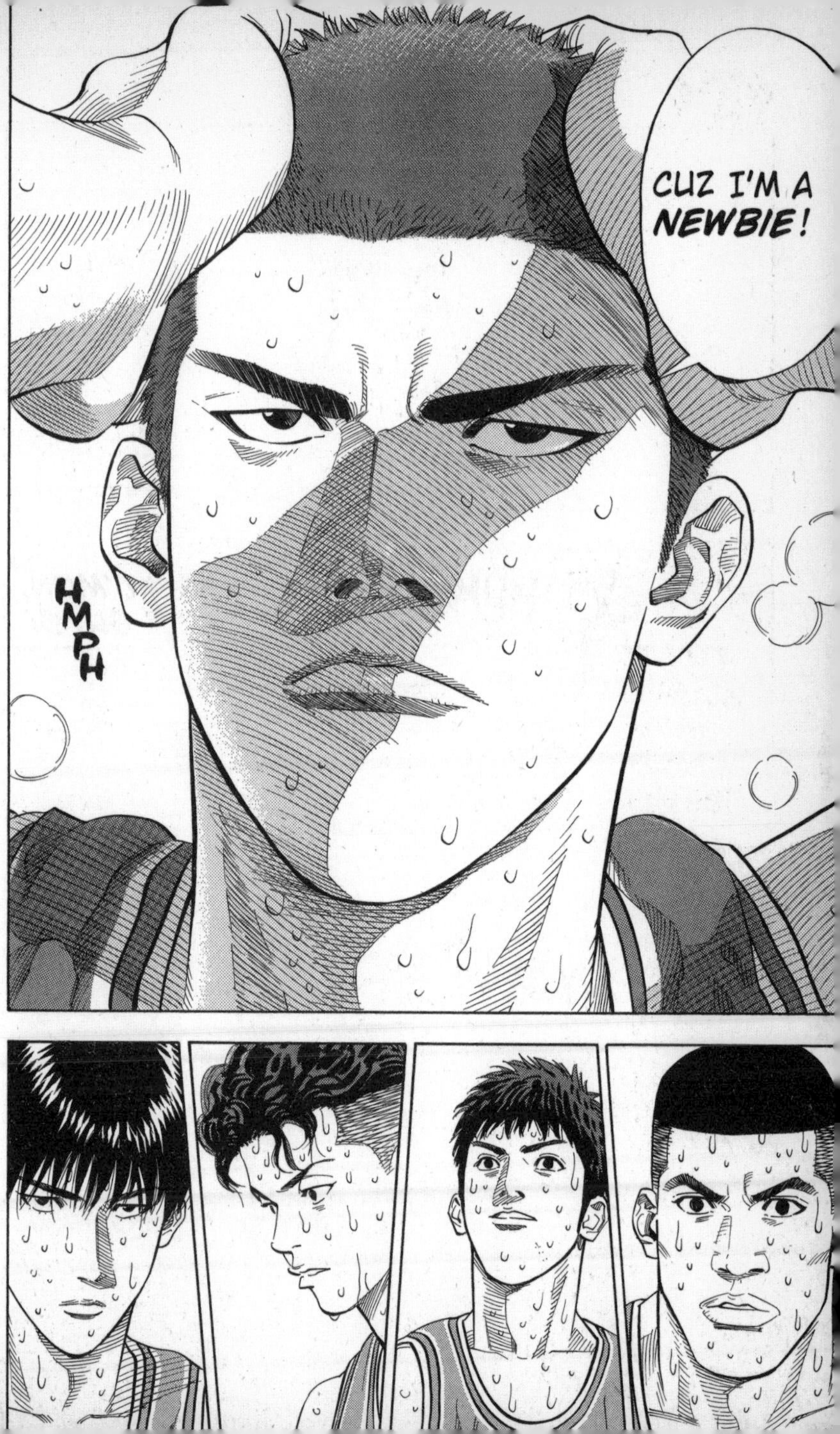
CUZ I'M A NEWBIE!
HMPH

READ THIS WAY

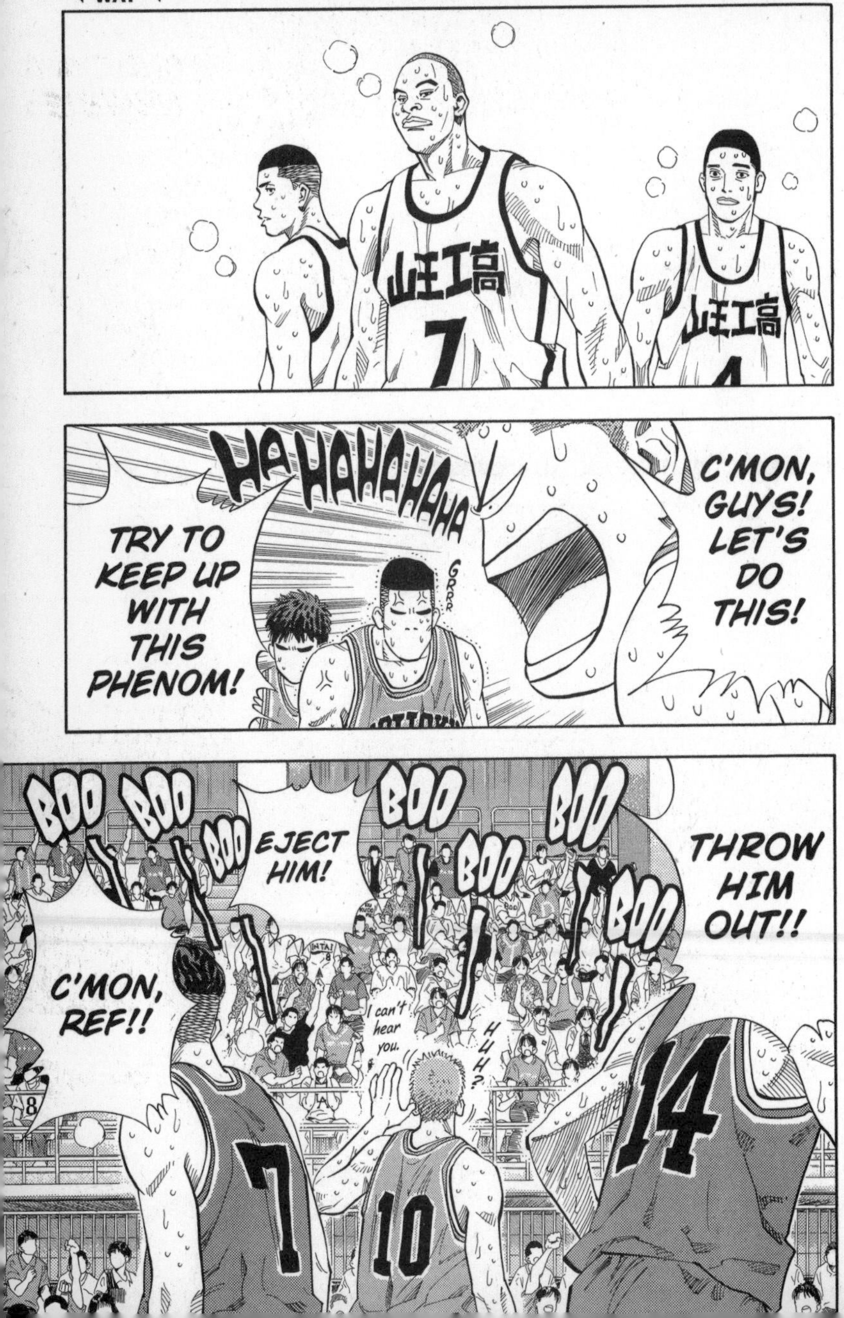
山王工高
7
山王工高
4
C'MON, GUYS! LET'S DO THIS!
HAHAHAHAHA
GRRR
TRY TO KEEP UP WITH THIS PHENOM!
THROW HIM OUT!!
BOO
BOO
BOO
BOO
EJECT HIM!
BOO
BOO
BOO
C'MON, REF!!
HUH?
I can't hear you.
14
10
7

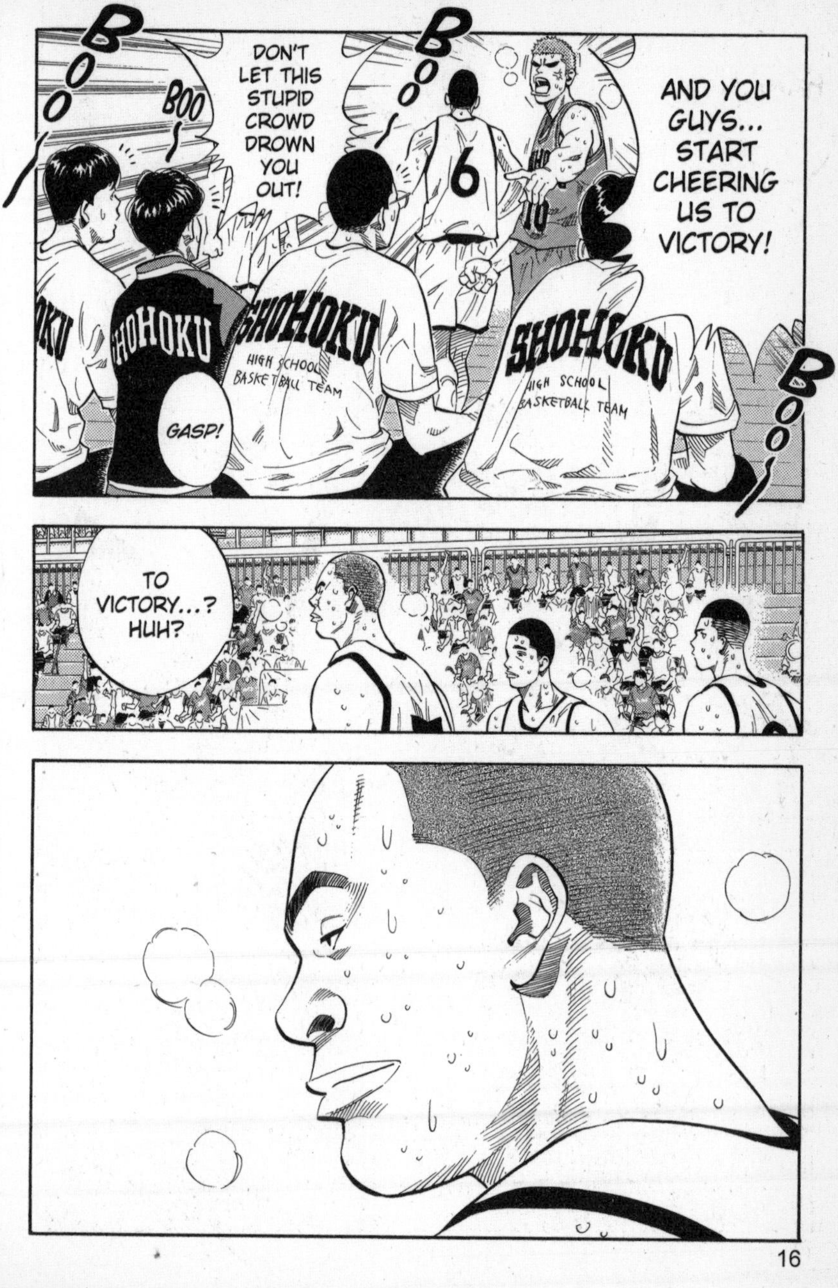
BOOO
AND YOU GUYS... START CHEERING US TO VICTORY!
BOOO
DON'T LET THIS STUPID CROWD DROWN YOU OUT!
BOO
BOOO
SHOHOKU HIGH SCHOOL BASKETBALL TEAM
SHOHOKU HIGH SCHOOL BASKETBALL TEAM
SHOHOKU
GASP!
TO VICTORY...? HUH?

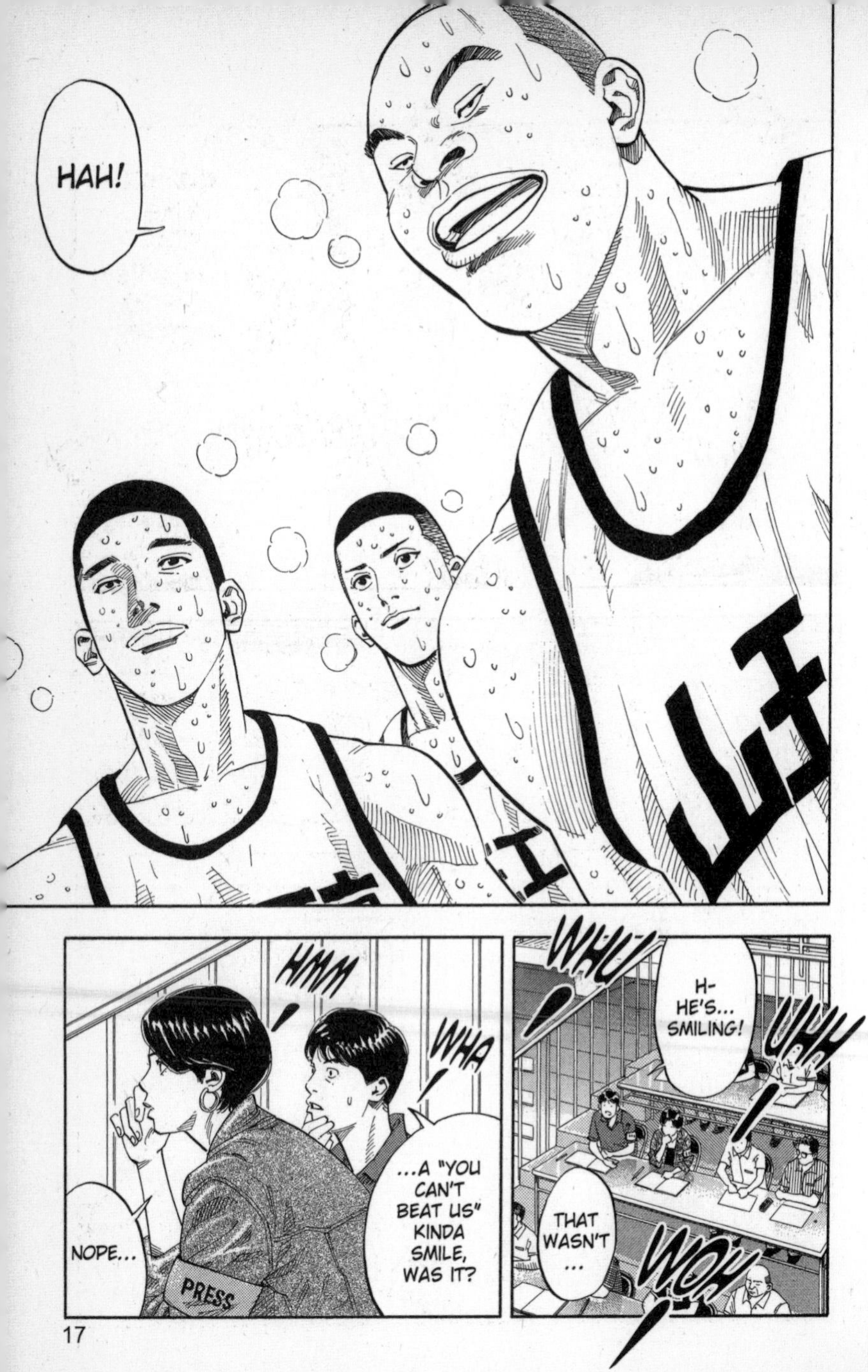
HAH!
WHU!
H- HE'S... SMILING!
UHH!
THAT WASN'T ...
WOH!
HMM!
WHA!
...A "YOU CAN'T BEAT US" KINDA SMILE, WAS IT?
NOPE...
PRESS

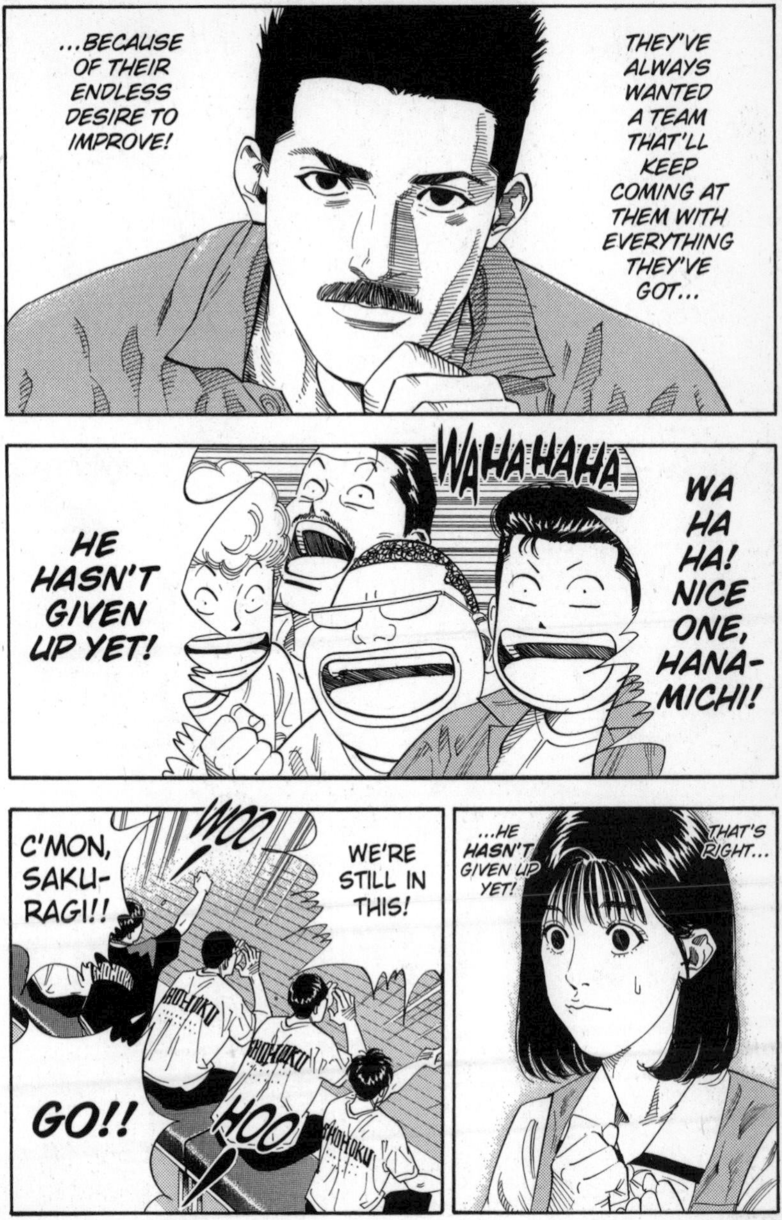
THEY'VE ALWAYS WANTED A TEAM THAT'LL KEEP COMING AT THEM WITH EVERYTHING THEY'VE GOT...
...BECAUSE OF THEIR ENDLESS DESIRE TO IMPROVE!
WAHAHAHA
WA HA HA! NICE ONE, HANA-MICHI!
HE HASN'T GIVEN UP YET!
THAT'S RIGHT...
...HE HASN'T GIVEN UP YET!
WOO
WE'RE STILL IN THIS!
C'MON, SAKU-RAGI!!
HOO
GO!!

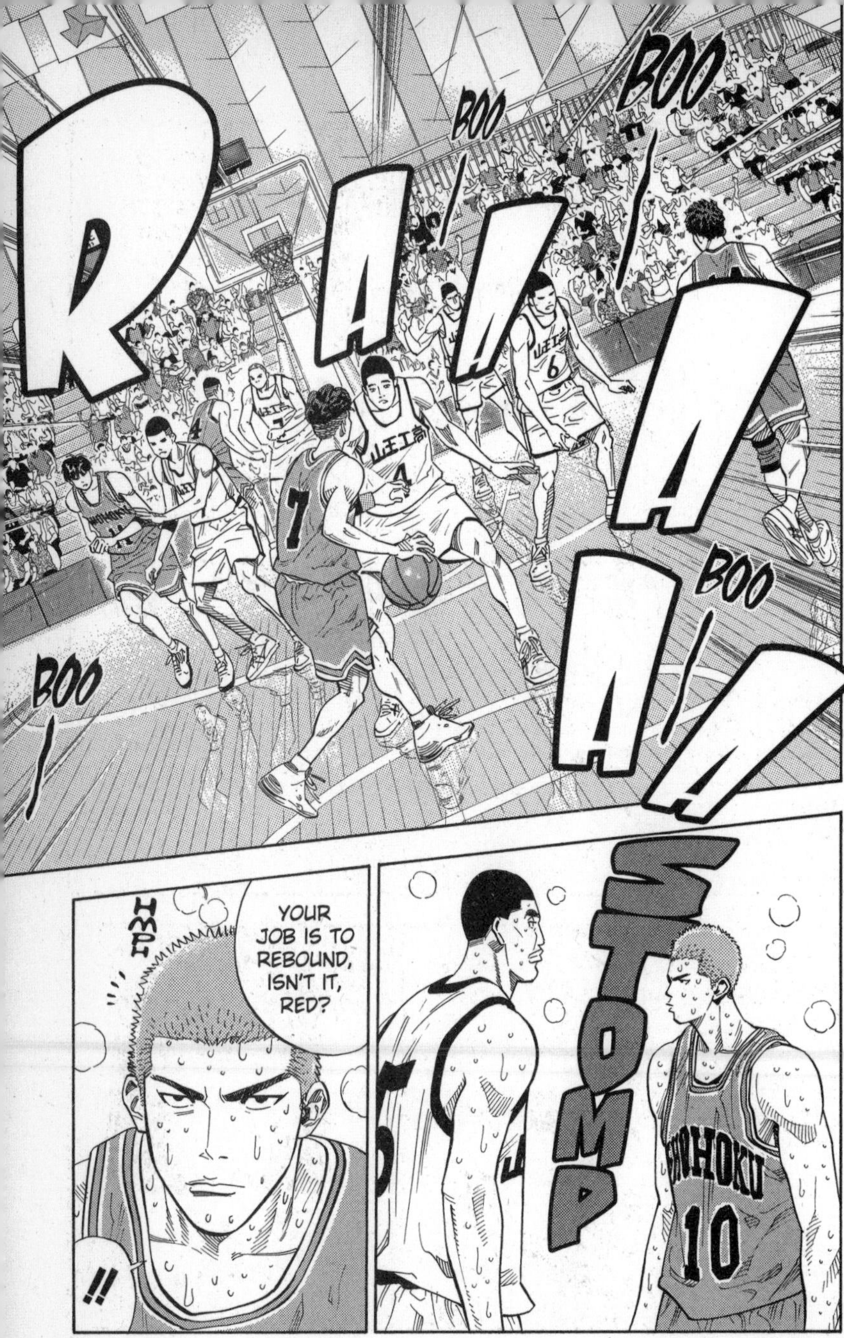
RAAAAA!!
BOO
BOO
BOO
BOO
STOMP
YOUR JOB IS TO REBOUND, ISN'T IT, RED?
HMP!
!!

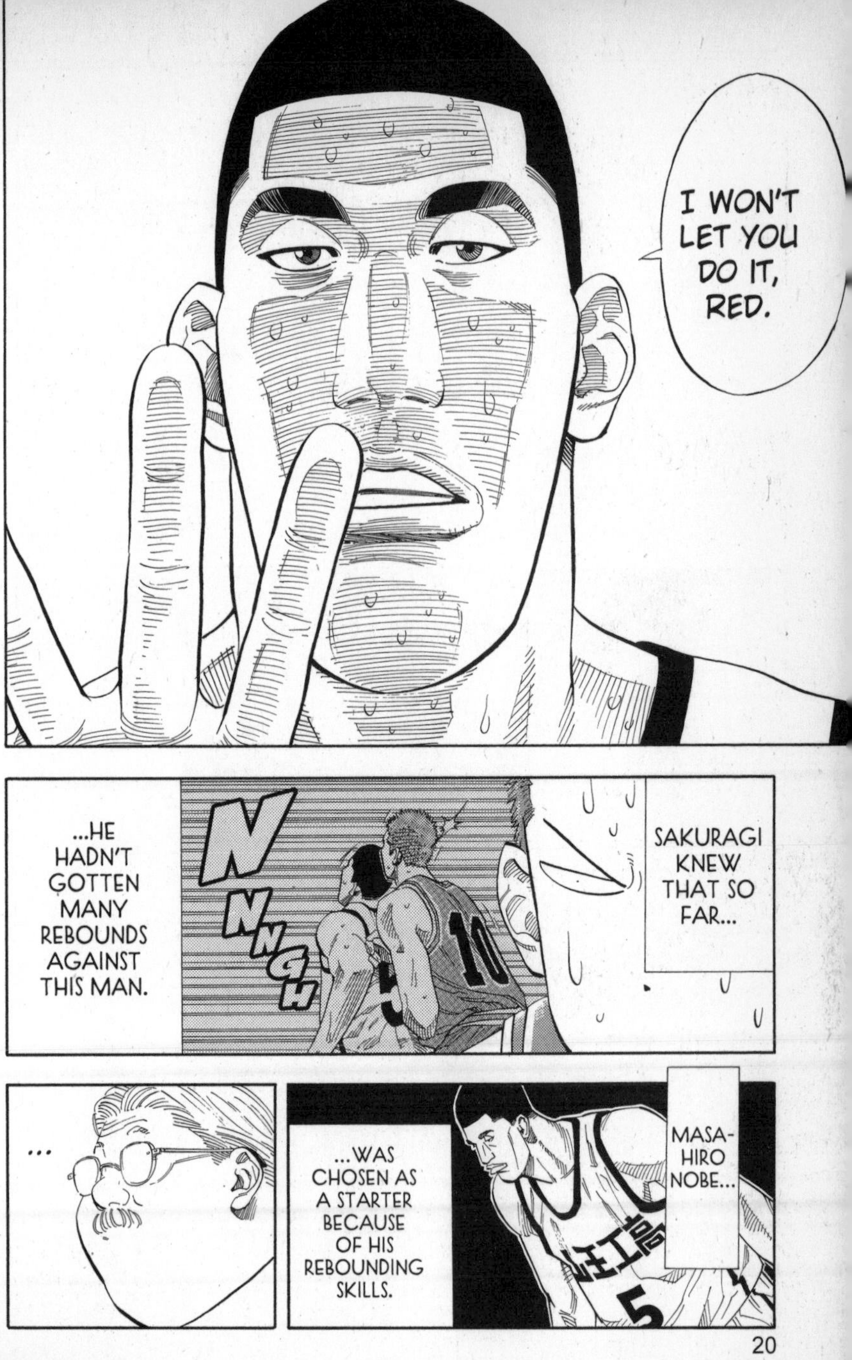
I WON'T LET YOU DO IT, RED.
SAKURAGI KNEW THAT SO FAR...
NNNGH
...HE HADN'T GOTTEN MANY REBOUNDS AGAINST THIS MAN.
MASA-HIRO NOBE...
...WAS CHOSEN AS A STARTER BECAUSE OF HIS REBOUNDING SKILLS.
...

READ THIS WAY

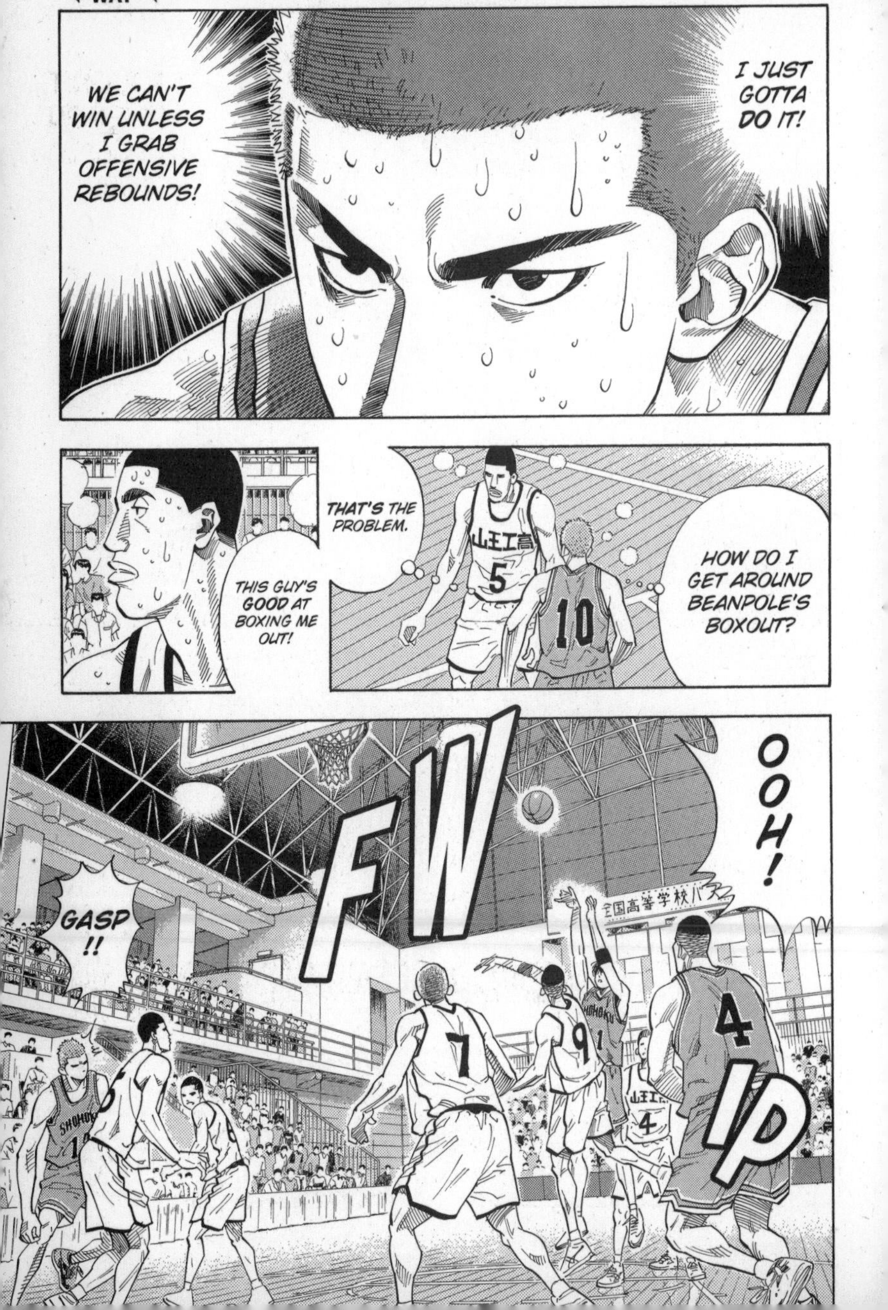

I JUST GOTTA DO IT!
WE CAN'T WIN UNLESS I GRAB OFFENSIVE REBOUNDS!
HOW DO I GET AROUND BEANPOLE'S BOXOUT?
THAT'S THE PROBLEM.
THIS GUY'S GOOD AT BOXING ME OUT!
OOOH!
FWIP
全国高等学校バス
GASP!!

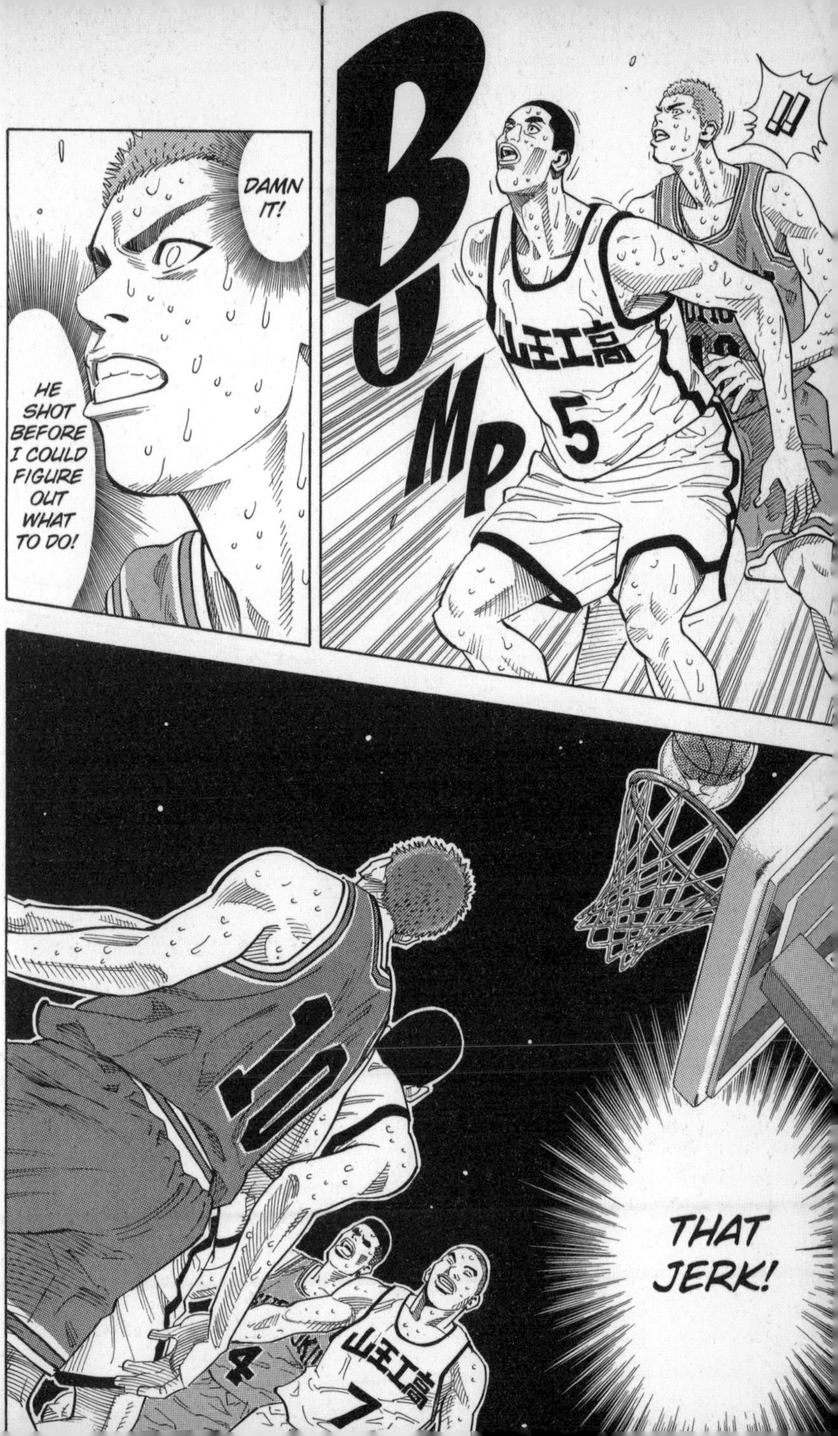
BUMP
!!
DAMN IT!
HE SHOT BEFORE I COULD FIGURE OUT WHAT TO DO!
THAT JERK!

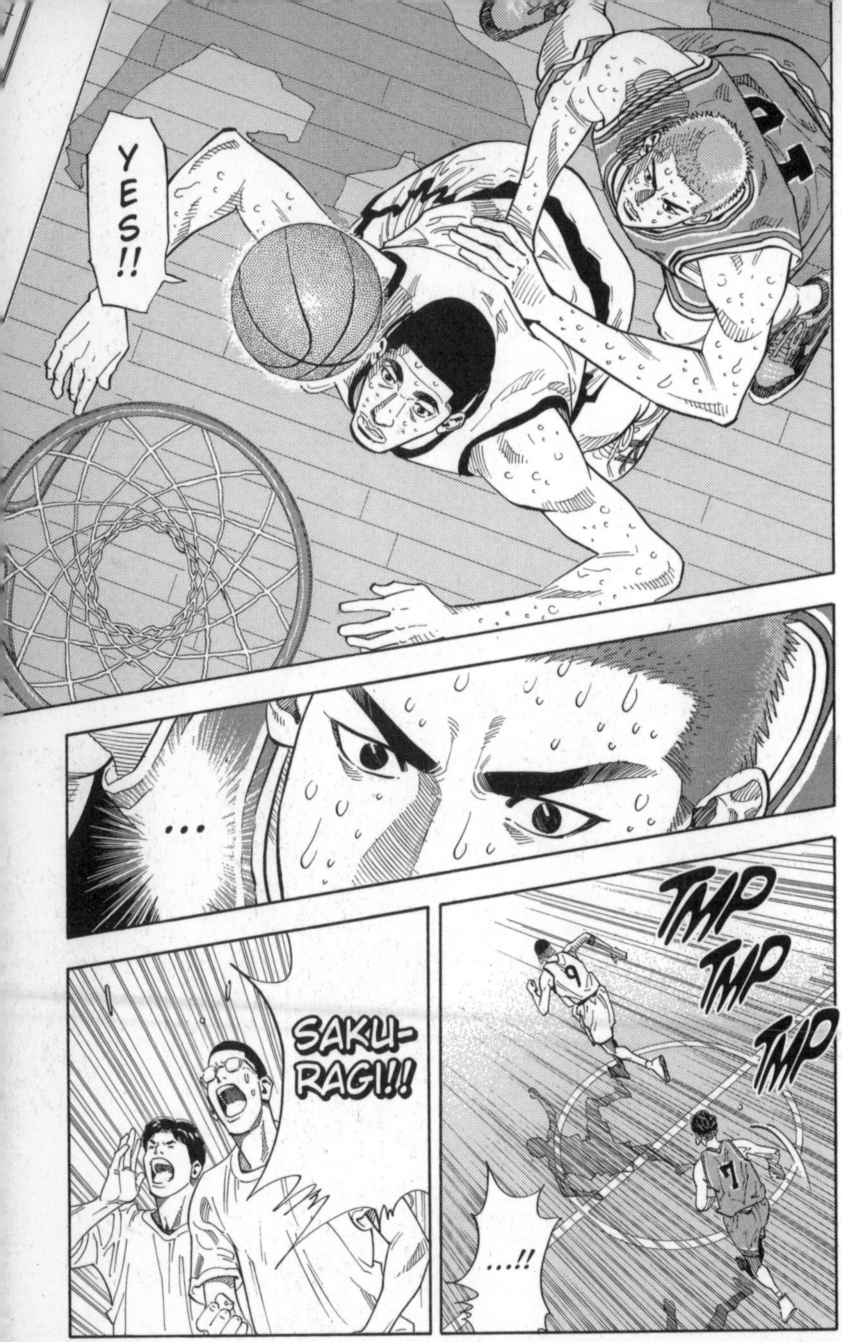
YES!!
...
TMP TMP TMP
...!!
SAKU-RAGI!!

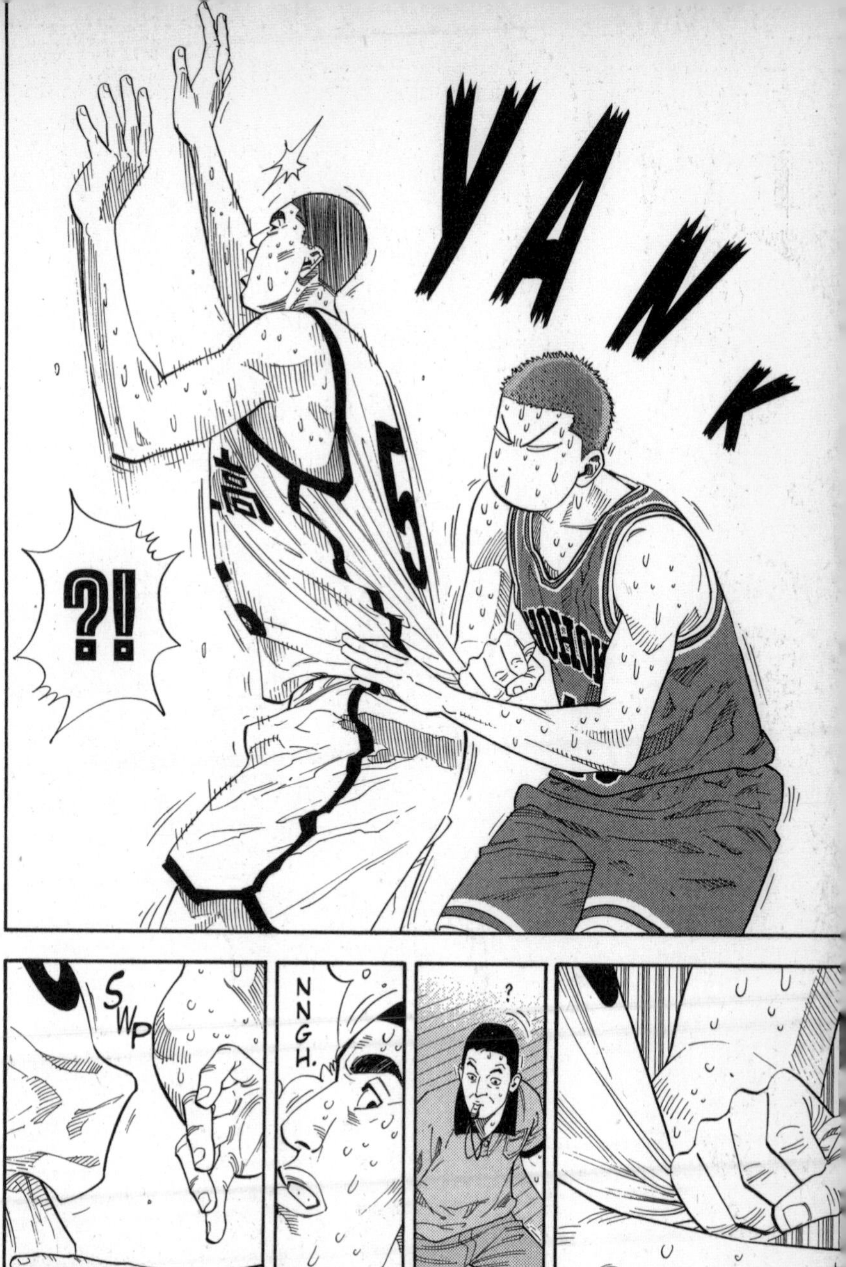
YANK
?!
?
NNGH.
SWP

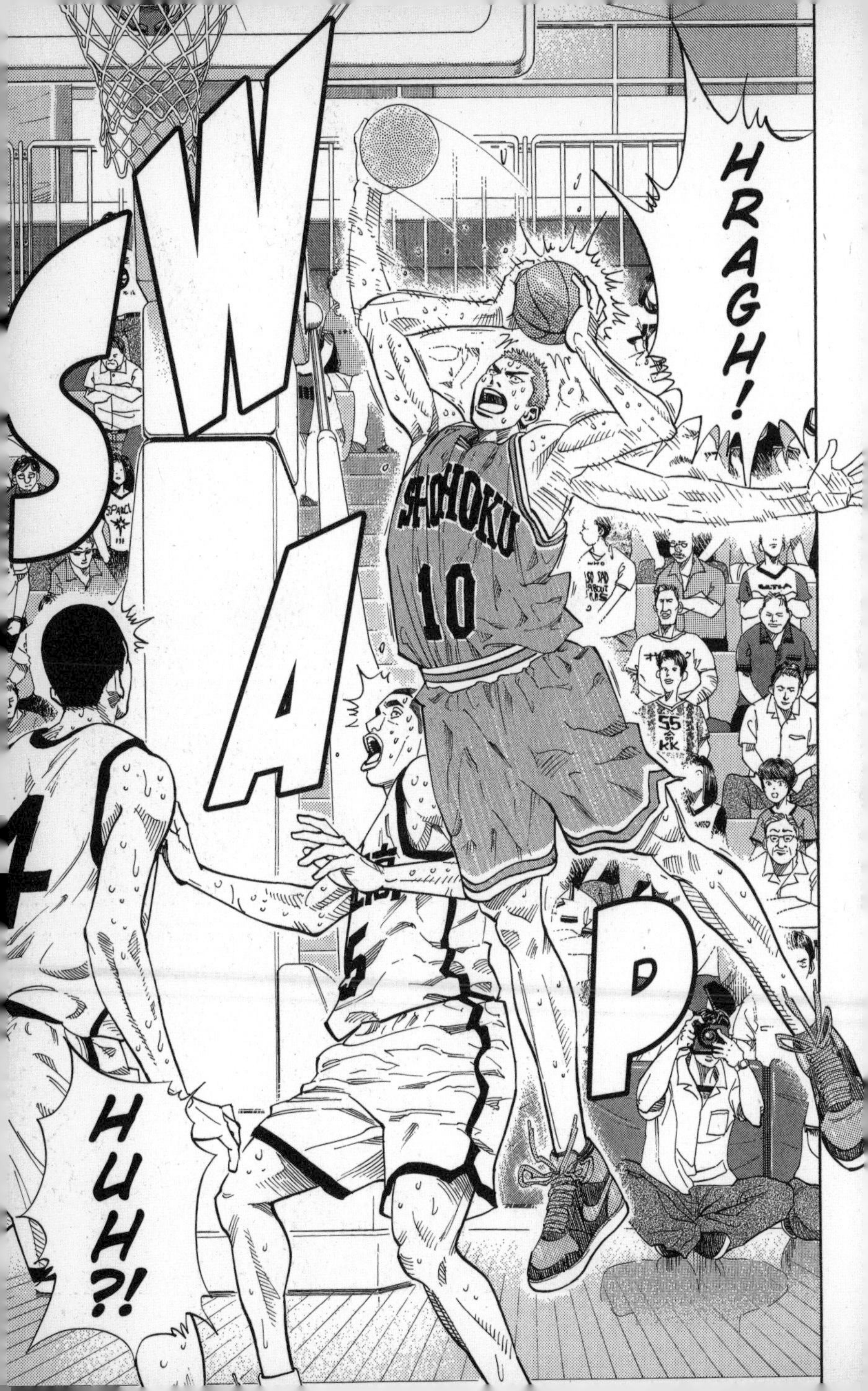
HRAGH!
SWAP
SHOHOKU
10
HUH?!

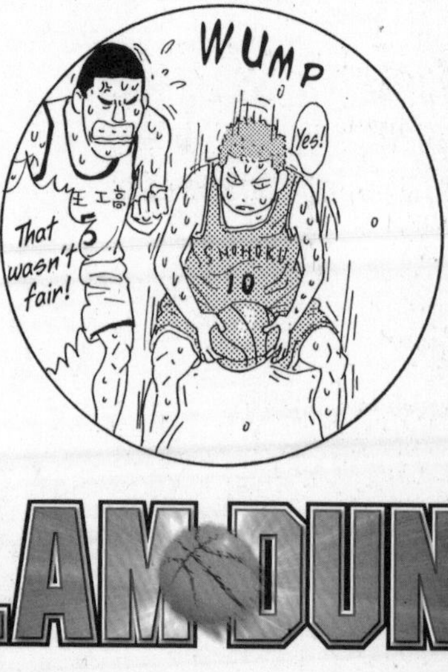
WUMP
Yes!
That wasn't fair!

SLAM DUNK

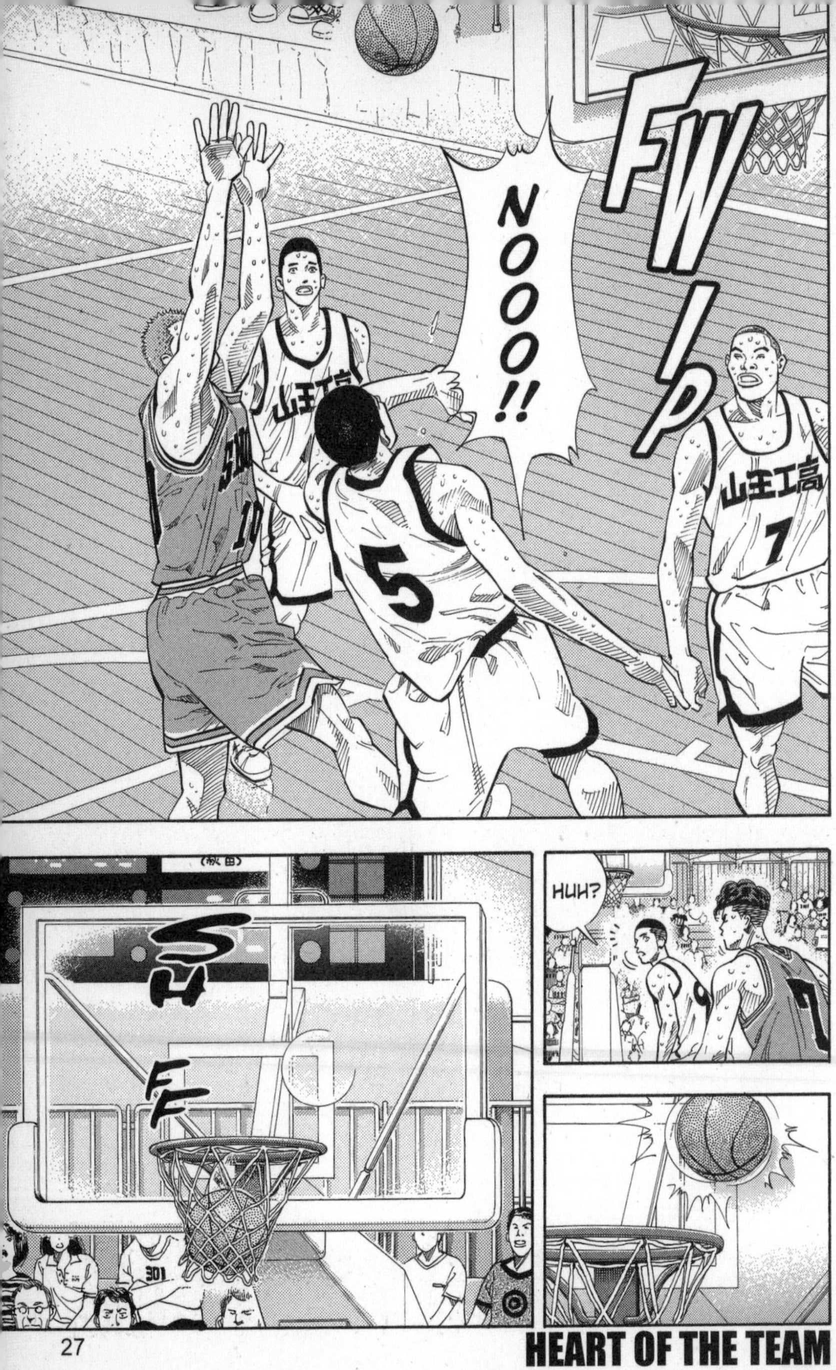
FWIP
NOOOO!!
HUH?
SHFF

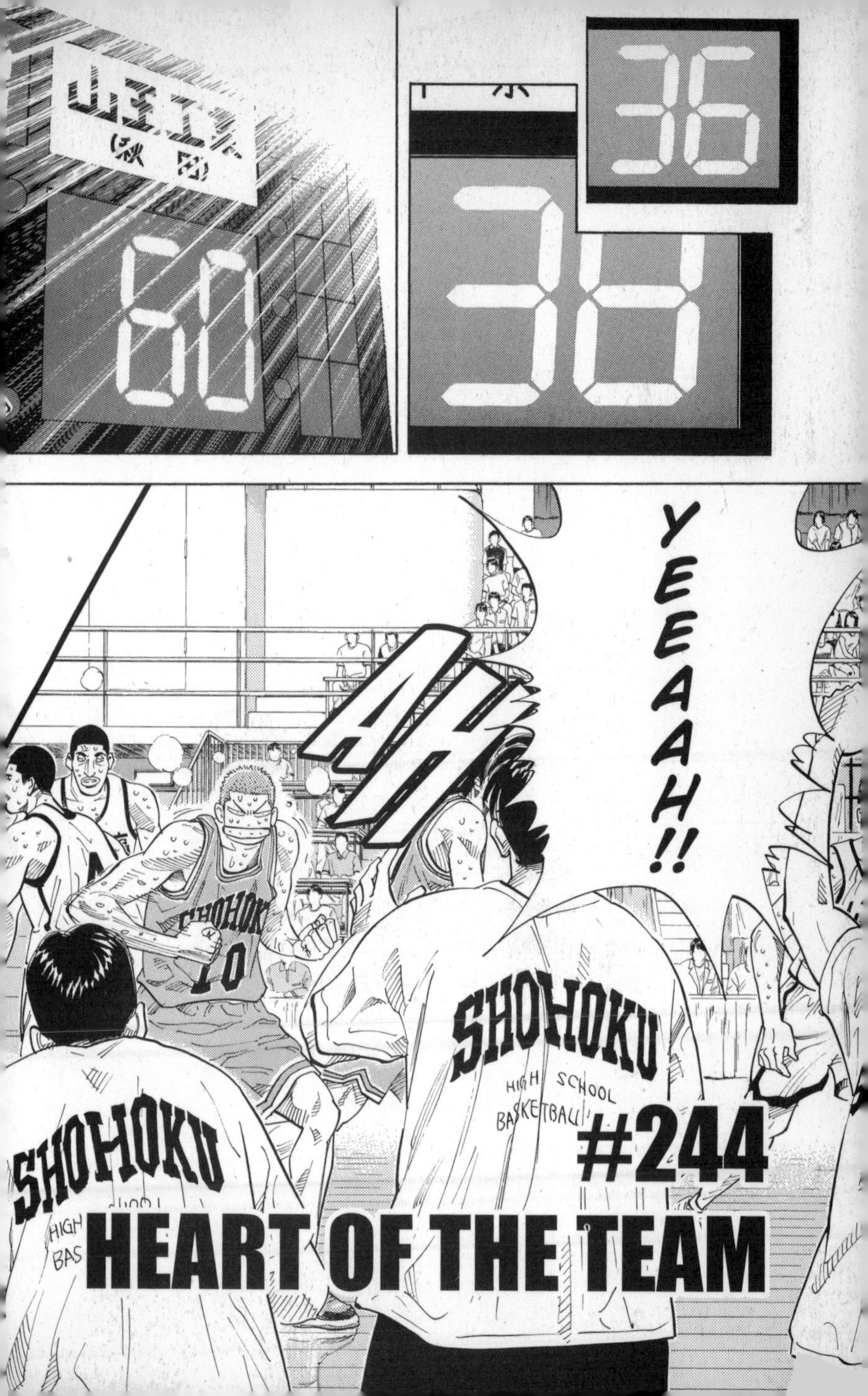
36
60
36
YEEAAH!!
AH
SHOHOKU
10
SHOHOKU
HIGH SCHOOL
BASKETBALL
SHOHOKU

#244 HEART OF THE TEAM

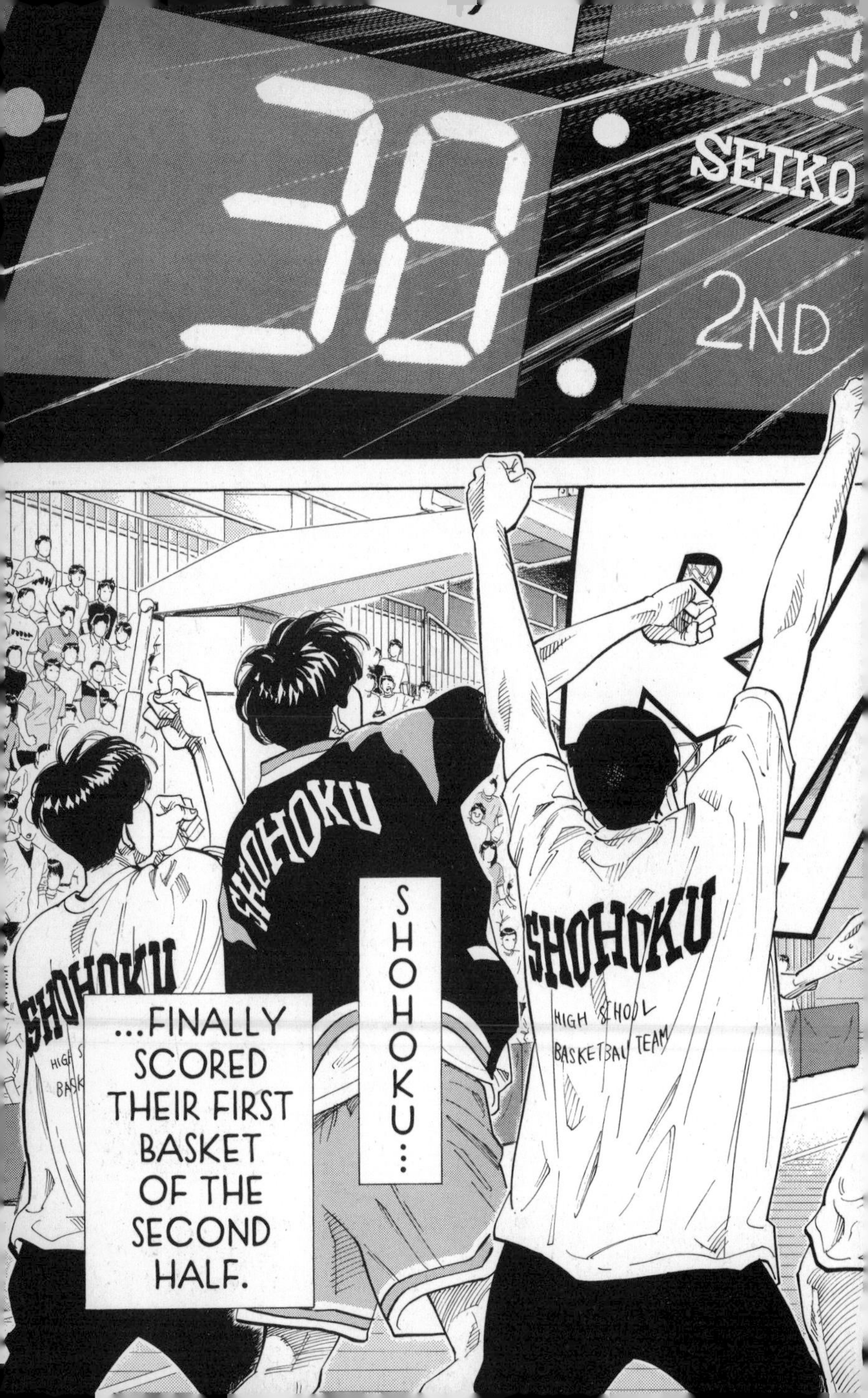
SEIKO
2ND
SHOHOKU...
...FINALLY SCORED THEIR FIRST BASKET OF THE SECOND HALF.

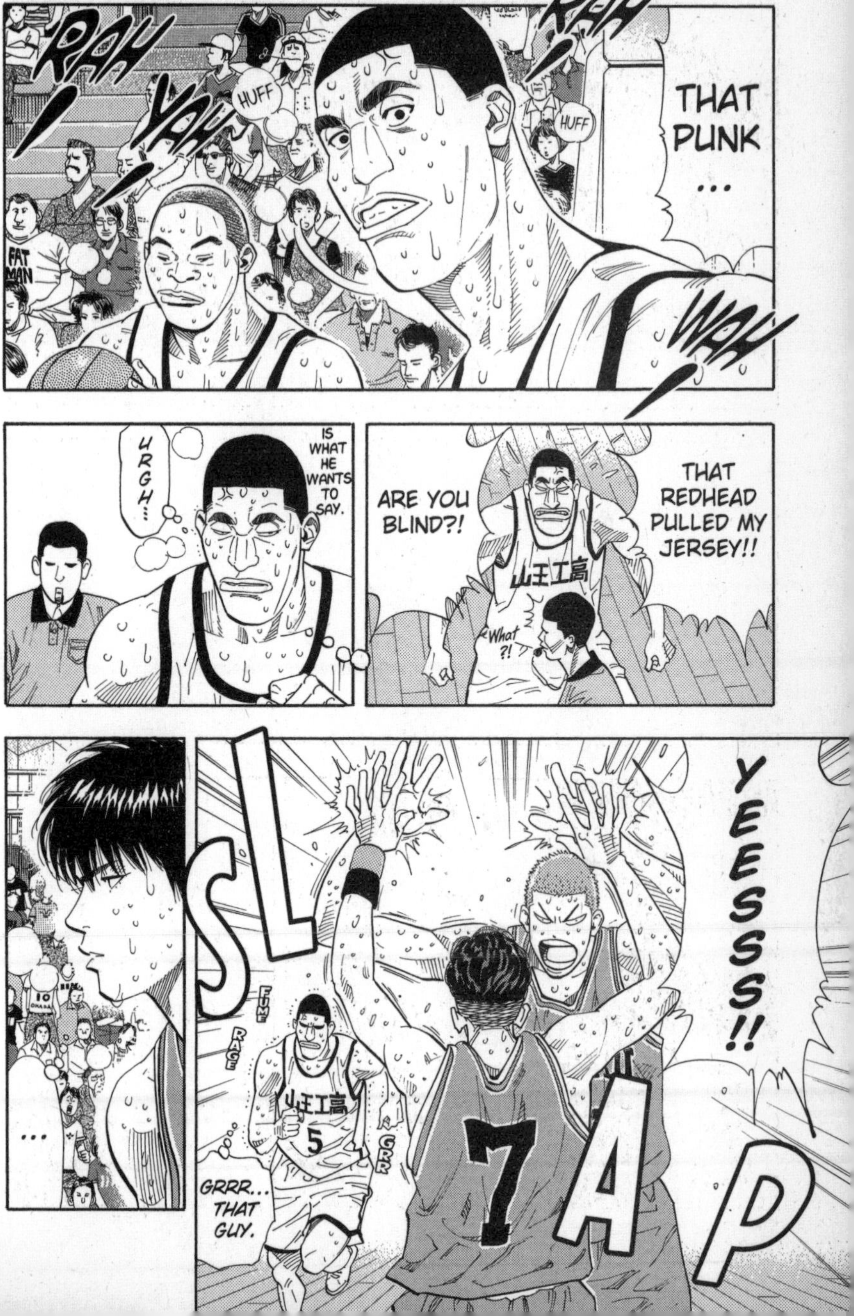
RAH!
THAT PUNK...
HUFF
WAH!
HUFF
YAH!
RAH!
FAT MAN
THAT REDHEAD PULLED MY JERSEY!!
ARE YOU BLIND?!
What?!
IS WHAT HE WANTS TO SAY.
URGH...
YEESSSS!!
SLAP
GRR
FUME
RAGE
GRRR... THAT GUY.
...

READ THIS WAY

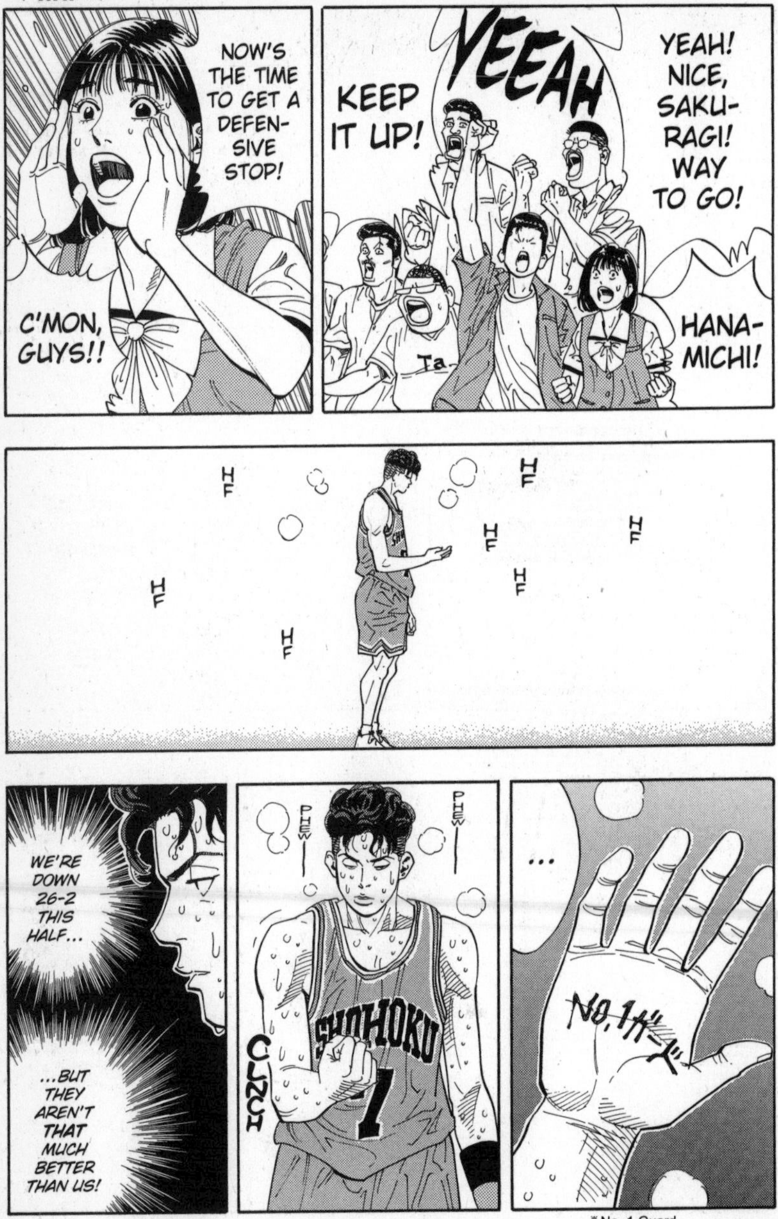
YEAH! NICE, SAKU-RAGI! WAY TO GO!
YEEAH
KEEP IT UP!
HANA-MICHI!
NOW'S THE TIME TO GET A DEFEN-SIVE STOP!
C'MON, GUYS!!
HF
HF
HF
HF
HF
HF
HF
...
No.1ガード
PHEW
PHEW
CLINCH
WE'RE DOWN 26-2 THIS HALF...
...BUT THEY AREN'T THAT MUCH BETTER THAN US!

※ No. 1 Guard

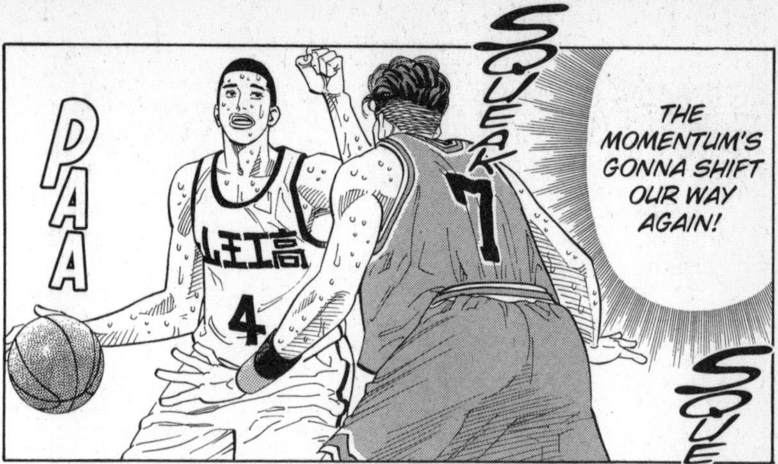
THE MOMENTUM'S GONNA SHIFT OUR WAY AGAIN!
SQUEAK
SQUEAK
PAA

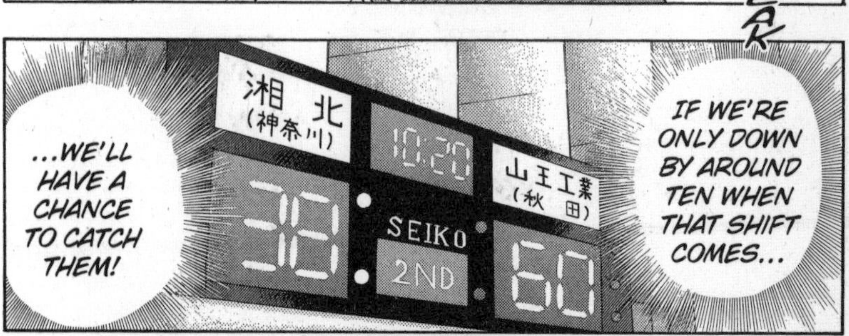
IF WE'RE ONLY DOWN BY AROUND TEN WHEN THAT SHIFT COMES...
...WE'LL HAVE A CHANCE TO CATCH THEM!
湘北
(神奈川)
10:20
山王工業
(秋田)
38
SEIKO
2ND
60

Scoreboard: Shohoku (Kanagawa) Sannoh Kogyo (Akita)

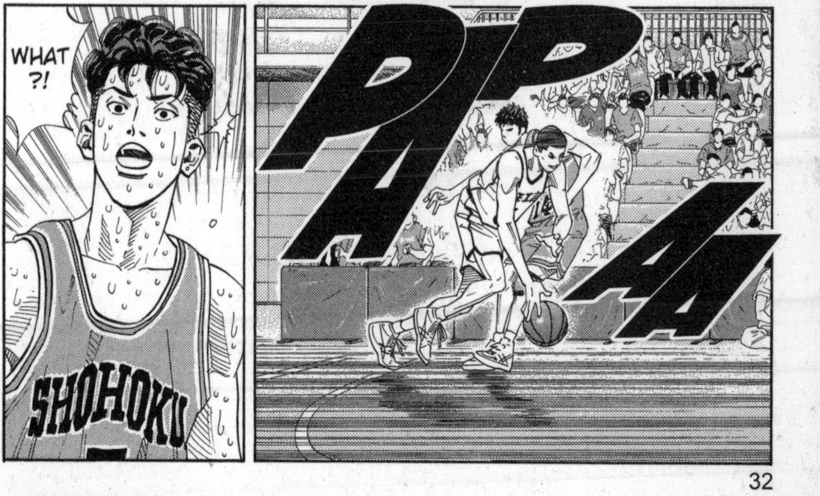
PAAA
WHAT?!
SHOHOKU

READ THIS WAY

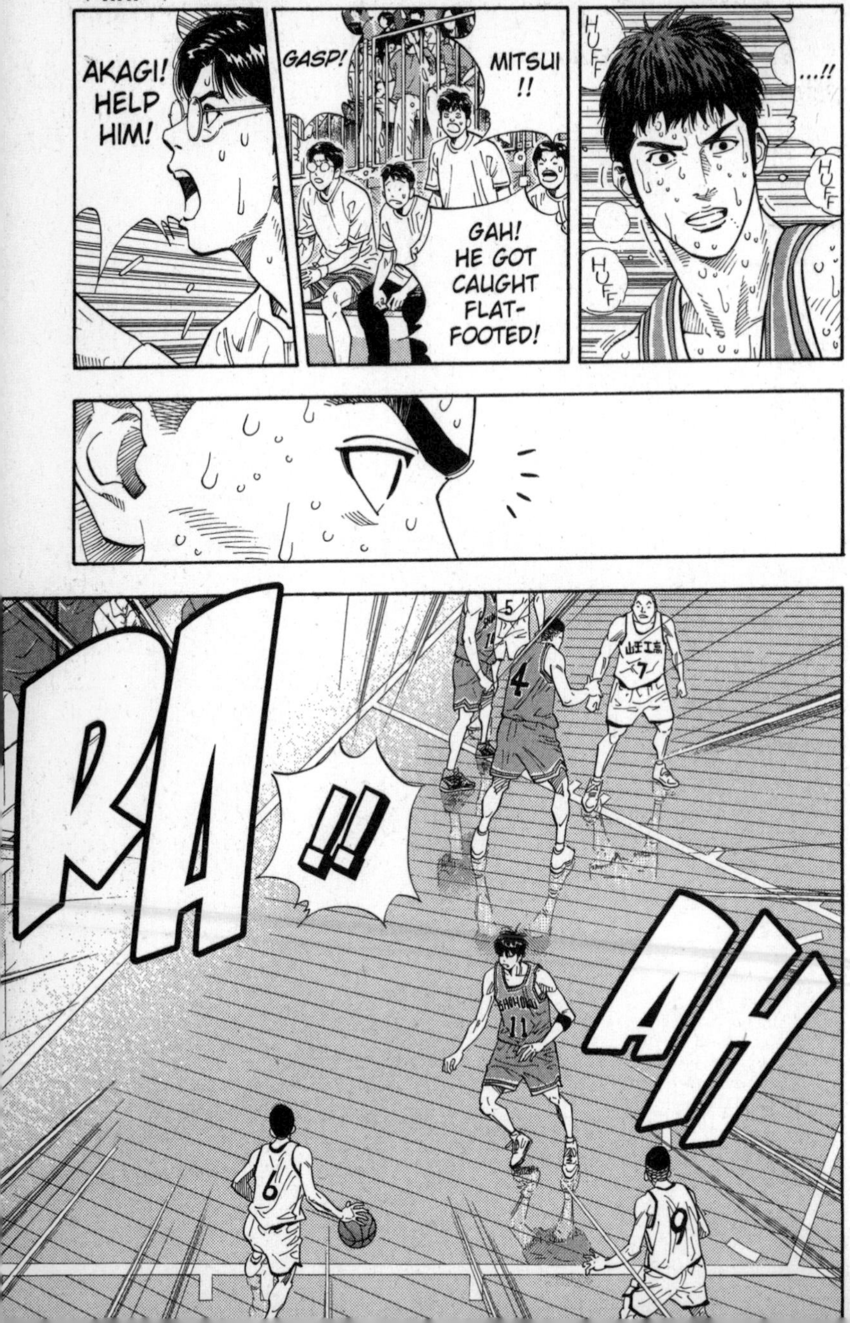
HUFF
...!!
HUFF
HUFF
GASP!
MITSUI !!
GAH! HE GOT CAUGHT FLAT-FOOTED!
AKAGI! HELP HIM!
RA
!!
AH

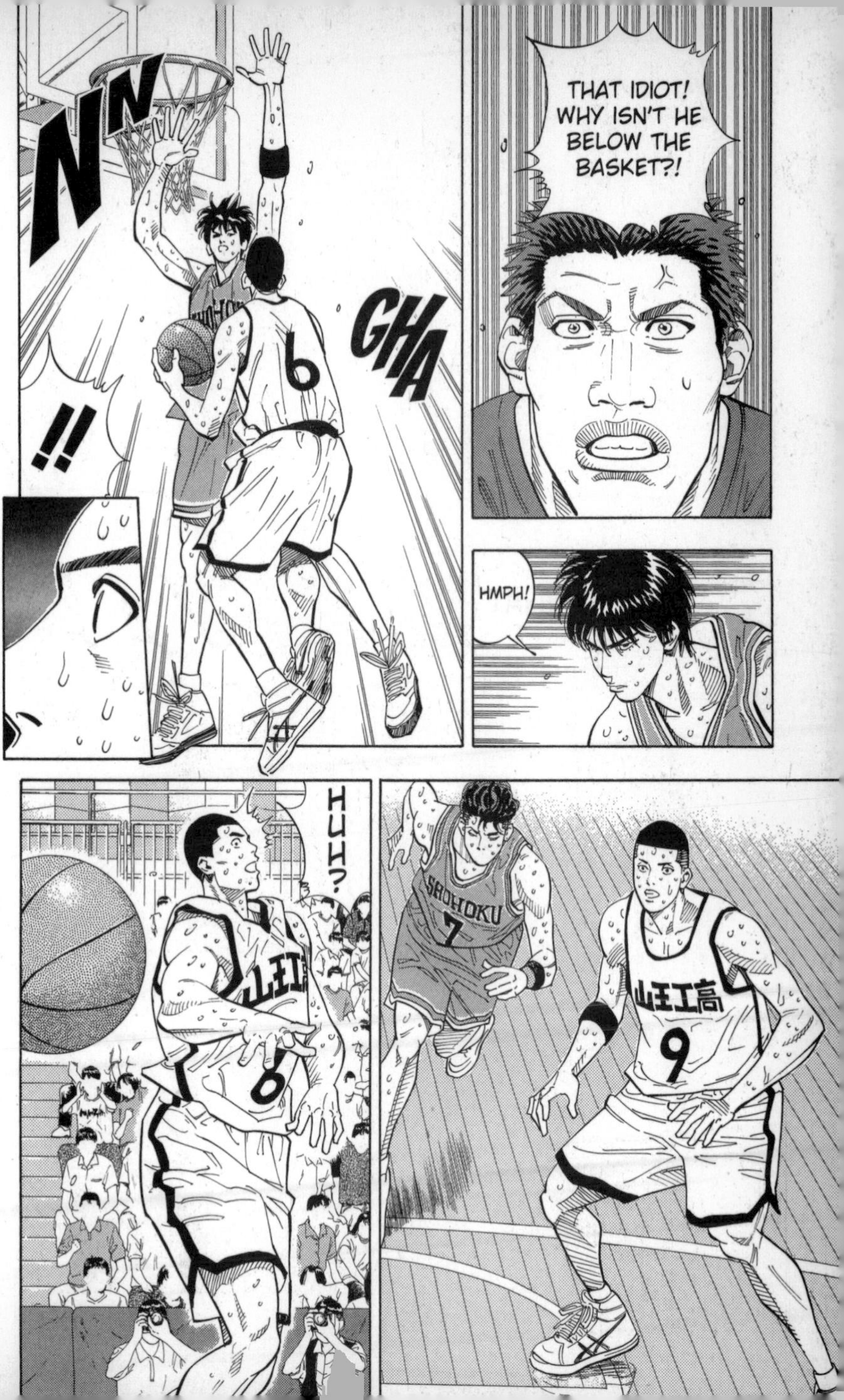
THAT IDIOT! WHY ISN'T HE BELOW THE BASKET?!
HMPH!
NN
GHA
!!
HUH?

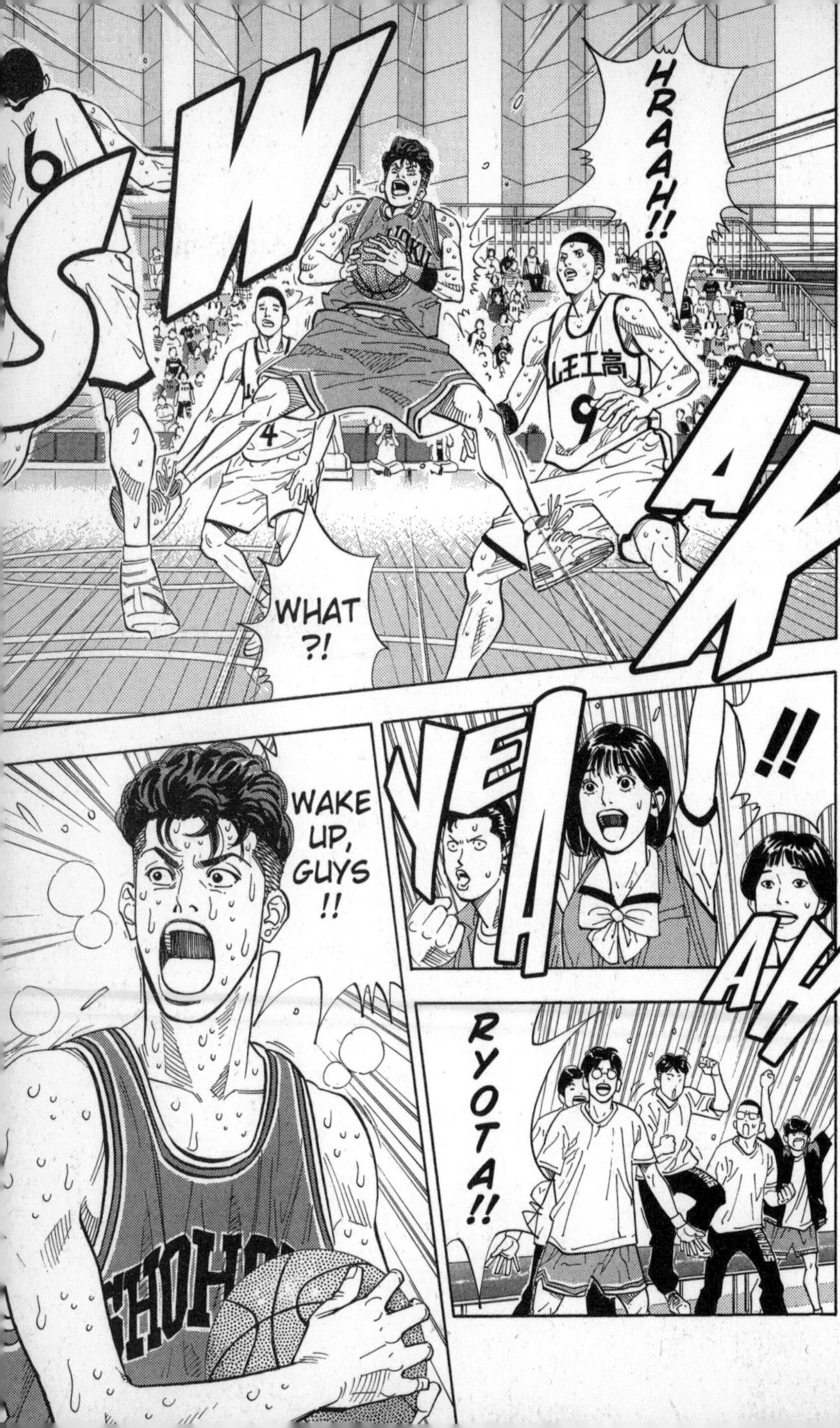
HRAAAH!!
WHAT ?!
RYOTA!!
WAKE UP, GUYS !!

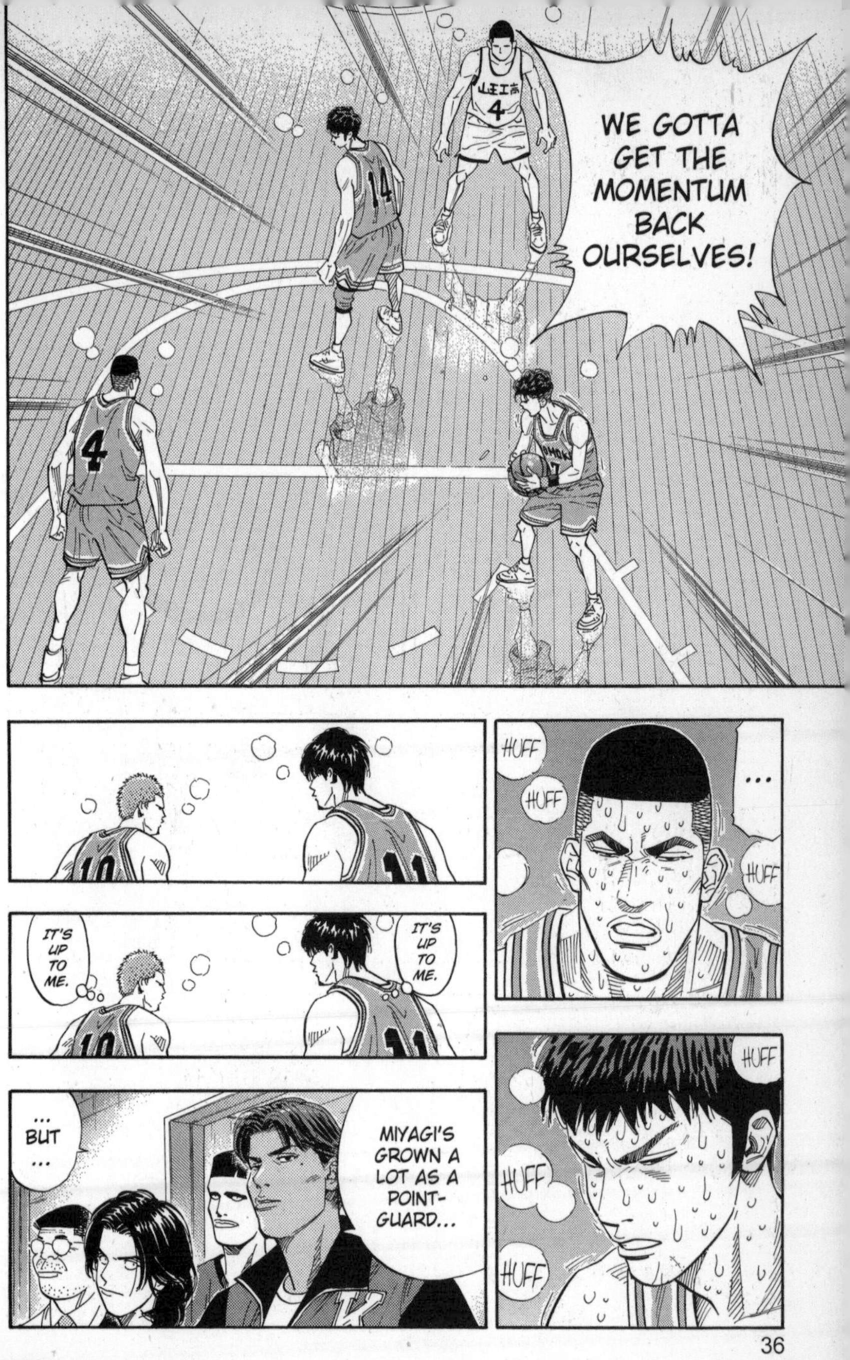
WE GOTTA GET THE MOMENTUM BACK OURSELVES!
...
HUFF
HUFF
HUFF
HUFF
HUFF
HUFF
IT'S UP TO ME.
IT'S UP TO ME.
MIYAGI'S GROWN A LOT AS A POINT-GUARD...
... BUT ...

READ THIS WAY

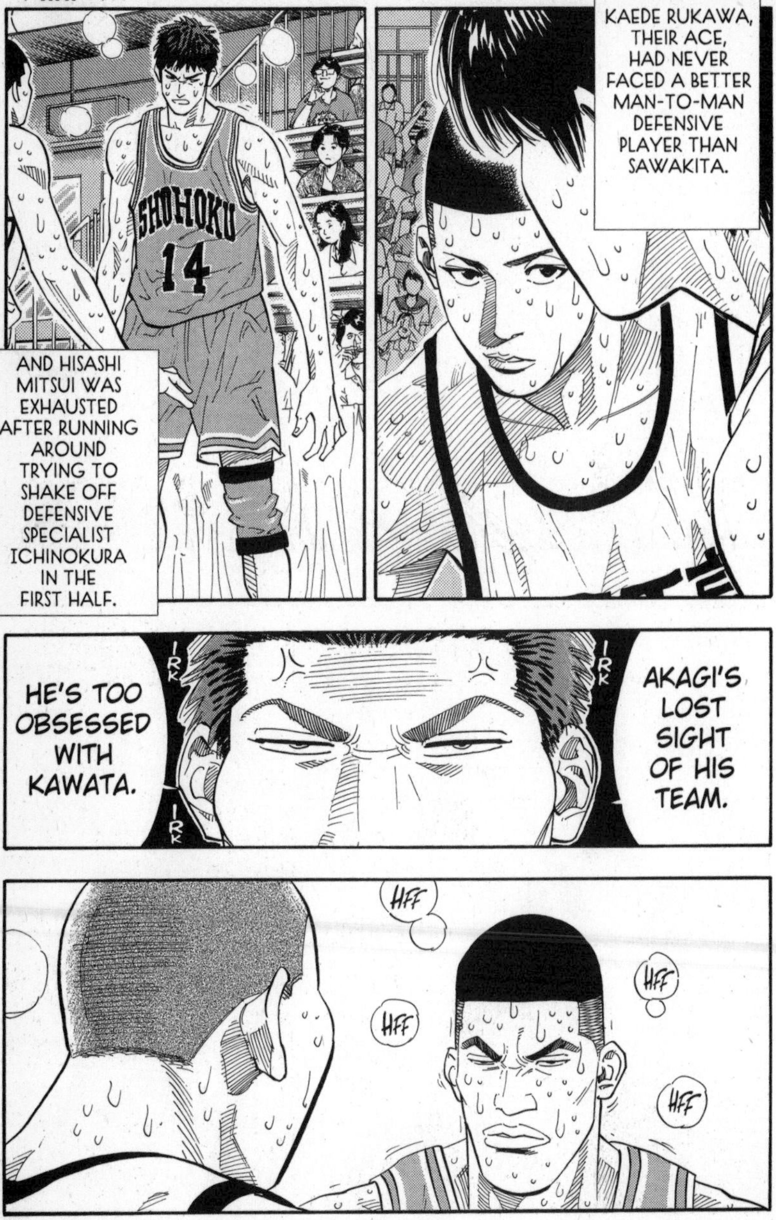

KAEDE RUKAWA, THEIR ACE, HAD NEVER FACED A BETTER MAN-TO-MAN DEFENSIVE PLAYER THAN SAWAKITA.
AND HISASHI MITSUI WAS EXHAUSTED AFTER RUNNING AROUND TRYING TO SHAKE OFF DEFENSIVE SPECIALIST ICHINOKURA IN THE FIRST HALF.
SHOHOKU
14
IRK
AKAGI'S LOST SIGHT OF HIS TEAM.
IRK
IRK
HE'S TOO OBSESSED WITH KAWATA.
HFF
HFF
HFF
HFF

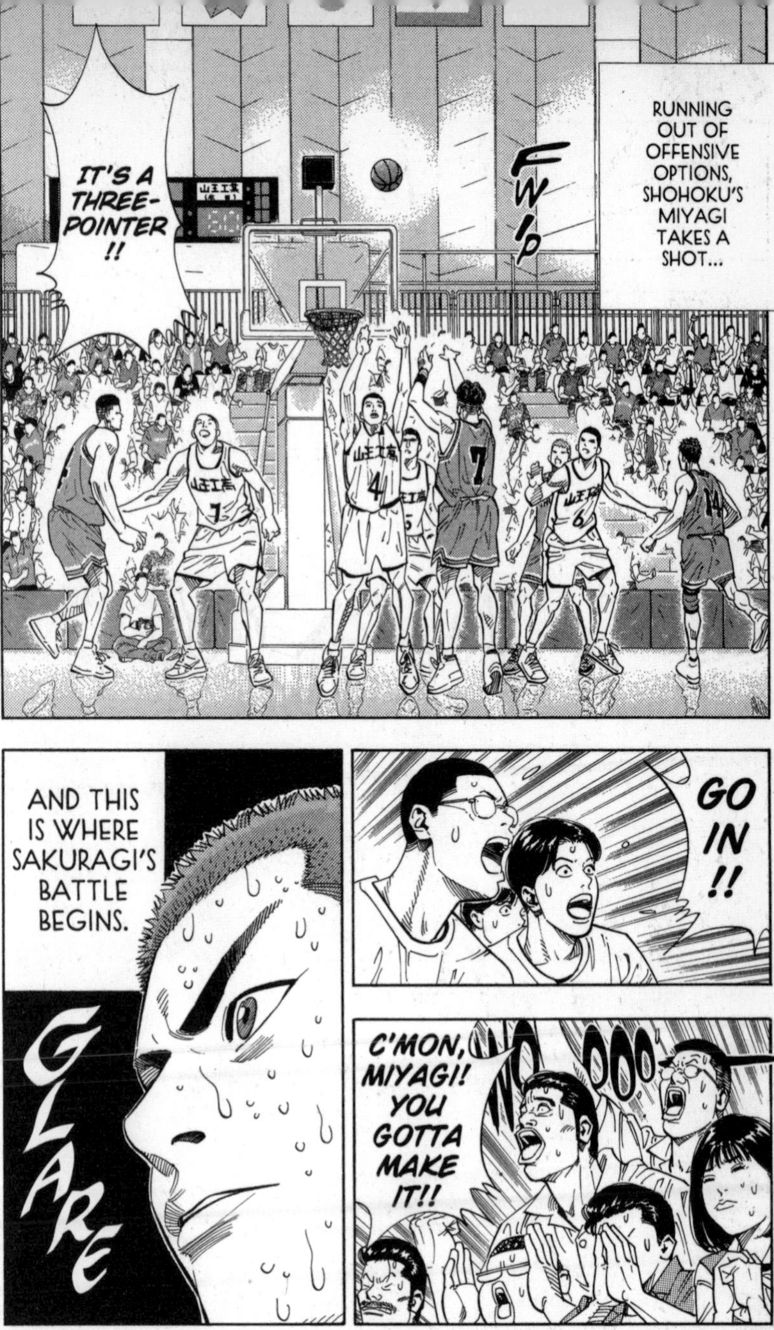
RUNNING OUT OF OFFENSIVE OPTIONS, SHOHOKU'S MIYAGI TAKES A SHOT...
FWIP
IT'S A THREE-POINTER!!
GO IN!!
C'MON, MIYAGI! YOU GOTTA MAKE IT!!
AND THIS IS WHERE SAKURAGI'S BATTLE BEGINS.
GLARE

READ THIS WAY

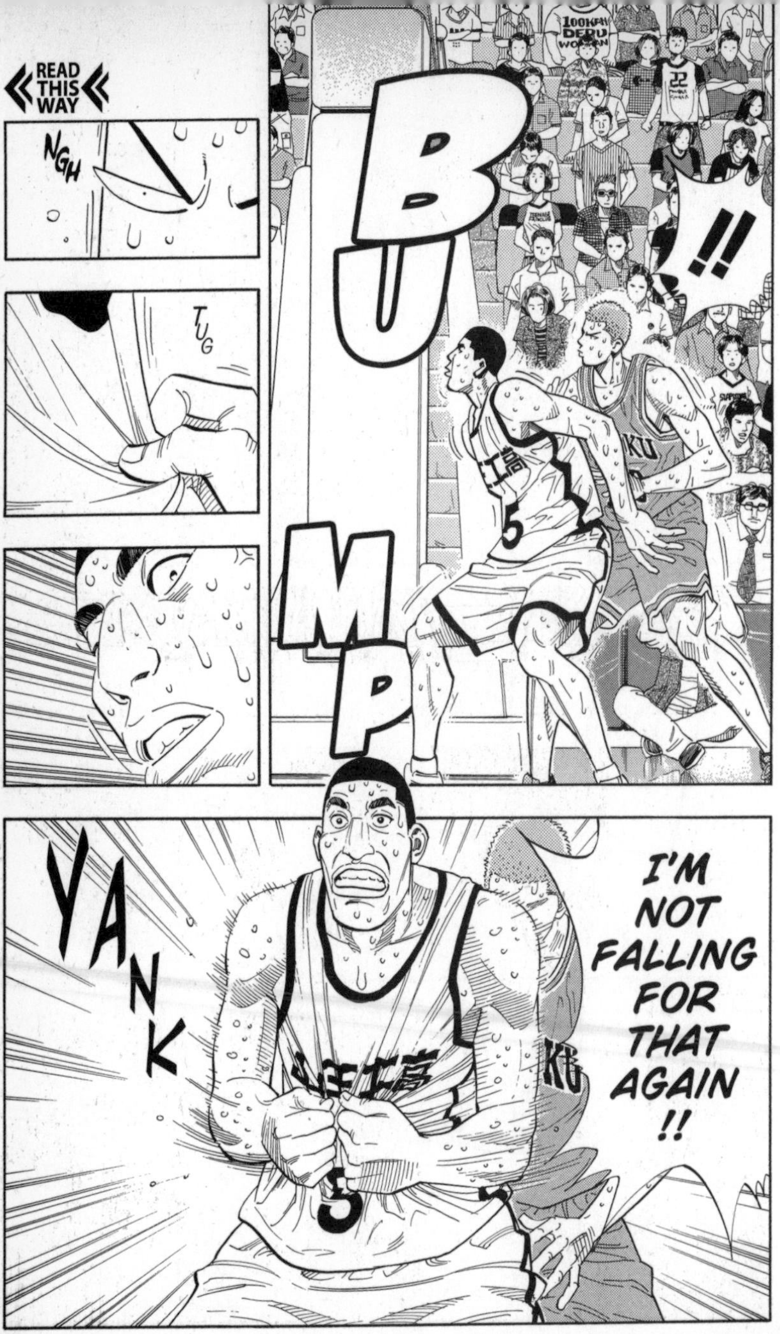
BUMP
!!
NGH
TUG
YANK
I'M NOT FALLING FOR THAT AGAIN!!

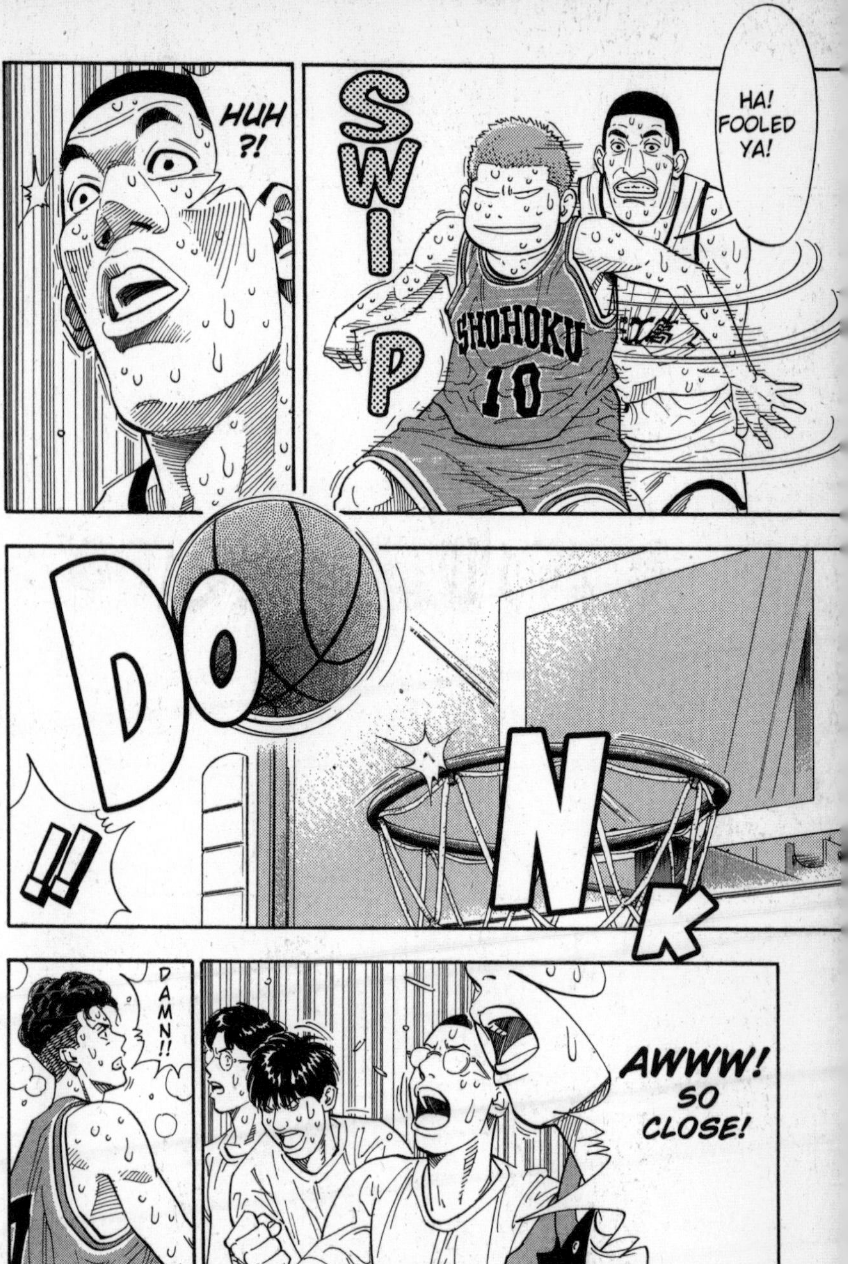
SWIP
HA! FOOLED YA!
HUH ?!
DONK!!
AWWW! SO CLOSE!
DAMN!!

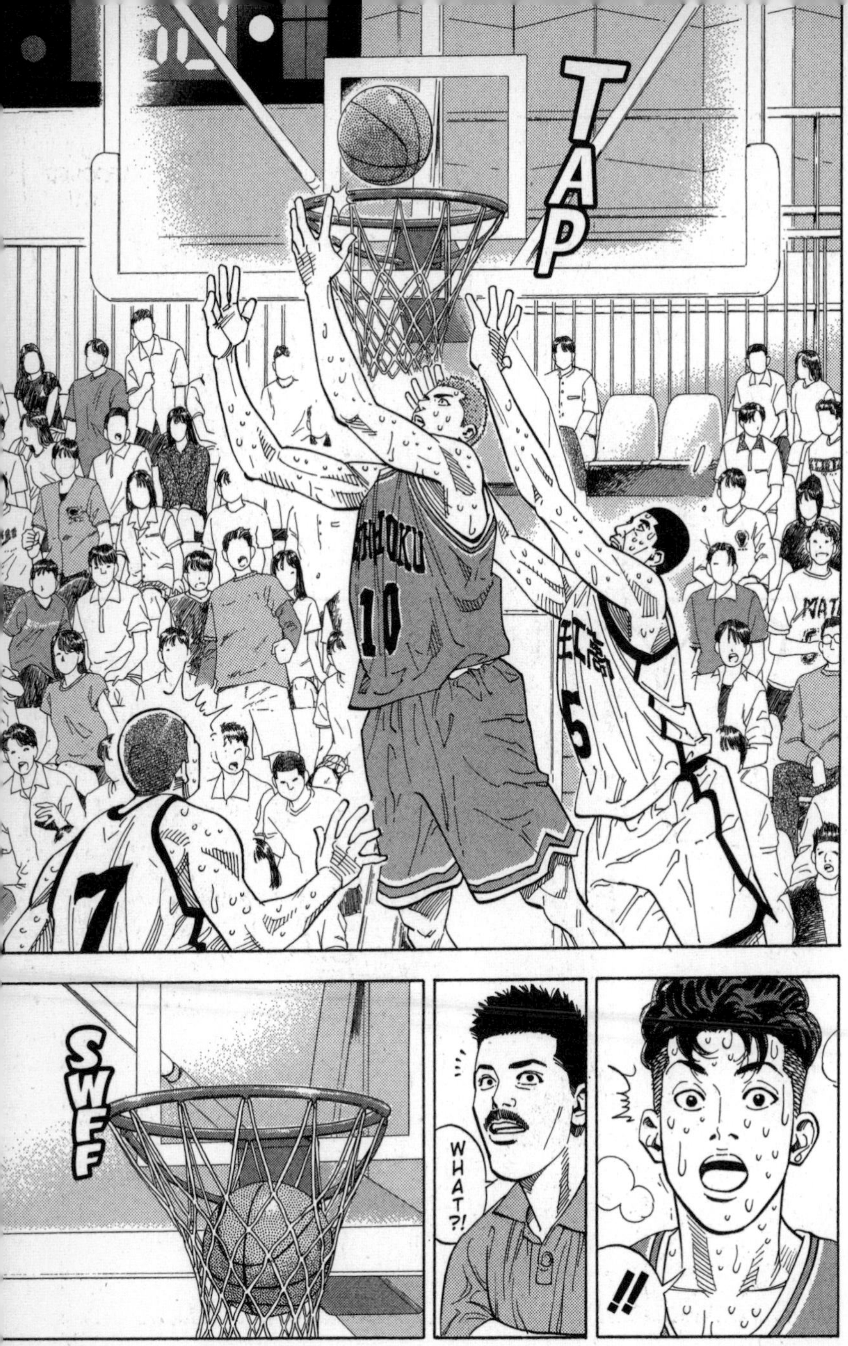
TAP
!!
WHAT?!
SWFF

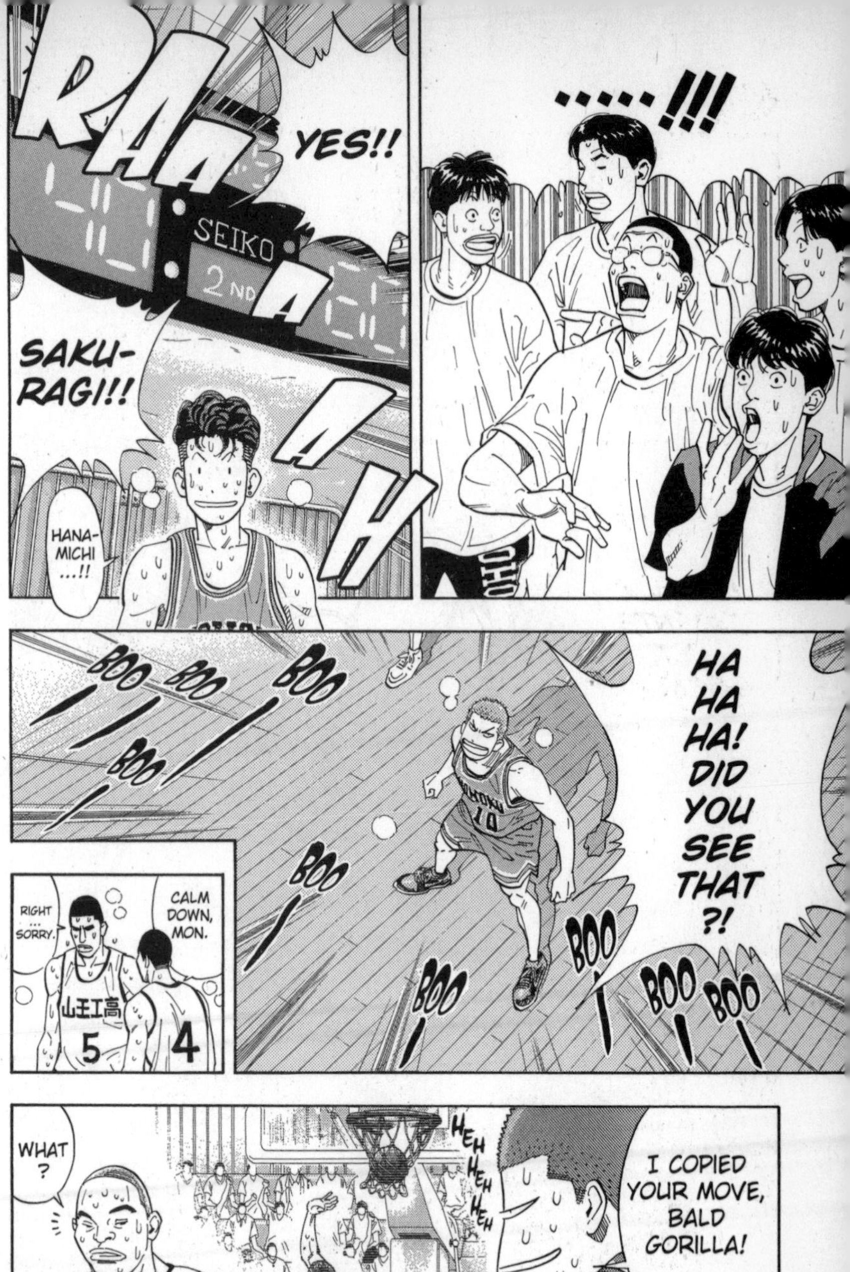
......!!!
RAAAAH
YES!!
SAKU-RAGI!!
HANA-MICHI ...!!
HA HA HA! DID YOU SEE THAT?!
BOO BOO BOO BOO BOO BOO BOO BOO BOO
CALM DOWN, MON.
RIGHT ... SORRY.
山王工高
HEH HEH HEH HEH
I COPIED YOUR MOVE, BALD GORILLA!
WHAT?

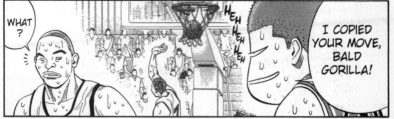

READ THIS WAY

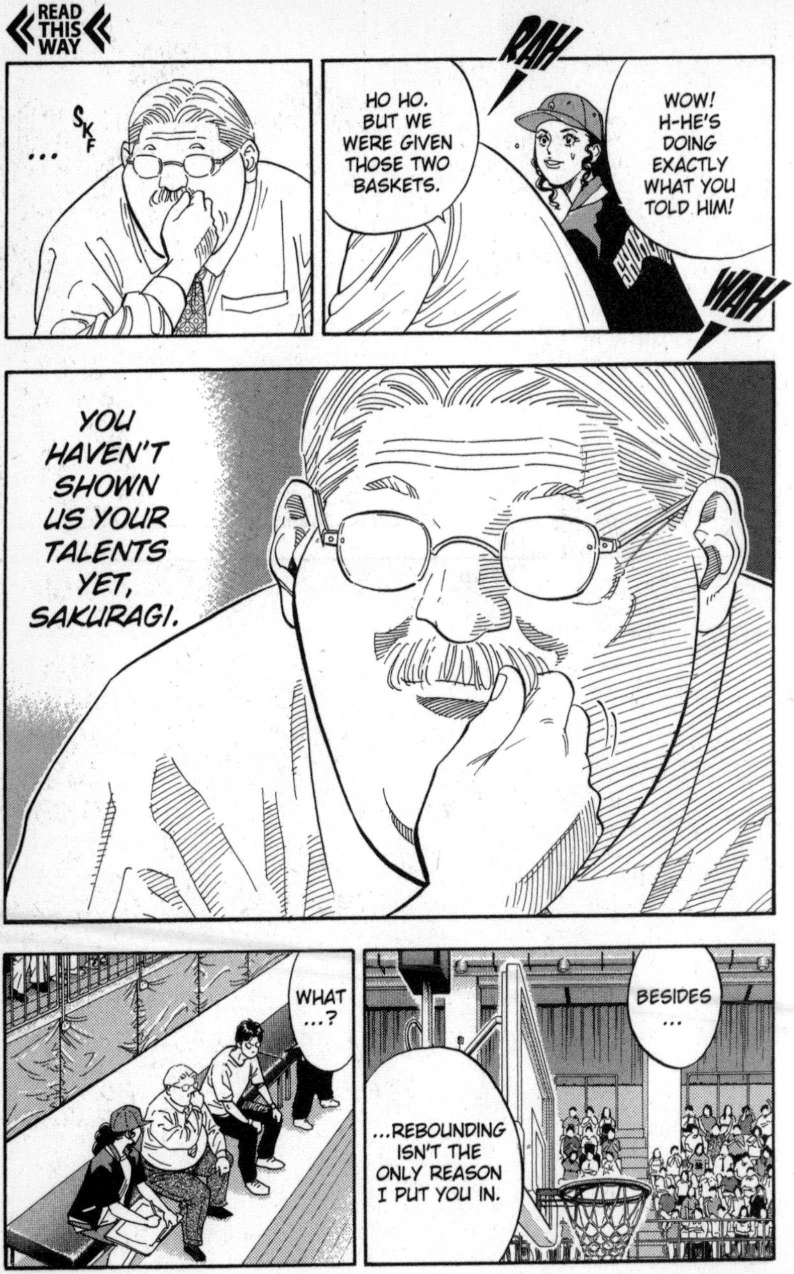
WOW! H-HE'S DOING EXACTLY WHAT YOU TOLD HIM!
RAH
HO HO. BUT WE WERE GIVEN THOSE TWO BASKETS.
WAH
...
SKF
YOU HAVEN'T SHOWN US YOUR TALENTS YET, SAKURAGI.
BESIDES ...
...REBOUNDING ISN'T THE ONLY REASON I PUT YOU IN.
WHAT ...?

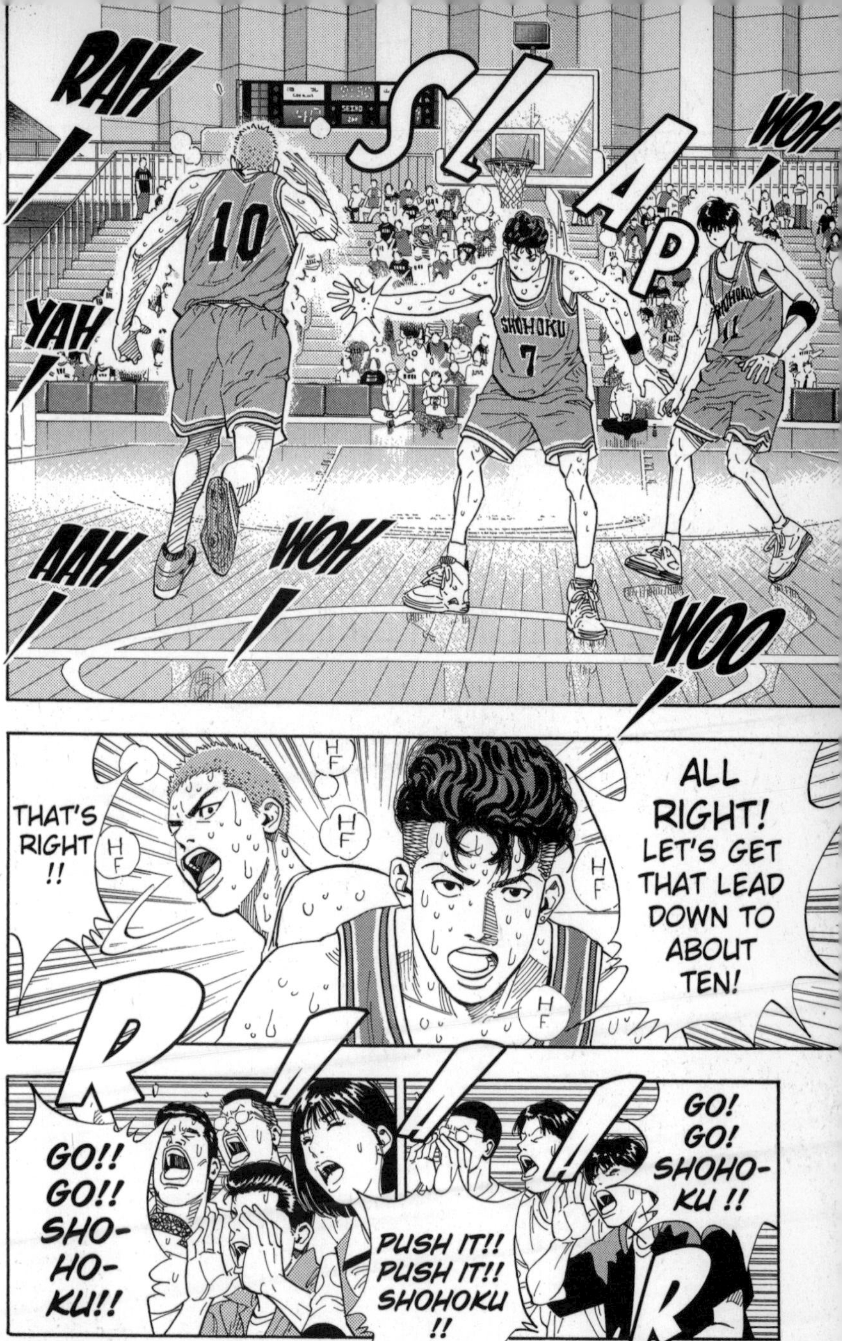
WOH
SLAP
RAH
YAH
WOO
WOH
AAH
ALL RIGHT! LET'S GET THAT LEAD DOWN TO ABOUT TEN!
HF
HF
HF
HF
THAT'S RIGHT!!
GO! GO! SHOHO-KU!!
R
PUSH IT!! PUSH IT!! SHOHOKU!!
GO!! GO!! SHO-HO-KU!!

READ THIS WAY

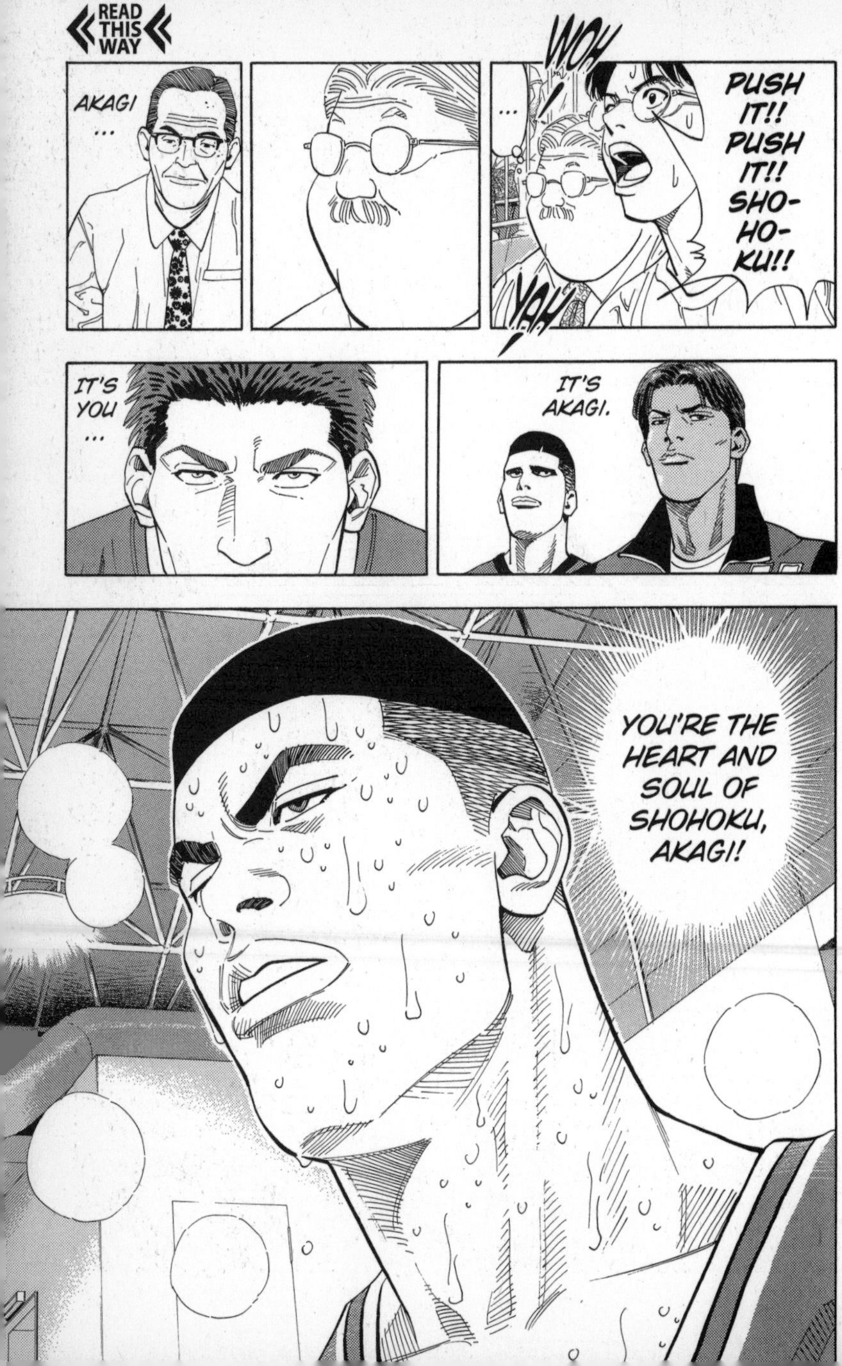
WOH
...
PUSH IT!! PUSH IT!! SHO-HO-KU!!
YAH
AKAGI ...
IT'S AKAGI.
IT'S YOU ...
YOU'RE THE HEART AND SOUL OF SHOHOKU, AKAGI!

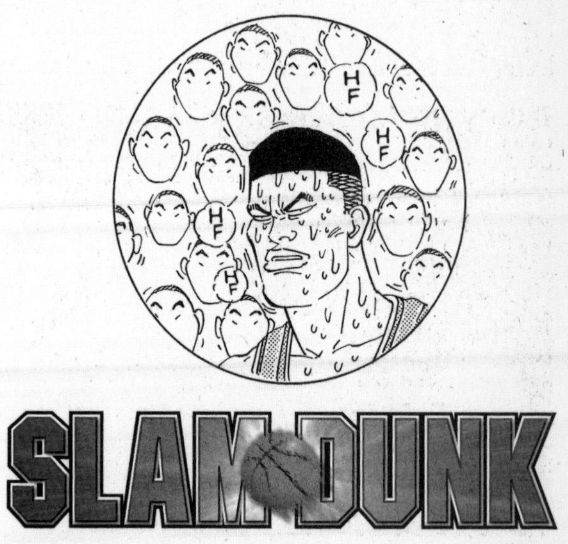
HF
HF
HF
HF

SLAM DUNK

OUT OF THE DARK

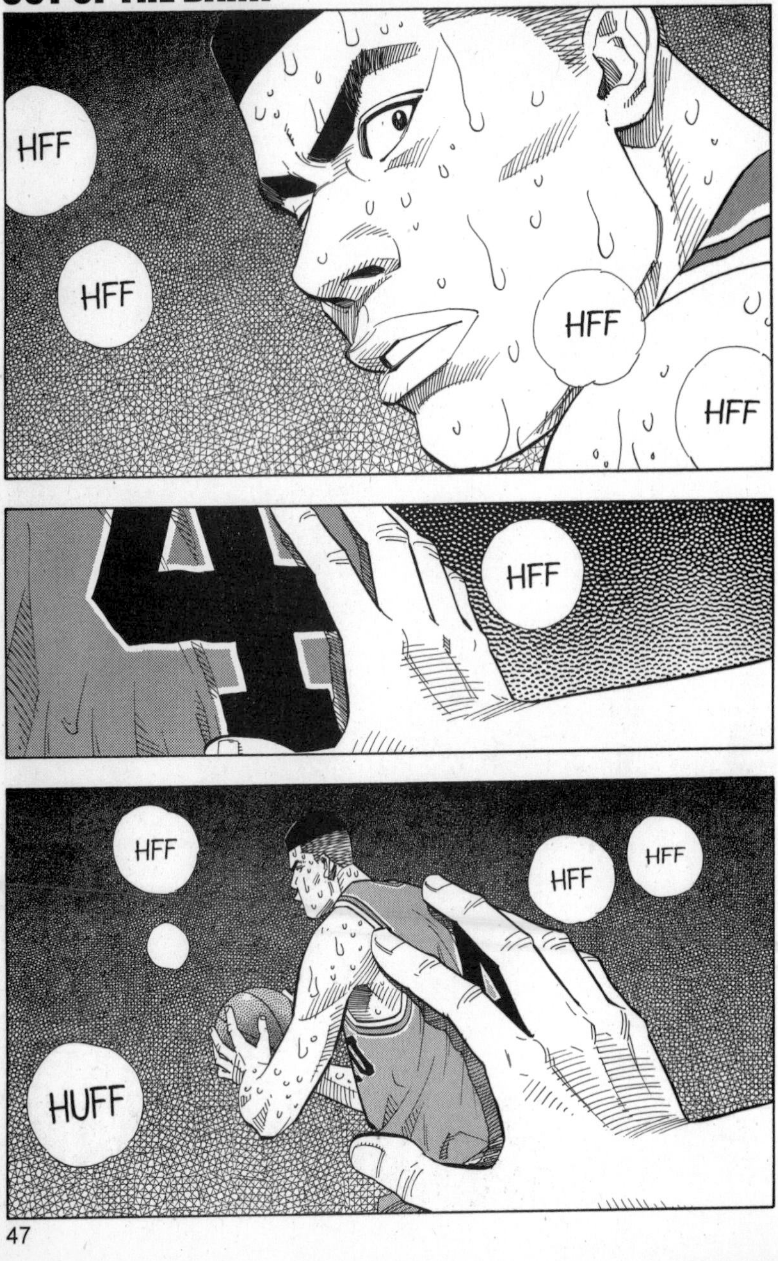
HFF
HFF
HFF
HFF
HFF
HFF
HFF
HFF
HUFF

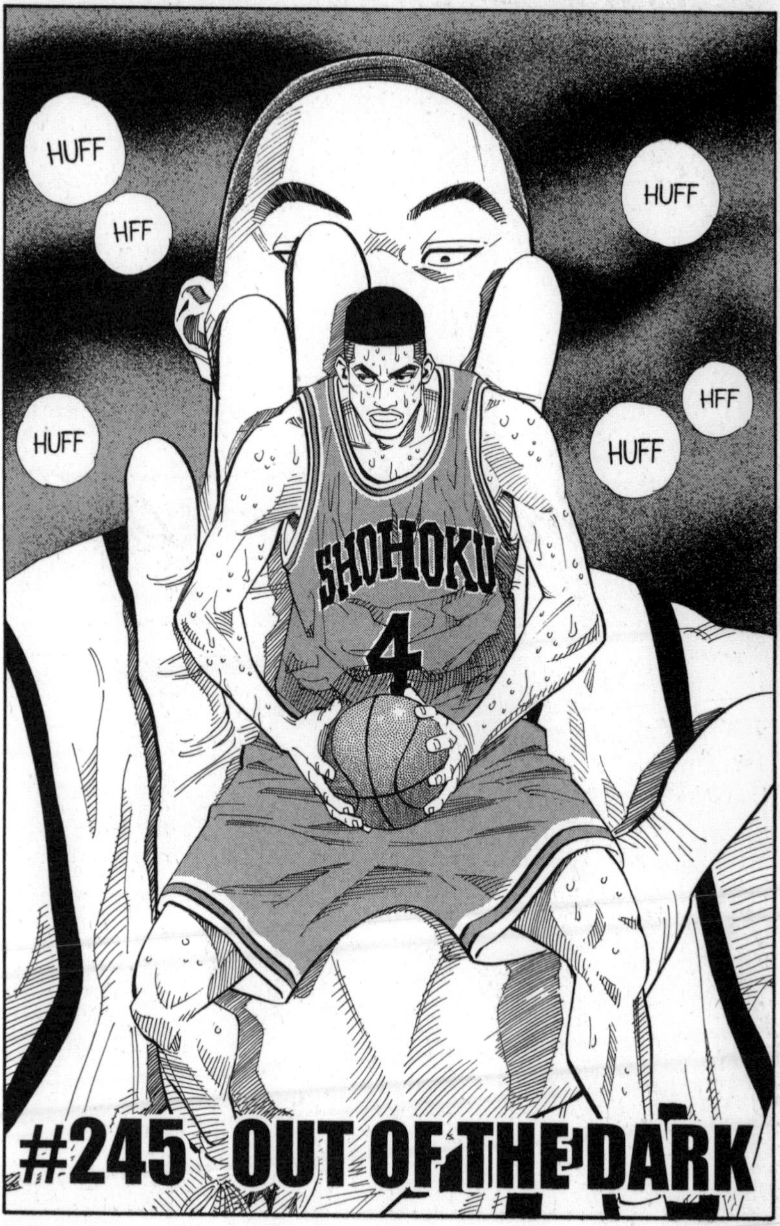
HUFF
HFF
HUFF
HUFF
HFF
HUFF
#245 OUT OF THE DARK

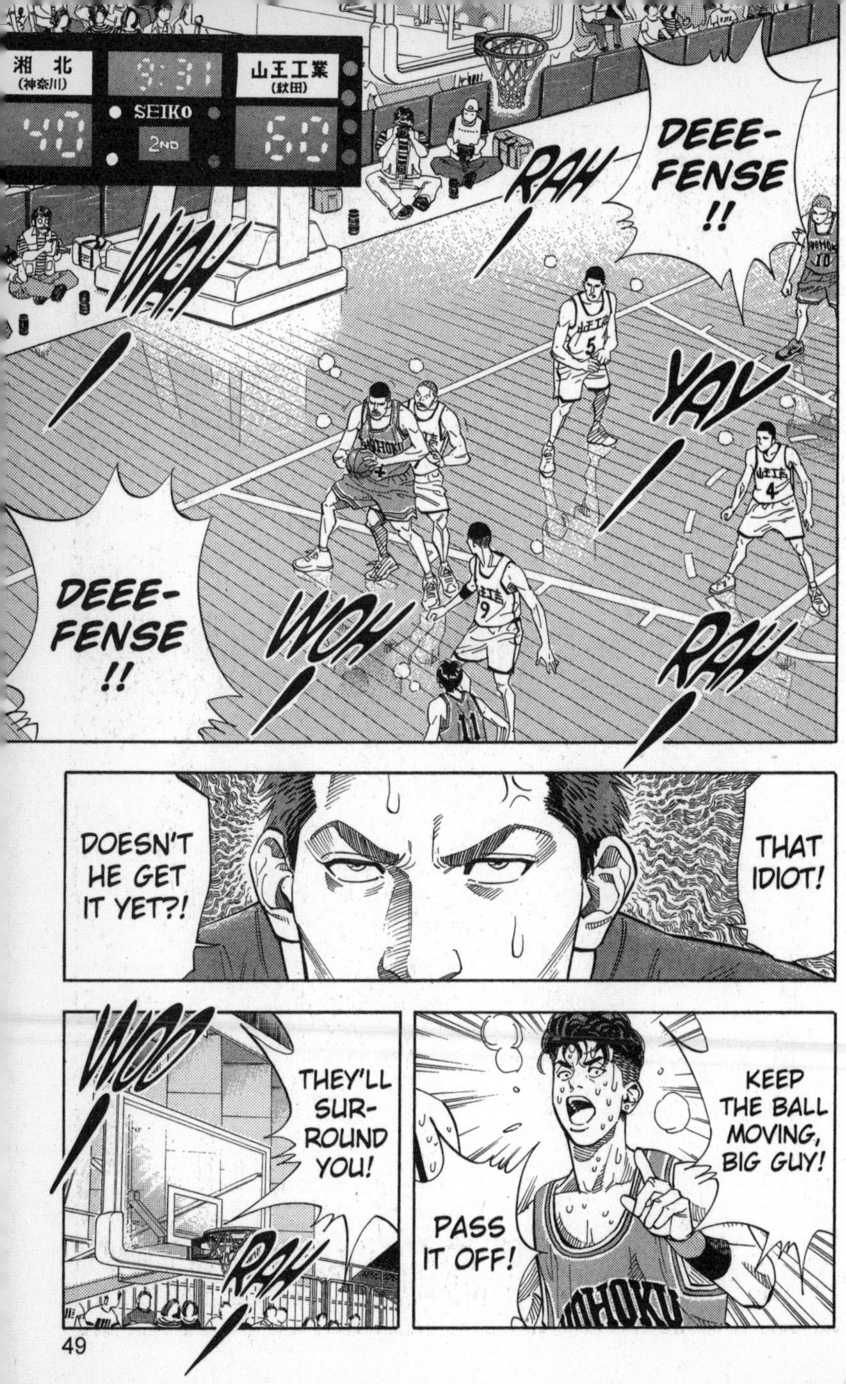
湘北
(神奈川)
9:31
SEIKO
2ND
40
山王工業
(秋田)
60
DEEEE-FENSE!!
RAH!
YAY!
WAH!
RAH!
WOH!
DEEEE-FENSE!!
THAT IDIOT!
DOESN'T HE GET IT YET?!
KEEP THE BALL MOVING, BIG GUY!
PASS IT OFF!
THEY'LL SUR-ROUND YOU!
WOO!
RAH!

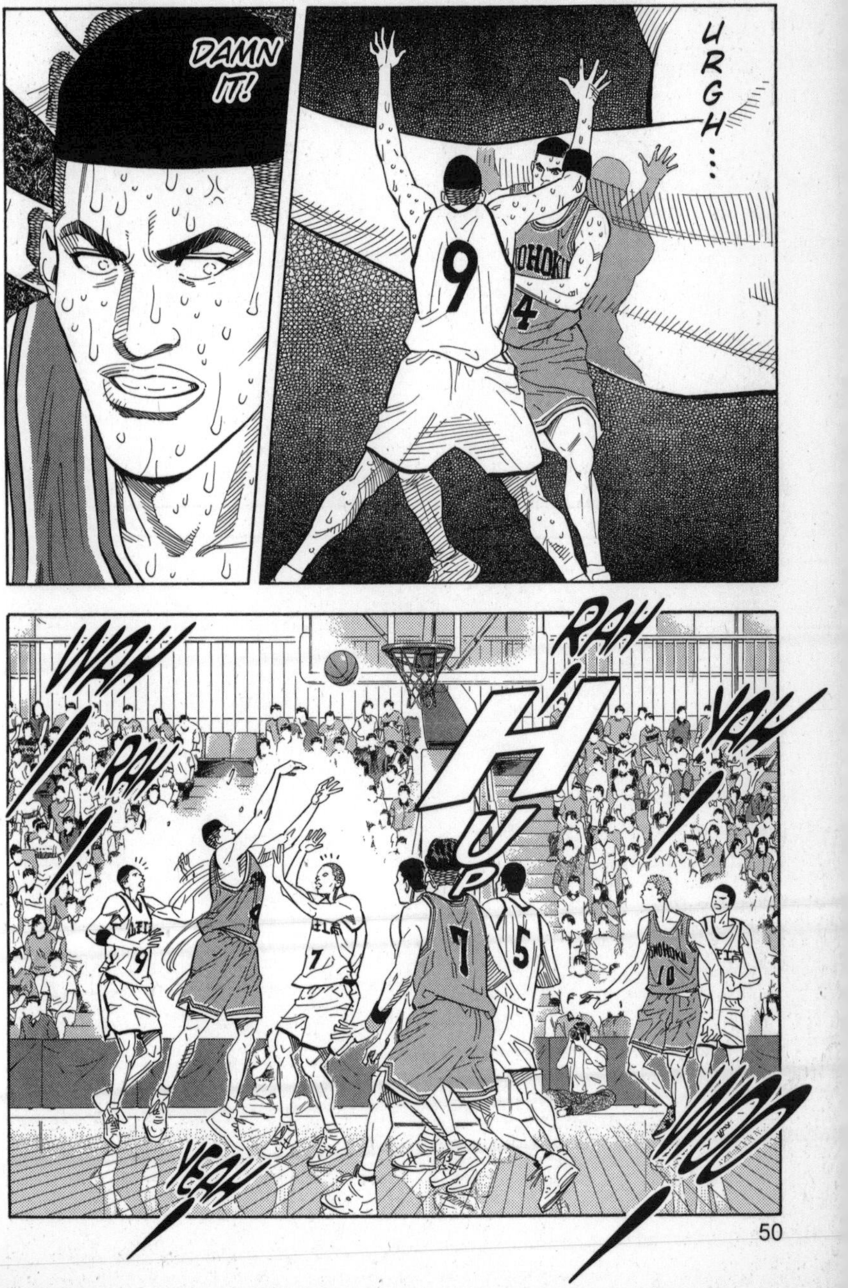
URGH...
DAMN IT!
RAH!
YAH!
HUP
WAH!
RAH!
WOOO!
YEAH!

READ THIS WAY

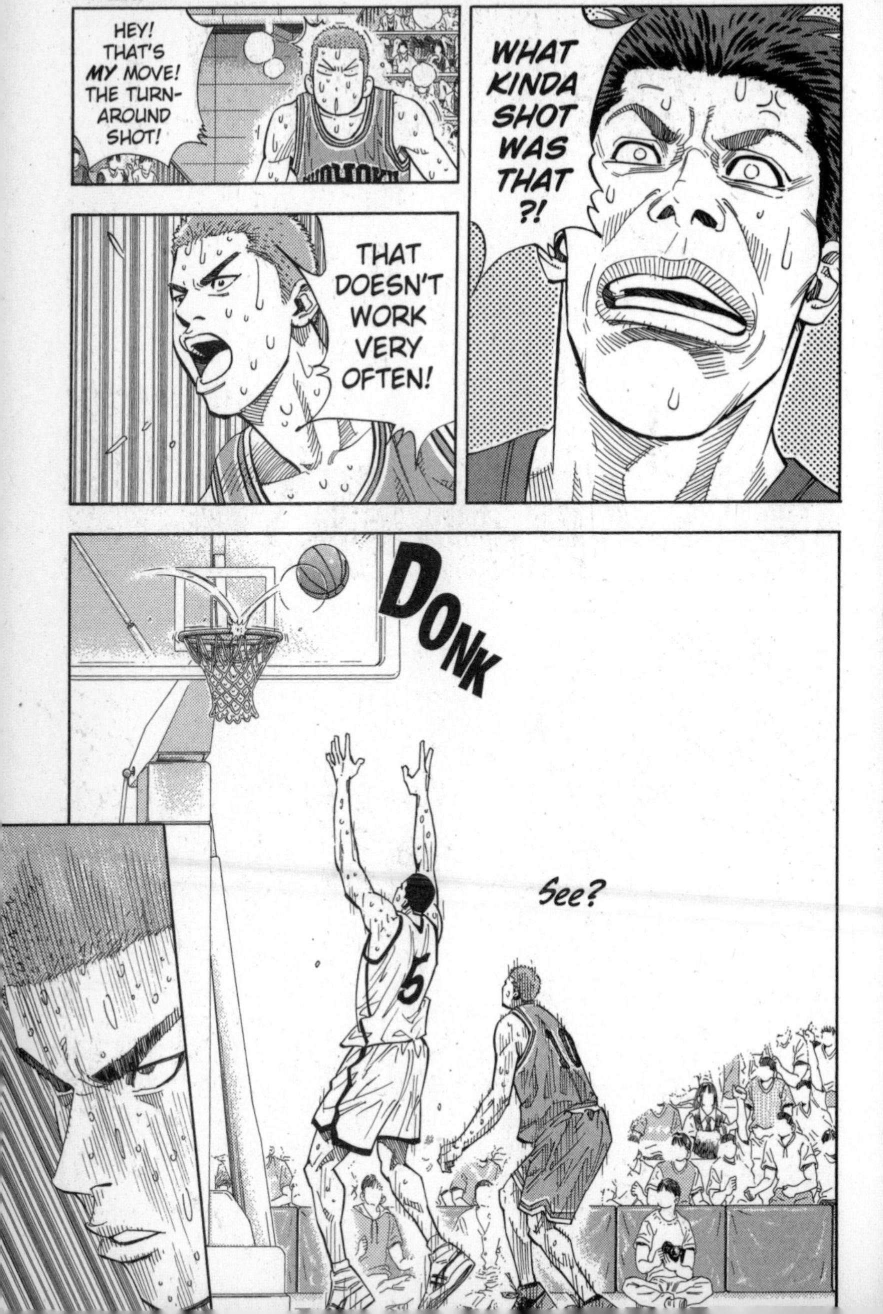
WHAT KINDA SHOT WAS THAT?!
HEY! THAT'S MY MOVE! THE TURN-AROUND SHOT!
THAT DOESN'T WORK VERY OFTEN!
DONK
See?

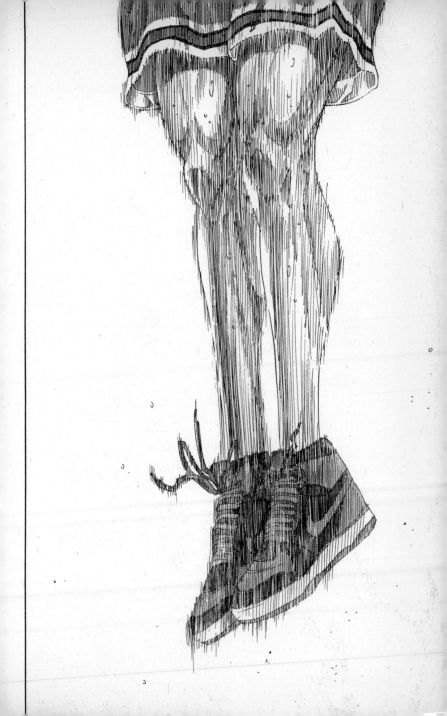

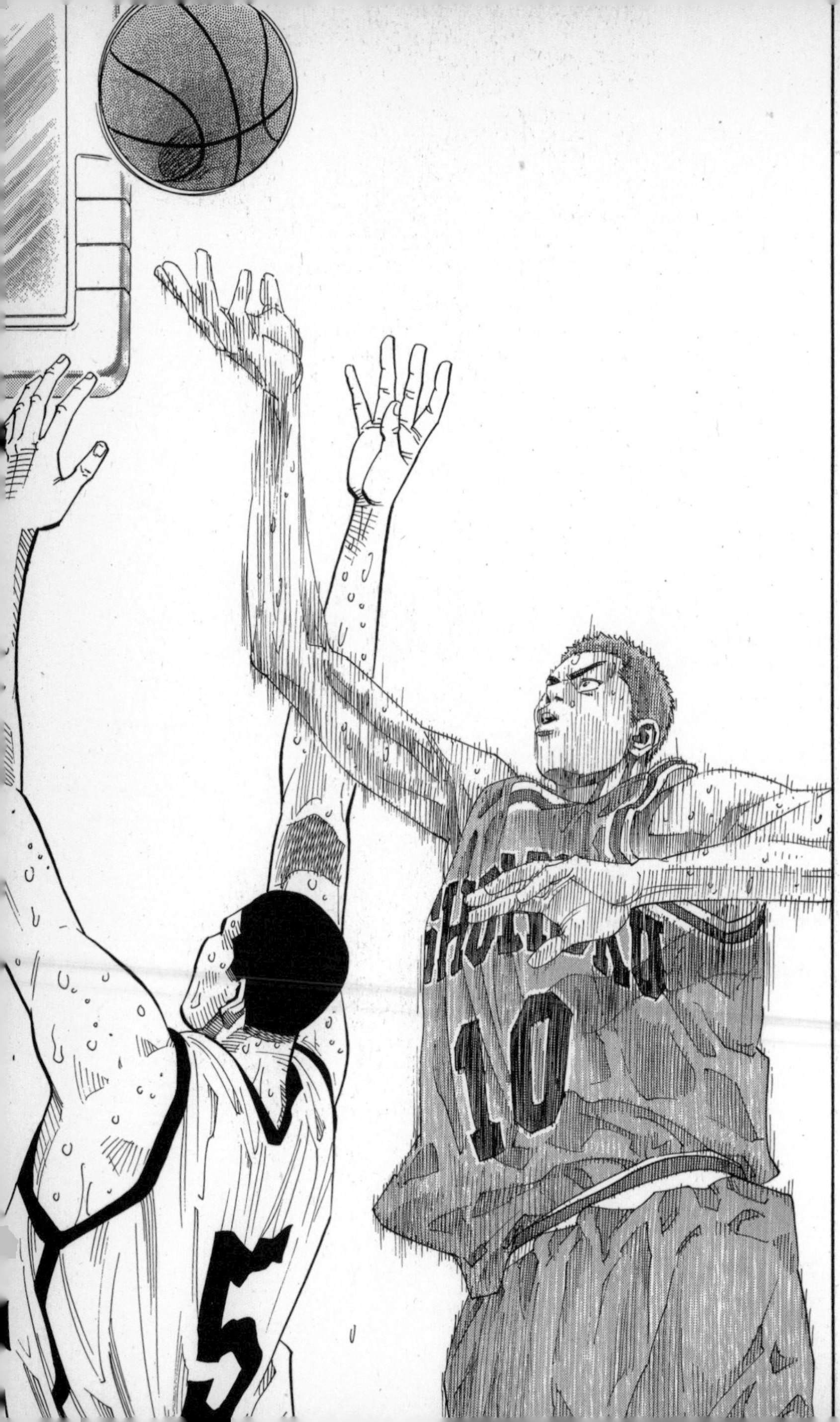

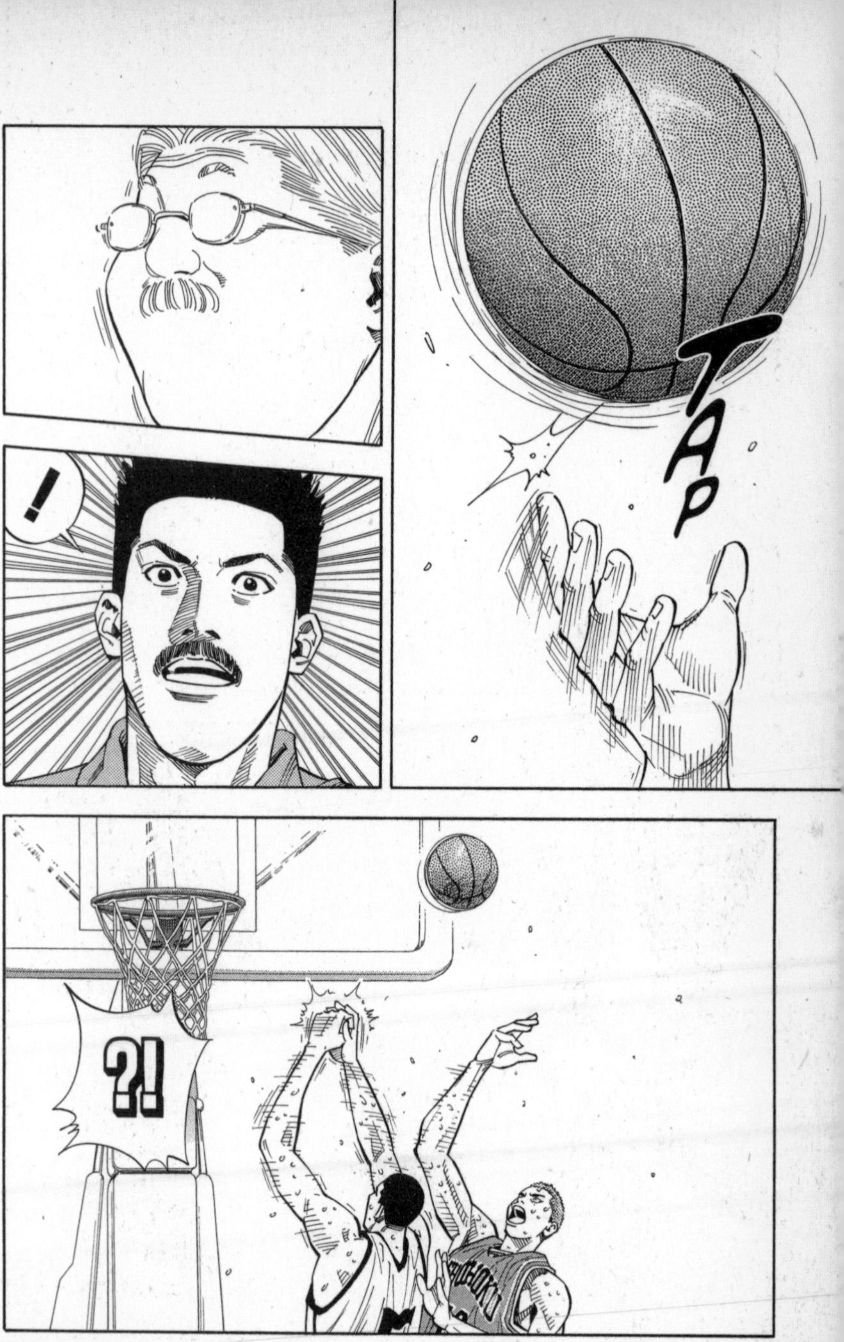
TAP
!
?!

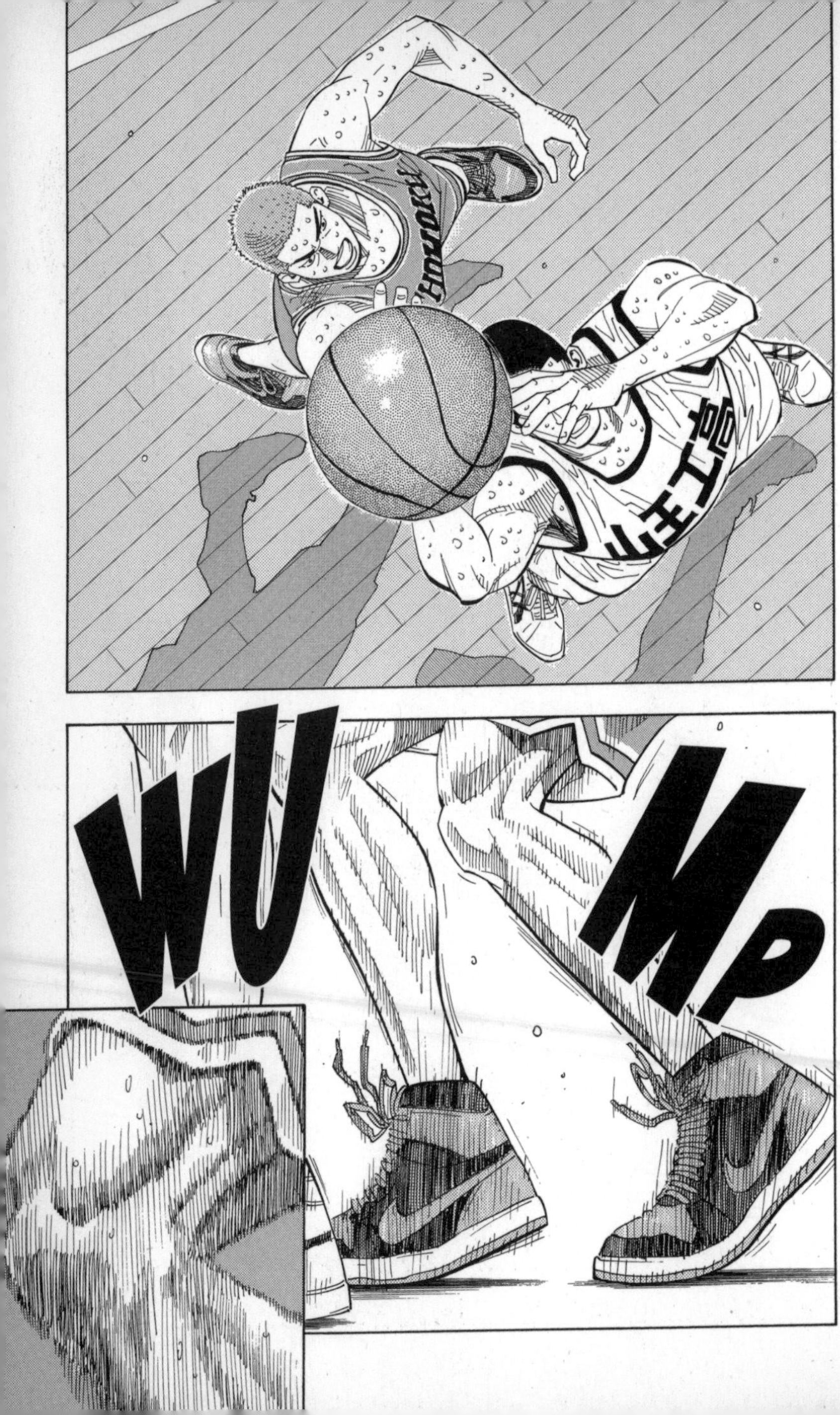
WUMP

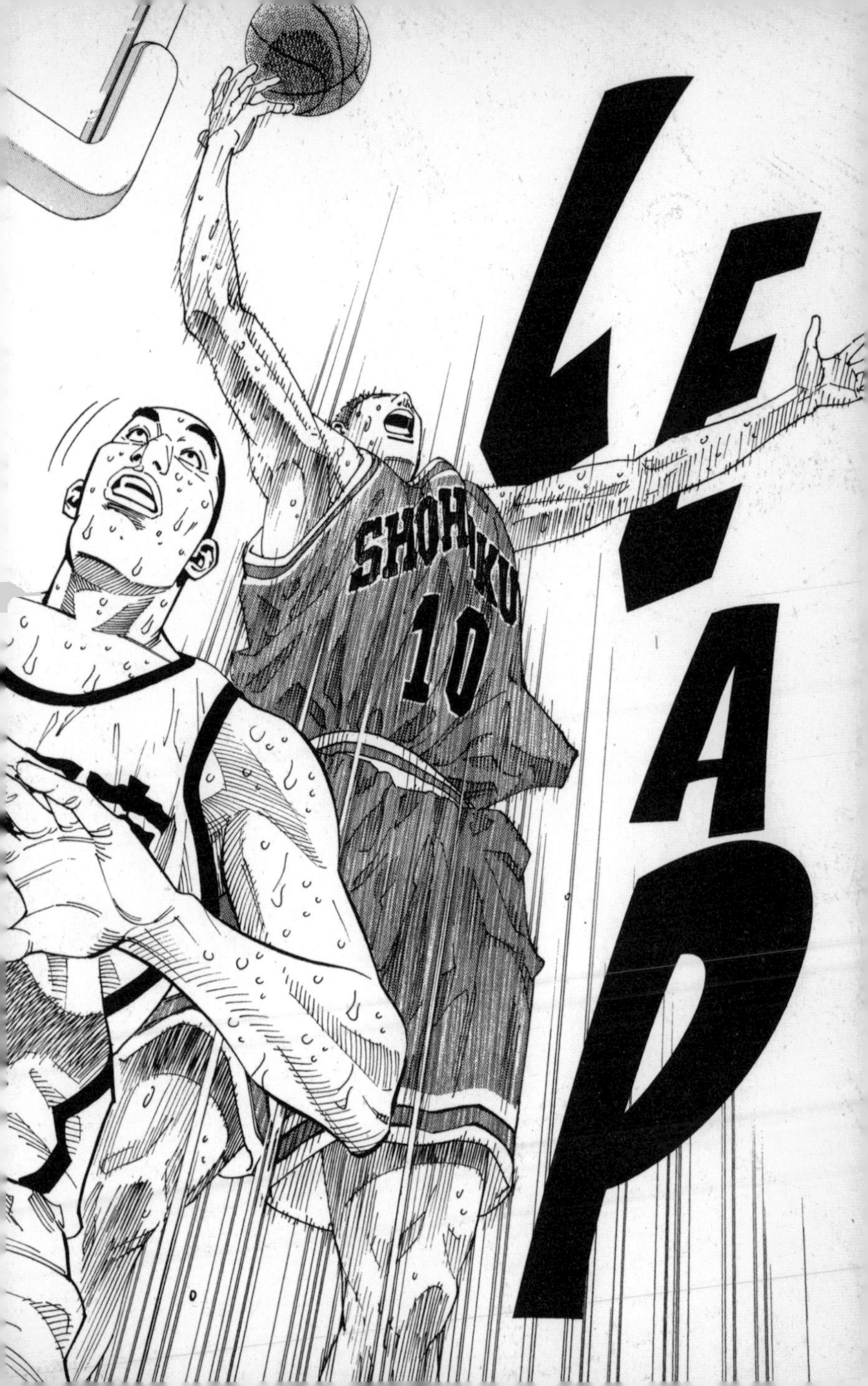
LEAP

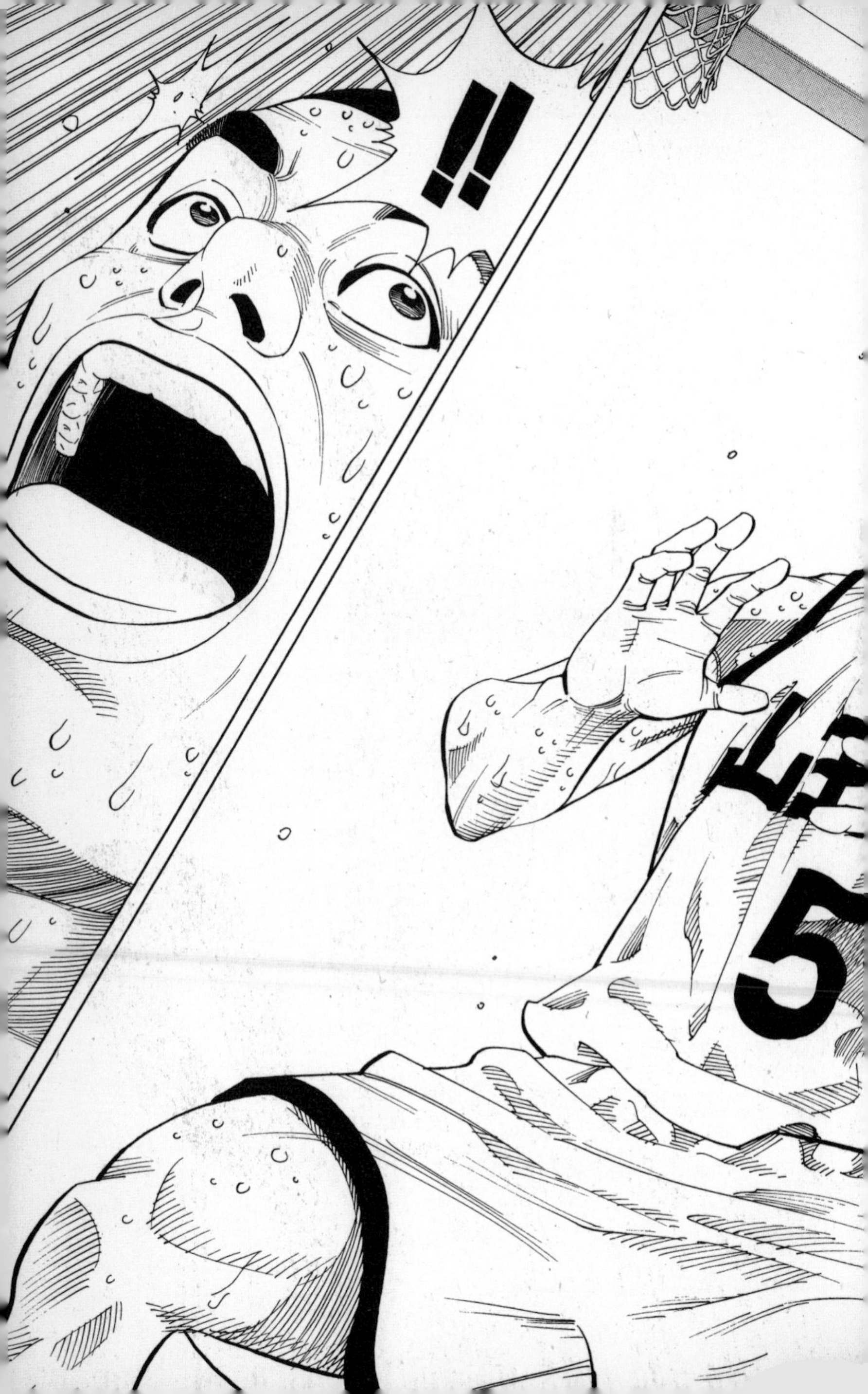
!!

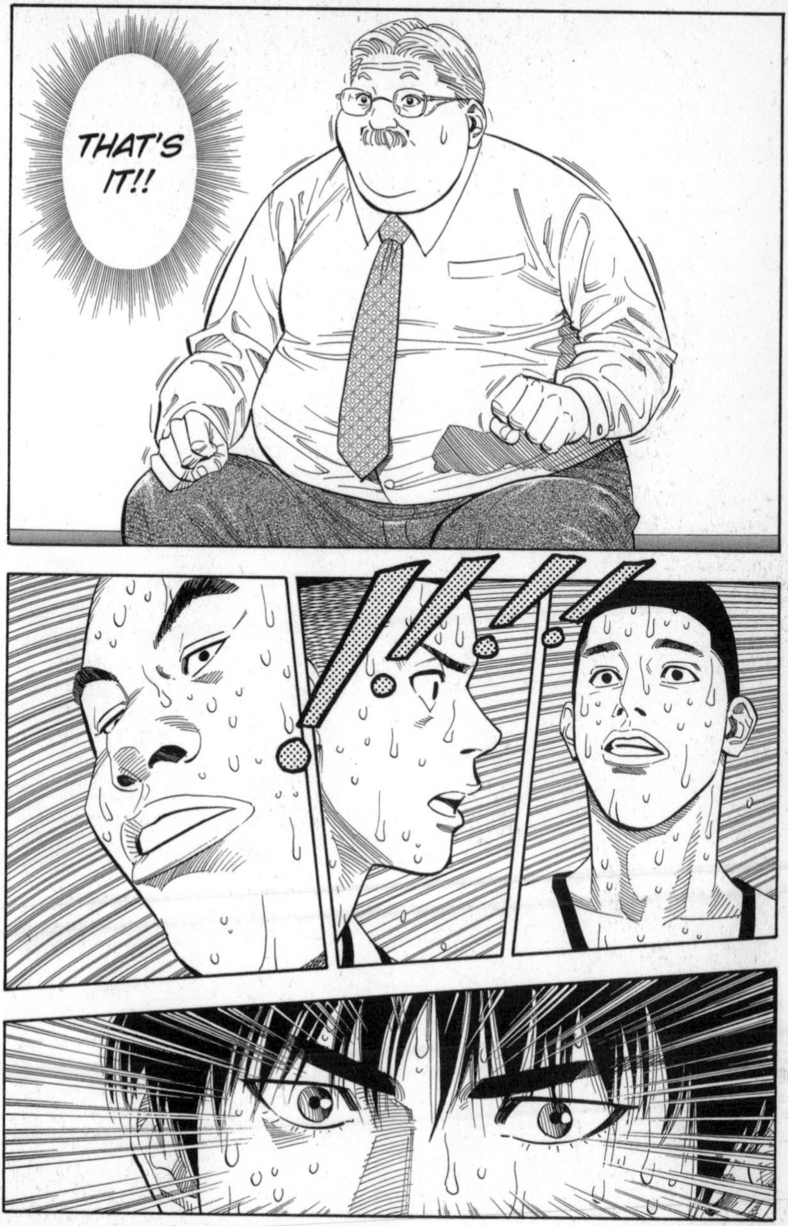
THAT'S IT!!

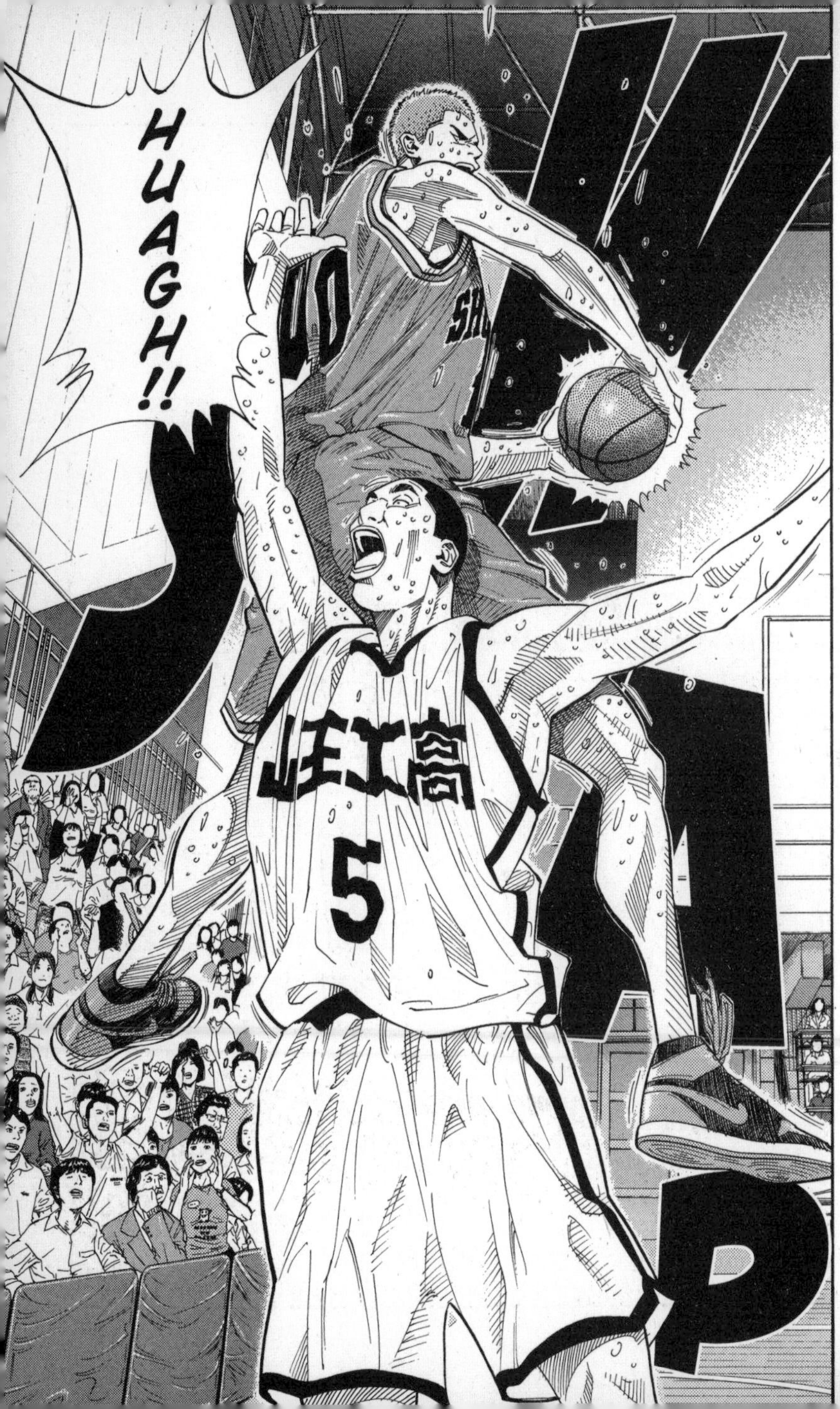
HUAGH!!
JUMP
山王工高
5

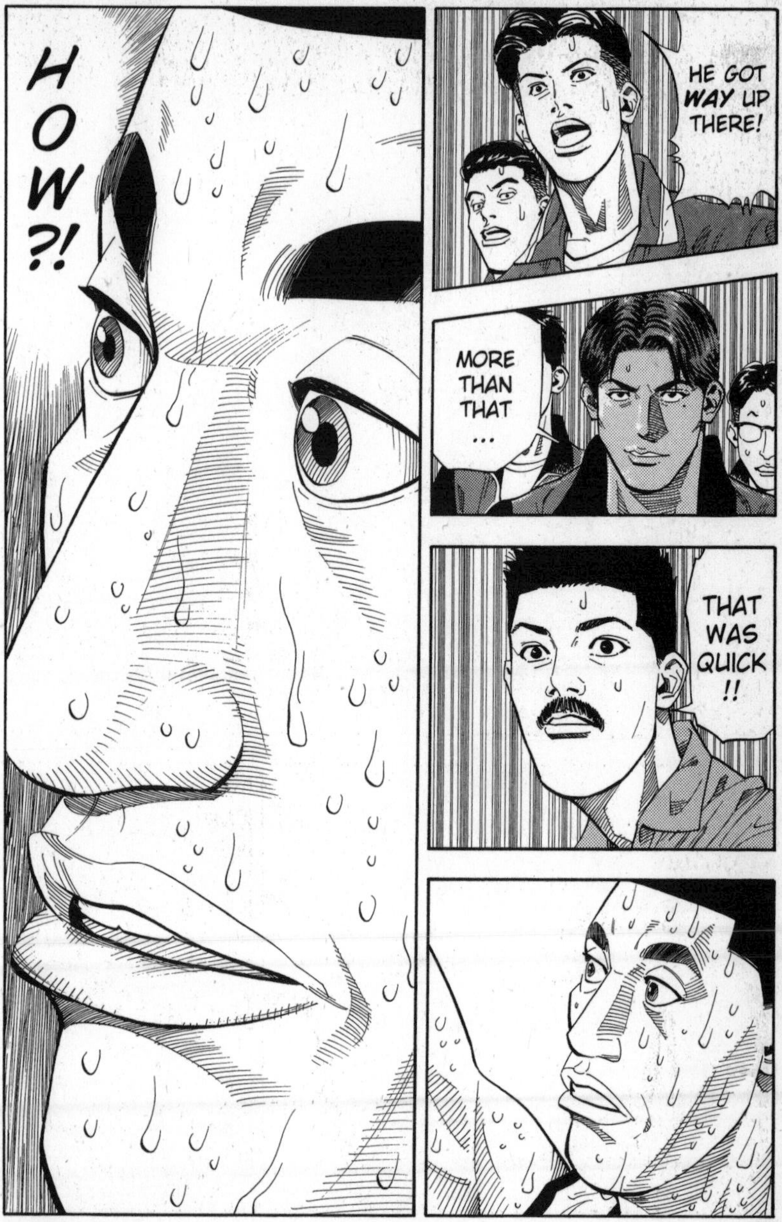
HE GOT WAY UP THERE!
MORE THAN THAT ...
THAT WAS QUICK !!
HOW?!

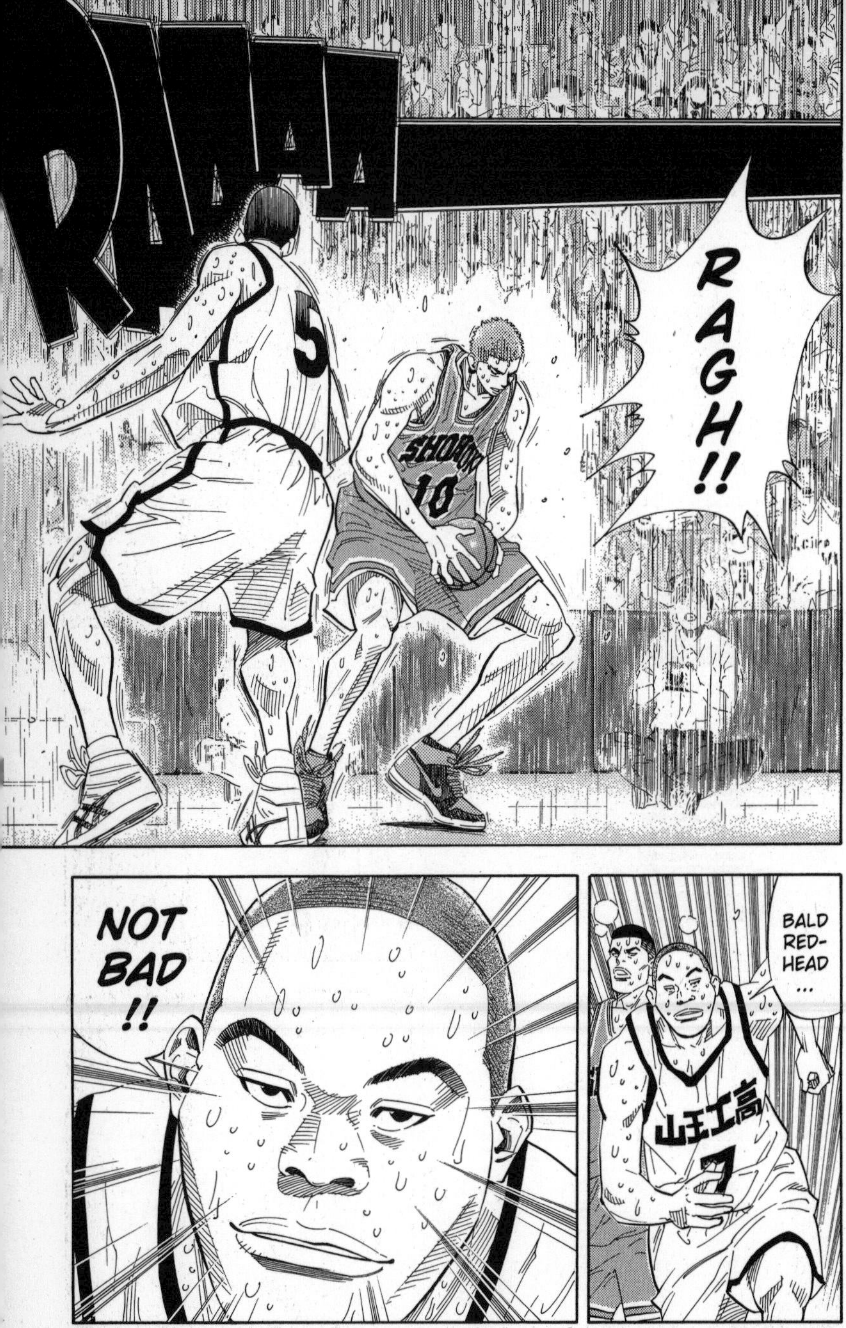
RAAAA
RAGH!!
BALD RED-HEAD ...
NOT BAD !!

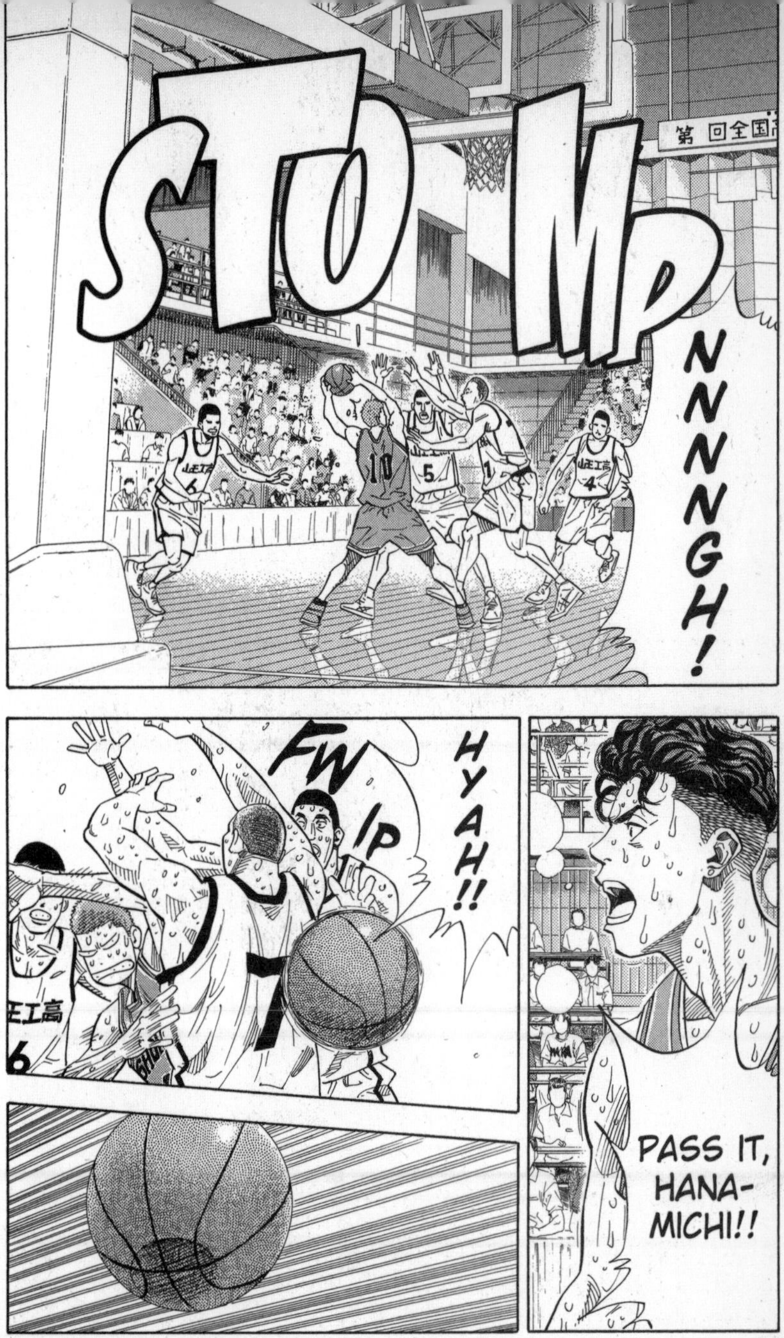
STOMP
NNNNNGH!
PASS IT, HANA-MICHI!!
HYAH!!
FWIP

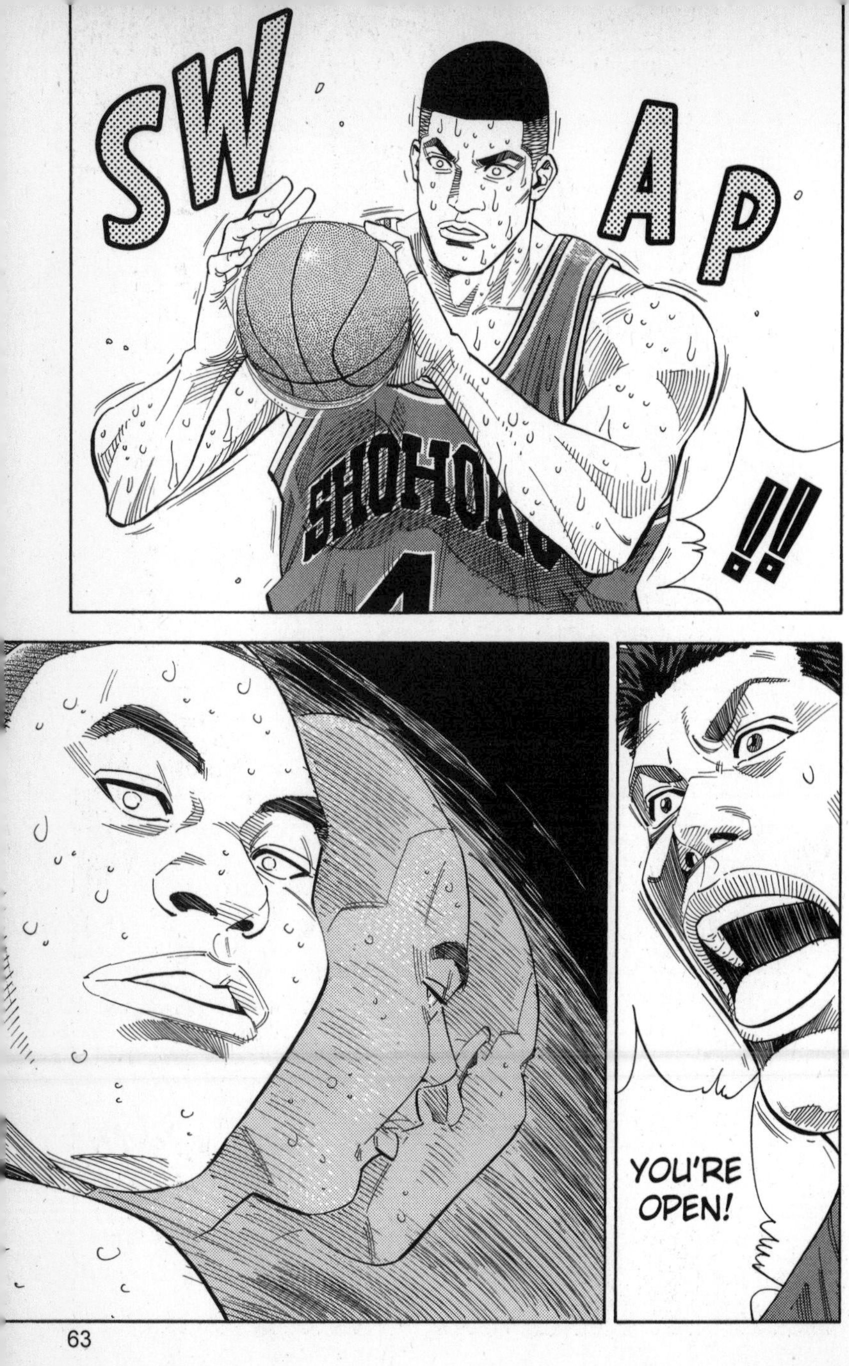
SWAP
!!
YOU'RE OPEN!

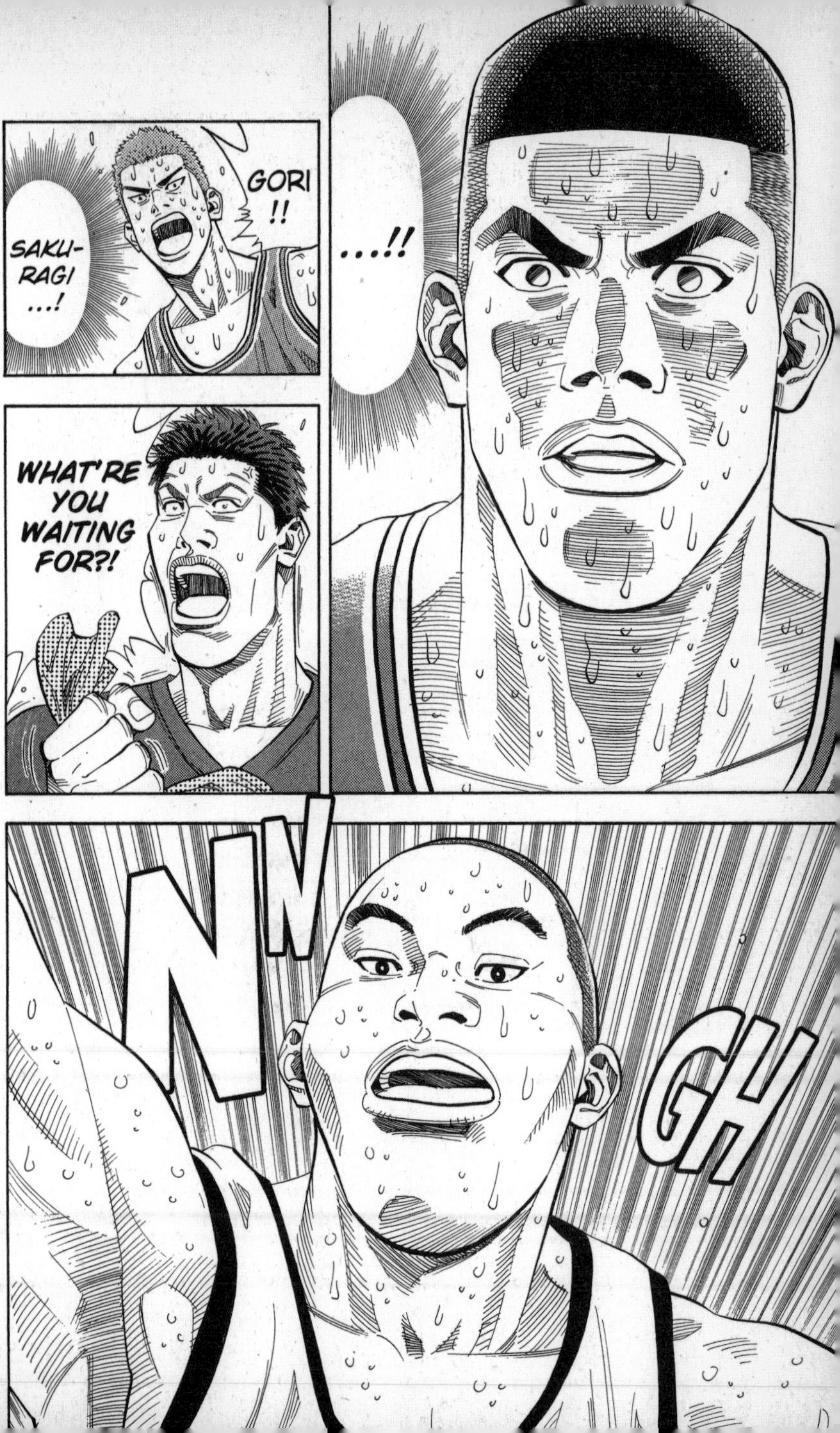
...!!
GORI !!
SAKU-RAGI ...!
WHAT'RE YOU WAITING FOR?!
NNGH

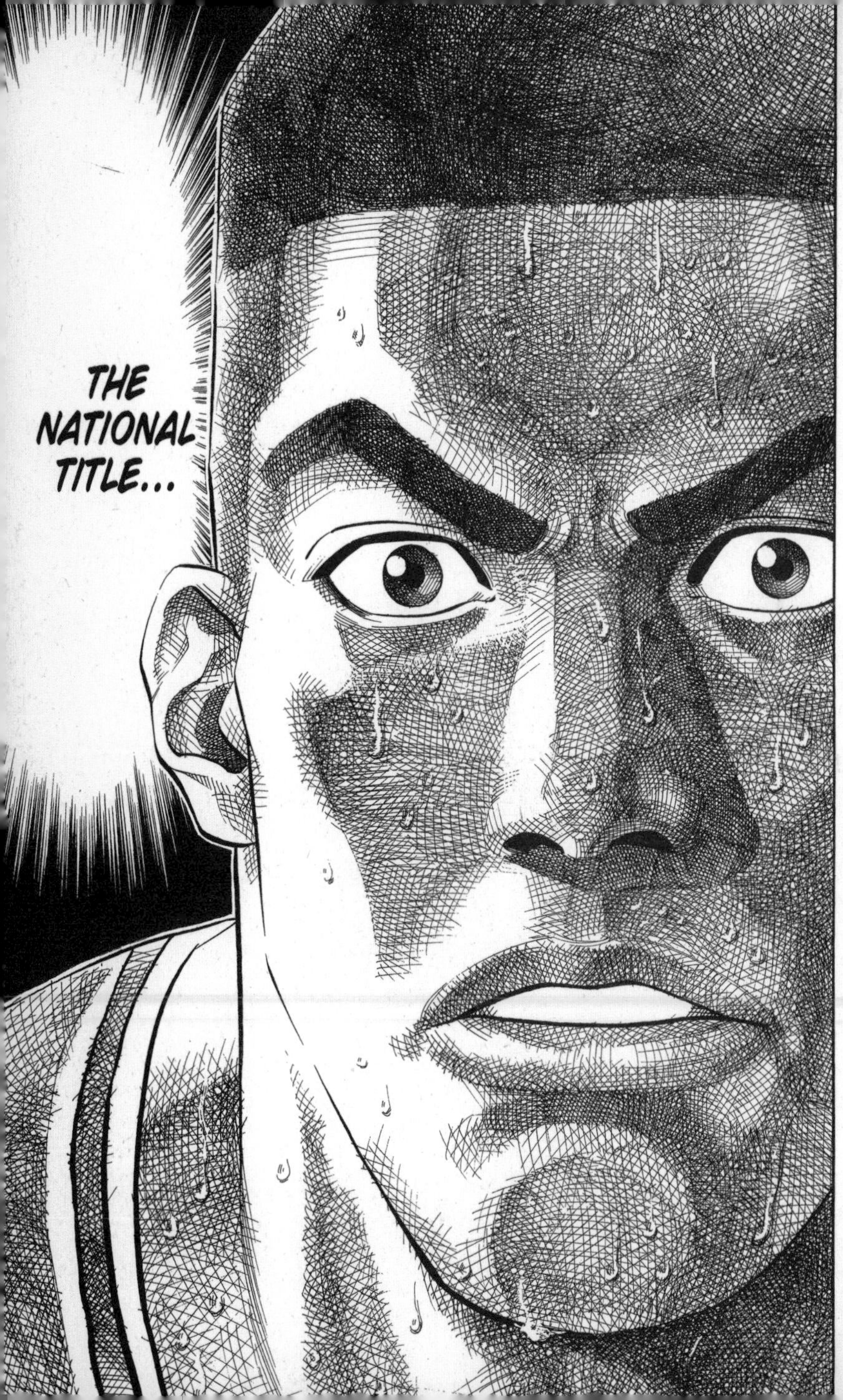
THE NATIONAL TITLE...

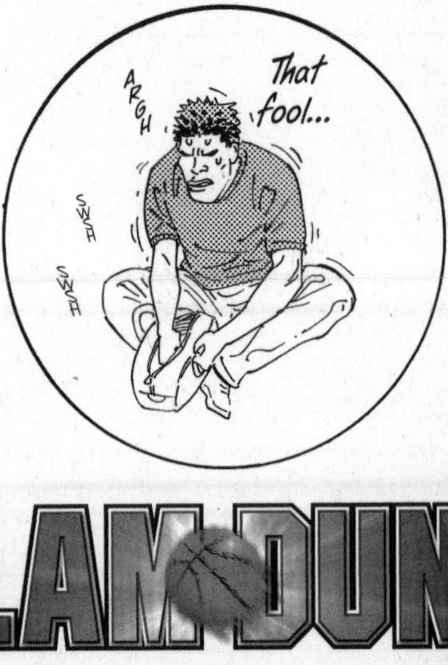
That fool...
ARGH
SWSH
SWSH

SLAM DUNK

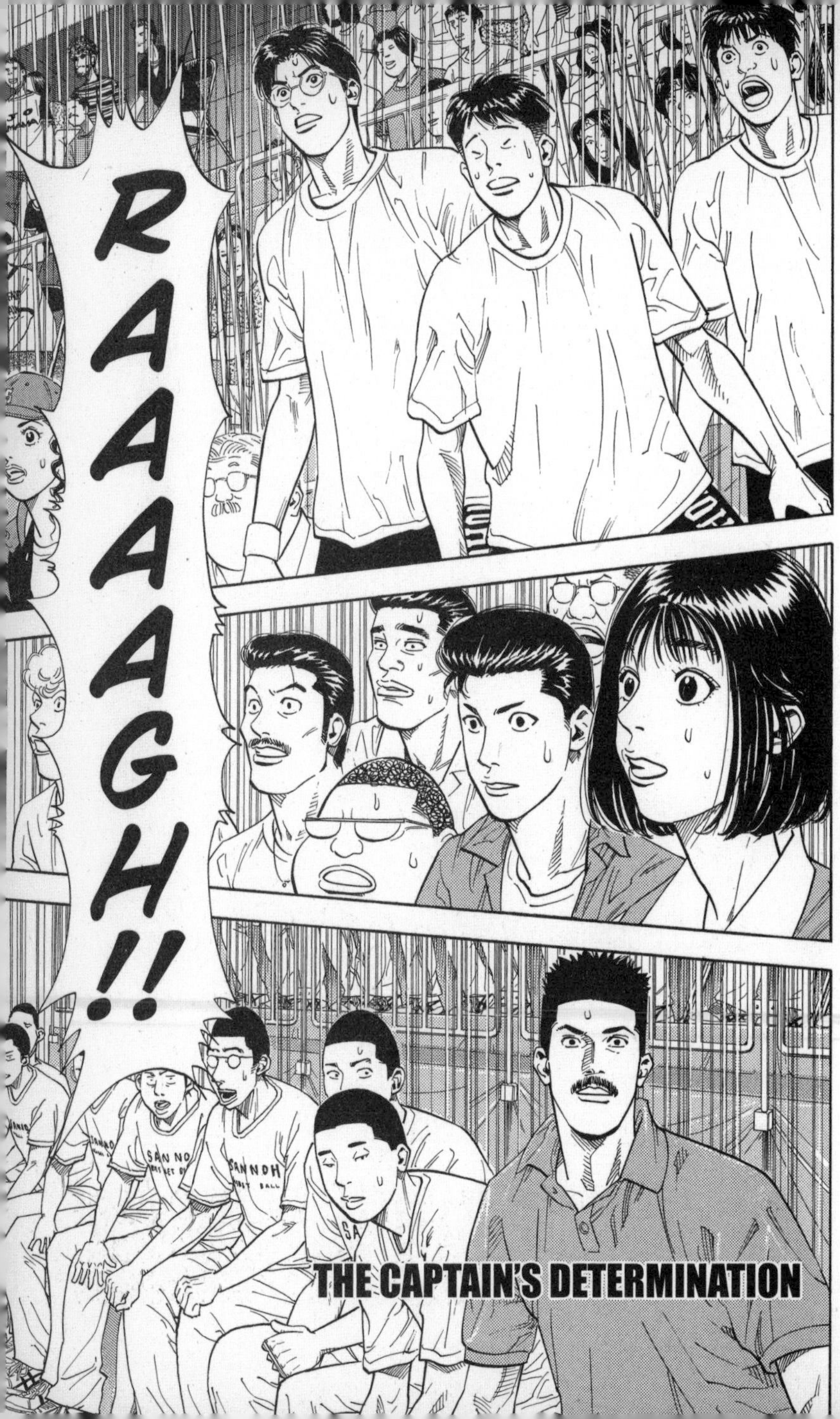
RAAAAGH!!
SANNOH
THE CAPTAIN'S DETERMINATION

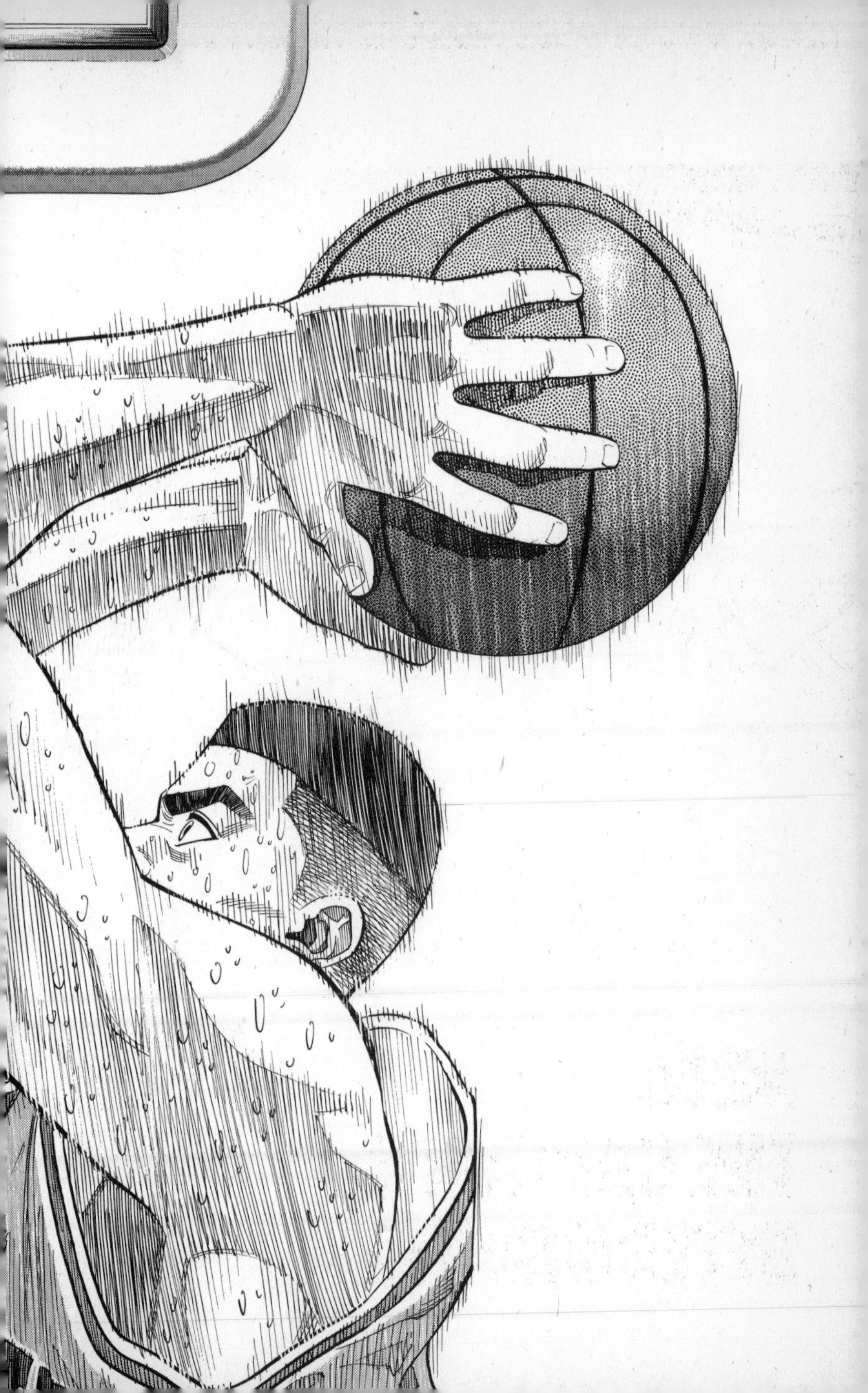

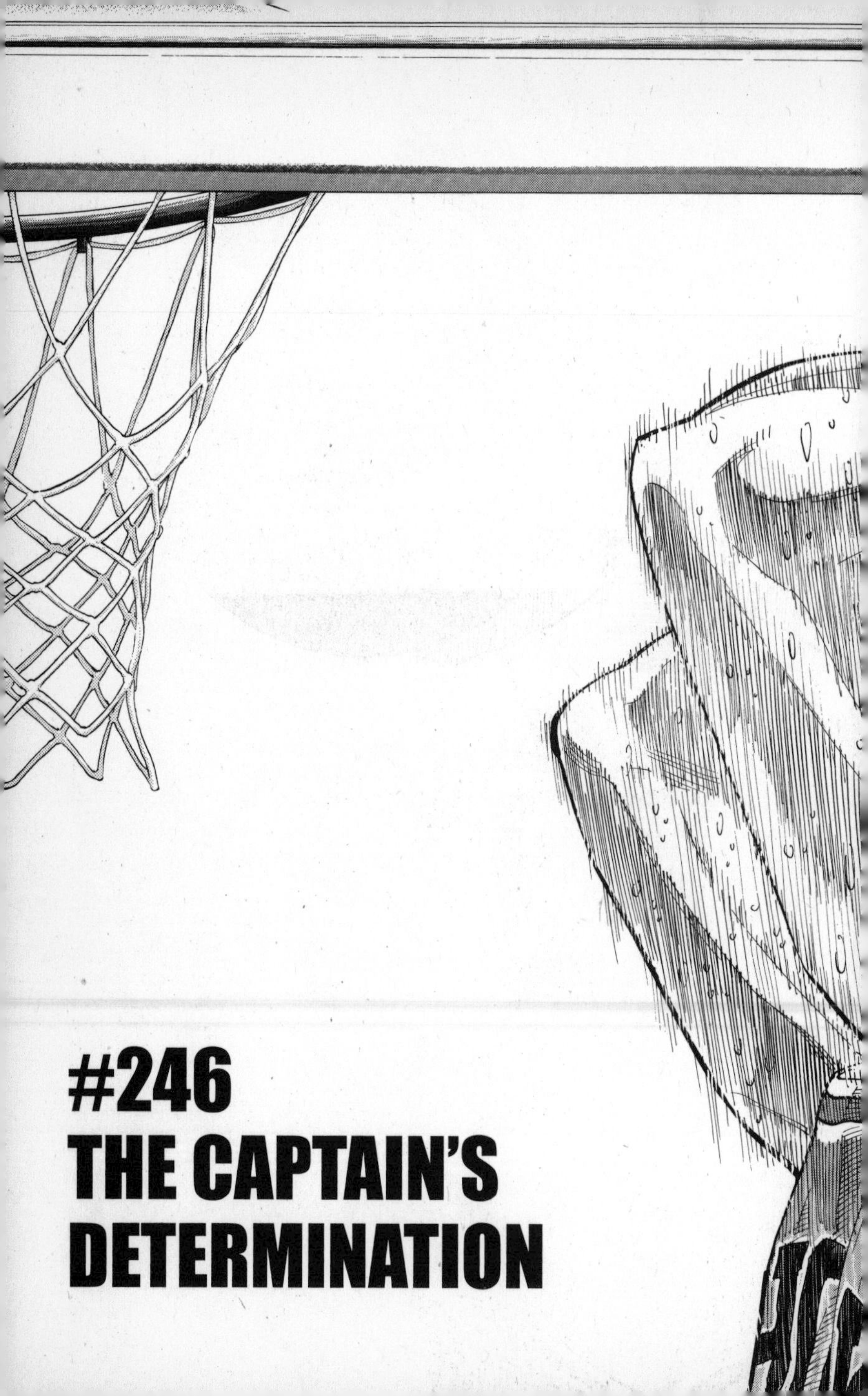
#246
THE CAPTAIN'S DETERMINATION

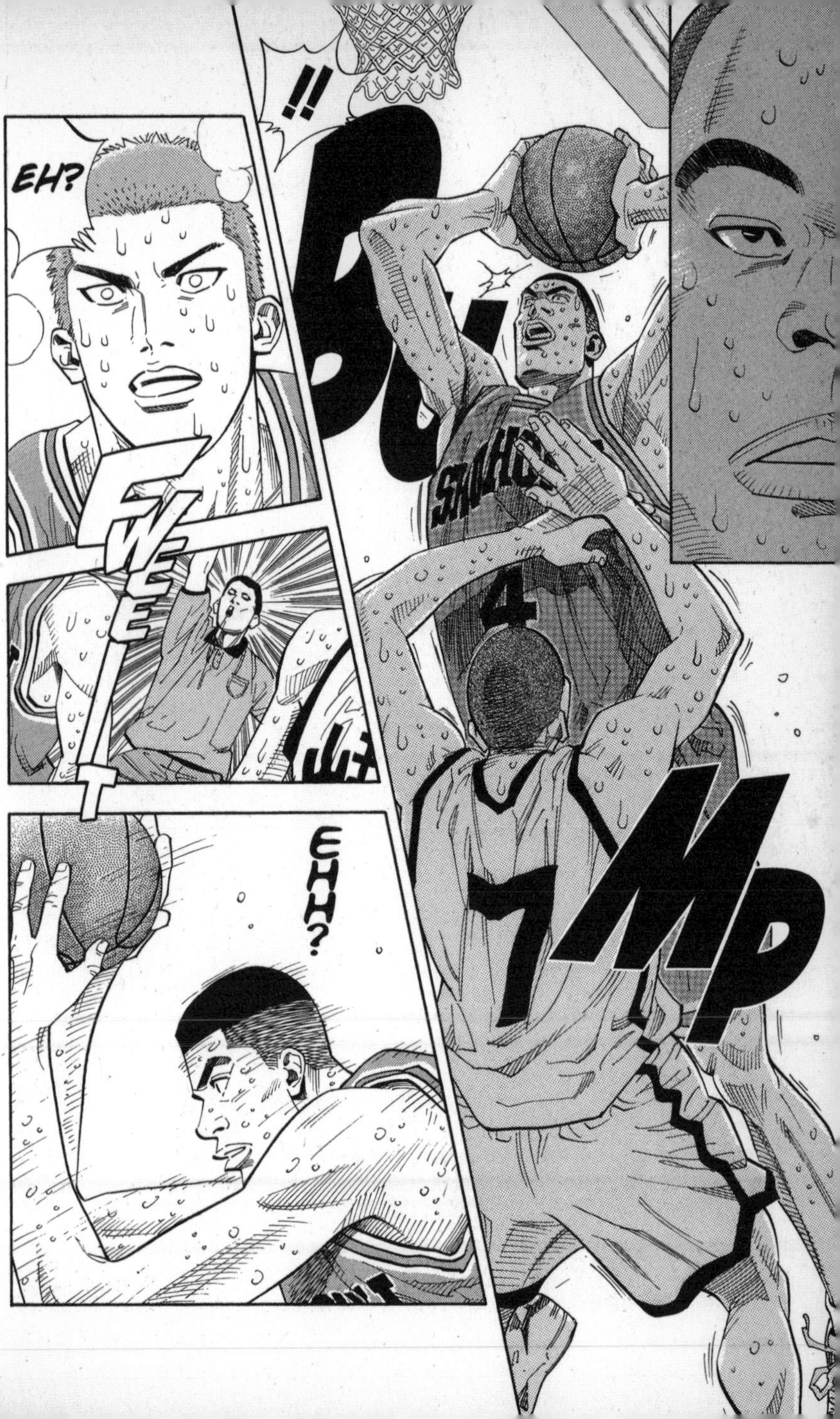
!!
EH?
FWEET
EHHH?

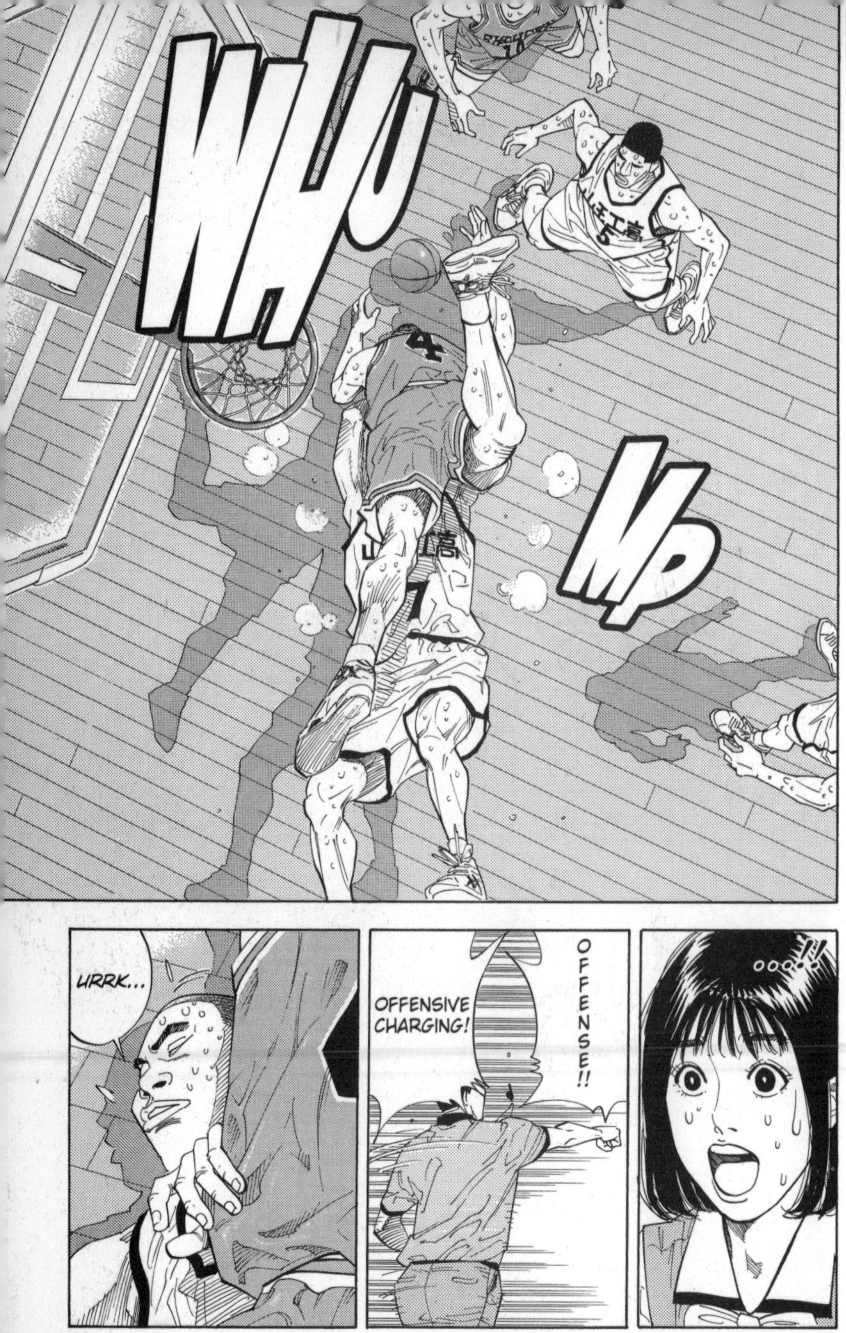
WHU
MP
ooo!!
OFFENSE!!
OFFENSIVE CHARGING!
URRK...

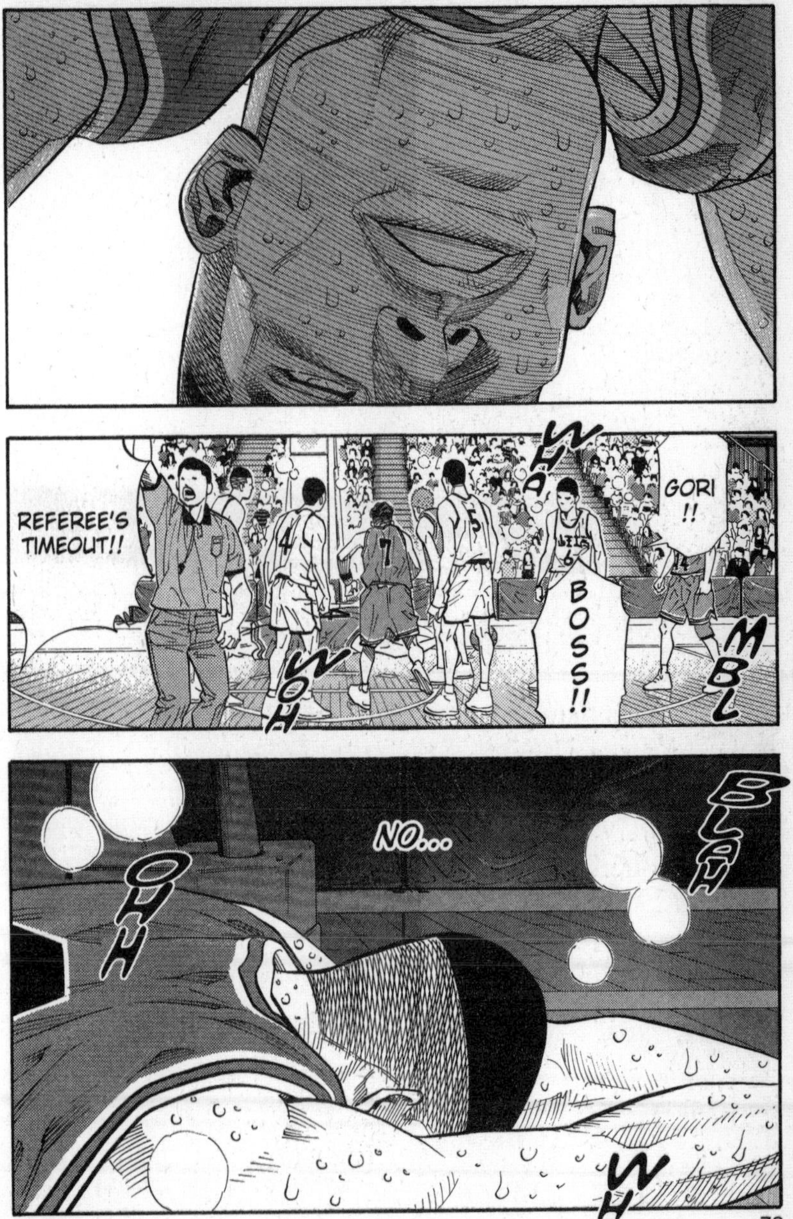
WHA
GORI!!
BOSS!!
MBL
WOH
REFEREE'S TIMEOUT!!
BLAH
NO...
OHH
WHA

READ THIS WAY

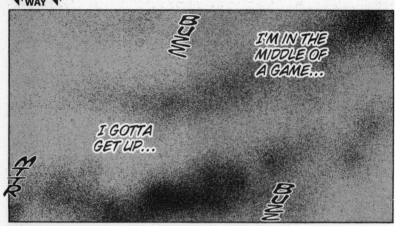

I'M IN THE MIDDLE OF A GAME...
BUZZ
I GOTTA GET UP...
BUZZ
MTTR
HMM
GET UP...
I HAVE TO GET UP...
MBL
WAH
...
MBL
SHFF
...HUH?
WHAT WAS THAT?

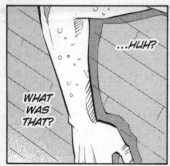

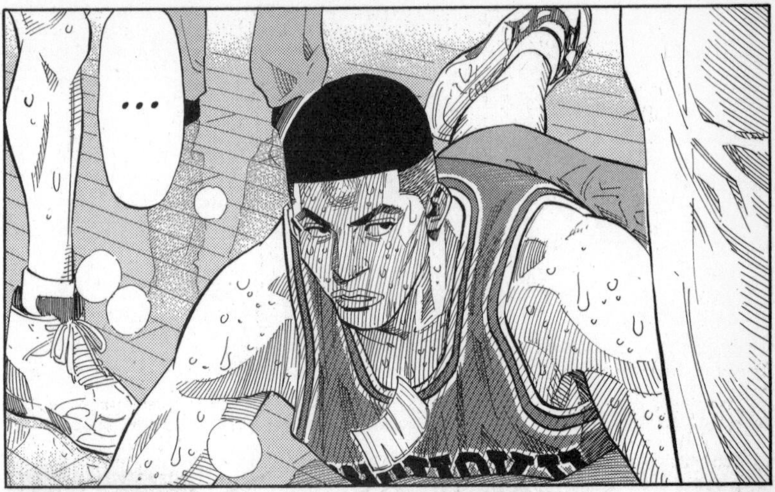
...
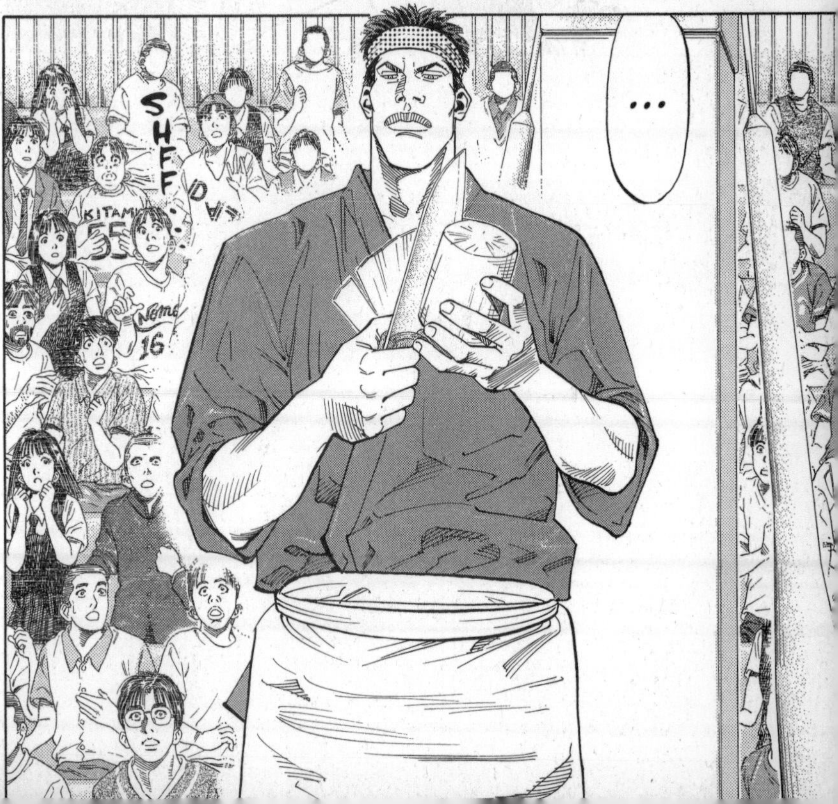
...
SHFF

SHFF...

40...

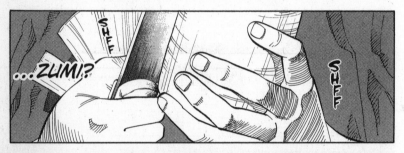

...ZUMI!?

SHFF

SHFF

MRMR

...?

SHFF

MUMBL

CHTR

A radish?

MUMBL

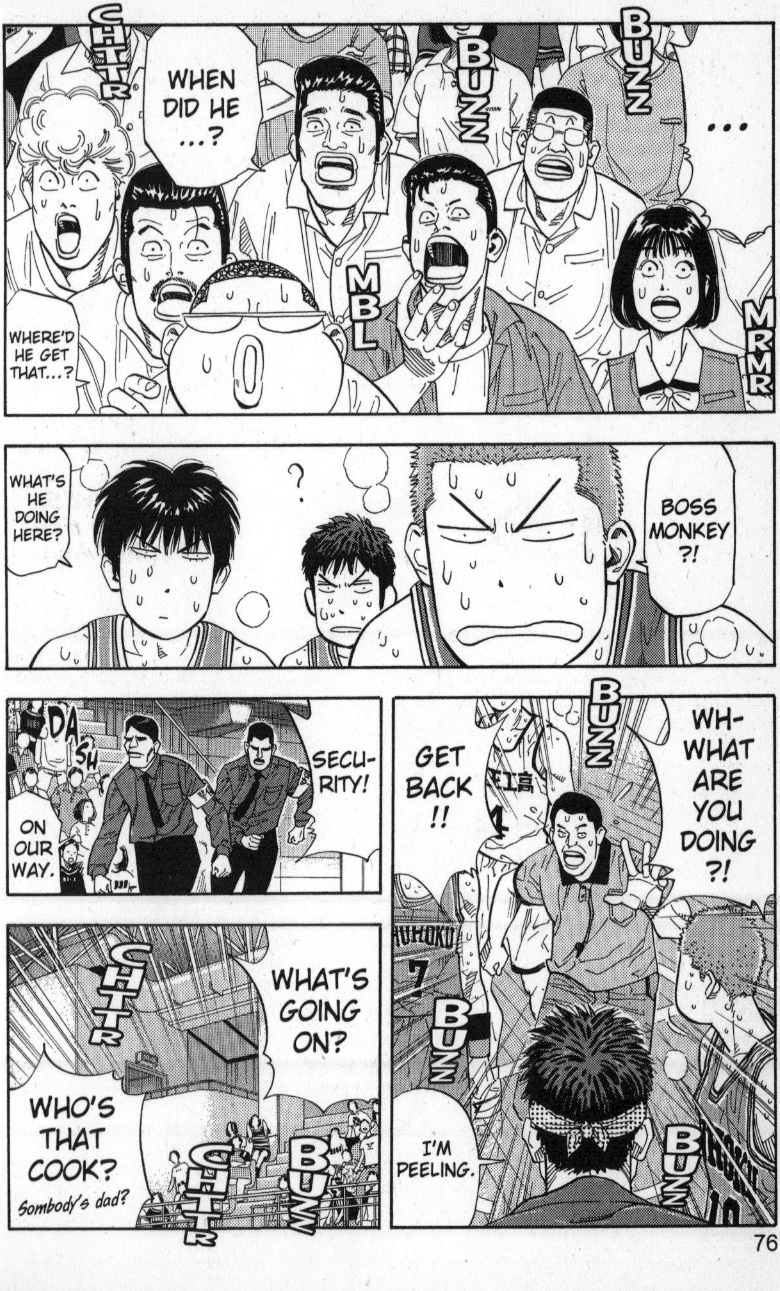
BUZZ
...
MRMR
BUZZ
WHEN DID HE ...?
CHTTR
MBL
WHERE'D HE GET THAT...?
BOSS MONKEY ?!
?
WHAT'S HE DOING HERE?
WH- WHAT ARE YOU DOING ?!
BUZZ
GET BACK !!
BUZZ
BUZZ
I'M PEELING.
SECU- RITY!
DASH
ON OUR WAY.
WHAT'S GOING ON?
CHTTR
BUZZ
CHTTR
WHO'S THAT COOK?
Sombody's dad?

READ THIS WAY

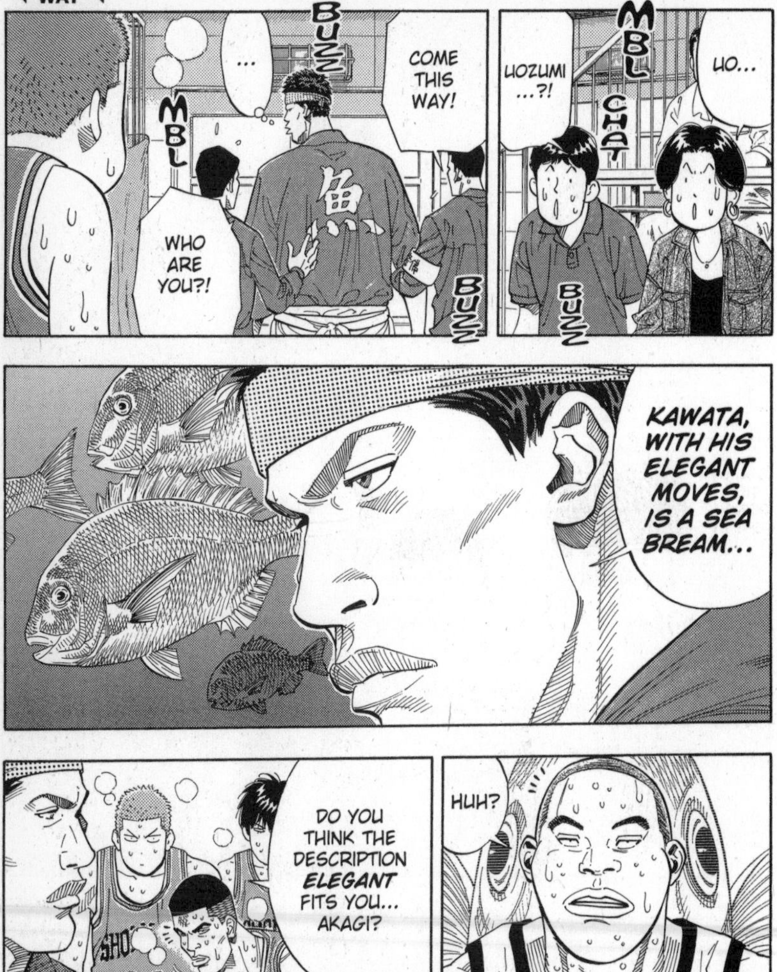
UO...
UOZUMI ...?!
MBL
CHAT
BUZZ
COME THIS WAY!
BUZZ
...
MBL
WHO ARE YOU?!
BUZZ
KAWATA, WITH HIS ELEGANT MOVES, IS A SEA BREAM...
HUH?
IS THAT AKAGI'S DAD...?
He's huge...
No he isn't.
DO YOU THINK THE DESCRIPTION ELEGANT FITS YOU... AKAGI?

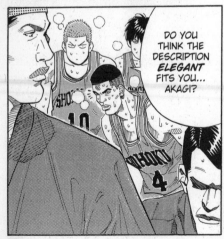

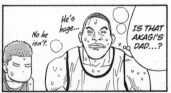

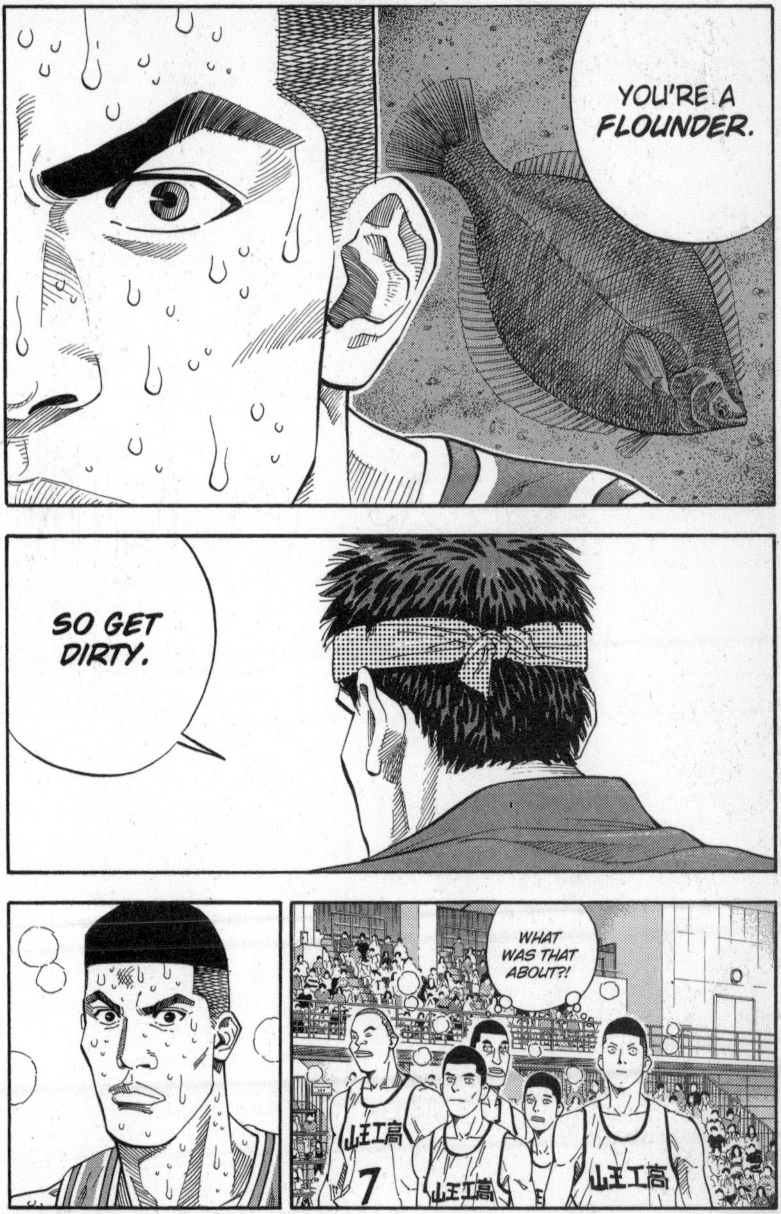
YOU'RE A FLOUNDER.
SO GET DIRTY.
WHAT WAS THAT ABOUT?!

READ THIS WAY

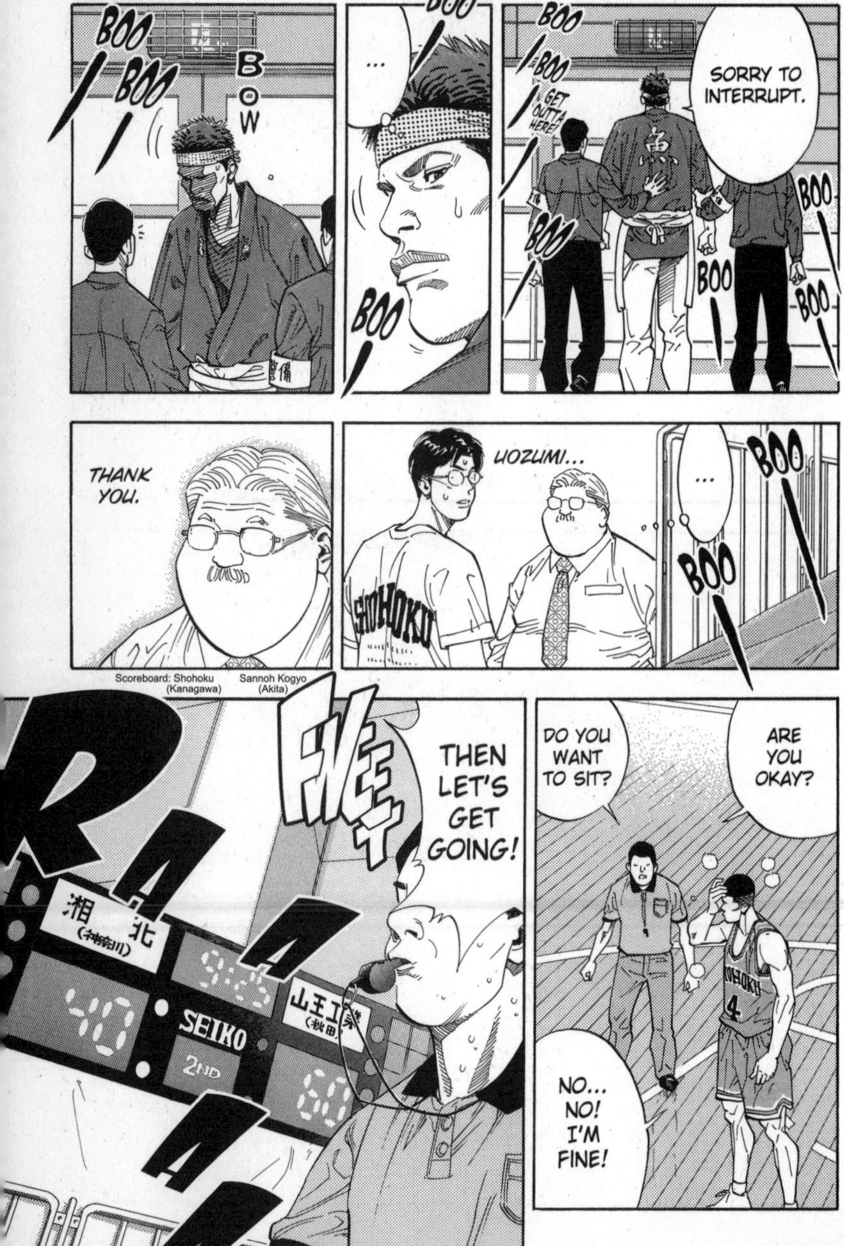
BOO
BOO
GET OUTTA HERE!
SORRY TO INTERRUPT.
BOO
BOO
BOO
BOO
BOO
...
BOO
BOO
BOO
BOW
UOZUMI...
...
BOO
BOO
THANK YOU.
Scoreboard: Shohoku (Kanagawa) Sannoh Kogyo (Akita)
ARE YOU OKAY?
DO YOU WANT TO SIT?
NO... NO! I'M FINE!
FWEEET
THEN LET'S GET GOING!
湘北 (神奈川)
9:25
山王工業 (秋田)
40
SEIKO
2ND
60
RAAAAA

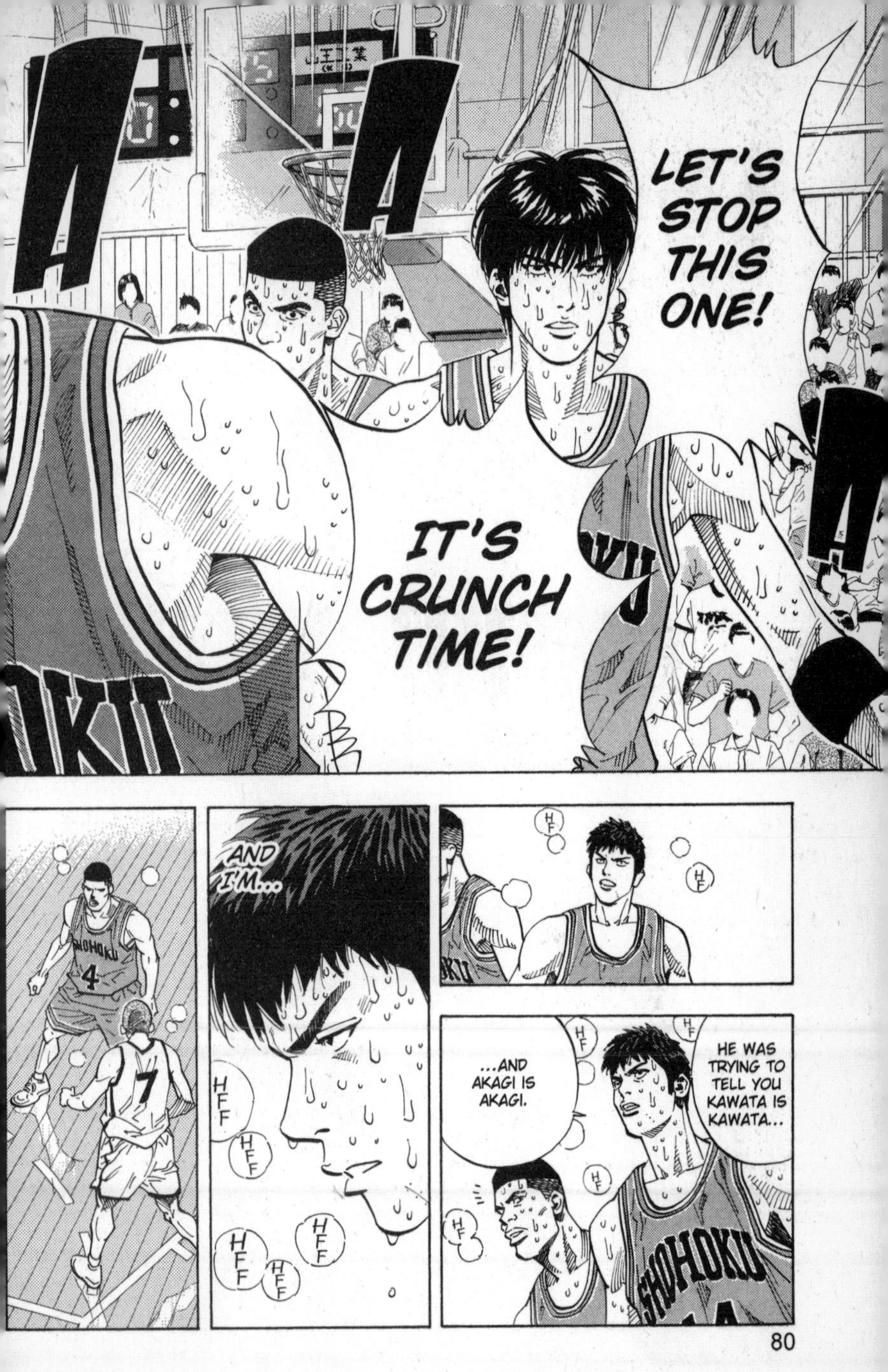

AAAA
LET'S STOP THIS ONE!
IT'S CRUNCH TIME!
HF
HF
HF
HF
HE WAS TRYING TO TELL YOU KAWATA IS KAWATA...
...AND AKAGI IS AKAGI.
HF
HF
AND I'M...
HFF
HFF
HFF
HFF
HFF

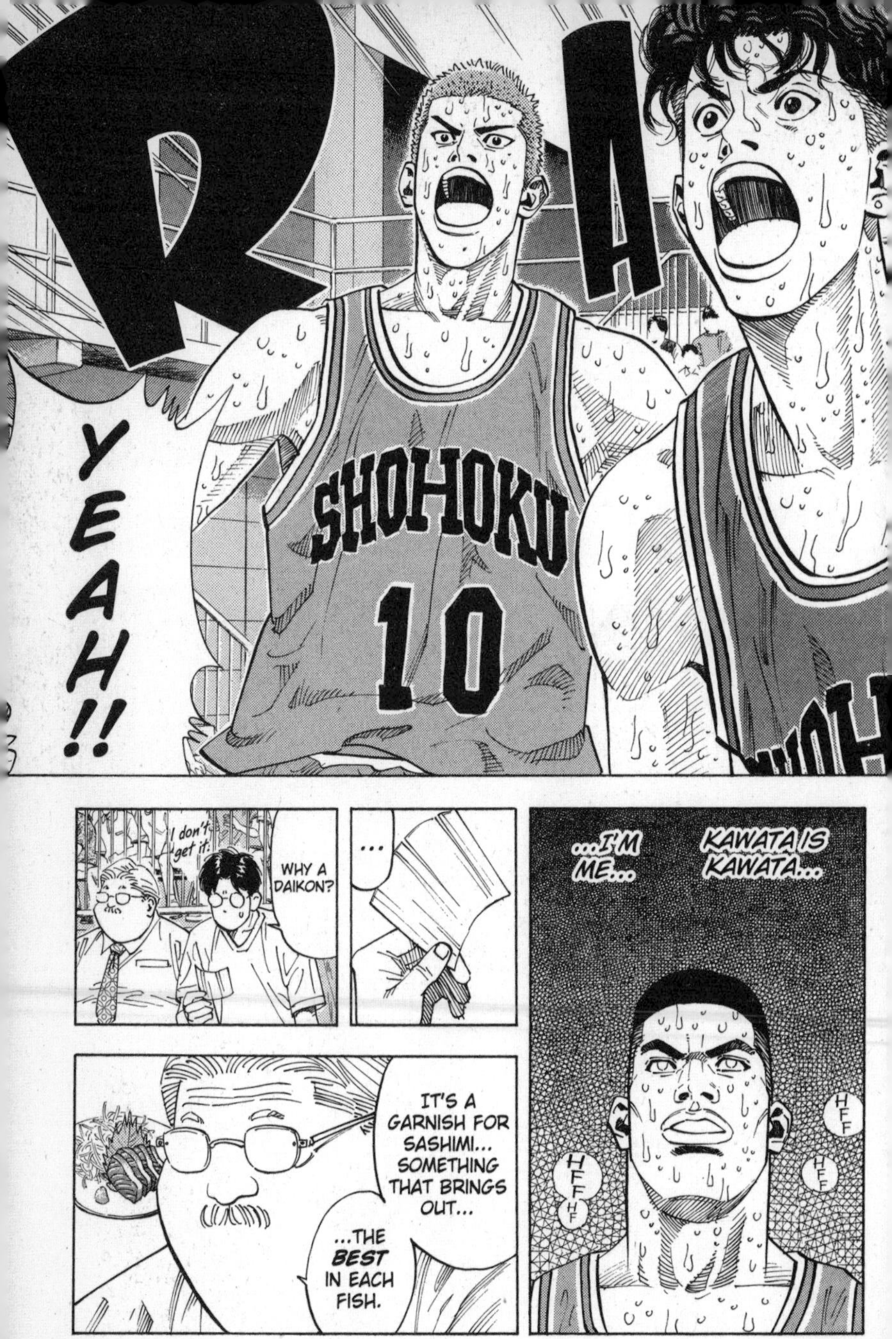
RA
YEAH!!
KAWATA IS KAWATA...
...I'M ME...
HFF
HFF
HFF HF
HFF
...
WHY A DAIKON?
I don't get it.
IT'S A GARNISH FOR SASHIMI... SOMETHING THAT BRINGS OUT...
...THE BEST IN EACH FISH.

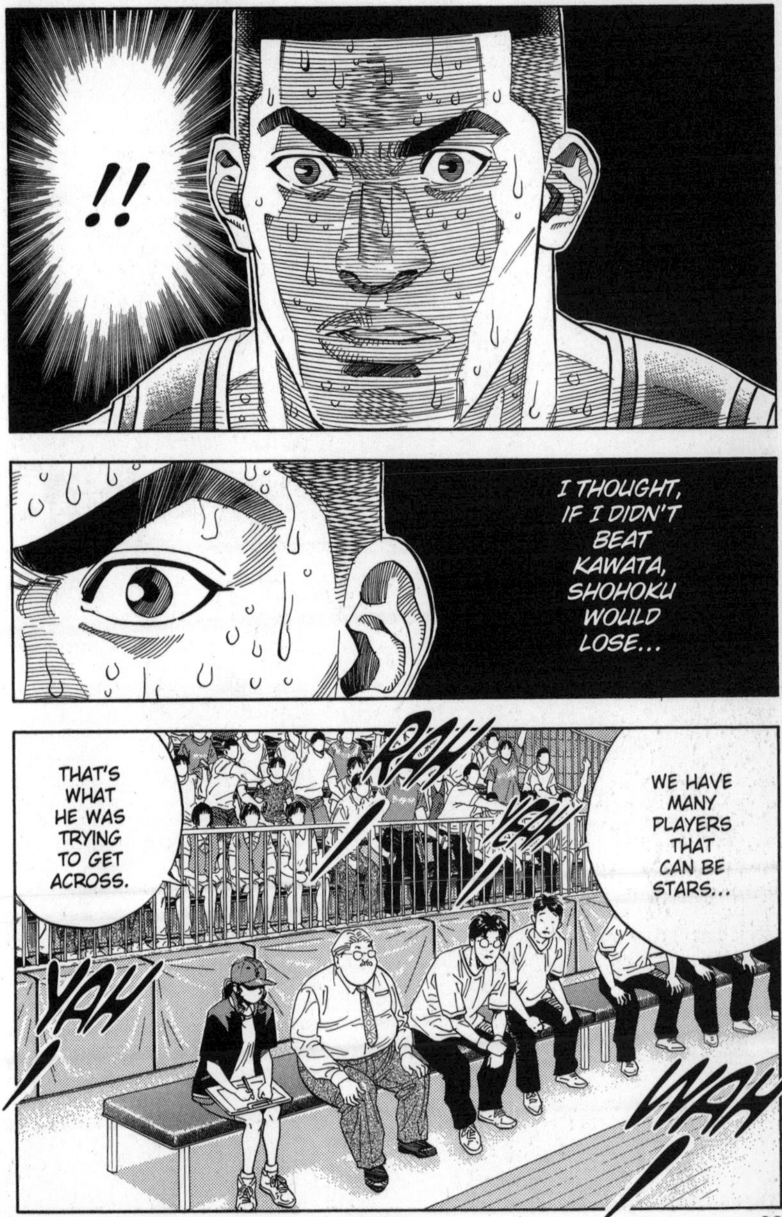
!!
I THOUGHT, IF I DIDN'T BEAT KAWATA, SHOHOKU WOULD LOSE...
WE HAVE MANY PLAYERS THAT CAN BE STARS...
RAH
YAH
THAT'S WHAT HE WAS TRYING TO GET ACROSS.
YAH
WAH

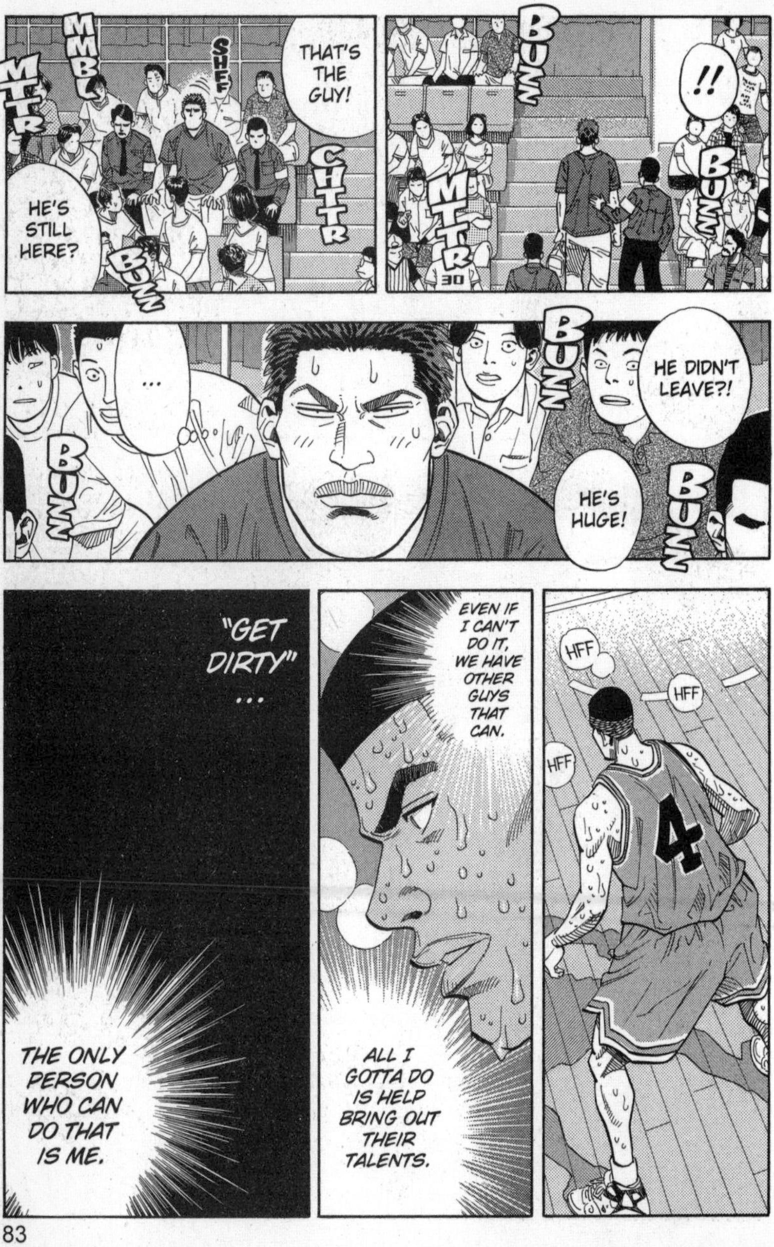

!!
BUZZ
MTTR
BUZZ
THAT'S THE GUY!
SHEF
MMBL
MTTR
CHTTR
HE'S STILL HERE?
BUZZ
HE DIDN'T LEAVE?!
BUZZ
HE'S HUGE!
BUZZ
...
BUZZ
HFF
HFF
HFF
EVEN IF I CAN'T DO IT, WE HAVE OTHER GUYS THAT CAN.
ALL I GOTTA DO IS HELP BRING OUT THEIR TALENTS.
"GET DIRTY"...
THE ONLY PERSON WHO CAN DO THAT IS ME.

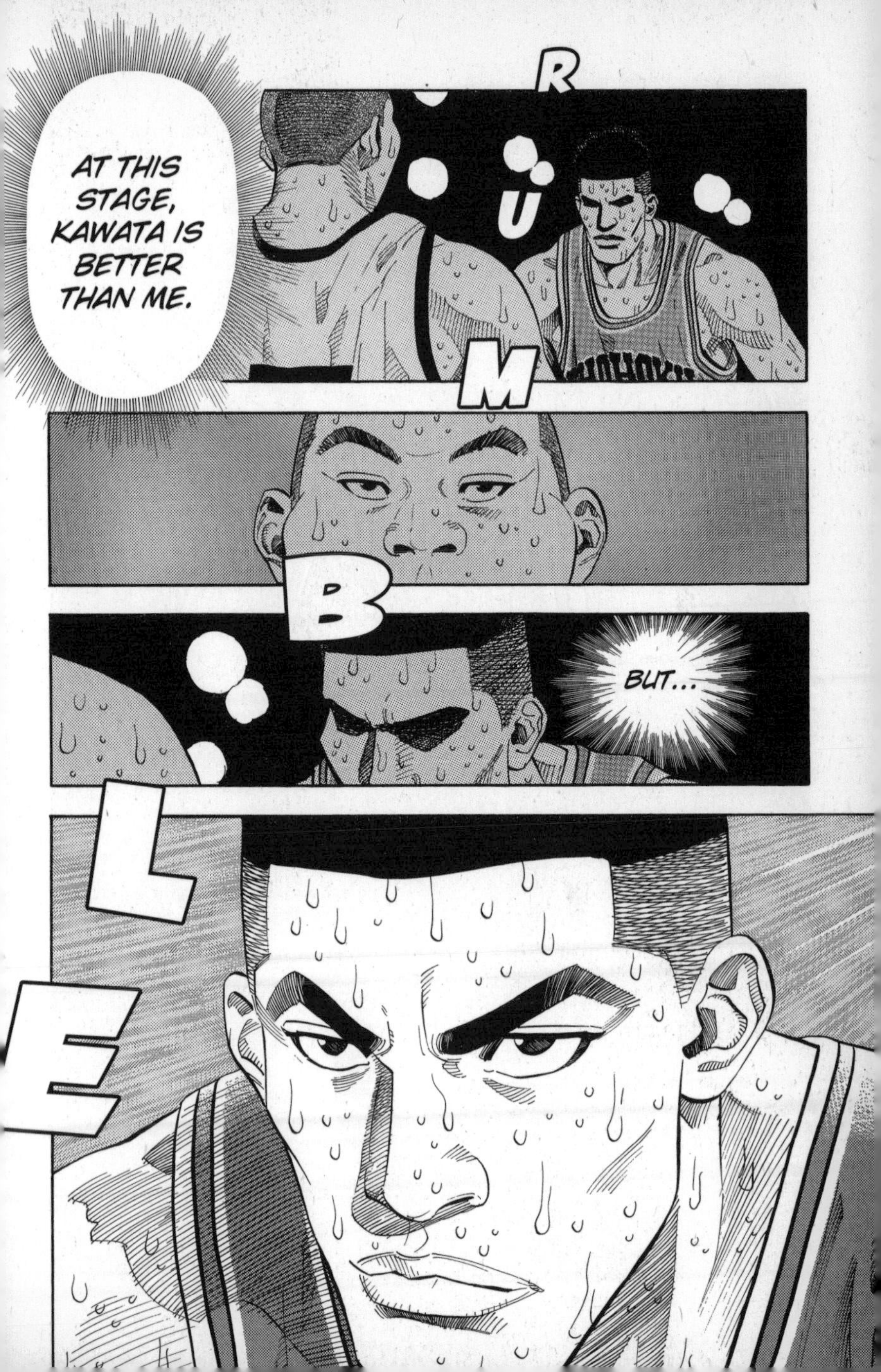
R
U
AT THIS STAGE, KAWATA IS BETTER THAN ME.
M
B
BUT...
L
E

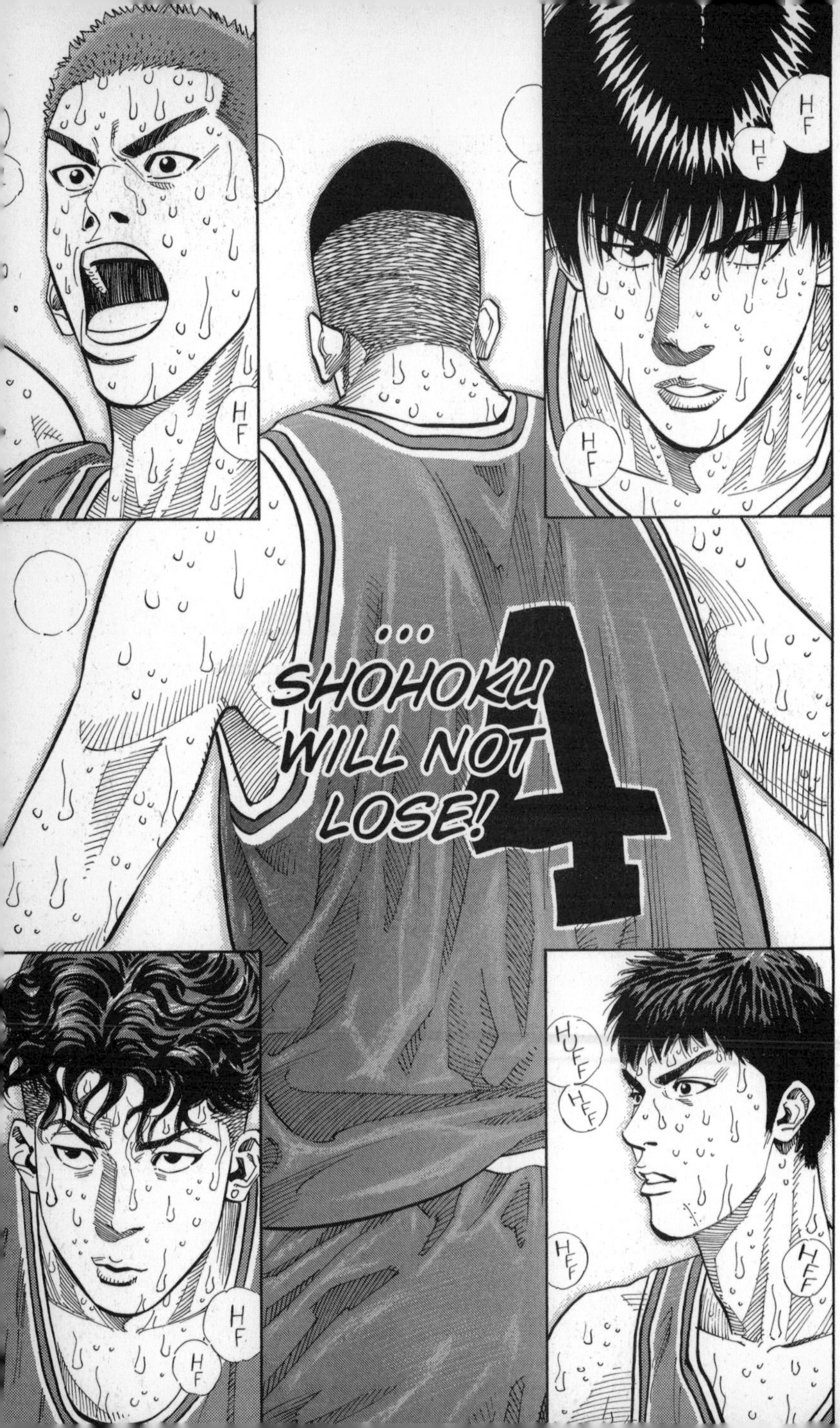
HF
HF
HF
HF
... SHOHOKU WILL NOT LOSE!
HUFF
HFF
HFF
HFF
HF
HF

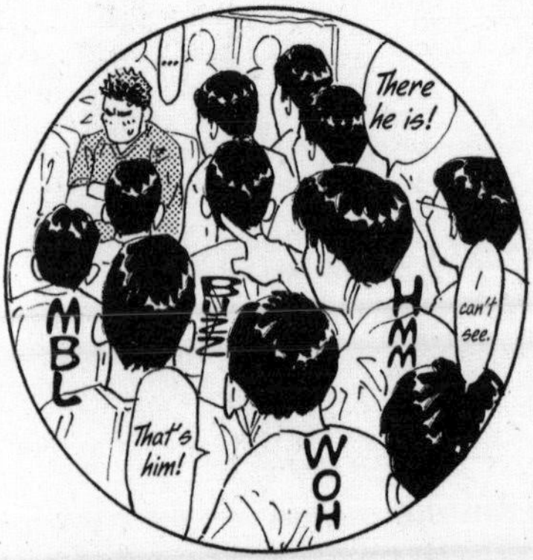
There he is!
...
I can't see.
HMM
BUZZ
MBL
WOH
That's him!

SLAM DUNK

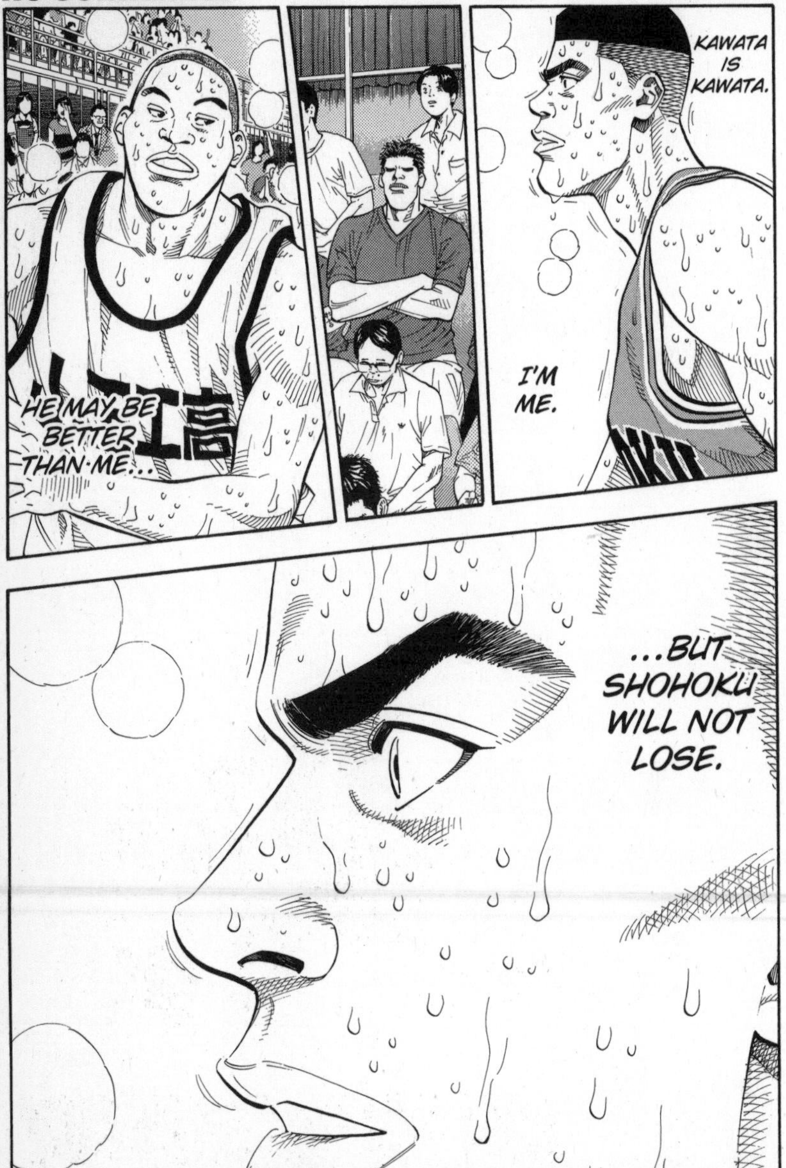
KAWATA IS KAWATA.
I'M ME.
HE MAY BE BETTER THAN ME...
...BUT SHOHOKU WILL NOT LOSE.

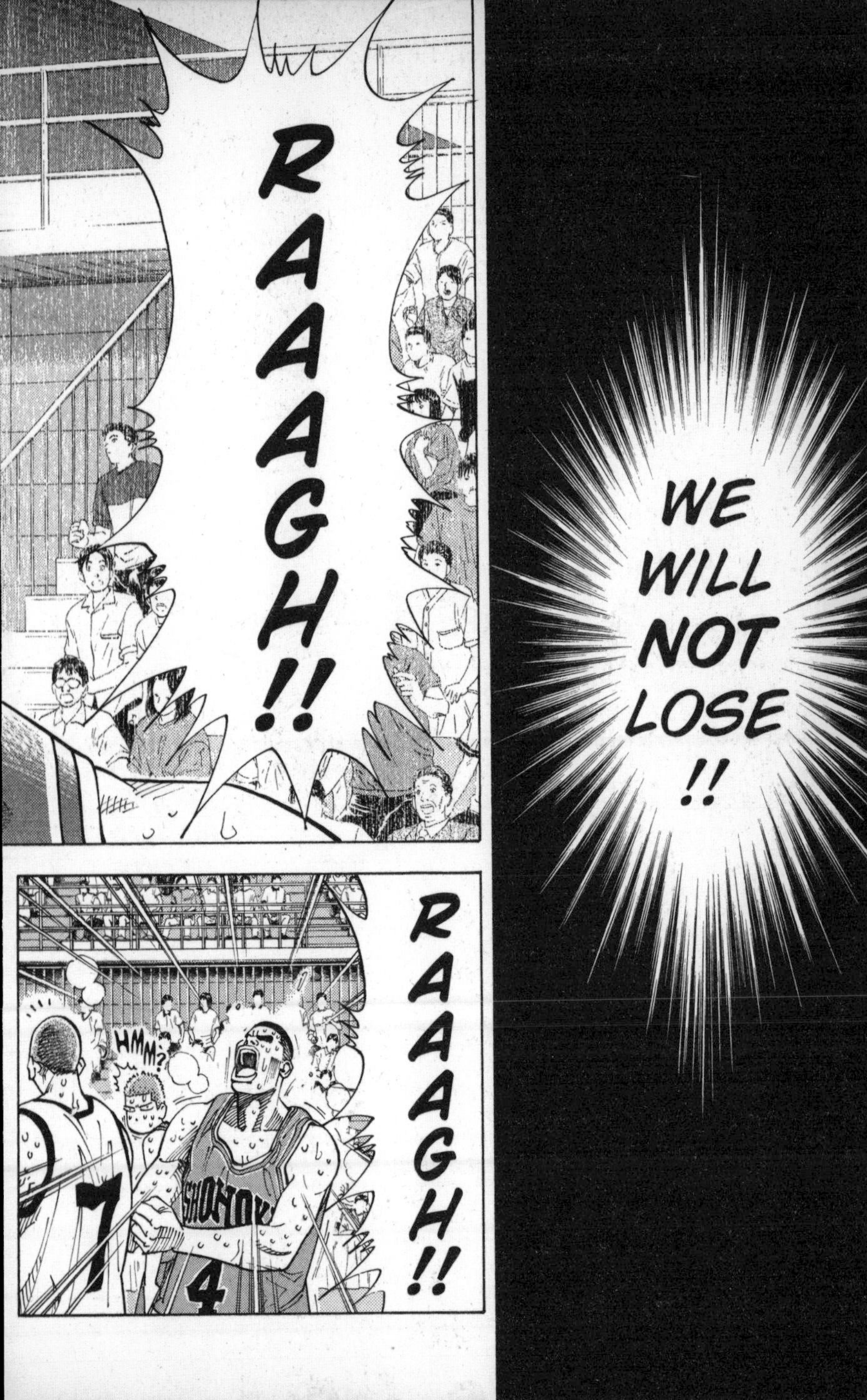
WE WILL NOT LOSE!!
RAAAGH!!
RAAAGH!!
HMM?

#247 NO SURRENDER

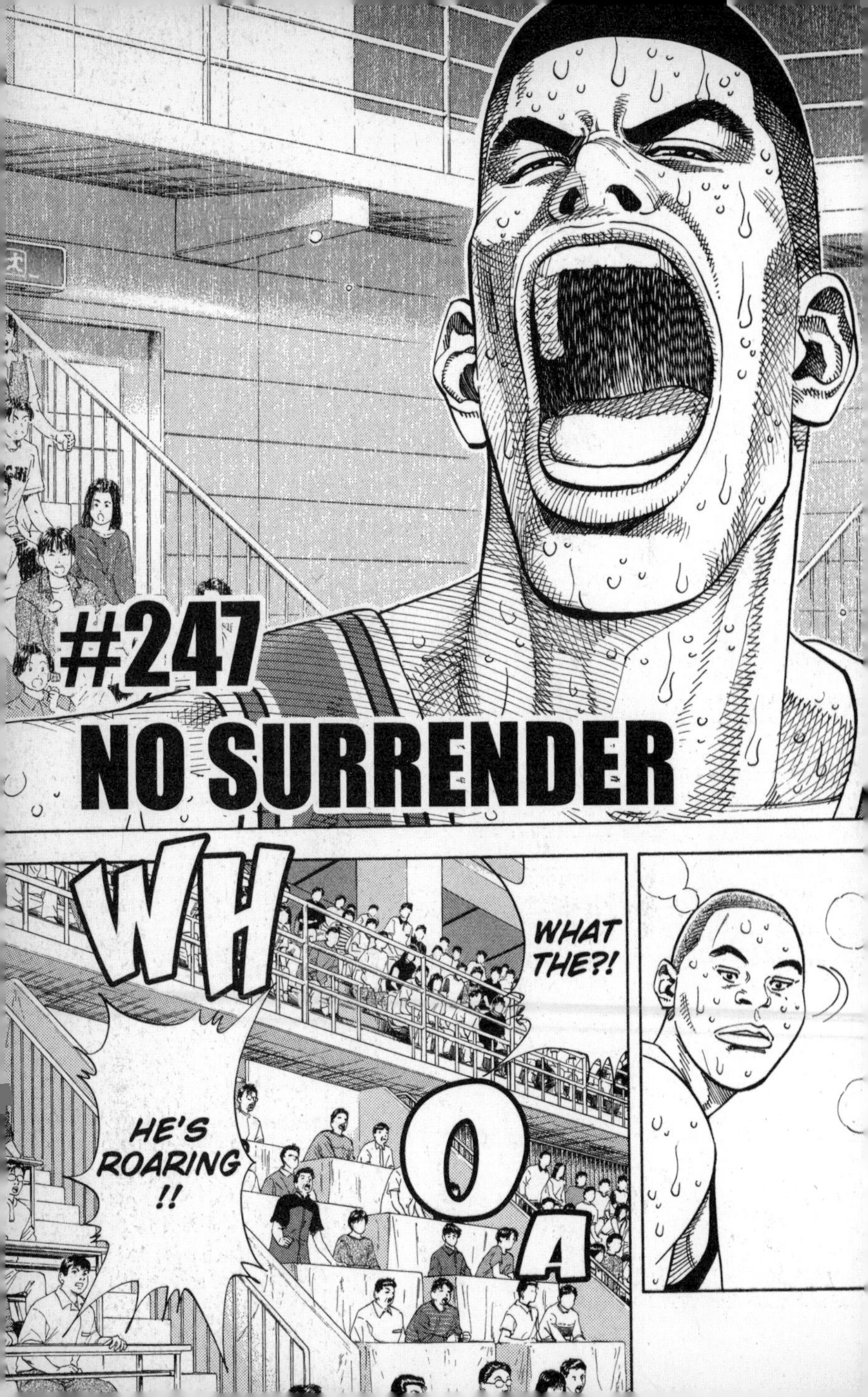
WHAT THE?!
WHOA
HE'S ROARING !!

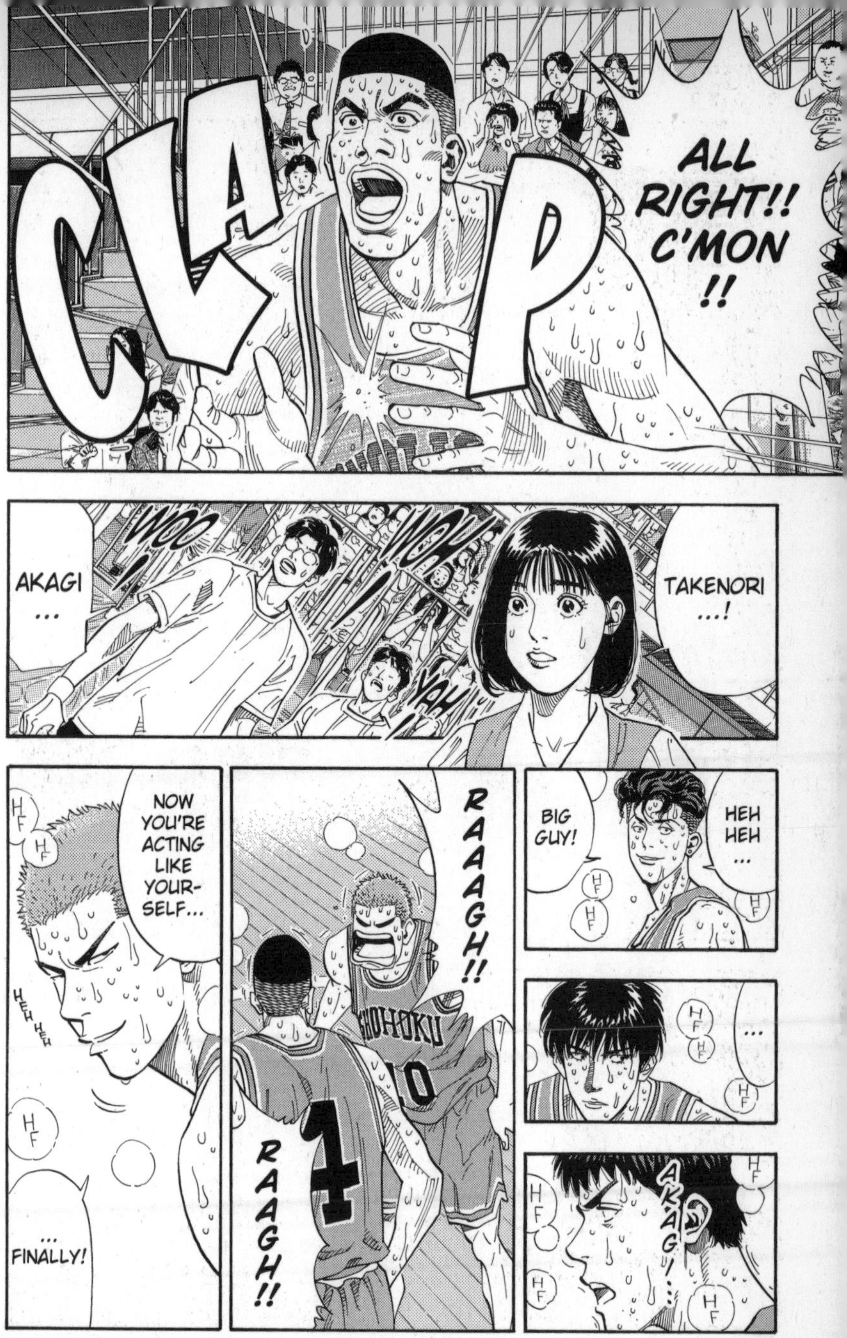
ALL RIGHT!! C'MON!!
CLAP
TAKENORI ...!
WOH
YAH
WOO
AKAGI ...
HEH HEH ...
BIG GUY!
HF HF
HF HF
...
HF HF
HF
AKAGI ...
HF HF
RAAAAGH!!
RAAAGH!!
NOW YOU'RE ACTING LIKE YOURSELF...
HF HF
HEH HEH
HF
... FINALLY!

READ THIS WAY

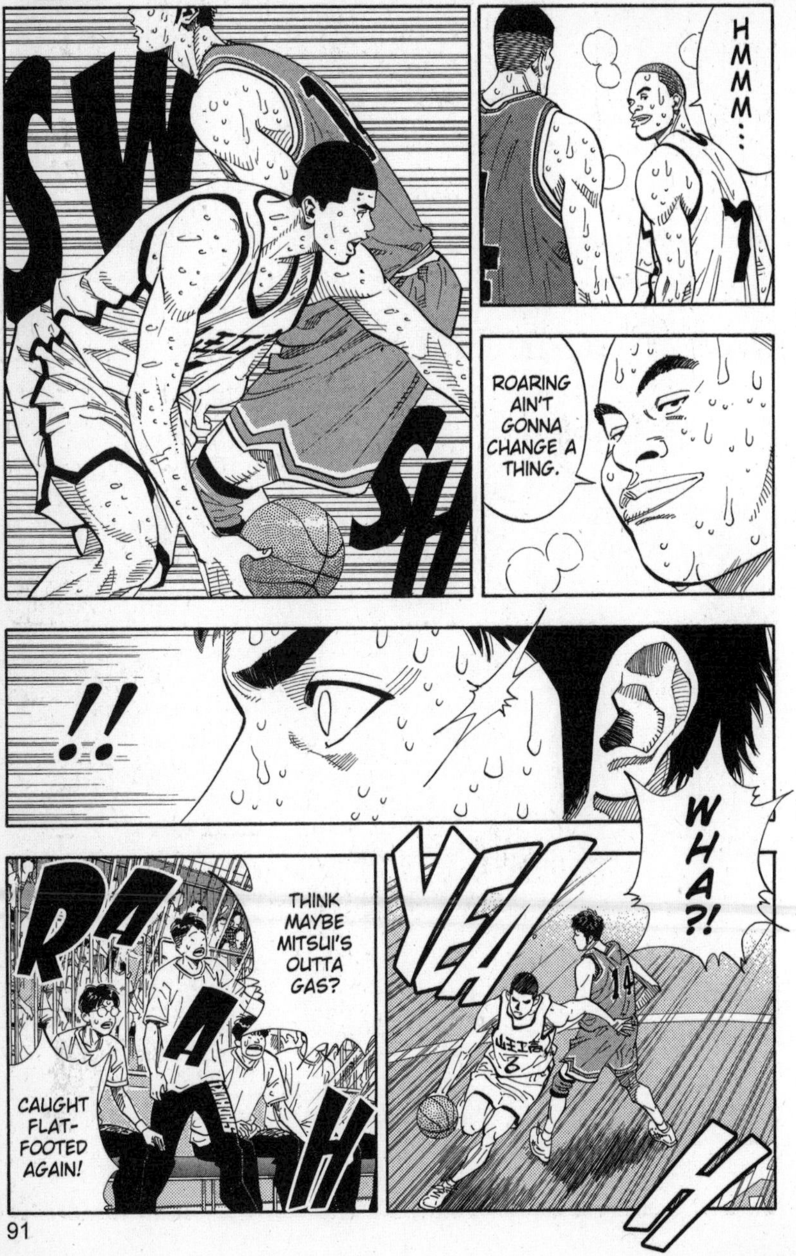
HMMM...
ROARING AIN'T GONNA CHANGE A THING.
SW
SH
!!
WHA?!
RAAH
THINK MAYBE MITSUI'S OUTTA GAS?
CAUGHT FLAT-FOOTED AGAIN!

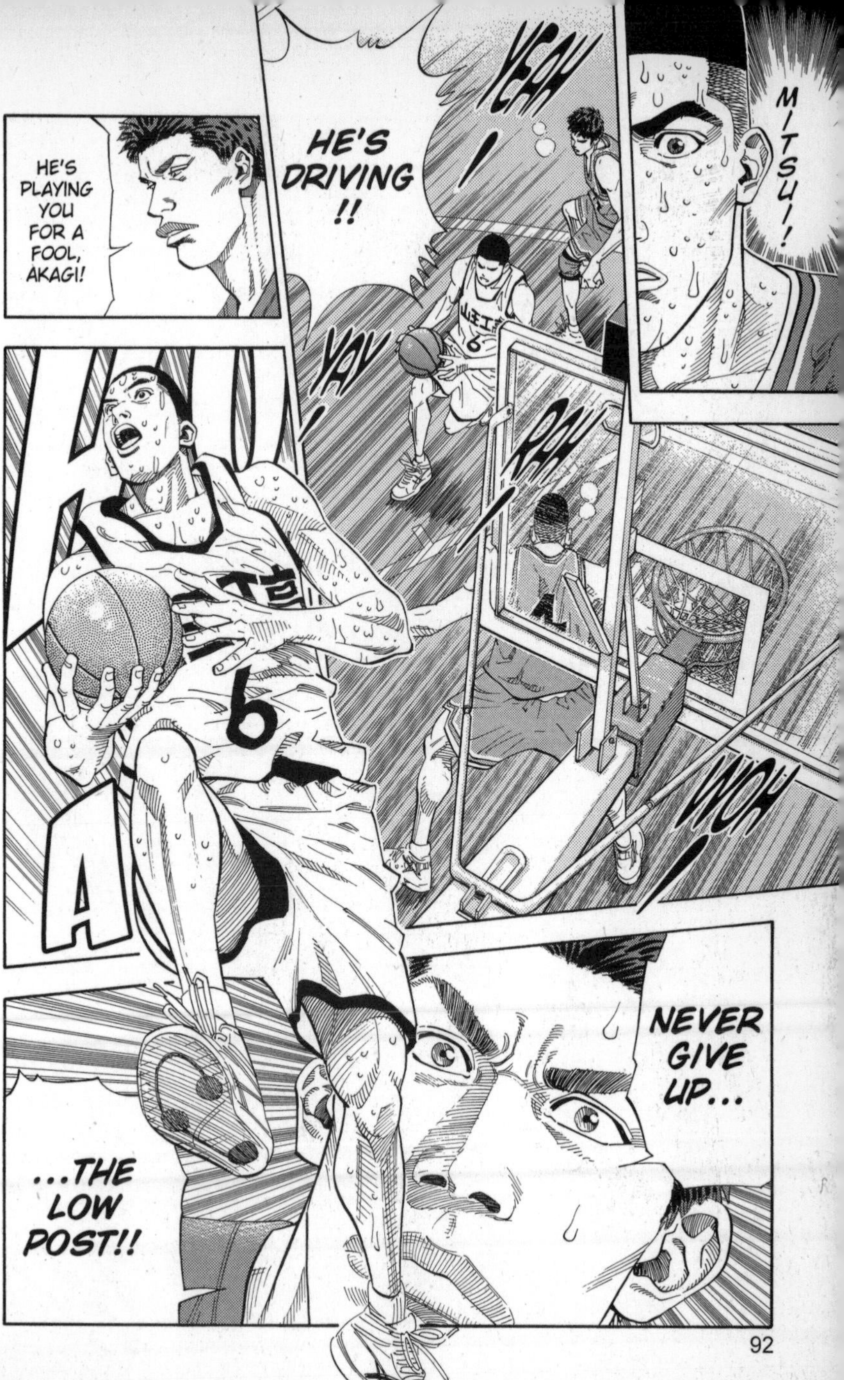
MITSUI!
YEAH!
HE'S DRIVING!!
YAY!
RAH!
WOH!
HE'S PLAYING YOU FOR A FOOL, AKAGI!
A
NEVER GIVE UP...
...THE LOW POST!!

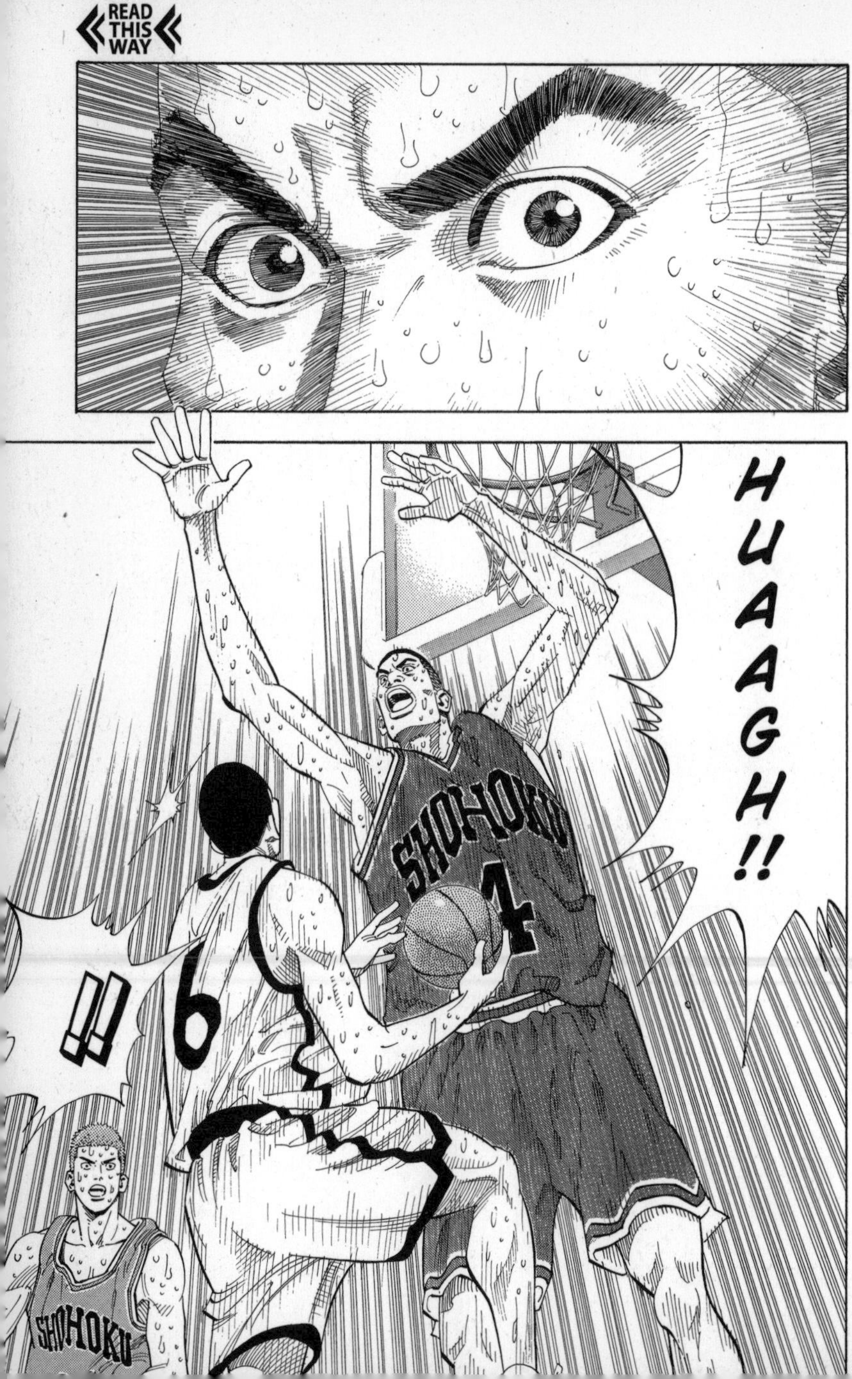

READ THIS WAY
HUAAAGH!!
SHOHOKU
4
6
!!
SHOHOKU

AKAGI!

!!

SHOHOKU
4

A DOUBLE CLUTCH!

S K C H

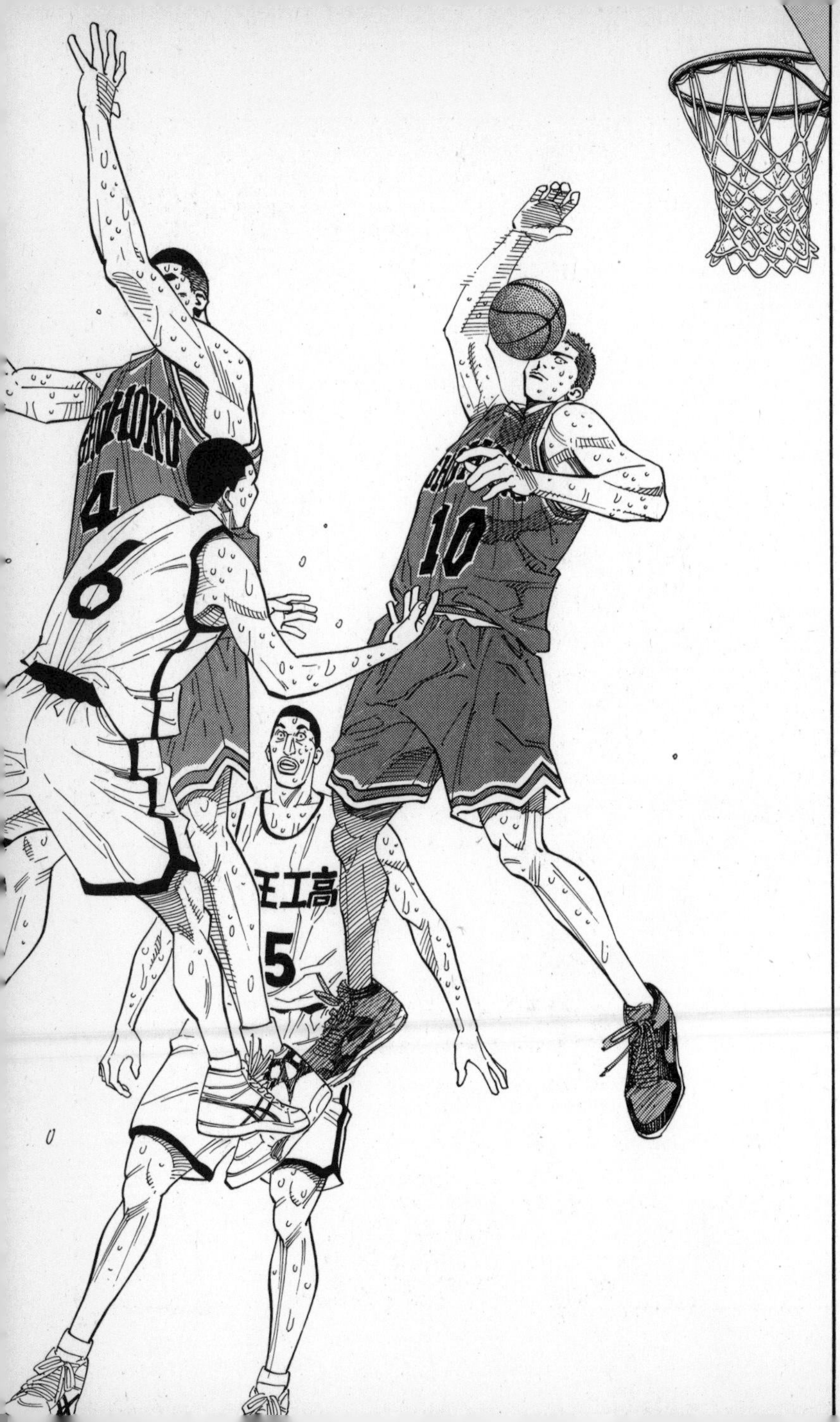

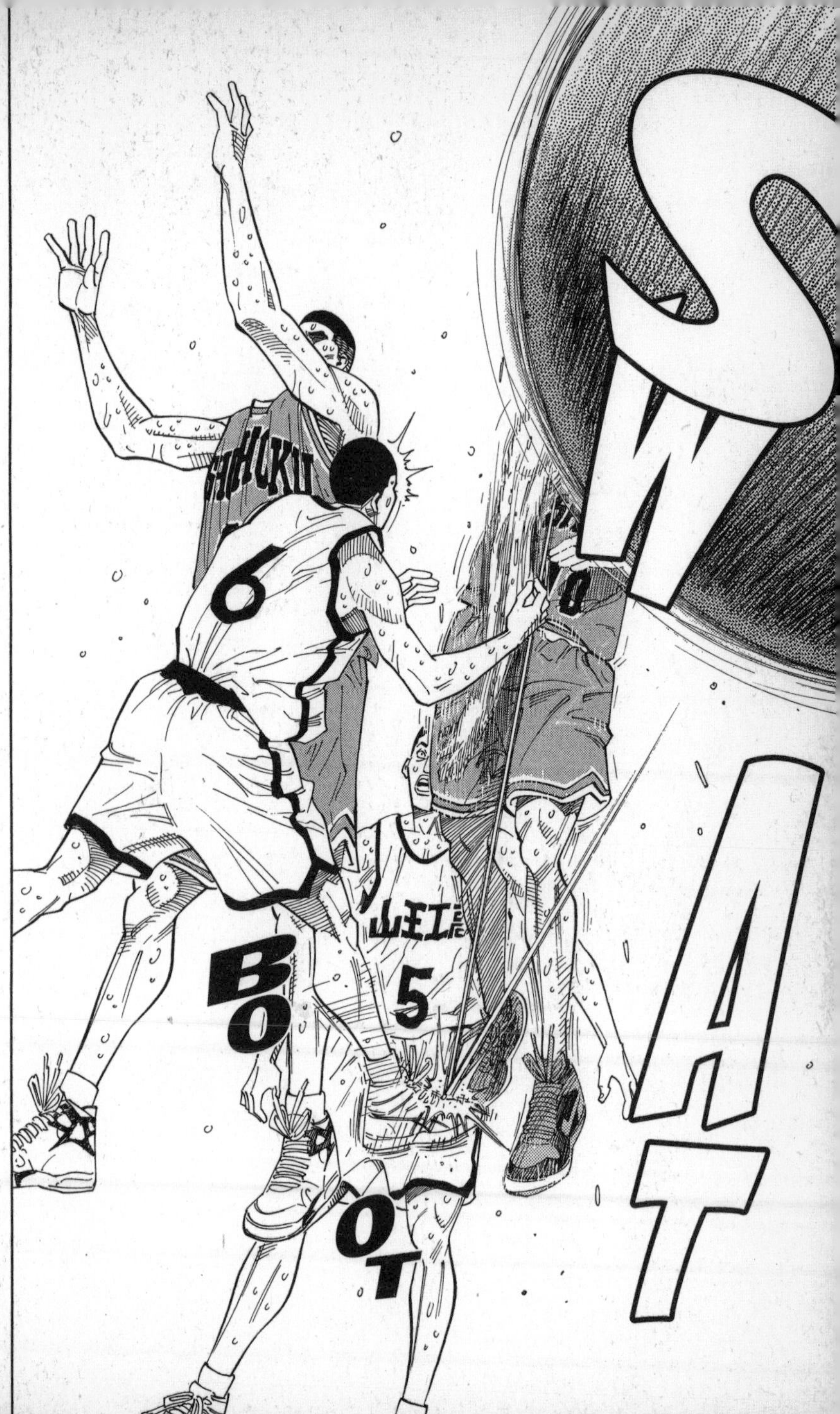
SWAT
BOOT

READ THIS WAY

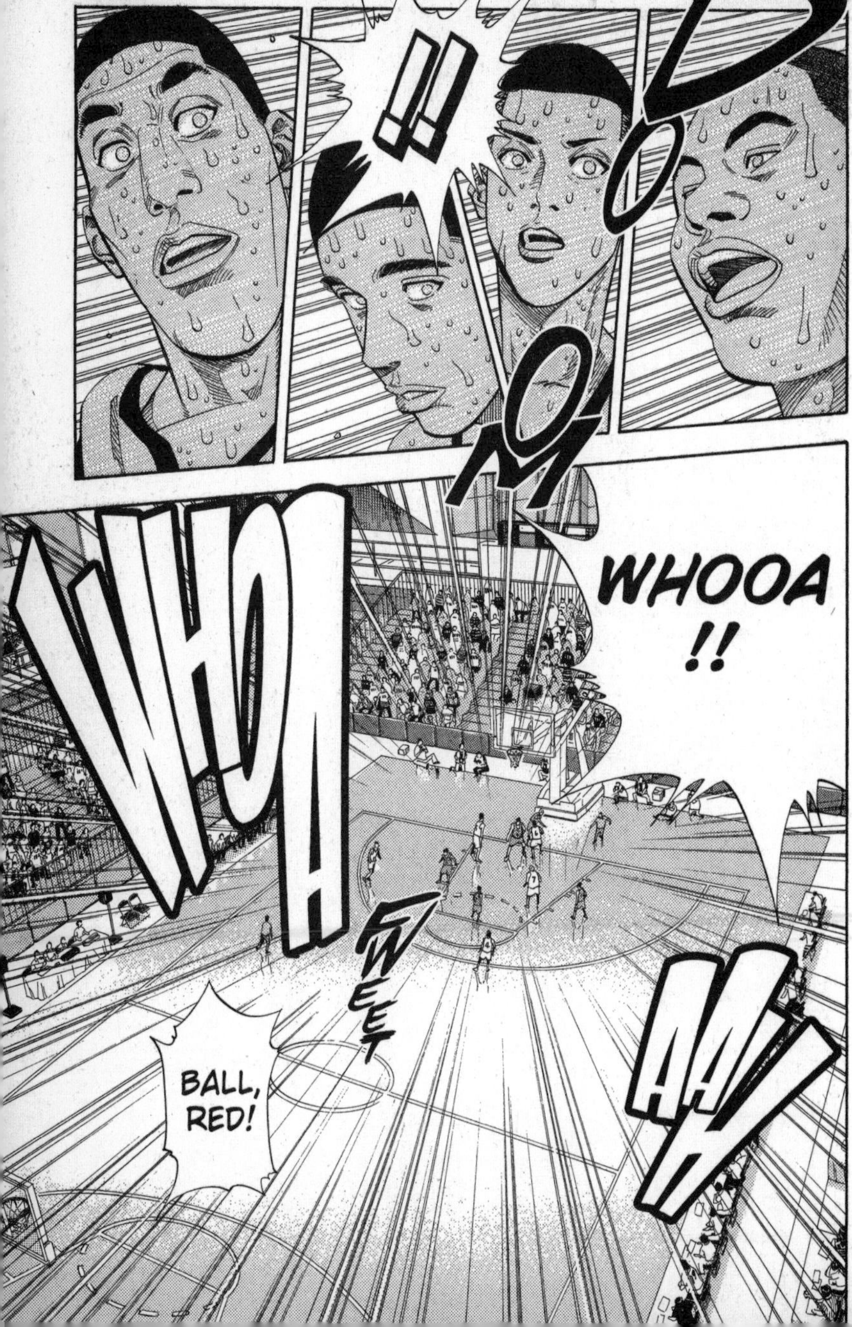
DOOM
!!
WHOOA !!
WHOA
AAH
FWEET
BALL, RED!

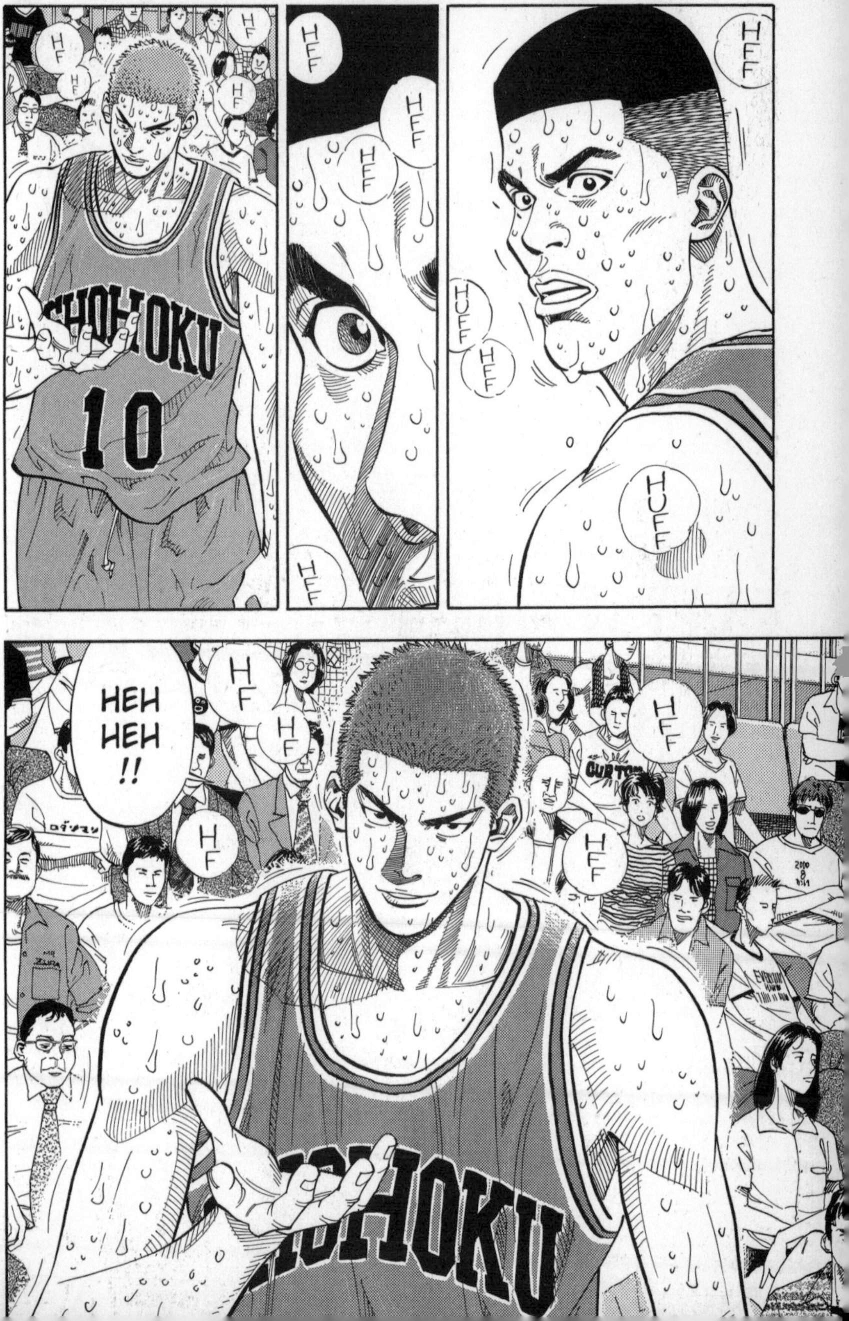
HFF
HUFF
HFF
HUFF
HFF
HFF
HFF
HFF
HF
HF
HF
HF
HFF
HFF
HF
HF
HEH HEH !!
HF

READ THIS WAY

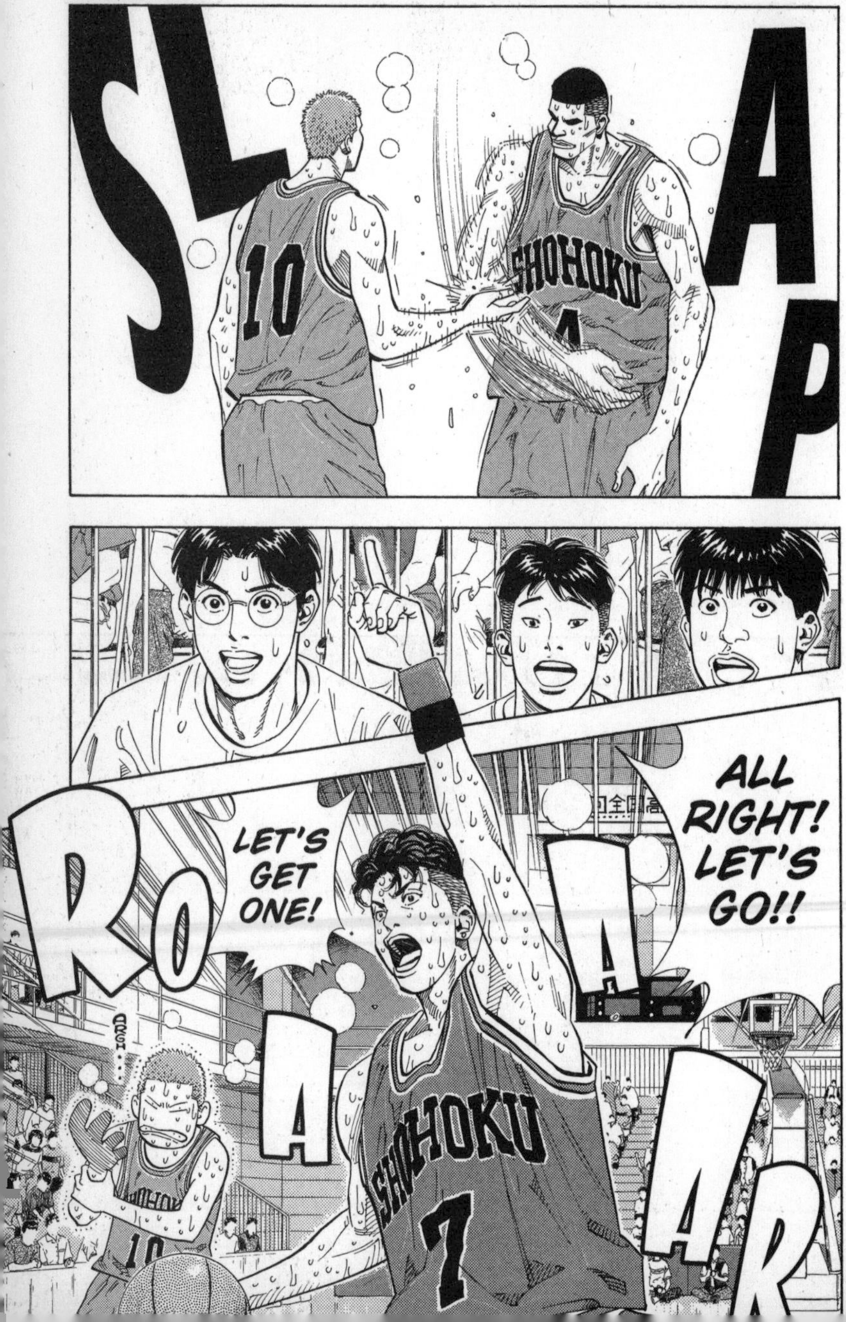
SLAP
ALL RIGHT! LET'S GO!!
LET'S GET ONE!
ROAAAR
ARGH...

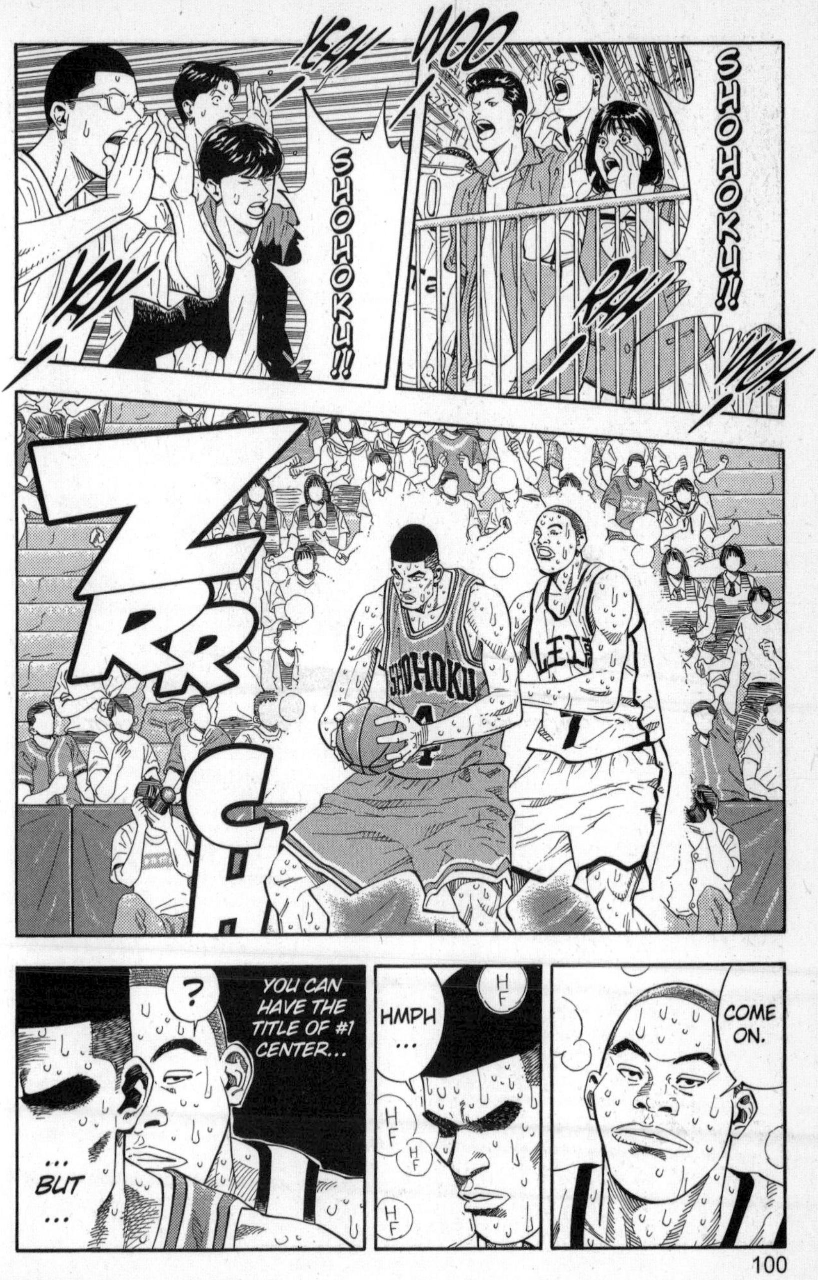
WOO!
SHOHOKU!!
RAH!
WOH!
YEAH!
SHOHOKU!!
YAY!
ZRR
CH
COME ON.
HMPH ...
HF
HF
HF
HF
HF
YOU CAN HAVE THE TITLE OF #1 CENTER...
?
... BUT ...

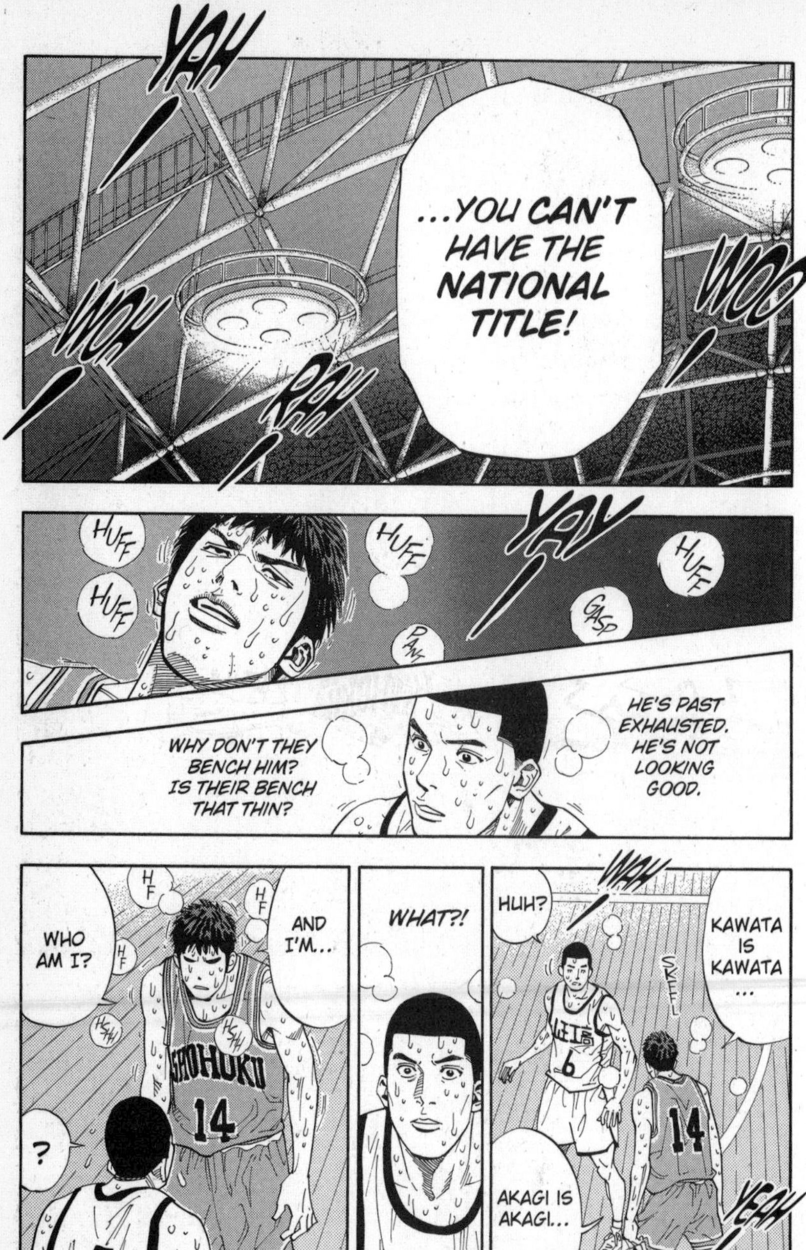
WOO!
...YOU CAN'T HAVE THE NATIONAL TITLE!
YAH!
RAH!
WOH!
YAY!
HUFF
GASP
HUFF
PANT
HUFF
HUFF
HE'S PAST EXHAUSTED. HE'S NOT LOOKING GOOD.
WHY DON'T THEY BENCH HIM? IS THEIR BENCH THAT THIN?
WAH!
KAWATA IS KAWATA...
HUH?
SKFFL
AKAGI IS AKAGI...
YEAH!
WHAT?!
AND I'M...
HF
HF
WHO AM I?
HF
HSHH
HSHH
?

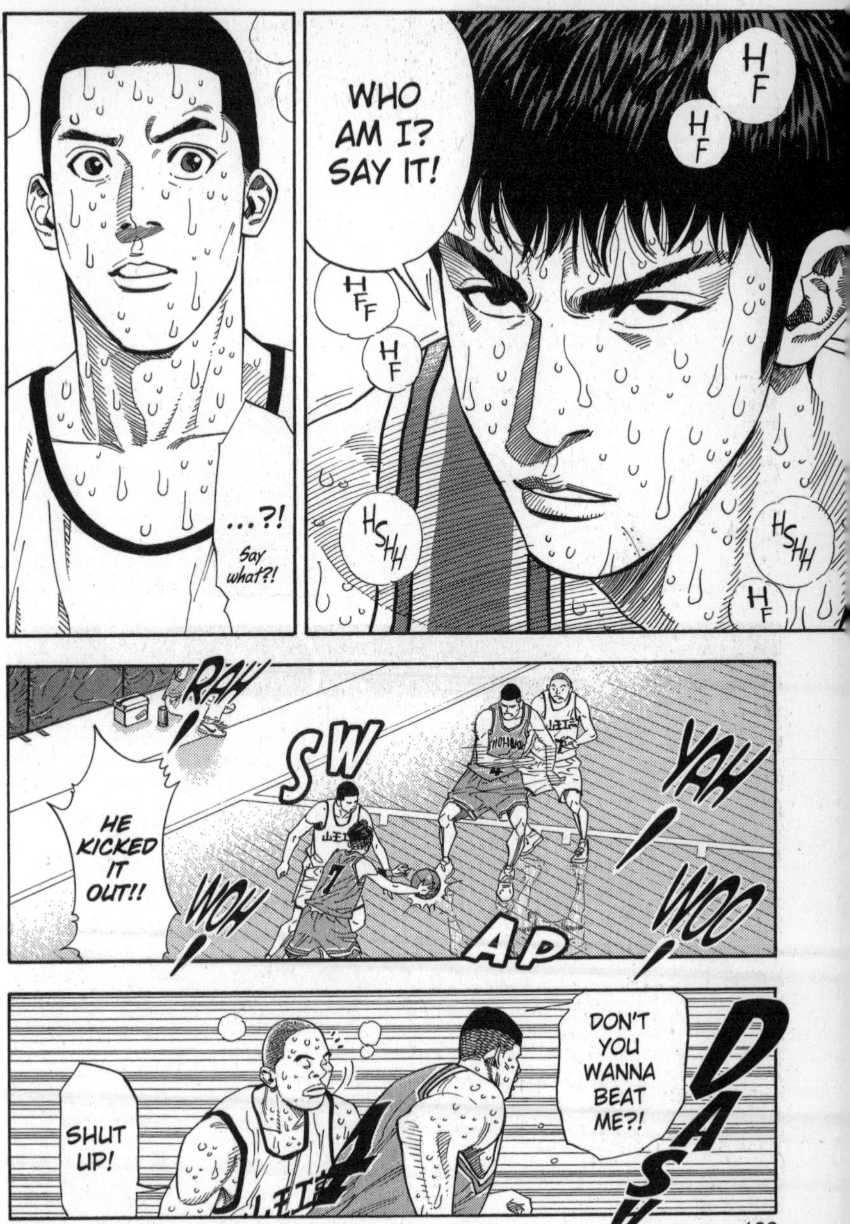
HF
HF
WHO AM I? SAY IT!
HFF
HF
HSHH
HSHH
HF
...?!
Say what?!
YAH!
WOO!
AP
SW
HE KICKED IT OUT!!
WOH!
RAH!
DASH
DON'T YOU WANNA BEAT ME?!
SHUT UP!

READ THIS WAY

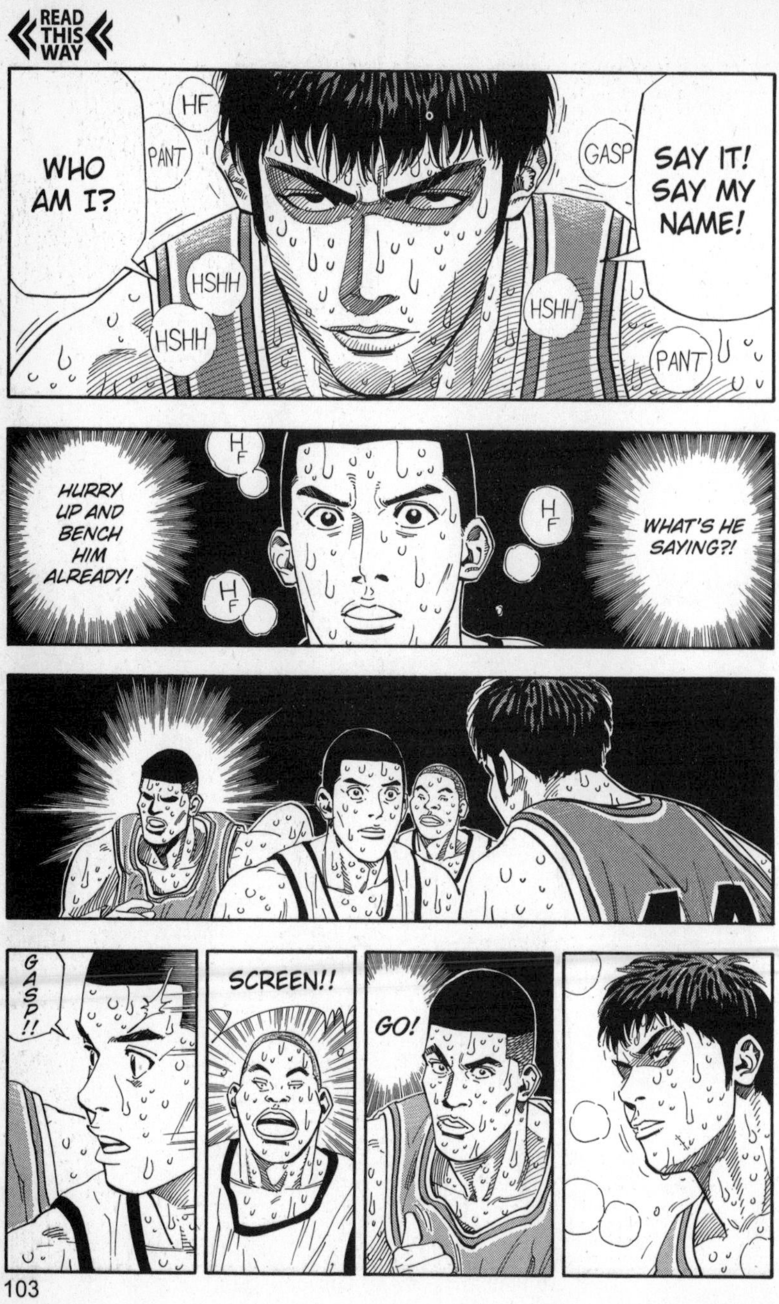
SAY IT! SAY MY NAME!
GASP
HF
PANT
WHO AM I?
HSHH
HSHH
HSHH
PANT
WHAT'S HE SAYING?!
HF
HF
HURRY UP AND BENCH HIM ALREADY!
HF
GO!
SCREEN!!
GASP!!

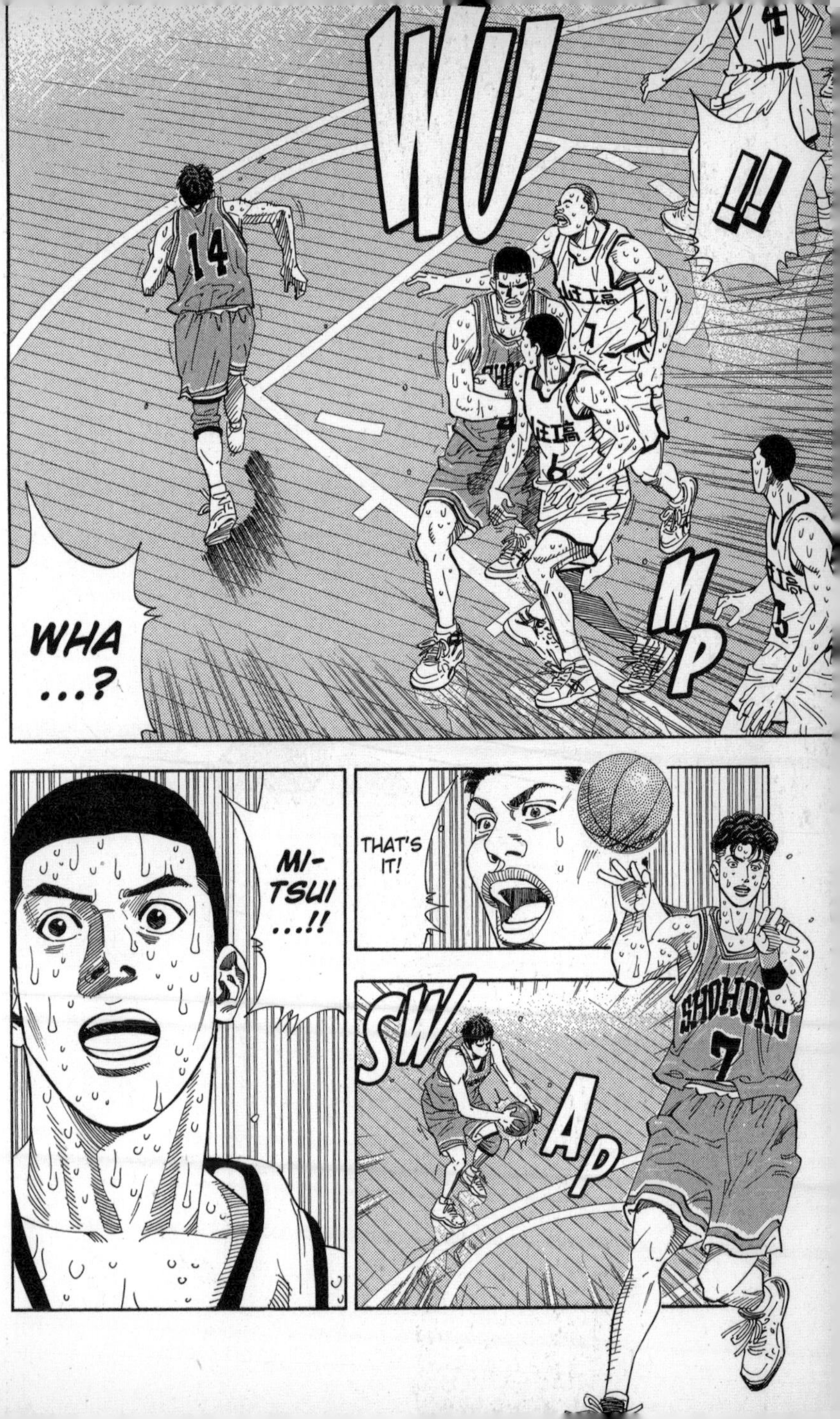
!!
WU
MP
WHA
...?
THAT'S
IT!
SW
AP
MI-
TSUI
...!!

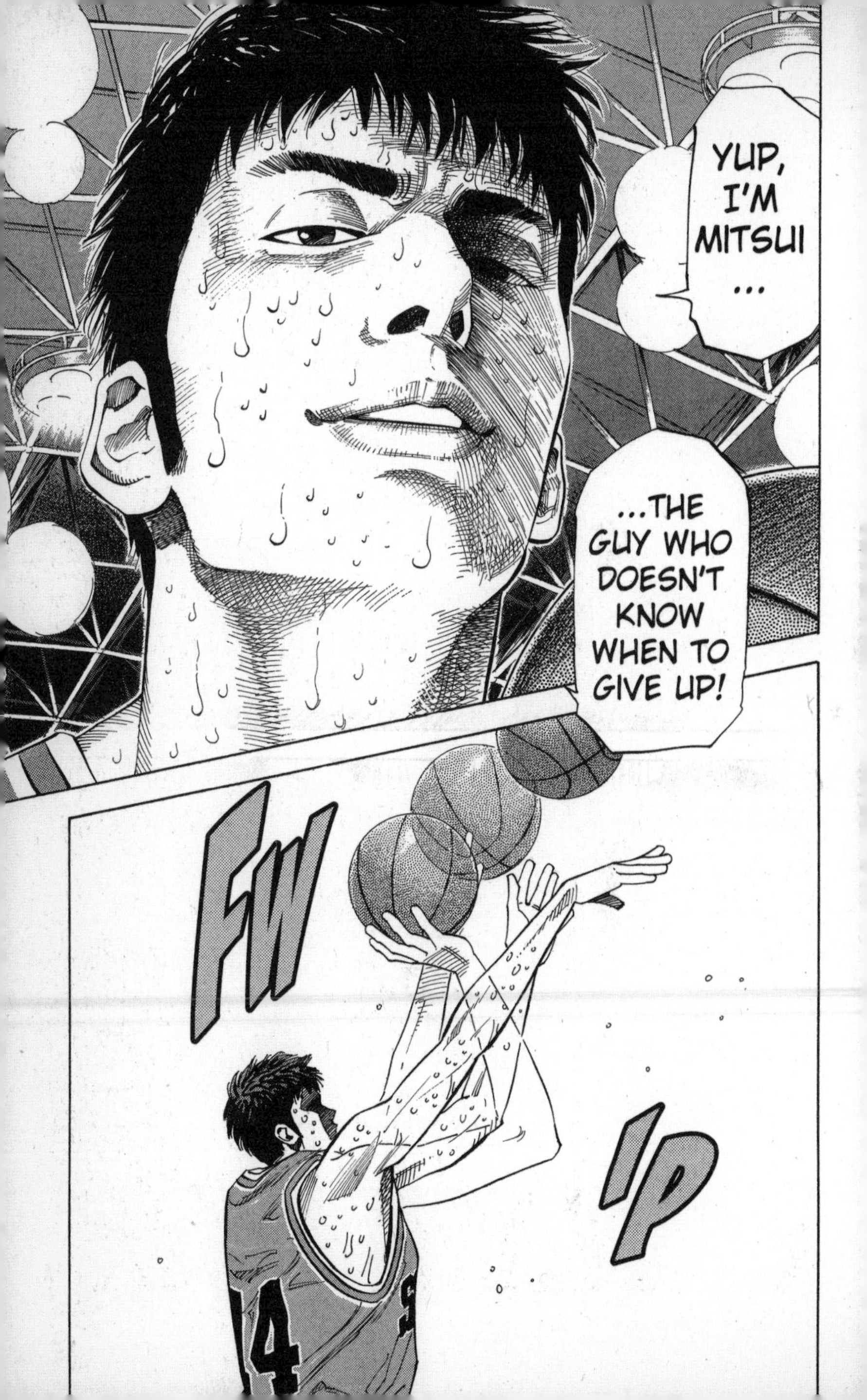
YUP, I'M MITSUI ...
...THE GUY WHO DOESN'T KNOW WHEN TO GIVE UP!
FWIP

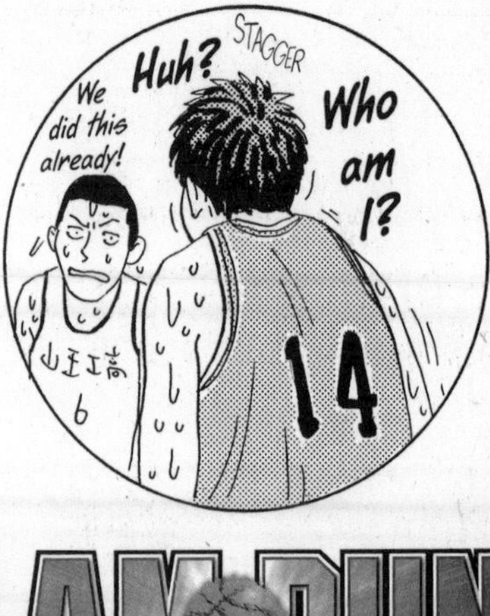
Who am I?
STAGGER
Huh?
We did this already!

SLAM DUNK

#248 TWO YEARS

湘北
47
60

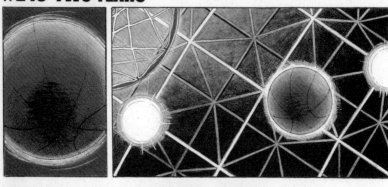

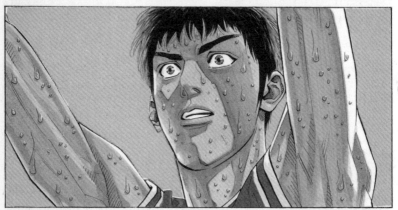

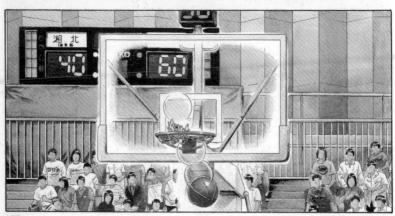

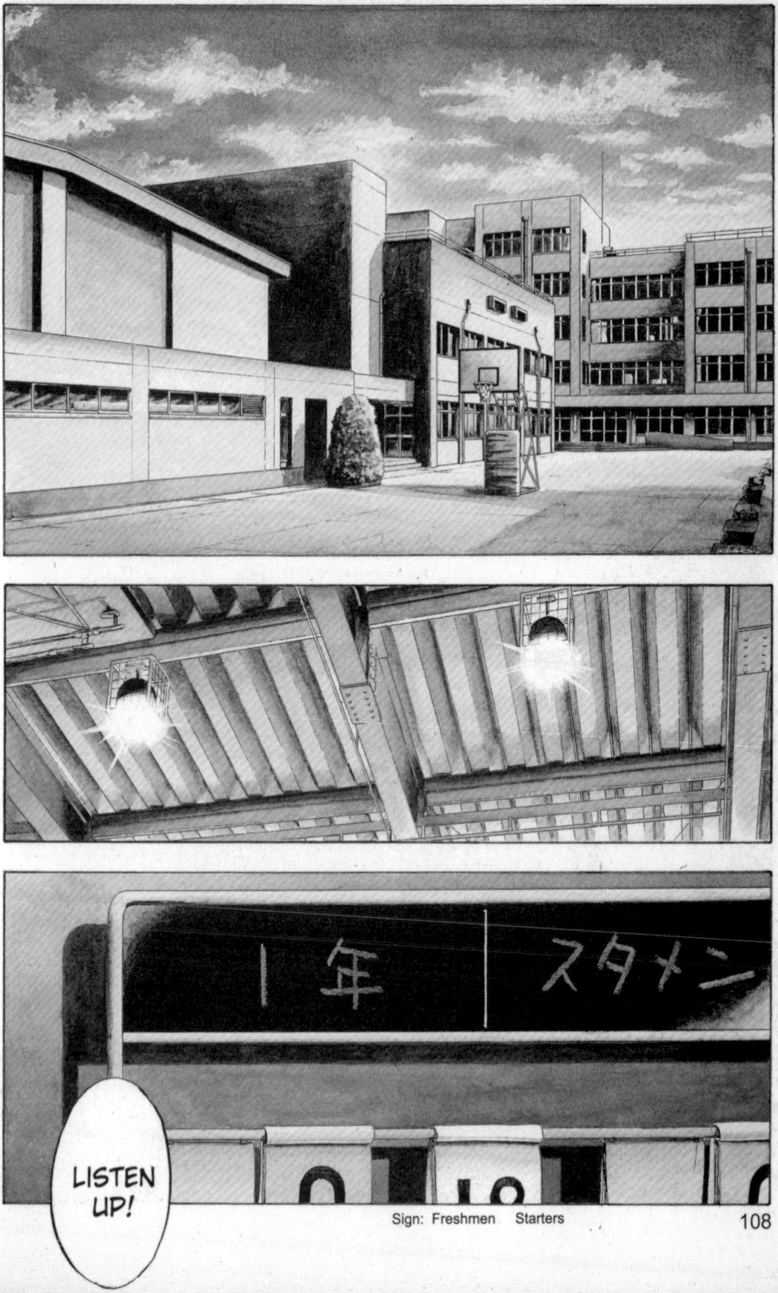
1年
スタメン
LISTEN UP!

Sign: Freshmen Starters

READ THIS WAY

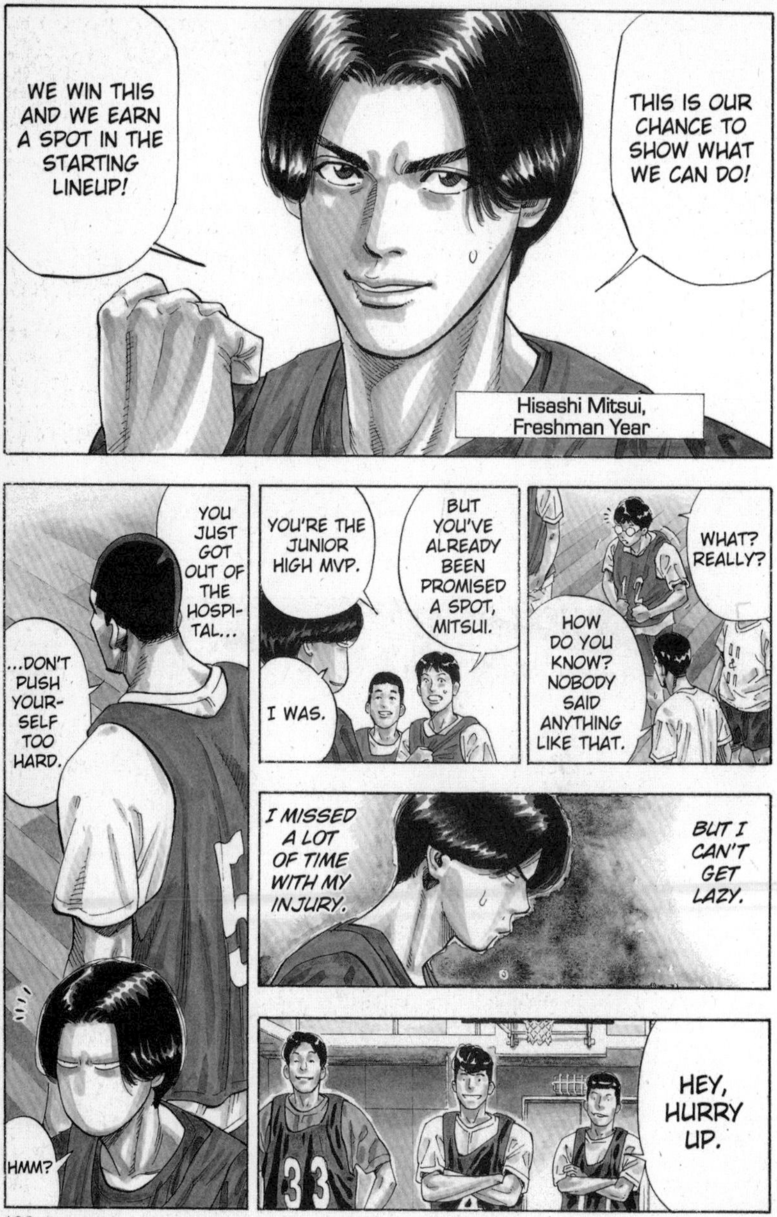

THIS IS OUR CHANCE TO SHOW WHAT WE CAN DO!
WE WIN THIS AND WE EARN A SPOT IN THE STARTING LINEUP!
Hisashi Mitsui, Freshman Year
WHAT? REALLY?
HOW DO YOU KNOW? NOBODY SAID ANYTHING LIKE THAT.
BUT YOU'VE ALREADY BEEN PROMISED A SPOT, MITSUI.
YOU'RE THE JUNIOR HIGH MVP.
I WAS.
I MISSED A LOT OF TIME WITH MY INJURY.
BUT I CAN'T GET LAZY.
HEY, HURRY UP.
YOU JUST GOT OUT OF THE HOSPITAL...
...DON'T PUSH YOURSELF TOO HARD.
HMM?

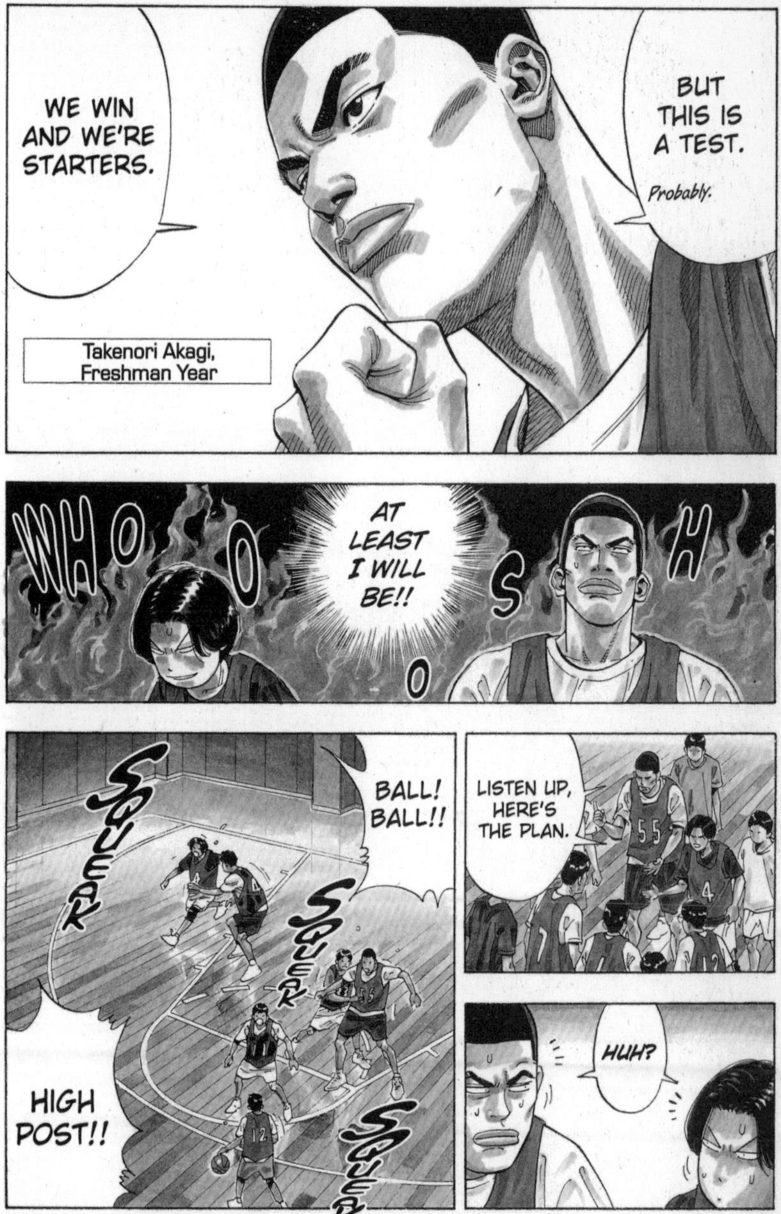
BUT THIS IS A TEST.
Probably.
WE WIN AND WE'RE STARTERS.
Takenori Akagi, Freshman Year
AT LEAST I WILL BE!!
WHOOOOSH
LISTEN UP, HERE'S THE PLAN.
HUH?
BALL! BALL!!
SQUEAK
SQUEAK
HIGH POST!!
SQUEAK

READ THIS WAY

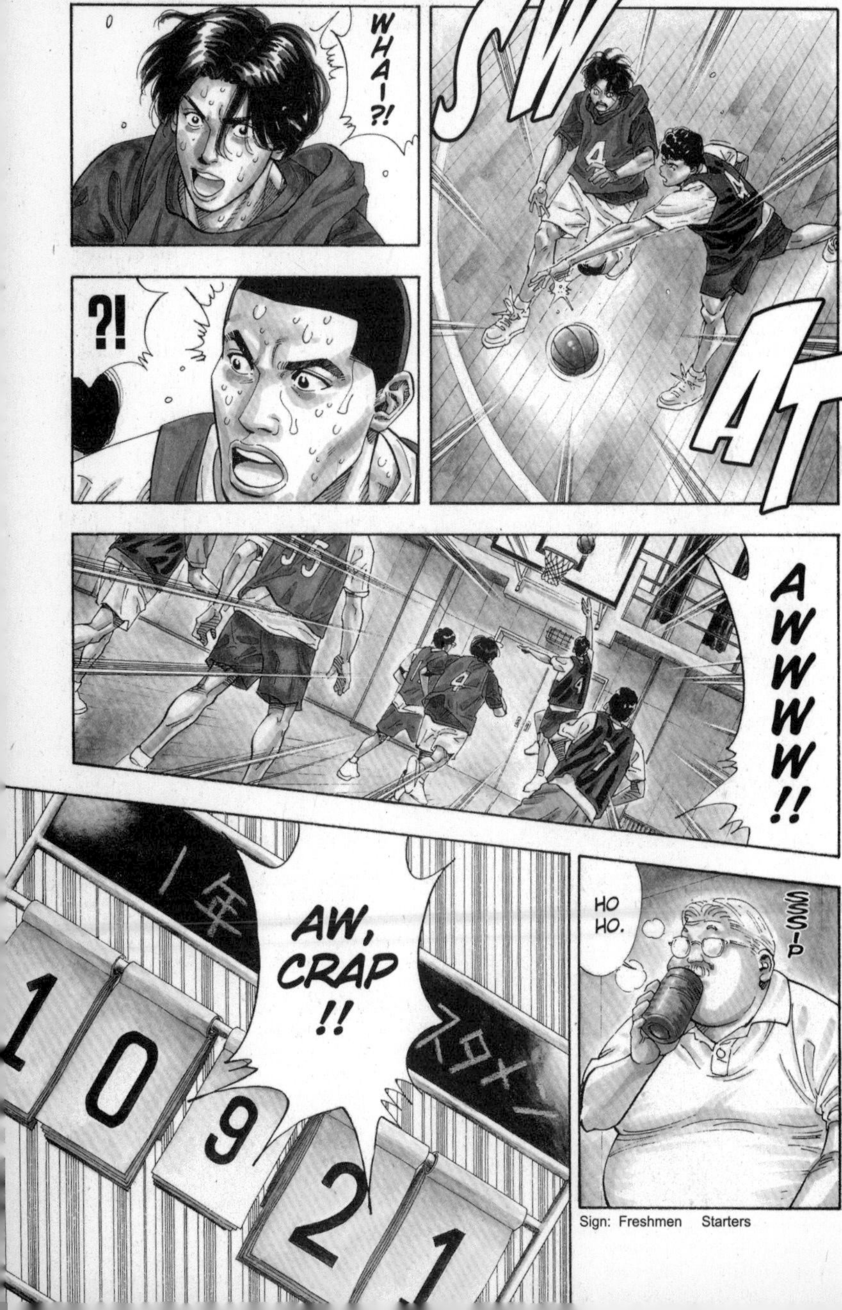
SWAT
WHAT?!
?!
AWWWWW!!
HO HO.
SSSIP
AW, CRAP!!
一年
10
9
スタメン
21

Sign: Freshmen Starters

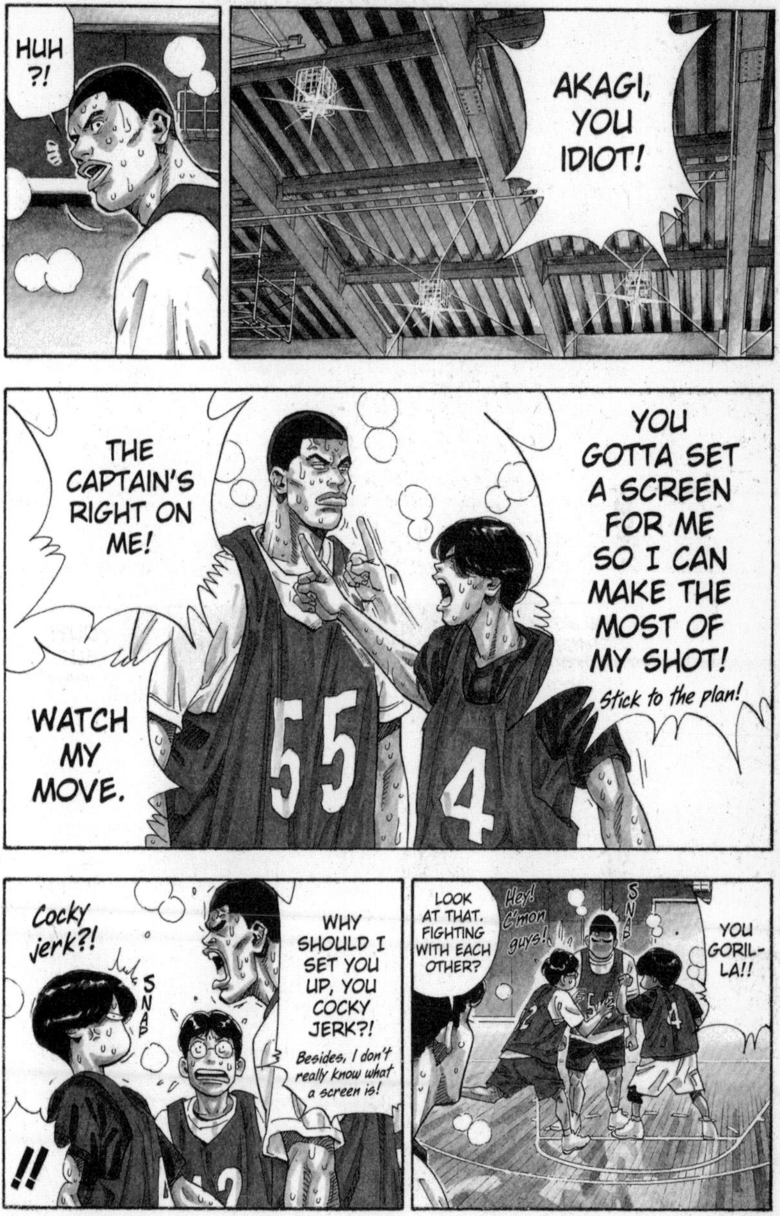
AKAGI, YOU IDIOT!
HUH ?!
YOU GOTTA SET A SCREEN FOR ME SO I CAN MAKE THE MOST OF MY SHOT!
Stick to the plan!
THE CAPTAIN'S RIGHT ON ME!
WATCH MY MOVE.
YOU GORIL-LA!!
SNAP
Hey! C'mon guys!
LOOK AT THAT. FIGHTING WITH EACH OTHER?
WHY SHOULD I SET YOU UP, YOU COCKY JERK?!
Besides, I don't really know what a screen is!
SNAP
Cocky jerk?!
!!

READ THIS WAY

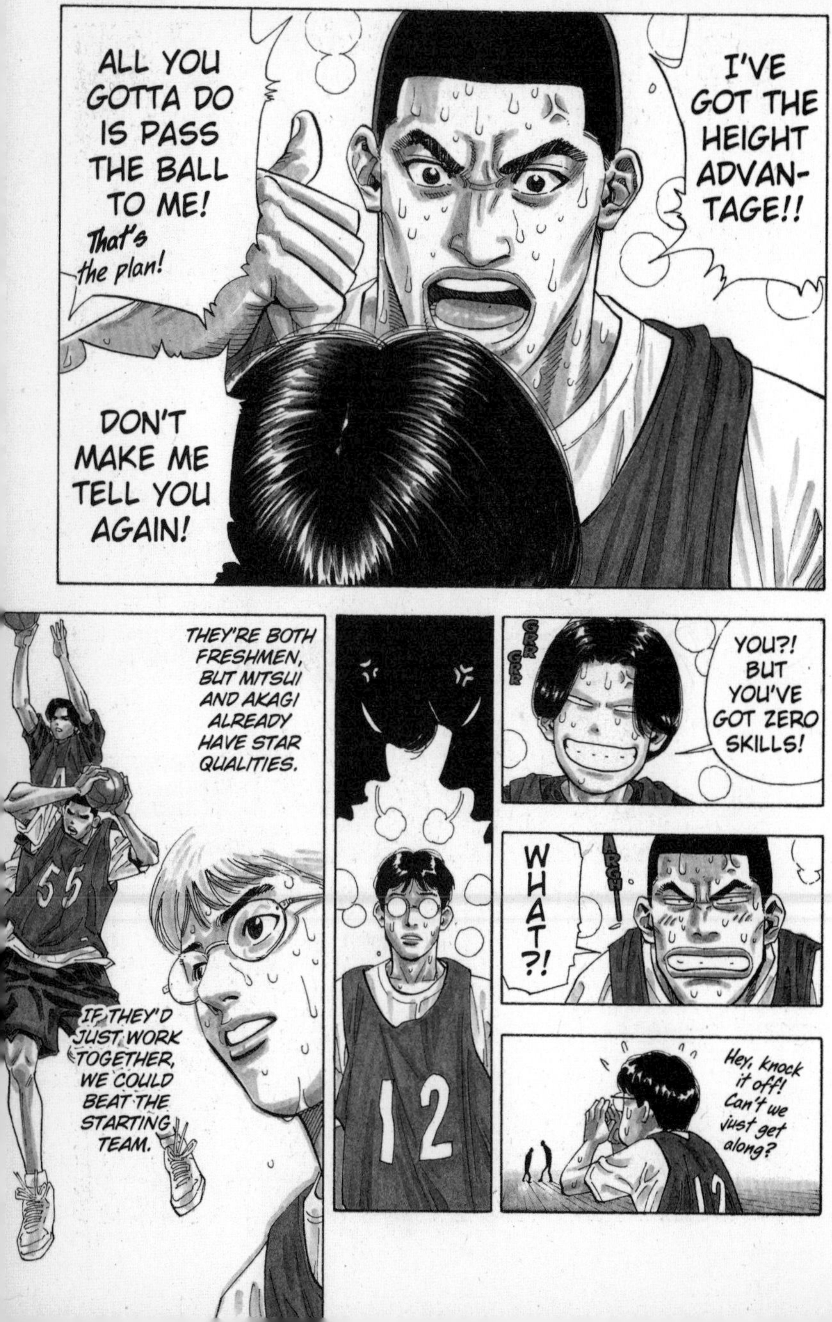
I'VE GOT THE HEIGHT ADVANTAGE!!
ALL YOU GOTTA DO IS PASS THE BALL TO ME!
That's the plan!
DON'T MAKE ME TELL YOU AGAIN!
GRR GRR
YOU?! BUT YOU'VE GOT ZERO SKILLS!
WHAT?!
ARGH
Hey, knock it off! Can't we just get along?
THEY'RE BOTH FRESHMEN, BUT MITSUI AND AKAGI ALREADY HAVE STAR QUALITIES.
IF THEY'D JUST WORK TOGETHER, WE COULD BEAT THE STARTING TEAM.

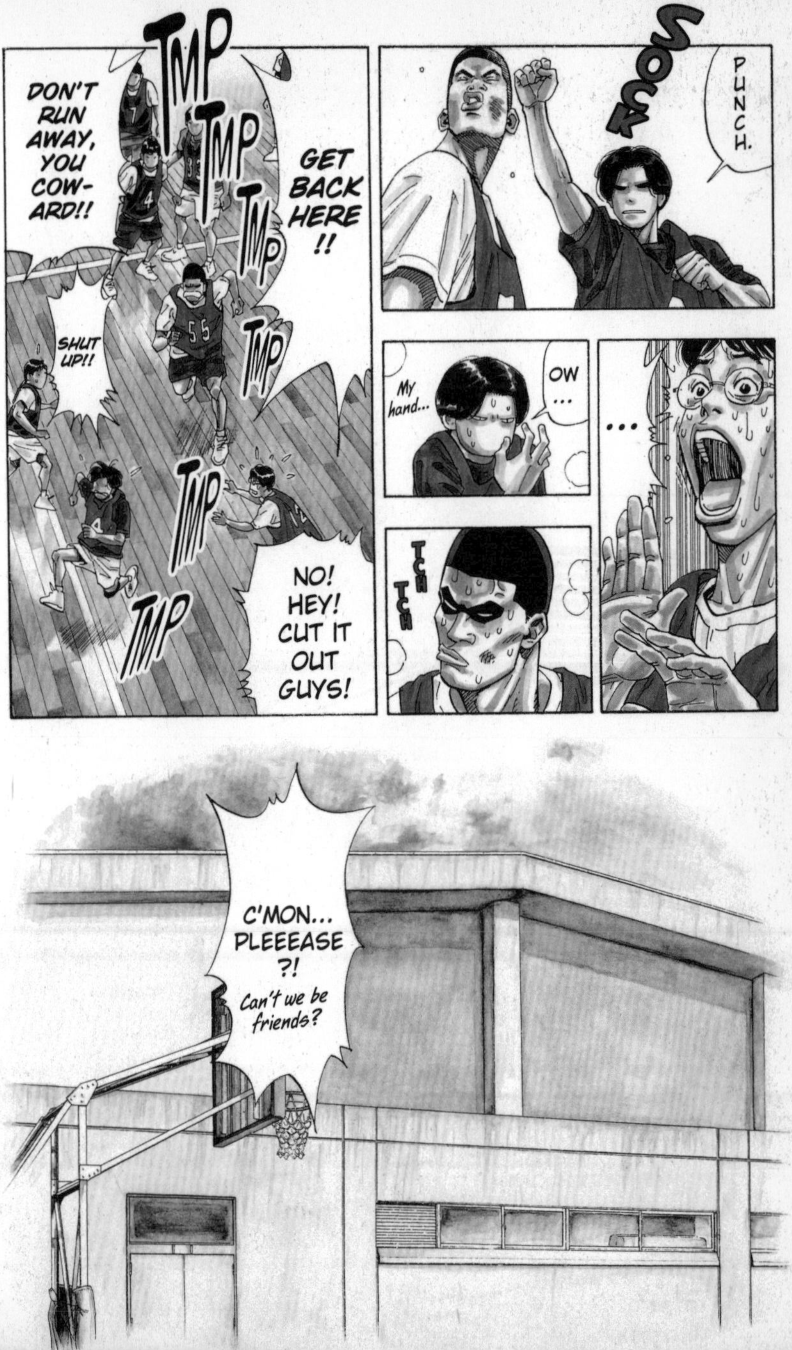
SOCK
PUNCH.
...
OW ...
My hand...
TCH TCH
GET BACK HERE !!
DON'T RUN AWAY, YOU COW-ARD!!
TMP TMP TMP TMP
SHUT UP!!
TMP TMP
NO! HEY! CUT IT OUT GUYS!
C'MON... PLEEEASE ?!
Can't we be friends?

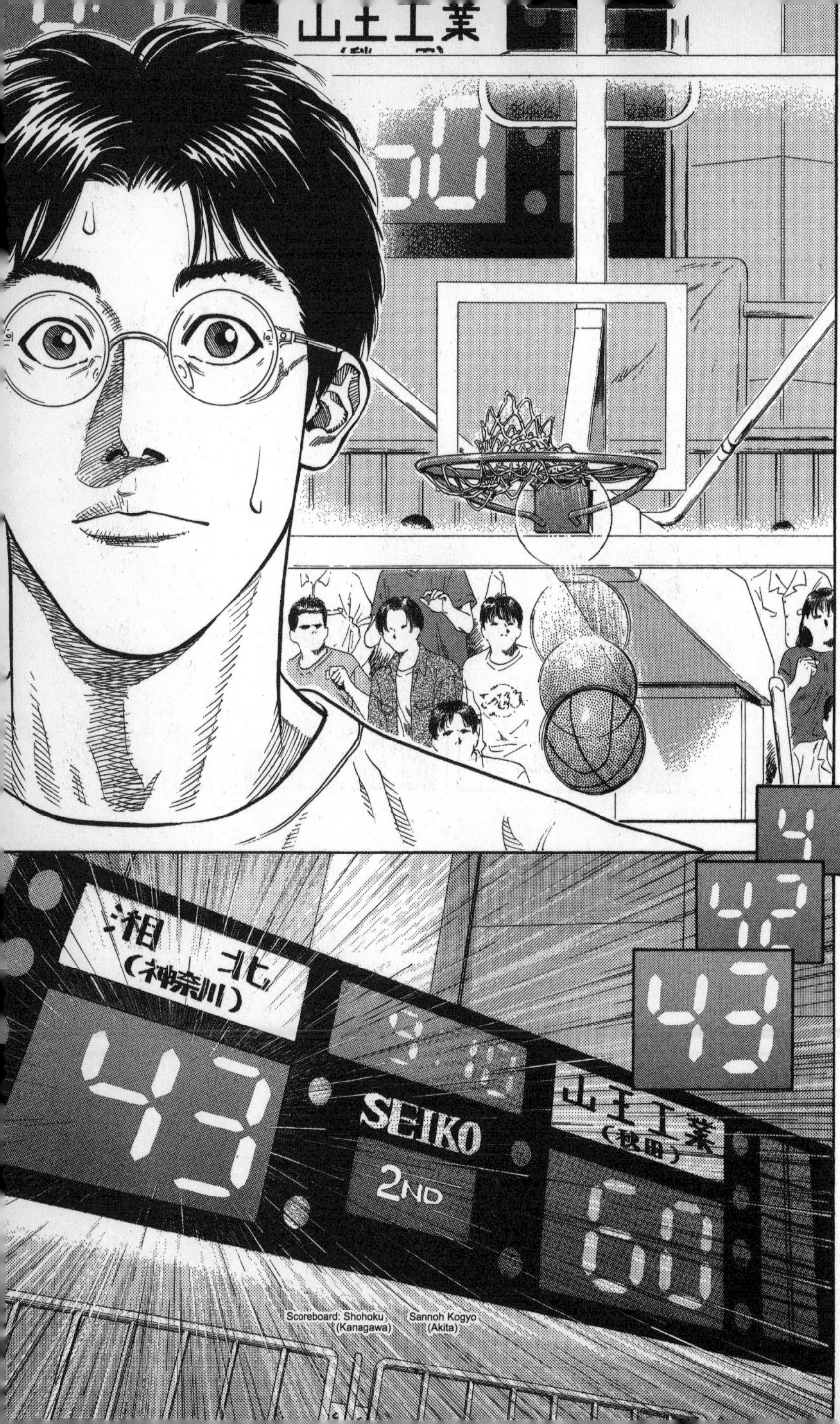
山王工業
41
42
43
湘北
(神奈川)
43
SEIKO
2ND
山王工業
(秋田)
60
Scoreboard: Shohoku (Kanagawa) Sannoh Kogyo (Akita)

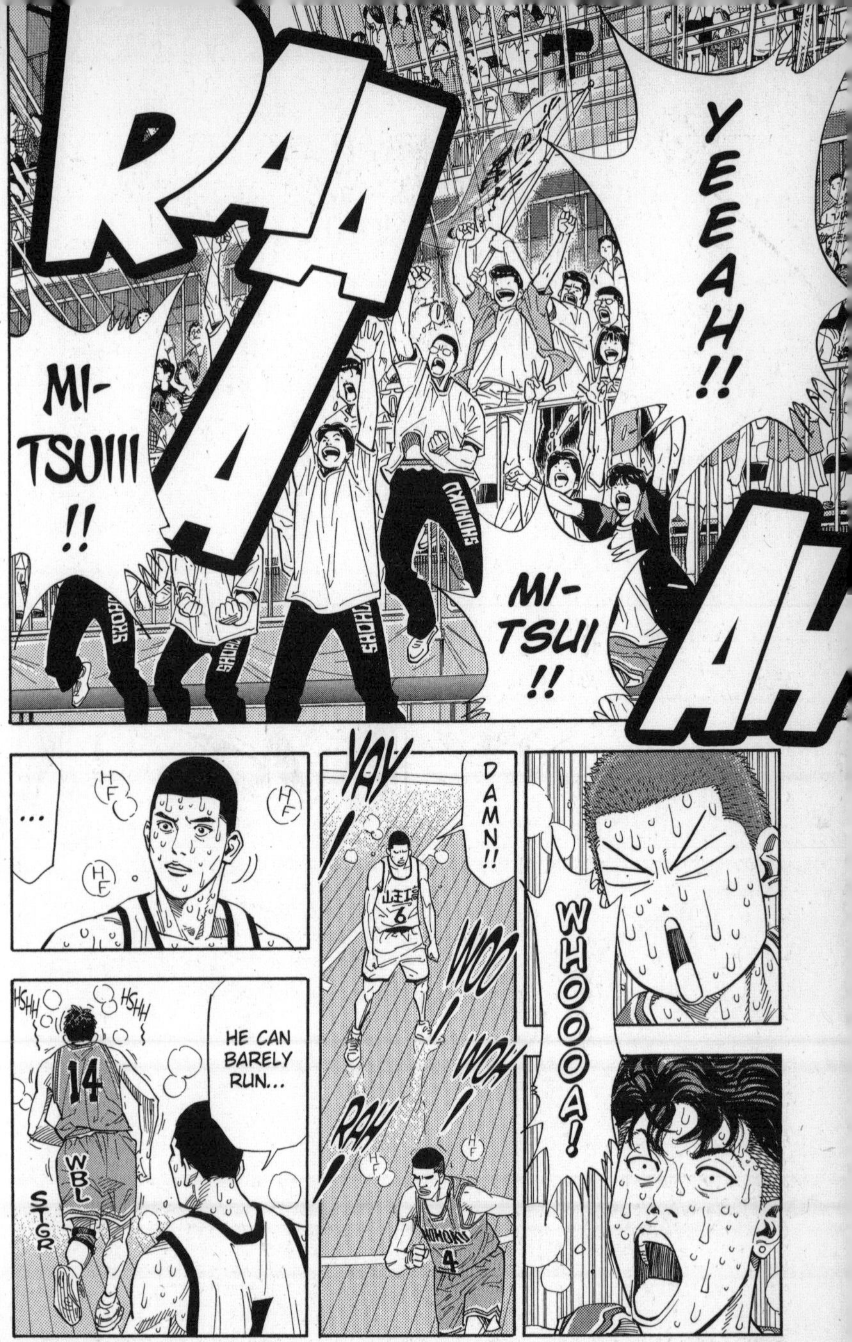
YEEAH!!
RAAAAH
MI-TSUI!!
MI-TSUIIII!!
WHOOOOA!
YAY!
DAMN!!
WOO! WOH! RAH!
HF
...
HF HF HF
HSHH HSHH
STGR
HE CAN BARELY RUN...

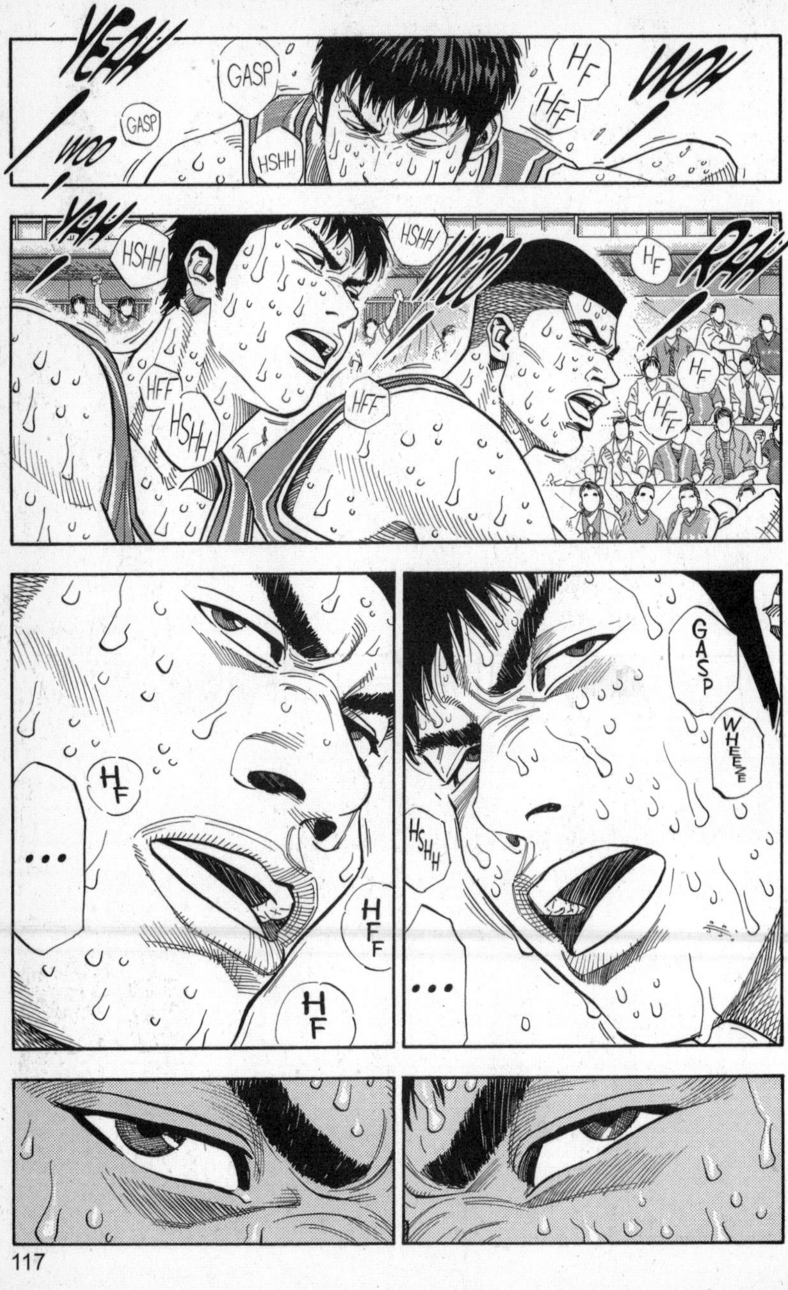
WOH!
HF
HFF
GASP
HSHH
GASP
YEAH!
WOO!
RAH!
HF
HF
HFF
HSHH
WOO!
HFF
HSHH
YAH!
HFF
HSHH
GASP
WHEEZE
HSHH
...
HF
HFF
HF
...

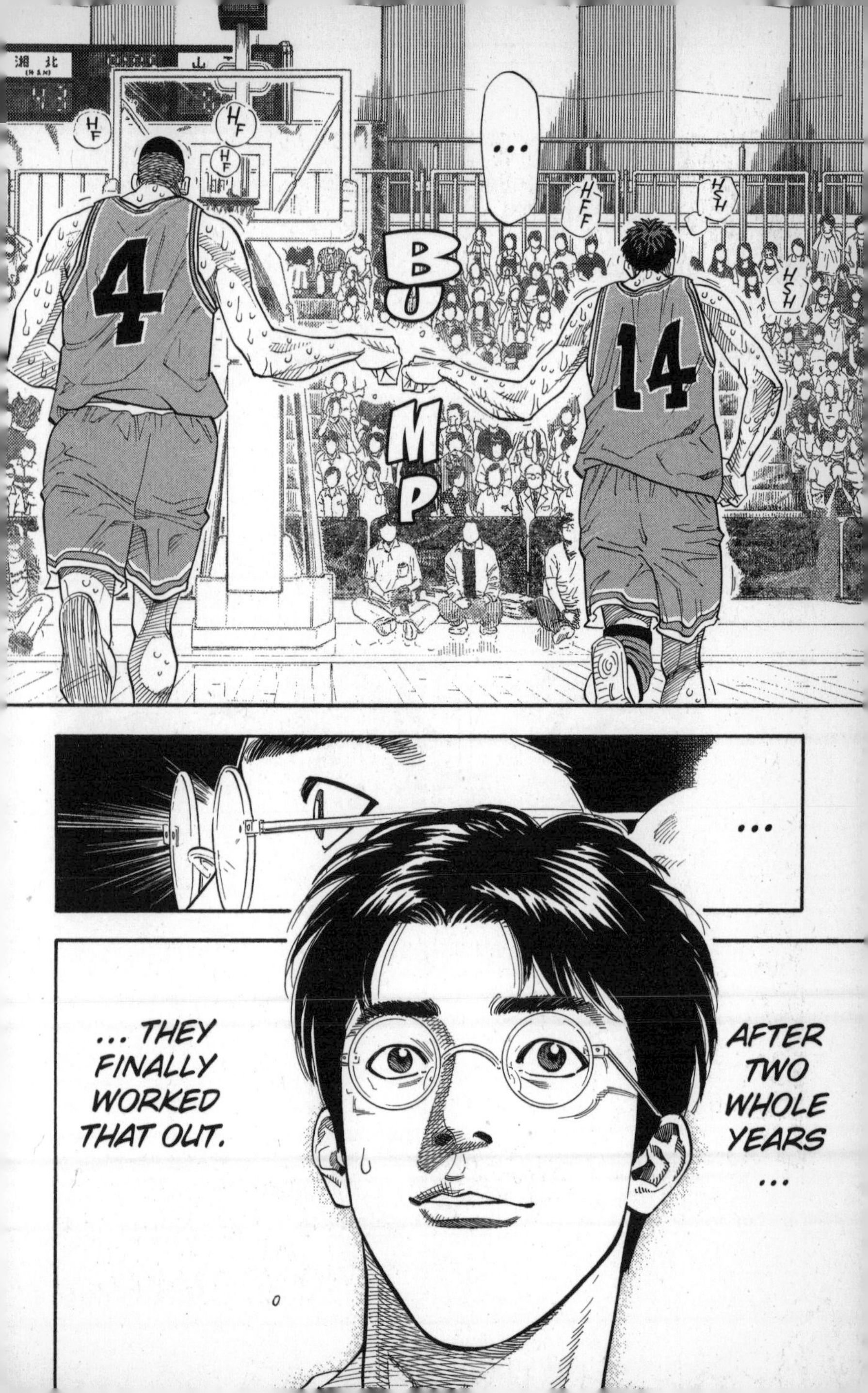
湘北
HSH
HSH
HFF
...
HF
HF
HF
BUMP
...
AFTER TWO WHOLE YEARS ...
... THEY FINALLY WORKED THAT OUT.

READ THIS WAY

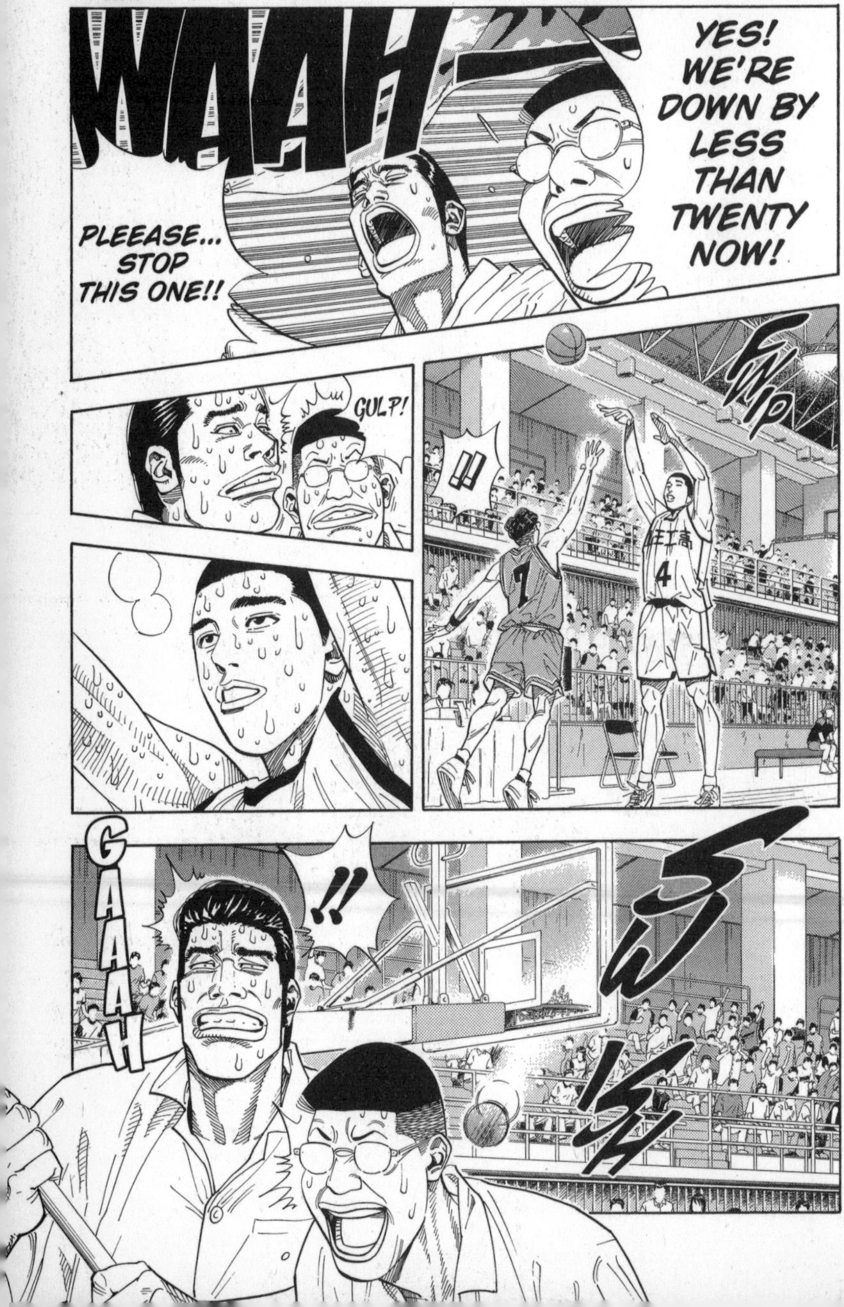
YES! WE'RE DOWN BY LESS THAN TWENTY NOW!
WAAH
PLEEASE... STOP THIS ONE!!
FWIP
!!
GULP!
SWISH
!!
GAAAAH

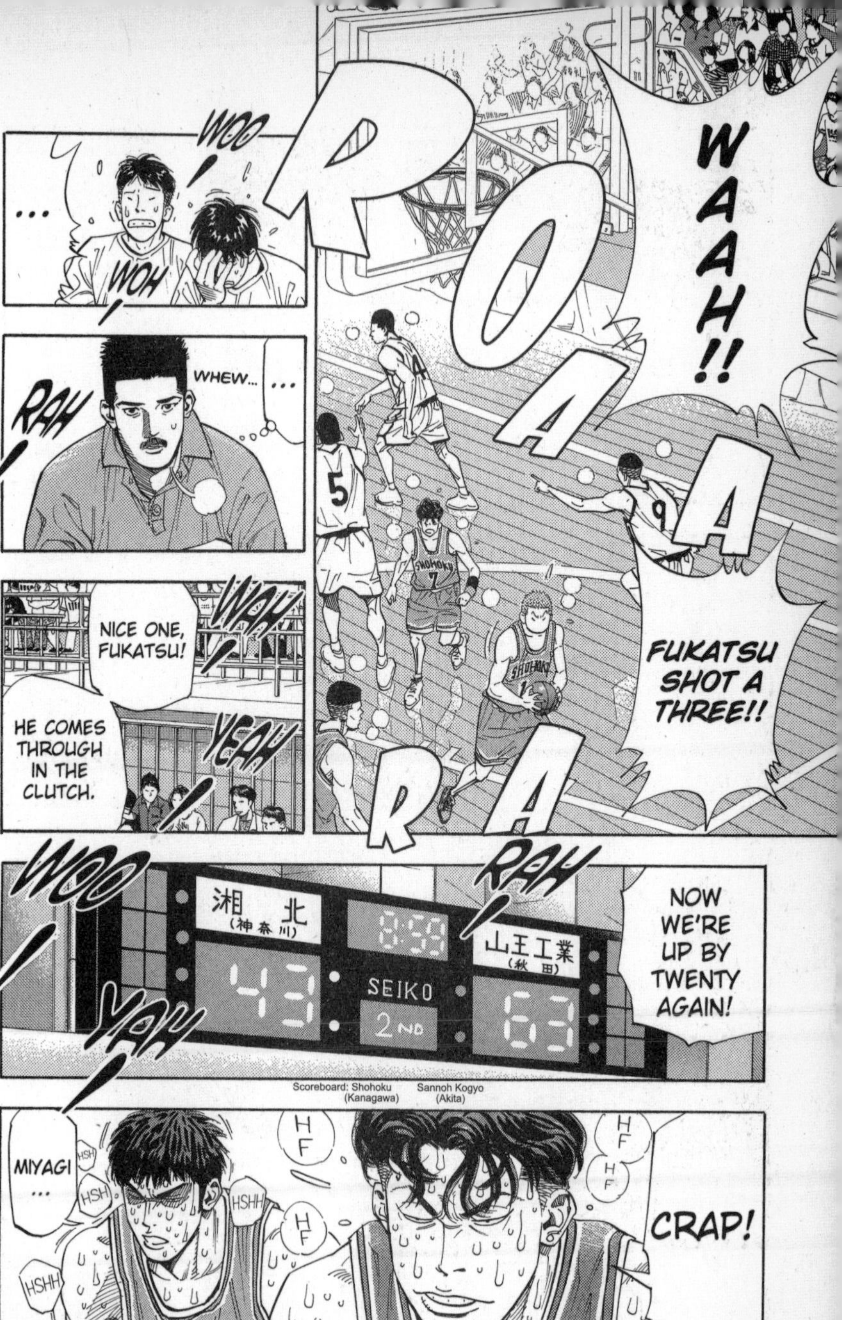
ROAAAAR
WAAAH!!
FUKATSU SHOT A THREE!!
WOO
WOH
...
RAH
WHEW...
...
WAH
NICE ONE, FUKATSU!
YEAH
HE COMES THROUGH IN THE CLUTCH.
RAH
NOW WE'RE UP BY TWENTY AGAIN!
WOO
YAH
湘北 (神奈川)
8:59
山王工業 (秋田)
43
SEIKO
2ND
63
HF
HF
HF
CRAP!
HF
HSHH
HSH
HSH
HSHH
MIYAGI ...
Scoreboard: Shohoku (Kanagawa) Sannoh Kogyo (Akita)

READ THIS WAY

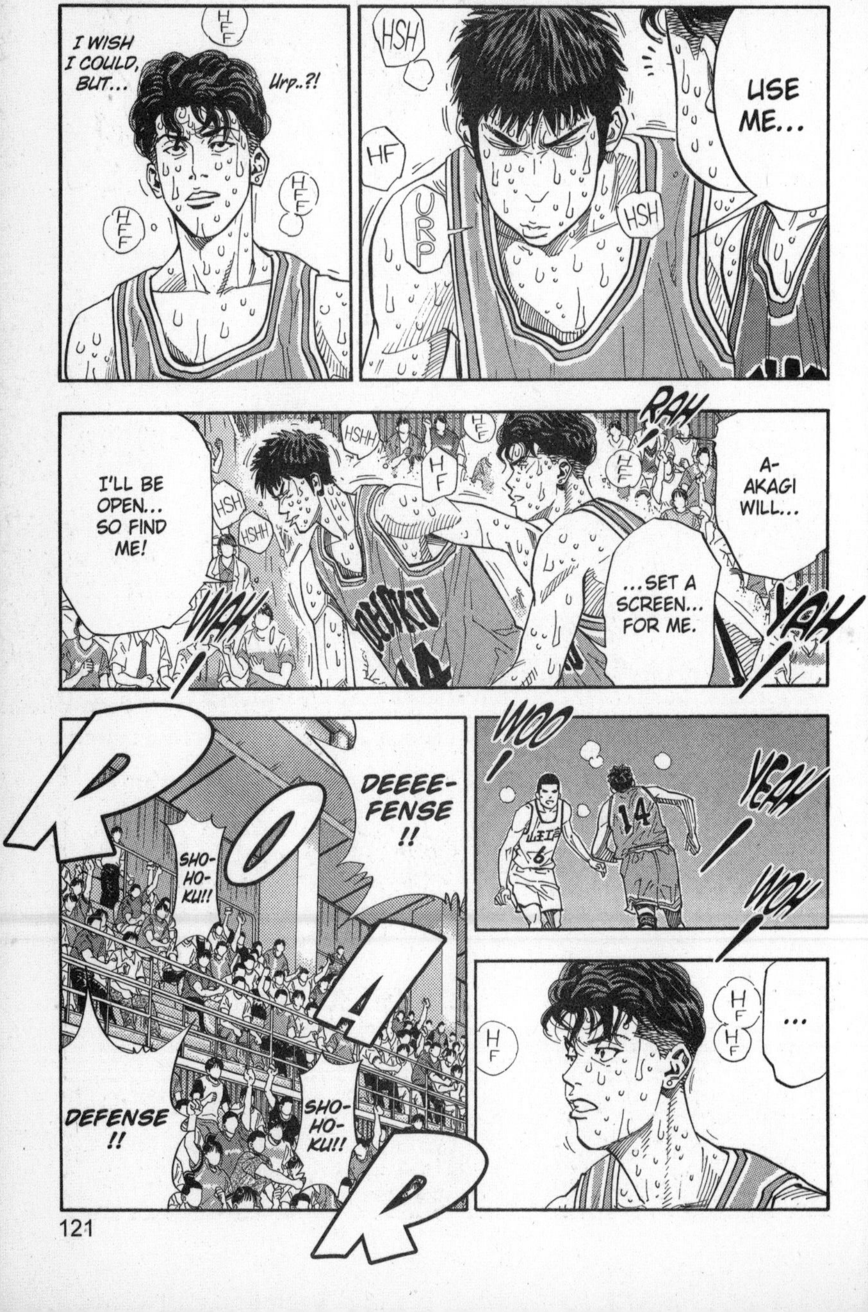
HSH
USE ME...
HF
URP
HSH
I WISH I COULD, BUT...
Urp..?!
HFF
HFF
HFF
RAH
A-AKAGI WILL...
...SET A SCREEN... FOR ME.
YAH
HFF
HF
HFF
HSHH
HSH
HSHH
I'LL BE OPEN... SO FIND ME!
WAH
WOO
YEAH
WOH
HF HF
...
HF
DEEEE-FENSE!!
SHO-HO-KU!!
DEFENSE!!
SHO-HO-KU!!
ROAR

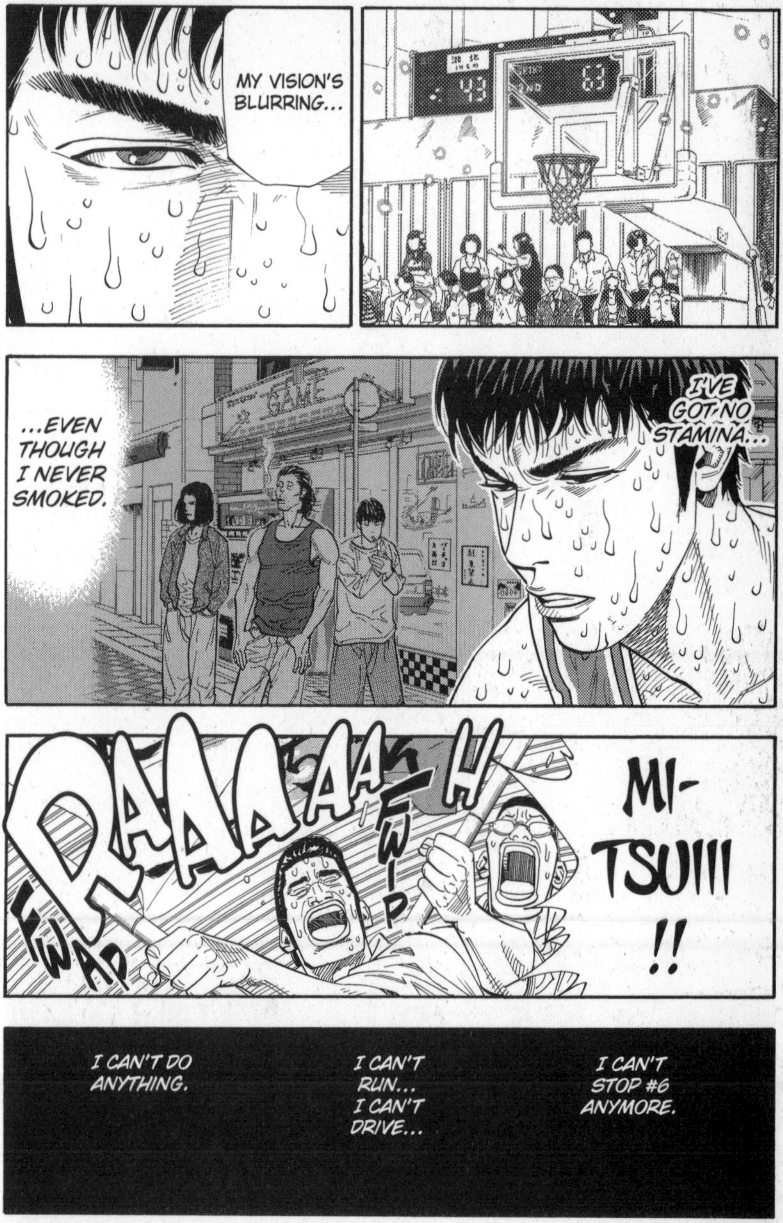
MY VISION'S BLURRING...
I'VE GOT NO STAMINA...
GAME
...EVEN THOUGH I NEVER SMOKED.
MI-TSUIII !!
FWIP
RAAAAAAH
FWAP
I CAN'T STOP #6 ANYMORE.
I CAN'T RUN... I CAN'T DRIVE...
I CAN'T DO ANYTHING.

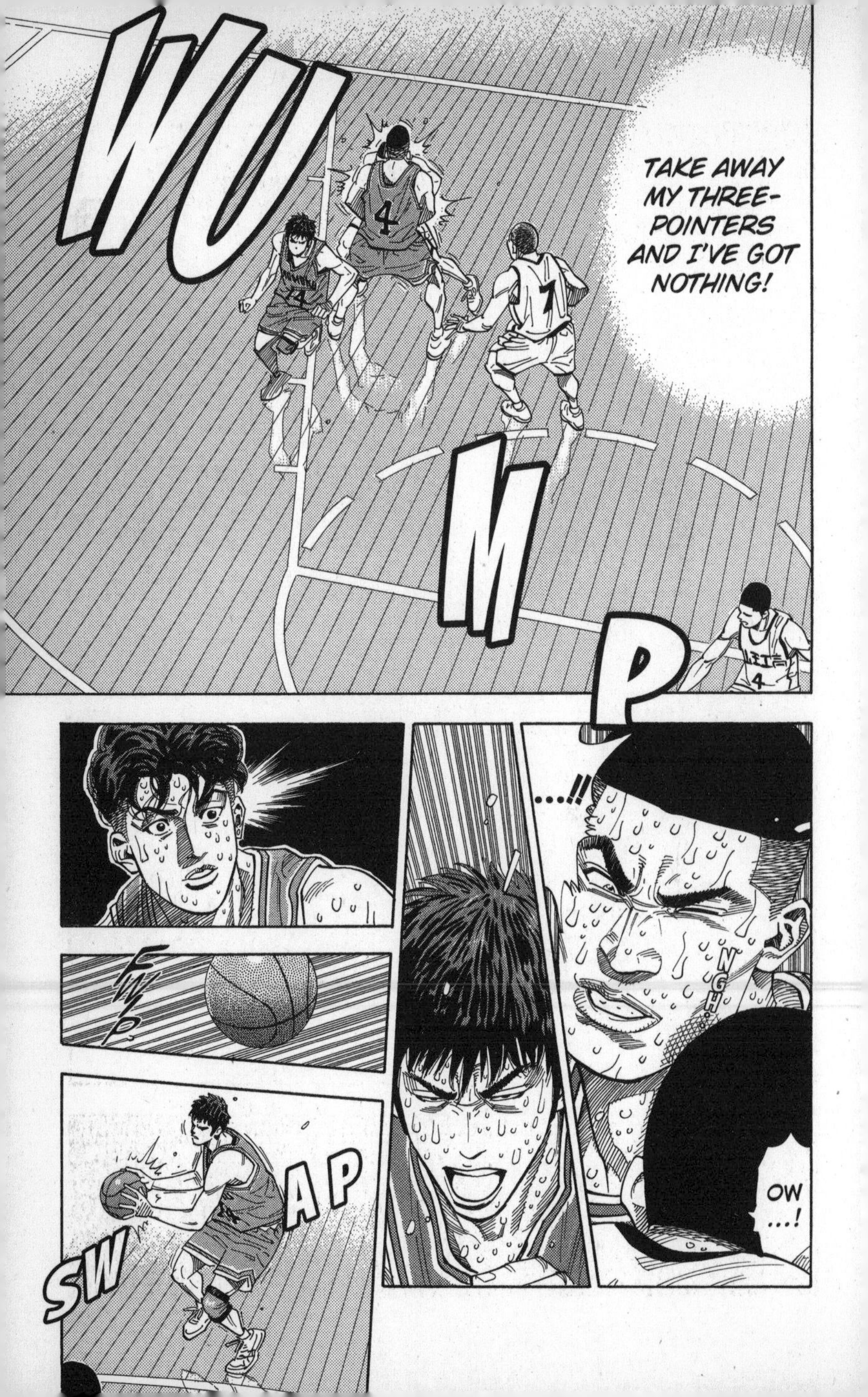
WUMP
TAKE AWAY MY THREE-POINTERS AND I'VE GOT NOTHING!
...!!
NGH...
OW ...!
FWIP
SWAP

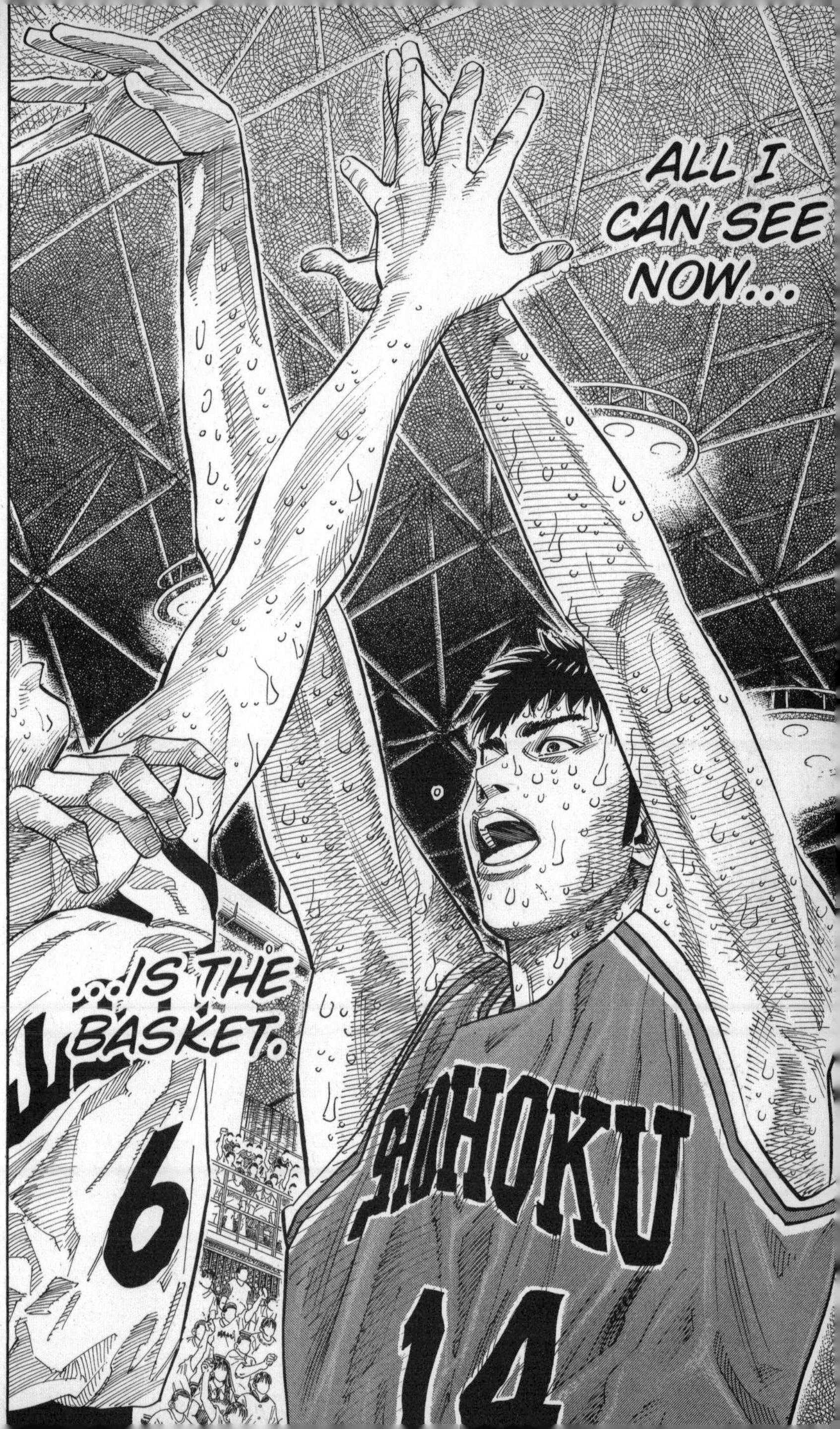
ALL I CAN SEE NOW...
...IS THE BASKET.
SHOHOKU
14
6

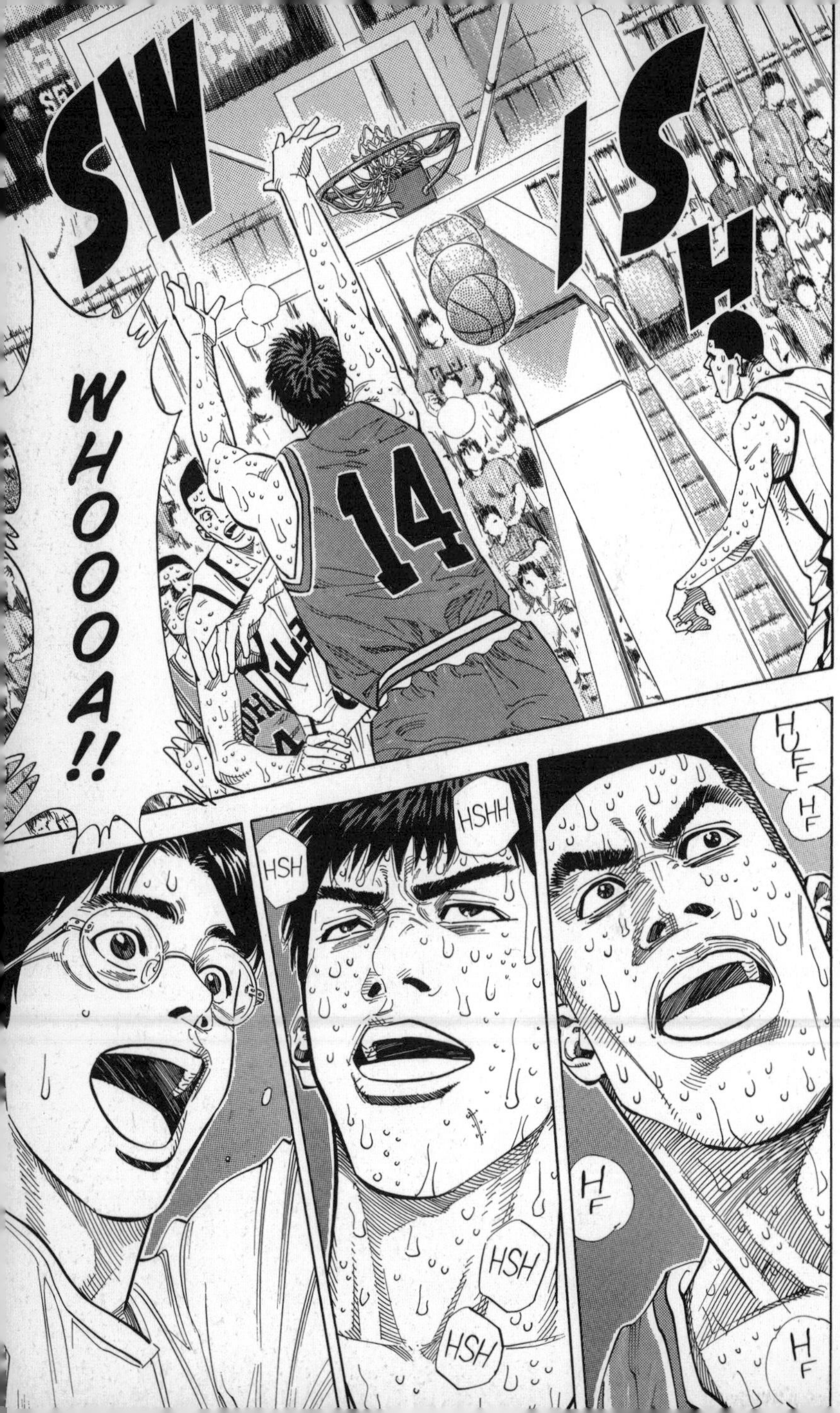
SWISH
WHOOOA!!
HUFF HF
HF
HF
HSHH
HSH
HSH
HSH

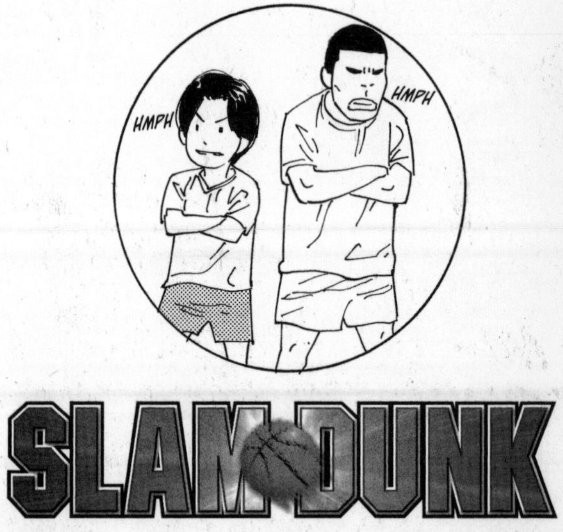
HMPH
HMPH

SLAM DUNK

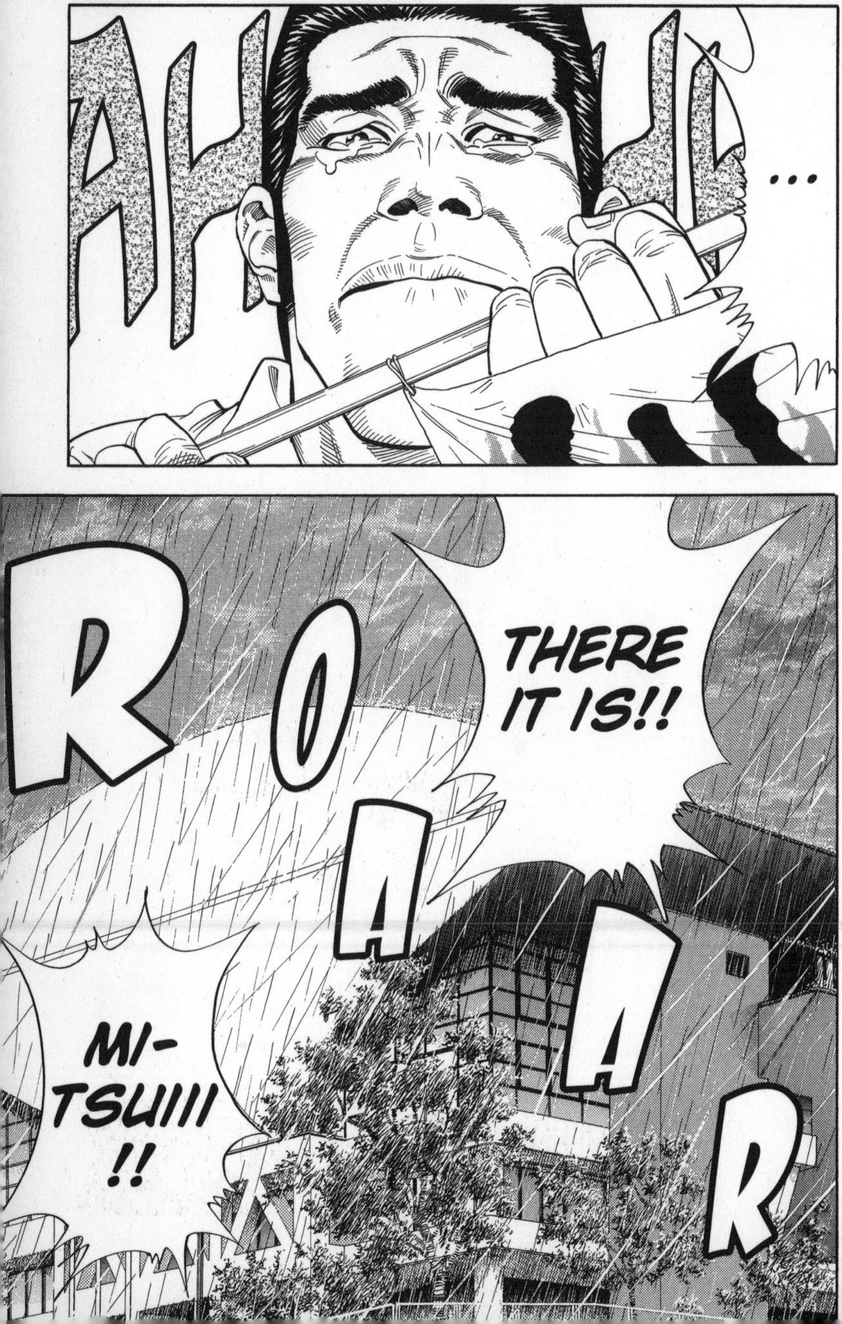
...
THERE IT IS!!
ROAAR
MI-TSUIII !!

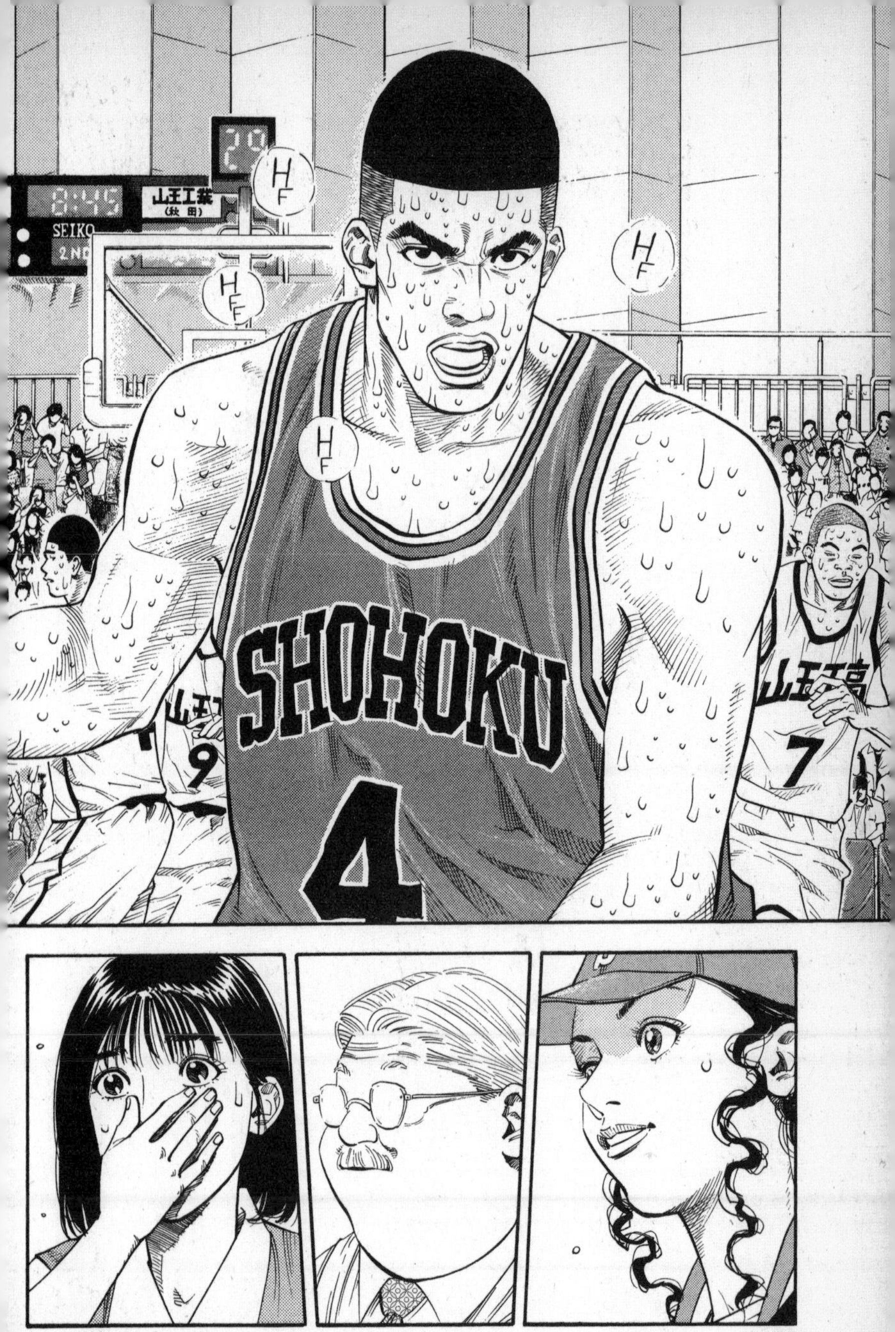
HF
HF
HF
HF
29
8:45
山王工業
(秋田)
SEIKO
SHOHOKU
4
7
9

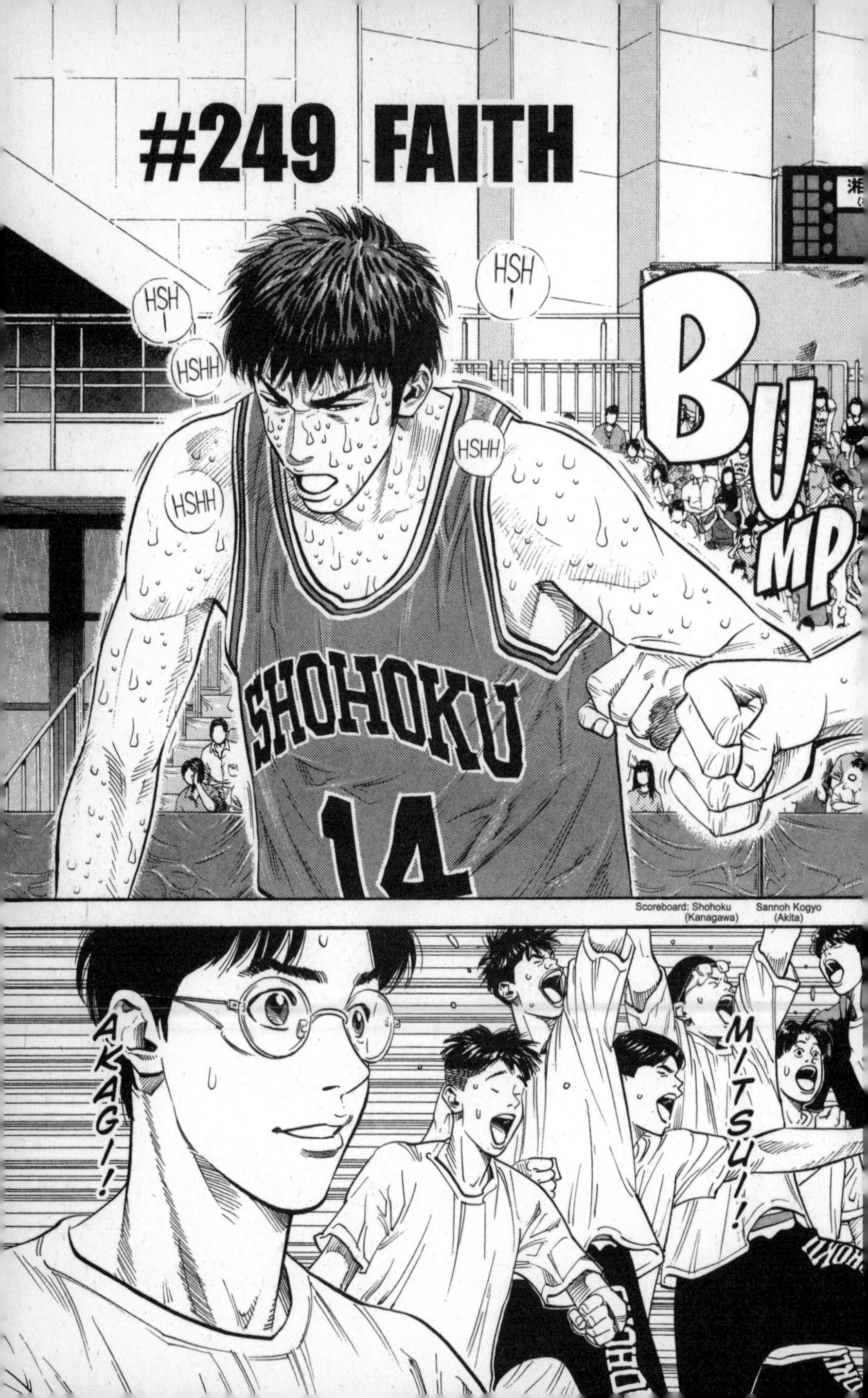
#249 FAITH
HSH!
HSH!
HSHH
HSHH
HSHH
BUMP
SHOHOKU
14
Scoreboard: Shohoku (Kanagawa) Sannoh Kogyo (Akita)
MITSUI!!
AKAGI!!

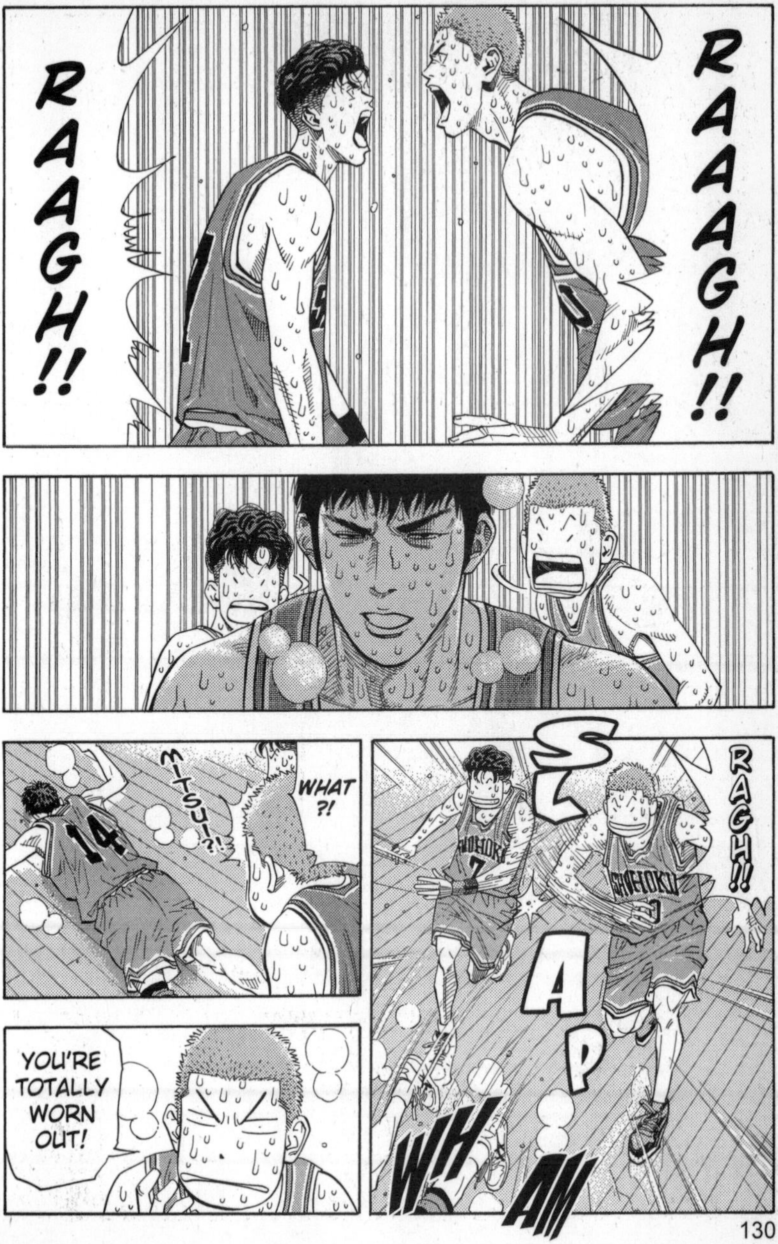
RAAAGH!!
RAAGH!!
RAGH!!
SLAP
WHAM
WHAT ?!
MITSUI?!
YOU'RE TOTALLY WORN OUT!

READ THIS WAY

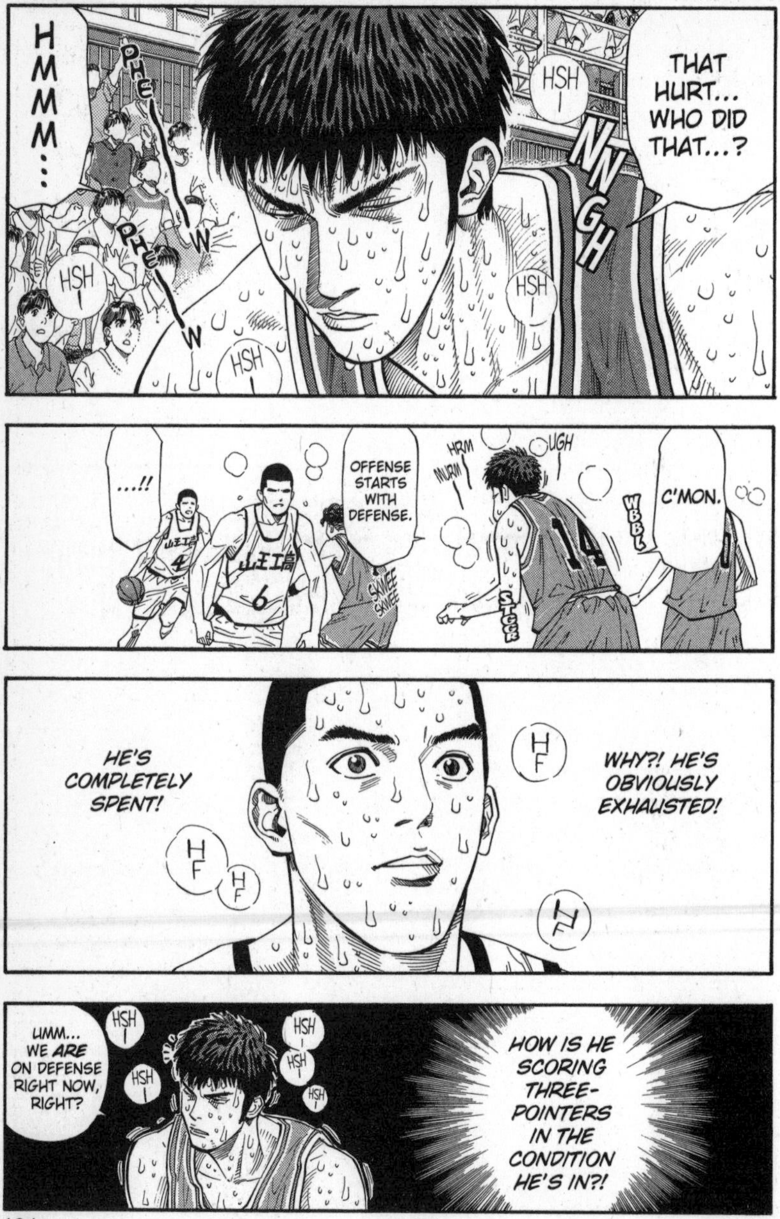
THAT HURT... WHO DID THAT...?
NNGH
HSH
HSH
PHEW
PHEW
HSH
HSH
HMMM...
C'MON.
WBBL
UGH
HRM
NURM
OFFENSE STARTS WITH DEFENSE.
SKWEE SKWEE
STGGR
...!!
WHY?! HE'S OBVIOUSLY EXHAUSTED!
HF
HE'S COMPLETELY SPENT!
HF
HF
HF
HOW IS HE SCORING THREE-POINTERS IN THE CONDITION HE'S IN?!
HSH
HSH
HSH
HSH
HSH
UMM... WE *ARE* ON DEFENSE RIGHT NOW, RIGHT?

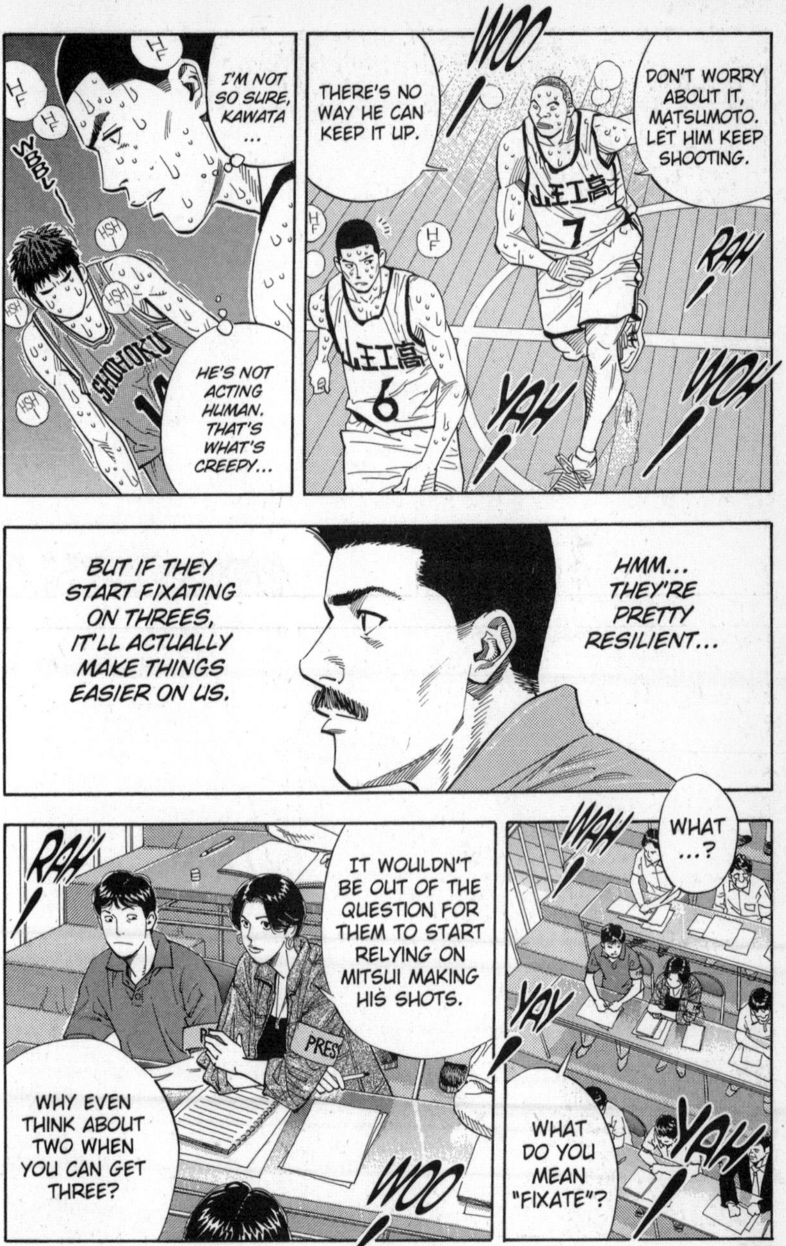
WOO
DON'T WORRY ABOUT IT, MATSUMOTO. LET HIM KEEP SHOOTING.
RAH
WOH
YAH
THERE'S NO WAY HE CAN KEEP IT UP.
HF
HF
I'M NOT SO SURE, KAWATA ...
HF
HF
HF
WBBL
HSH
HSH
HSH
HSH
HE'S NOT ACTING HUMAN. THAT'S WHAT'S CREEPY...
HMM... THEY'RE PRETTY RESILIENT...
BUT IF THEY START FIXATING ON THREES, IT'LL ACTUALLY MAKE THINGS EASIER ON US.
WAH
WHAT ...?
YAY
YAH
WHAT DO YOU MEAN "FIXATE"?
RAH
IT WOULDN'T BE OUT OF THE QUESTION FOR THEM TO START RELYING ON MITSUI MAKING HIS SHOTS.
WHY EVEN THINK ABOUT TWO WHEN YOU CAN GET THREE?
WOO

READ THIS WAY

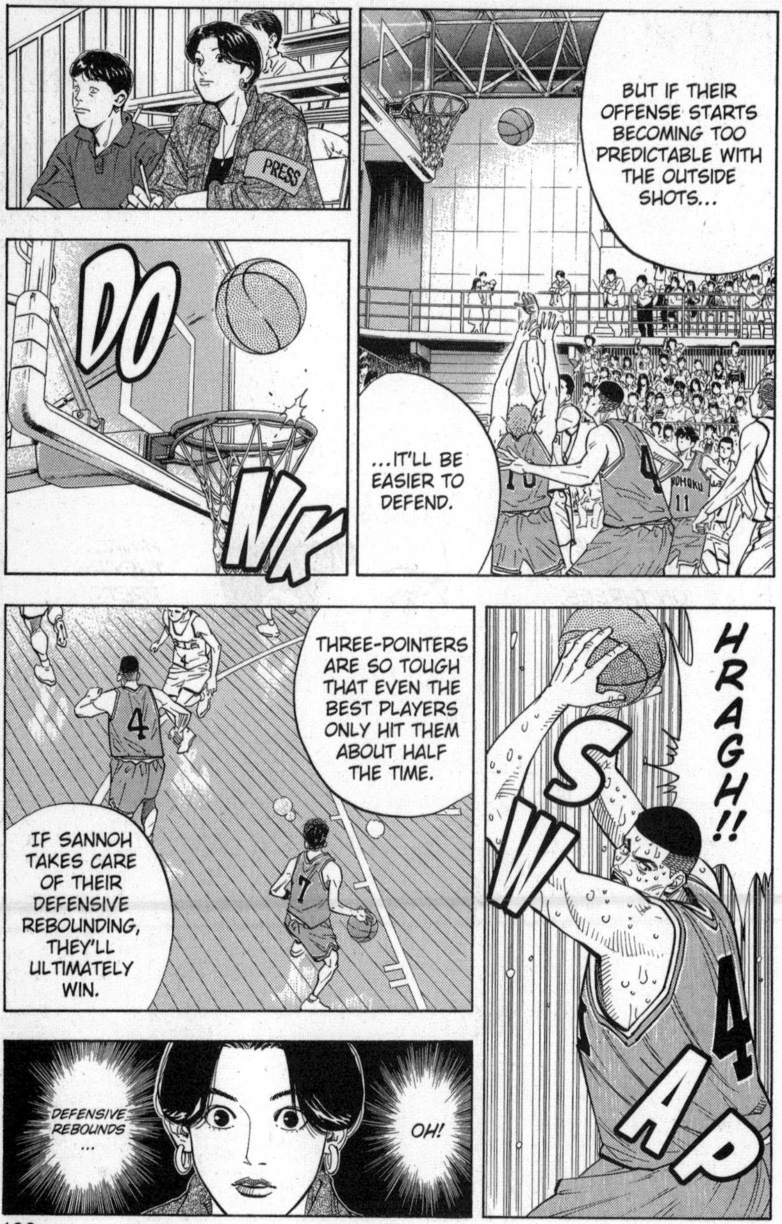

BUT IF THEIR OFFENSE STARTS BECOMING TOO PREDICTABLE WITH THE OUTSIDE SHOTS...
...IT'LL BE EASIER TO DEFEND.
DONK
HRAGH!!
SWAP
THREE-POINTERS ARE SO TOUGH THAT EVEN THE BEST PLAYERS ONLY HIT THEM ABOUT HALF THE TIME.
IF SANNOH TAKES CARE OF THEIR DEFENSIVE REBOUNDING, THEY'LL ULTIMATELY WIN.
OH!
DEFENSIVE REBOUNDS ...

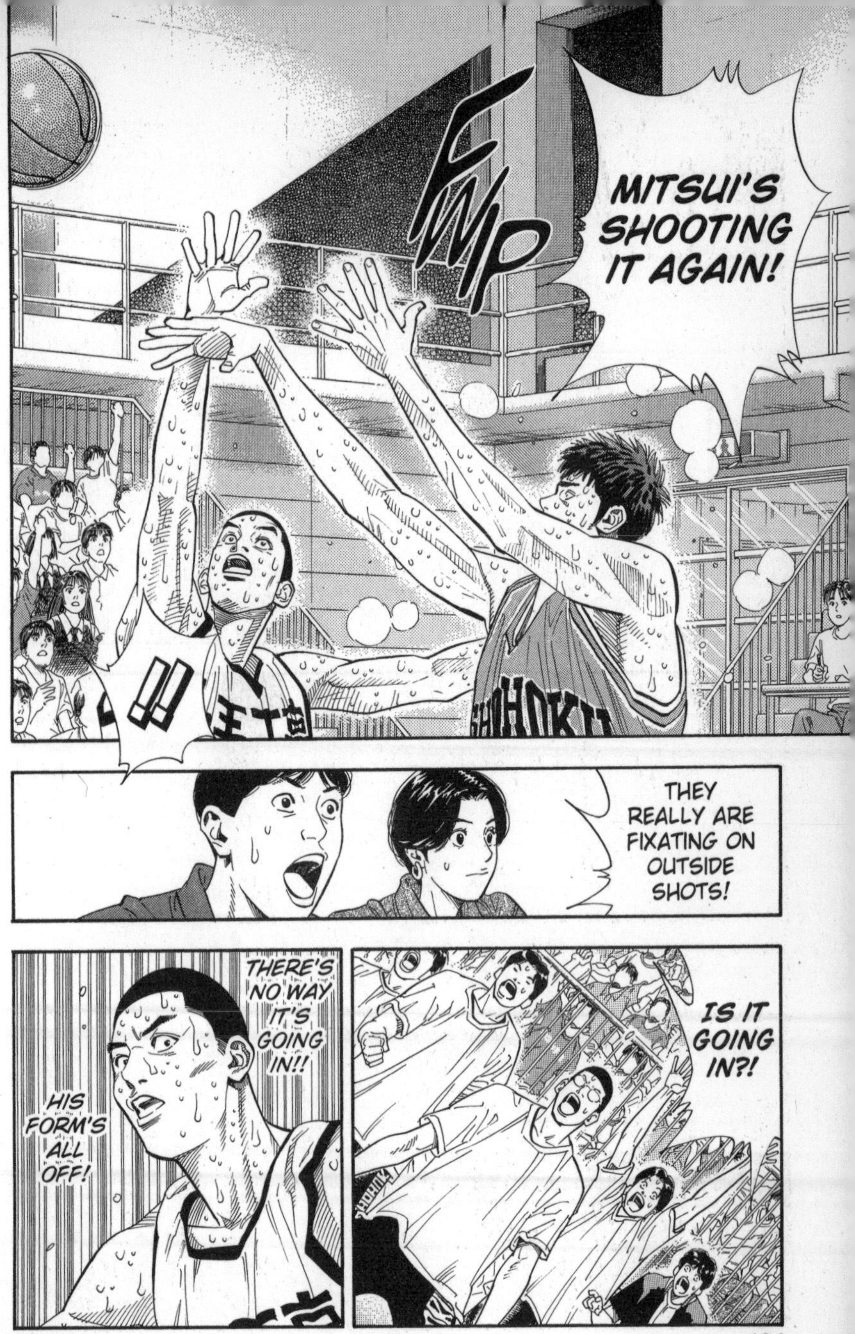
FWP
MITSUI'S SHOOTING IT AGAIN!
!!
THEY REALLY ARE FIXATING ON OUTSIDE SHOTS!
IS IT GOING IN?!
THERE'S NO WAY IT'S GOING IN!!
HIS FORM'S ALL OFF!

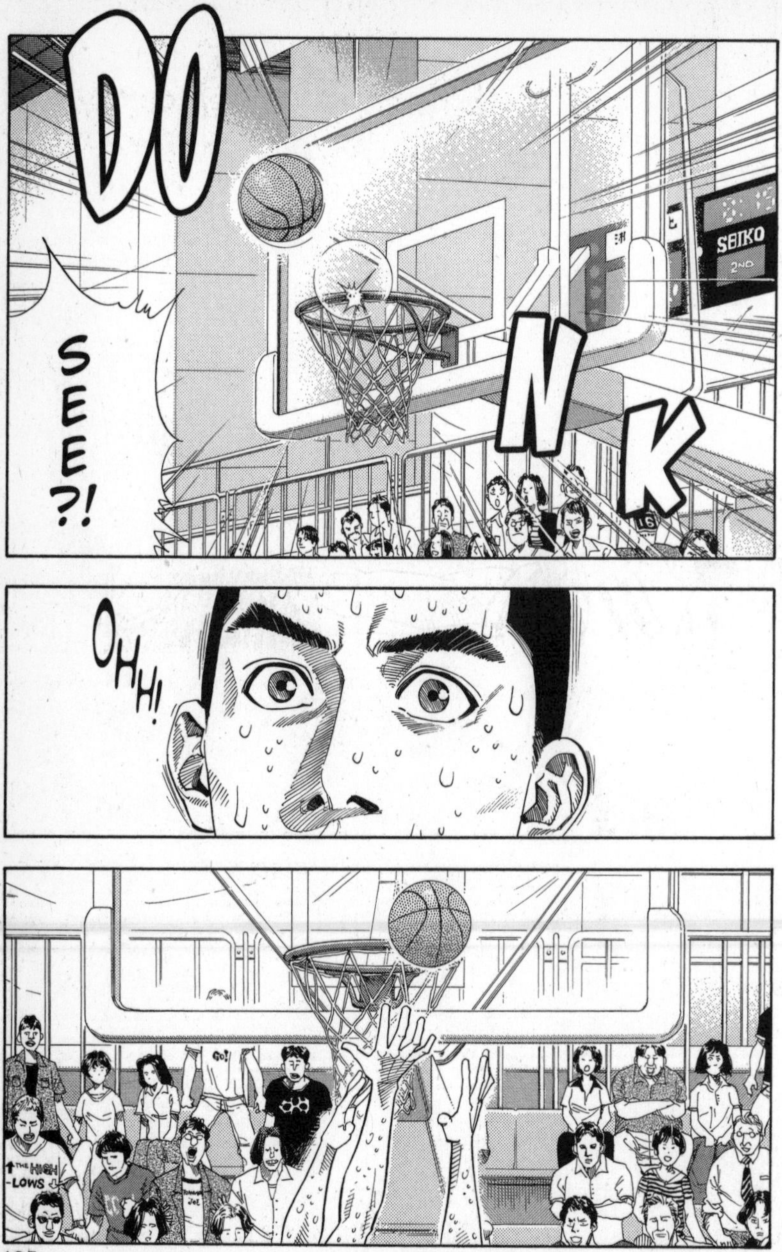
DO
N
K
SEE?!
OHH!

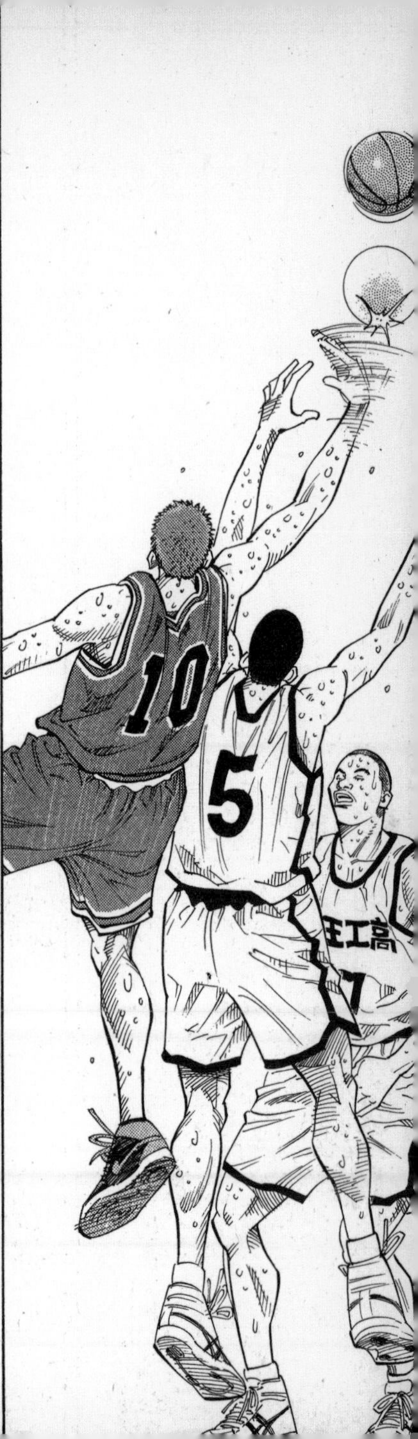
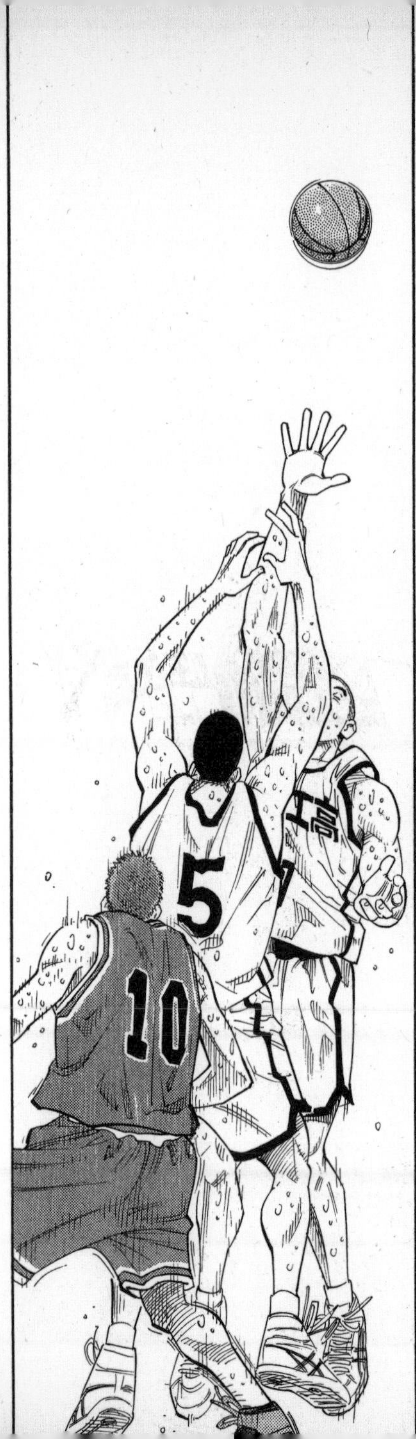

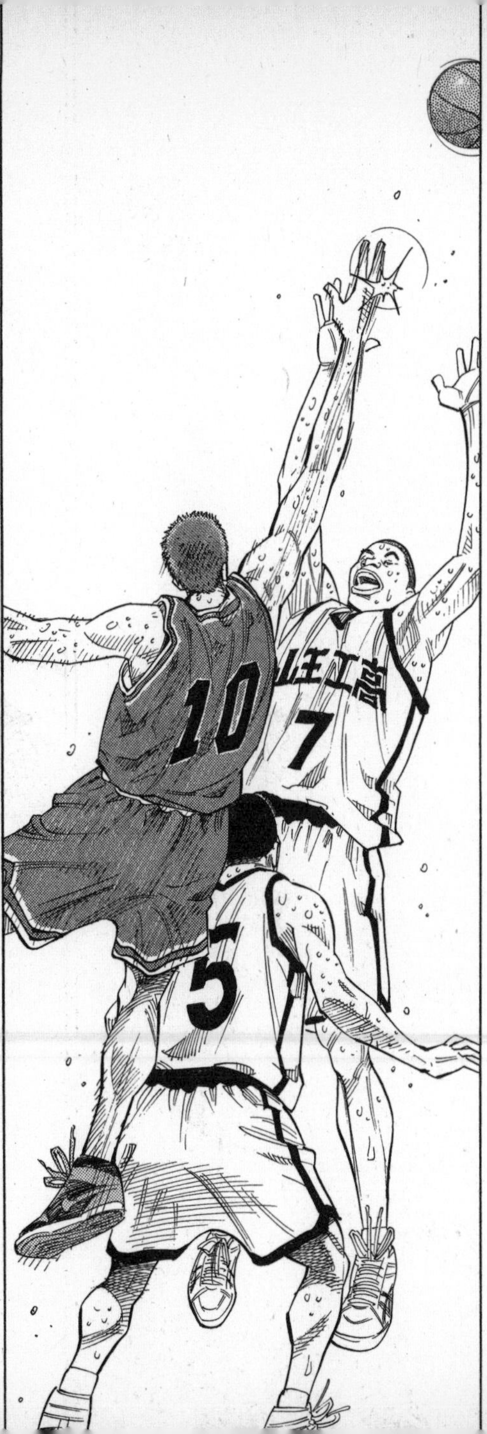
山王工高
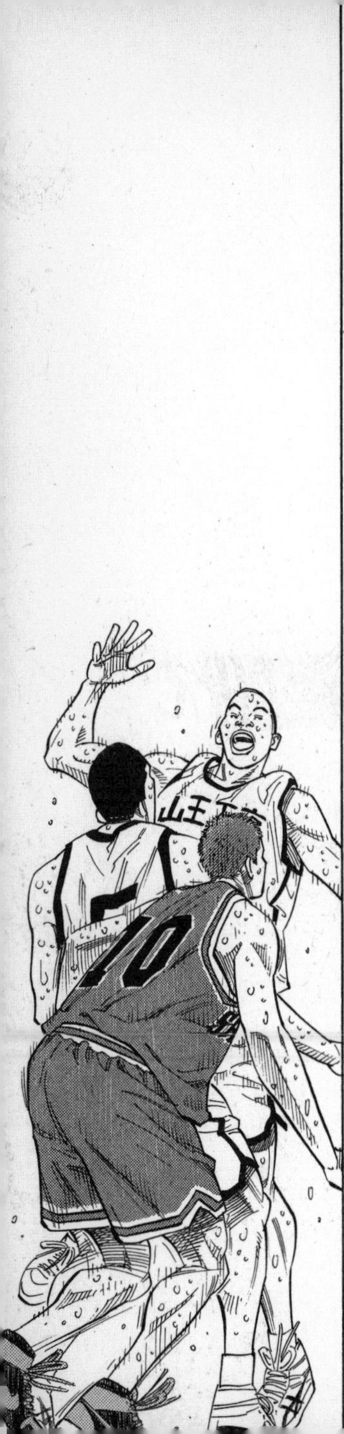

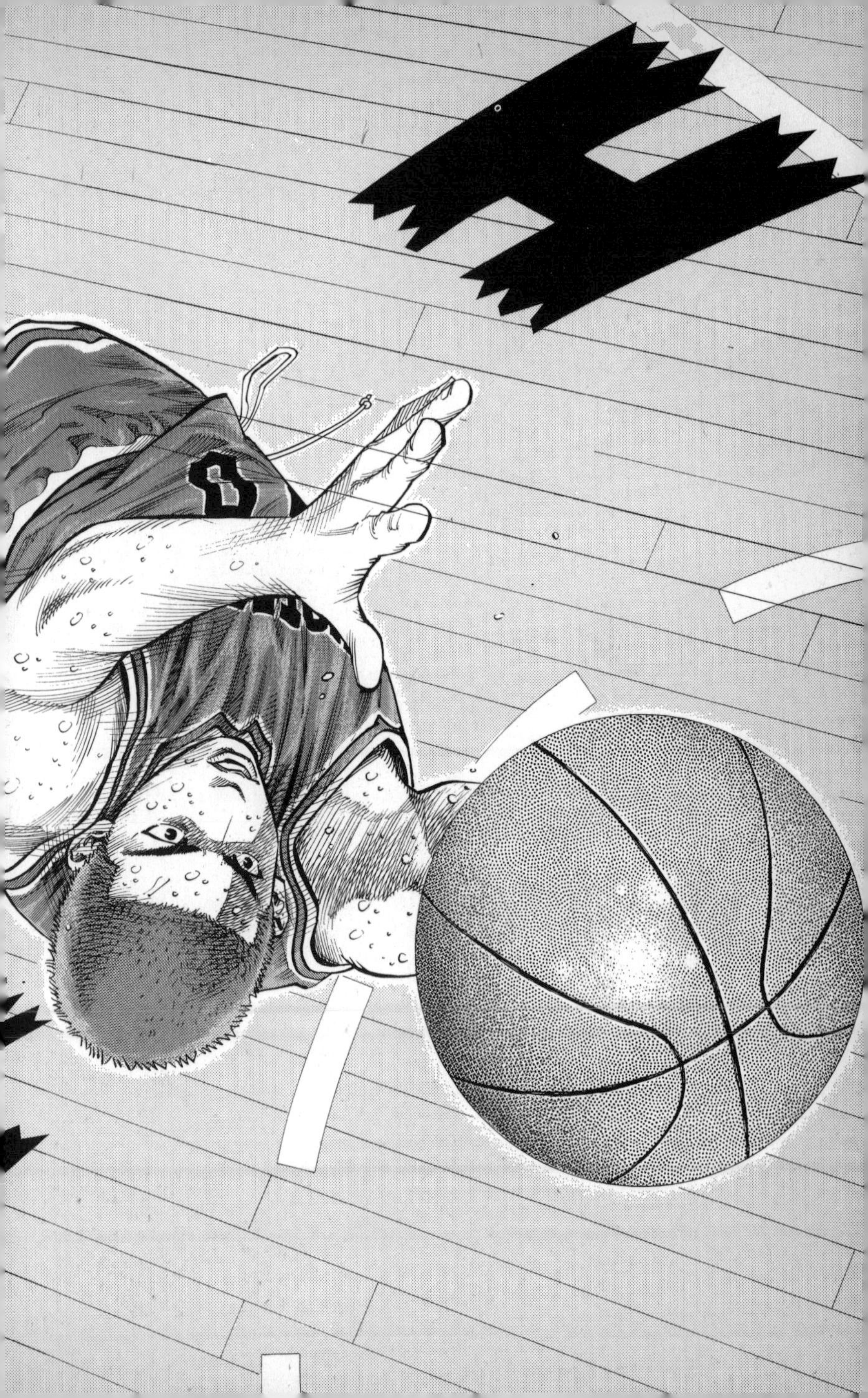

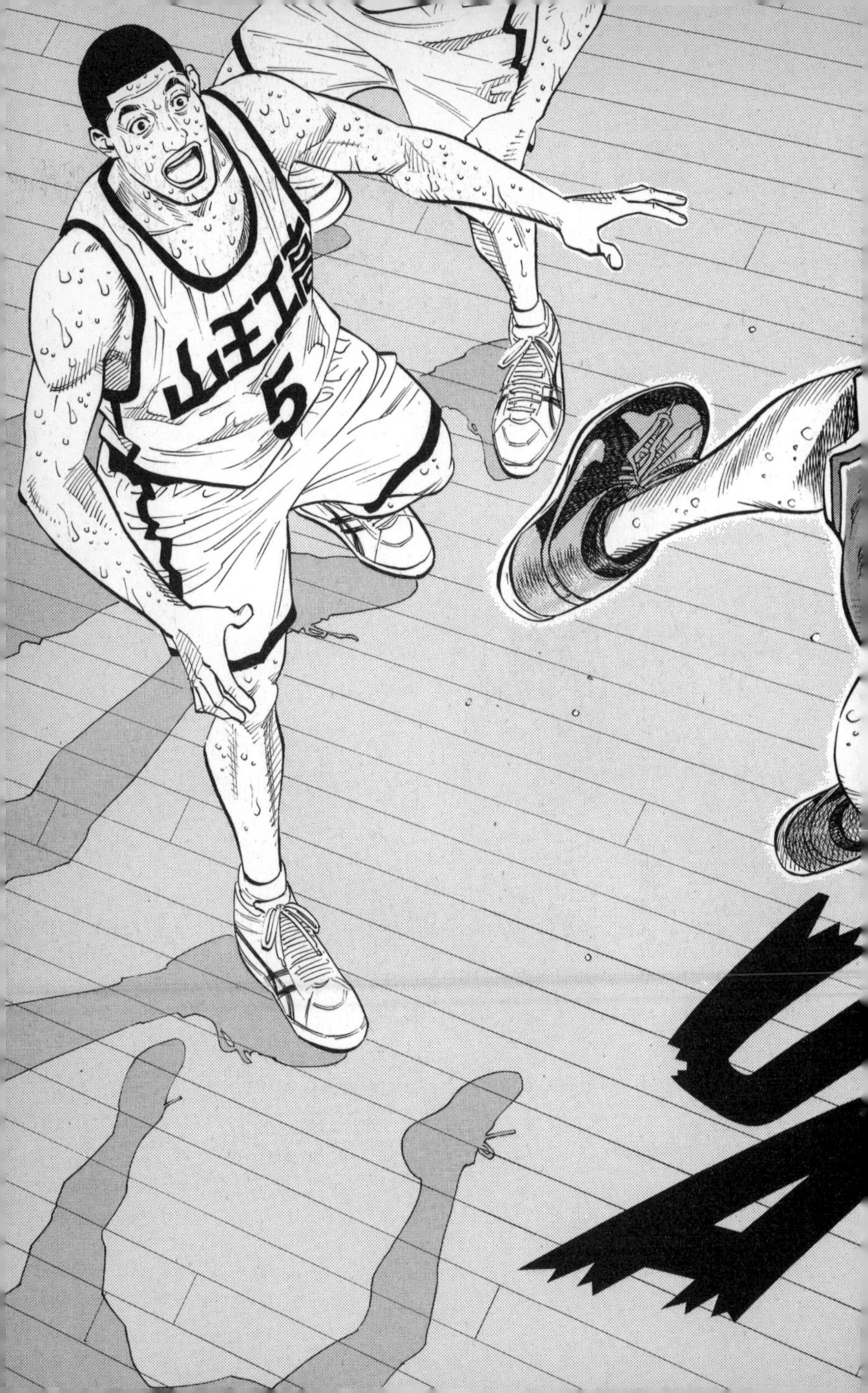

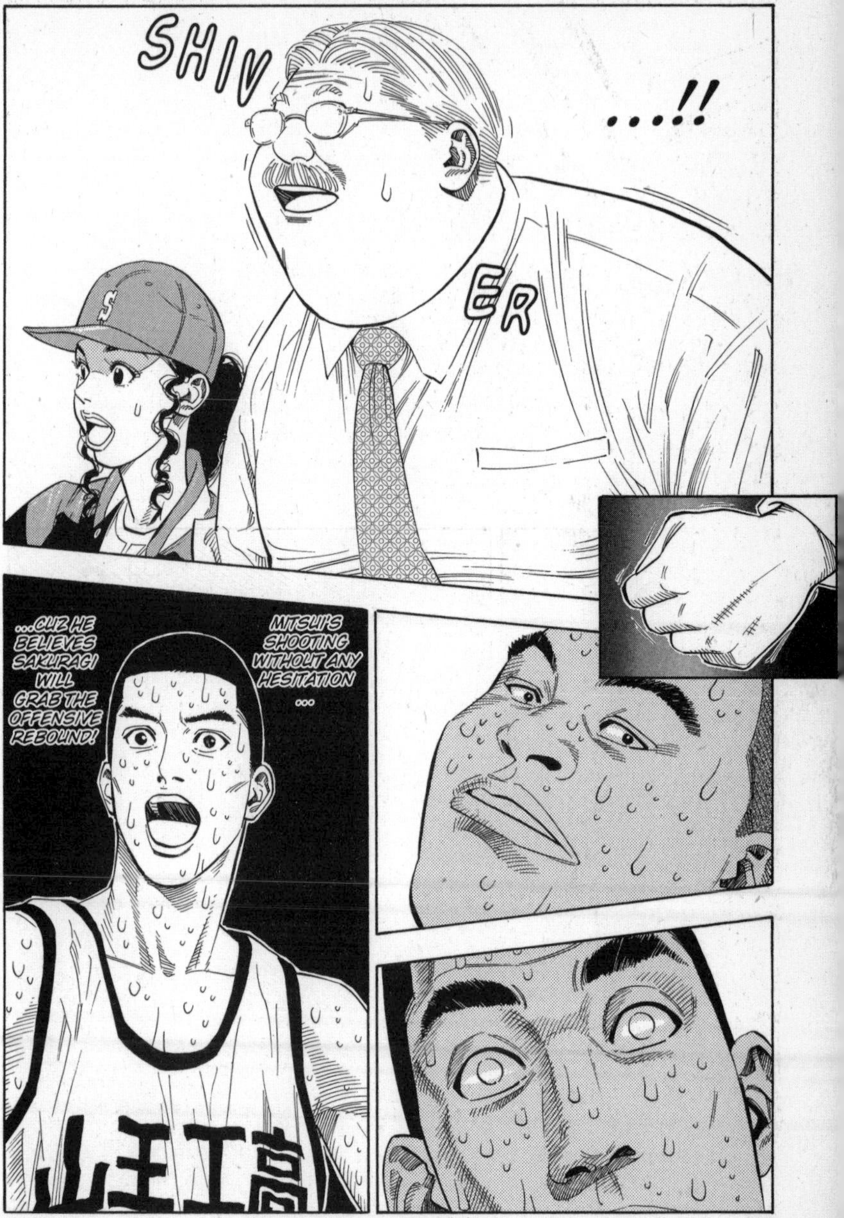

...!!
SHIVER
MITSUI'S SHOOTING WITHOUT ANY HESITATION ...
...CUZ HE BELIEVES SAKURAGI WILL GRAB THE OFFENSIVE REBOUND!
山王工高

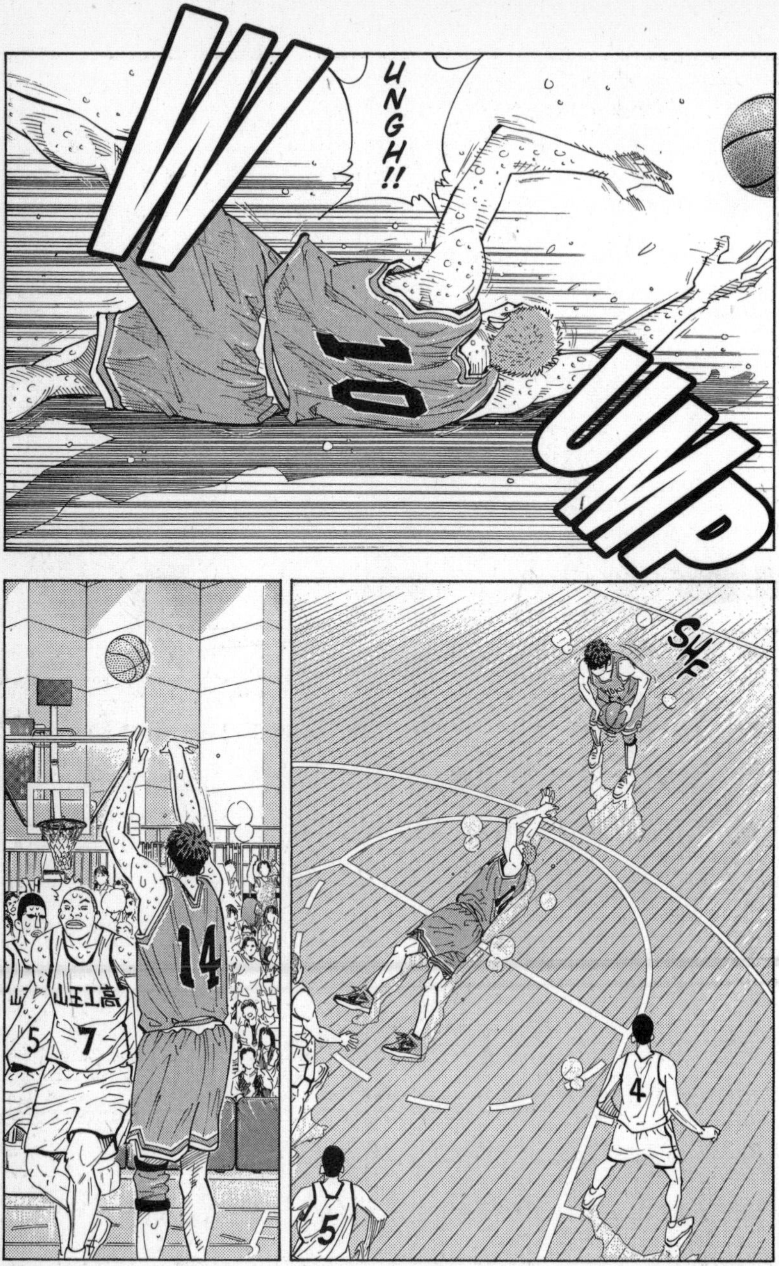
UNGH!!
WUMP
SHF

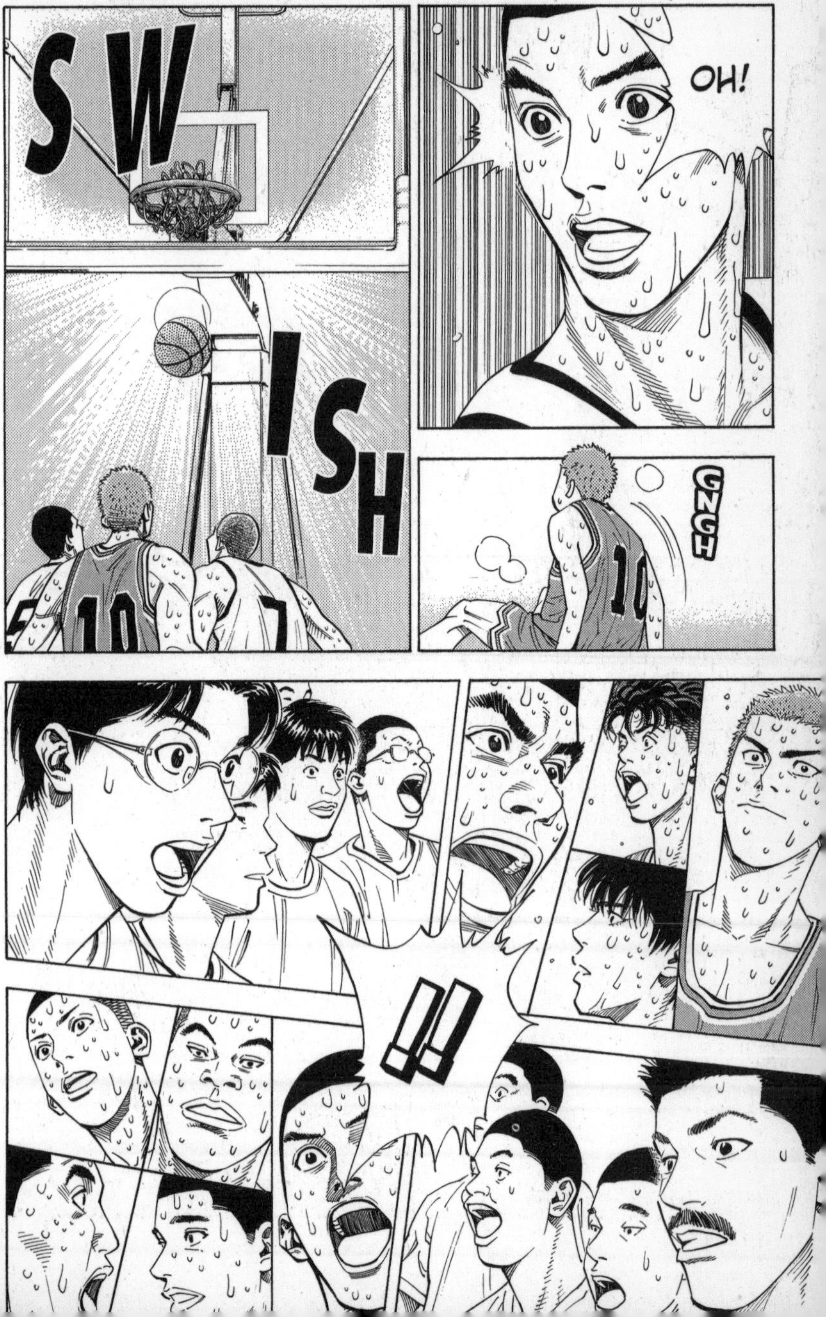
OH!
SWISH
GNGH
!!

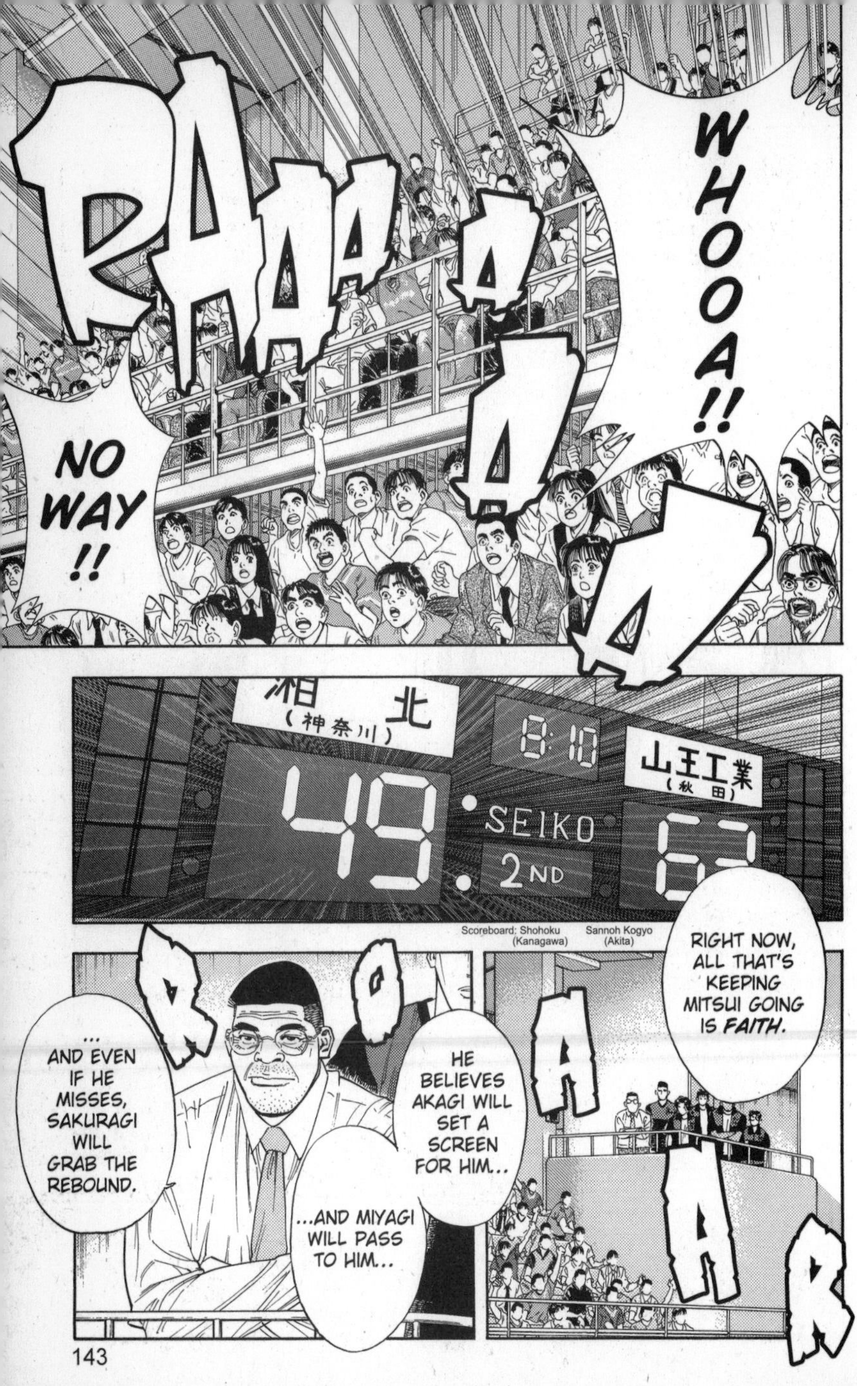
WHOOA!!
RAAAAAAA
NO WAY!!
湘北
(神奈川)
8:10
山王工業
(秋田)
49
SEIKO
2ND
Scoreboard: Shohoku (Kanagawa) Sannoh Kogyo (Akita)
RIGHT NOW, ALL THAT'S KEEPING MITSUI GOING IS *FAITH*.
HE BELIEVES AKAGI WILL SET A SCREEN FOR HIM...
...AND MIYAGI WILL PASS TO HIM...
... AND EVEN IF HE MISSES, SAKURAGI WILL GRAB THE REBOUND.
ROAAAR

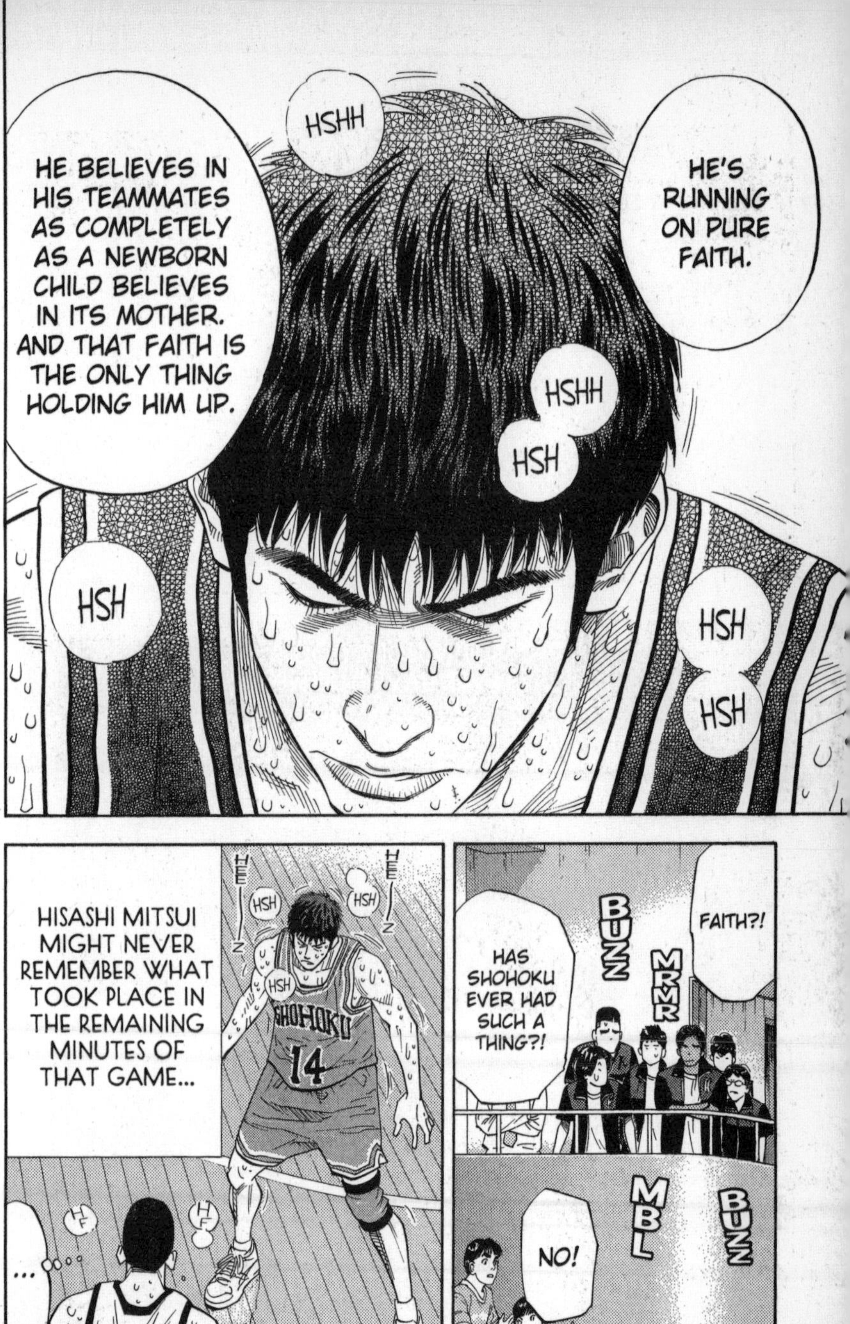
HE'S RUNNING ON PURE FAITH.
HSHH
HE BELIEVES IN HIS TEAMMATES AS COMPLETELY AS A NEWBORN CHILD BELIEVES IN ITS MOTHER. AND THAT FAITH IS THE ONLY THING HOLDING HIM UP.
HSHH
HSH
HSH
HSH
HSH
FAITH?!
BUZZ
MRMR
HAS SHOHOKU EVER HAD SUCH A THING?!
BUZZ
MBL
NO!
HE-Z
HSH
HSH
HE-Z
HISASHI MITSUI MIGHT NEVER REMEMBER WHAT TOOK PLACE IN THE REMAINING MINUTES OF THAT GAME...
HSH
SHOHOKU
14
HF
HF
...

READ THIS WAY

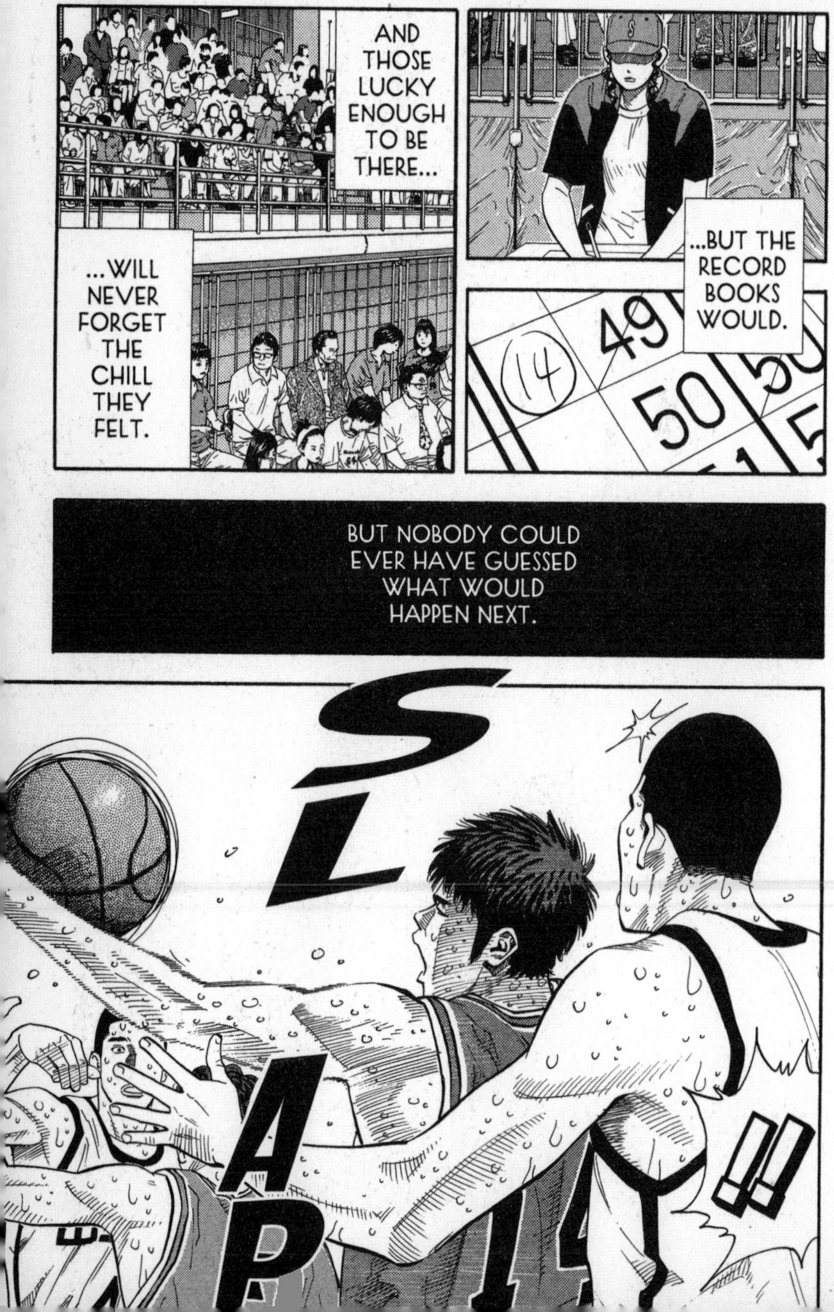

...BUT THE RECORD BOOKS WOULD.
AND THOSE LUCKY ENOUGH TO BE THERE...
...WILL NEVER FORGET THE CHILL THEY FELT.
BUT NOBODY COULD EVER HAVE GUESSED WHAT WOULD HAPPEN NEXT.
SLAP
!!

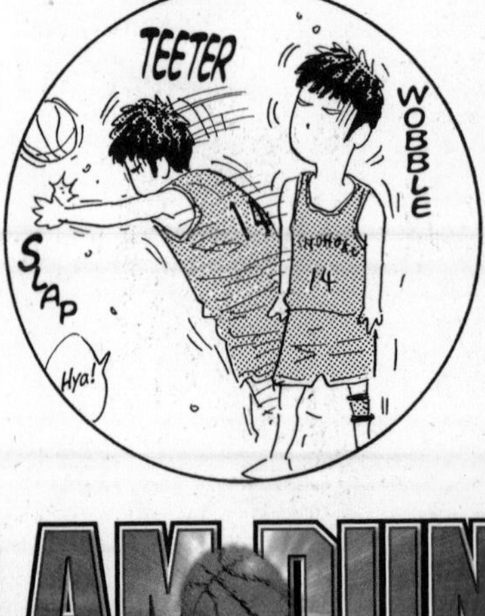
TEETER
WOBBLE
SLAP
Hya!

SLAM DUNK

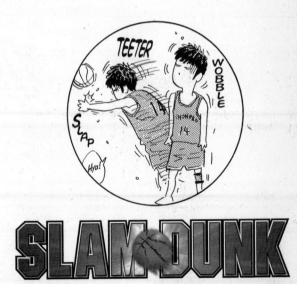

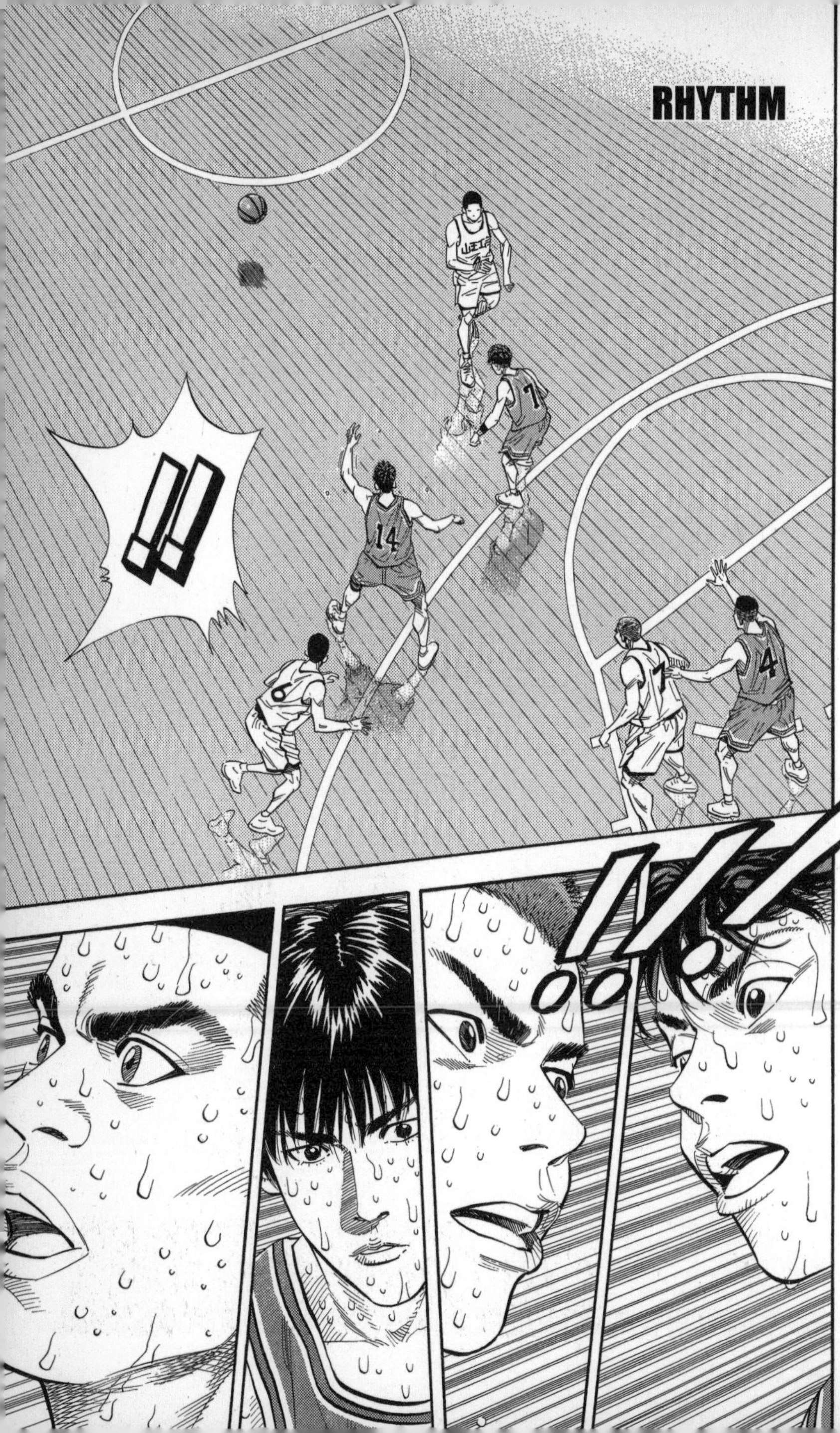
RHYTHM
!!
!!

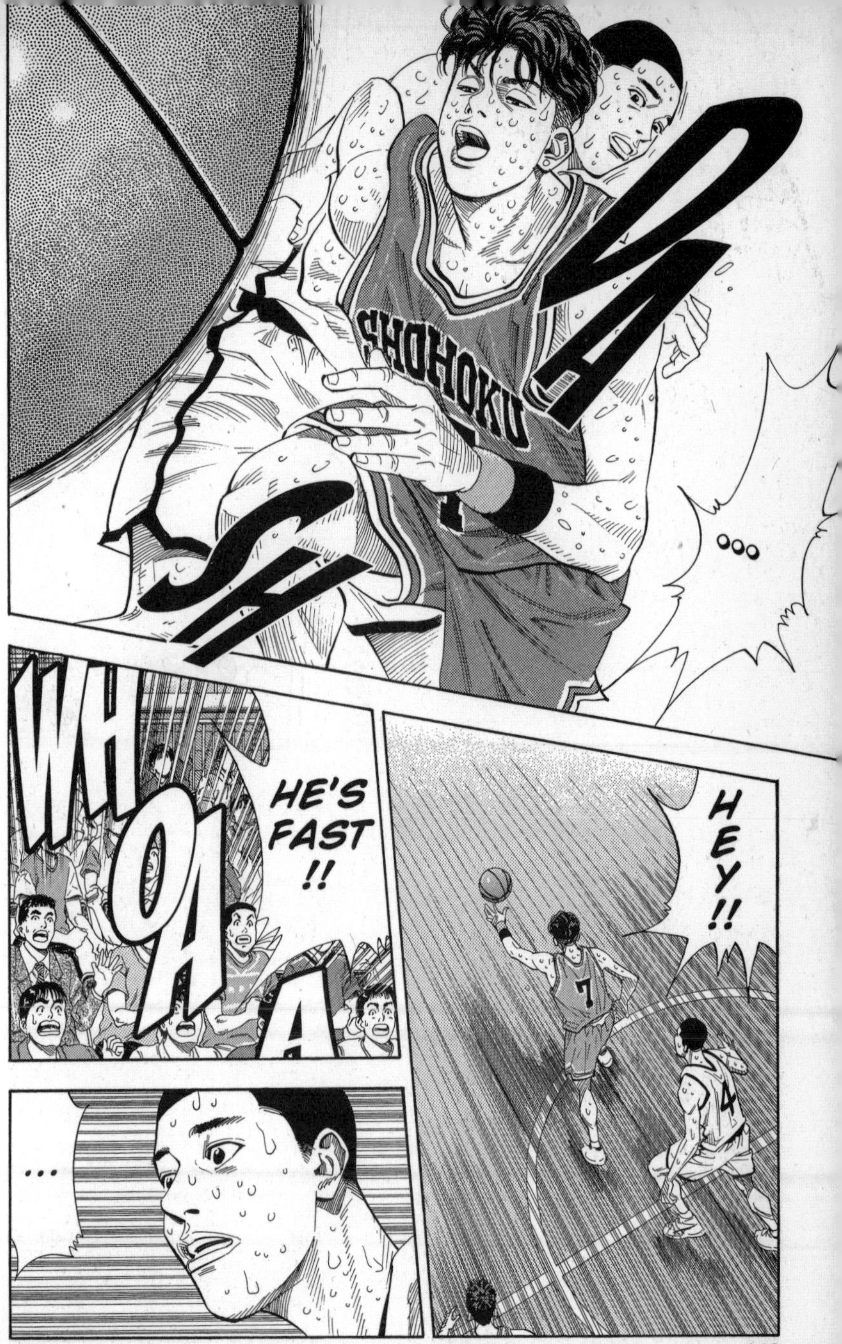
...
HEY!!
HE'S FAST!!
WHOA
...

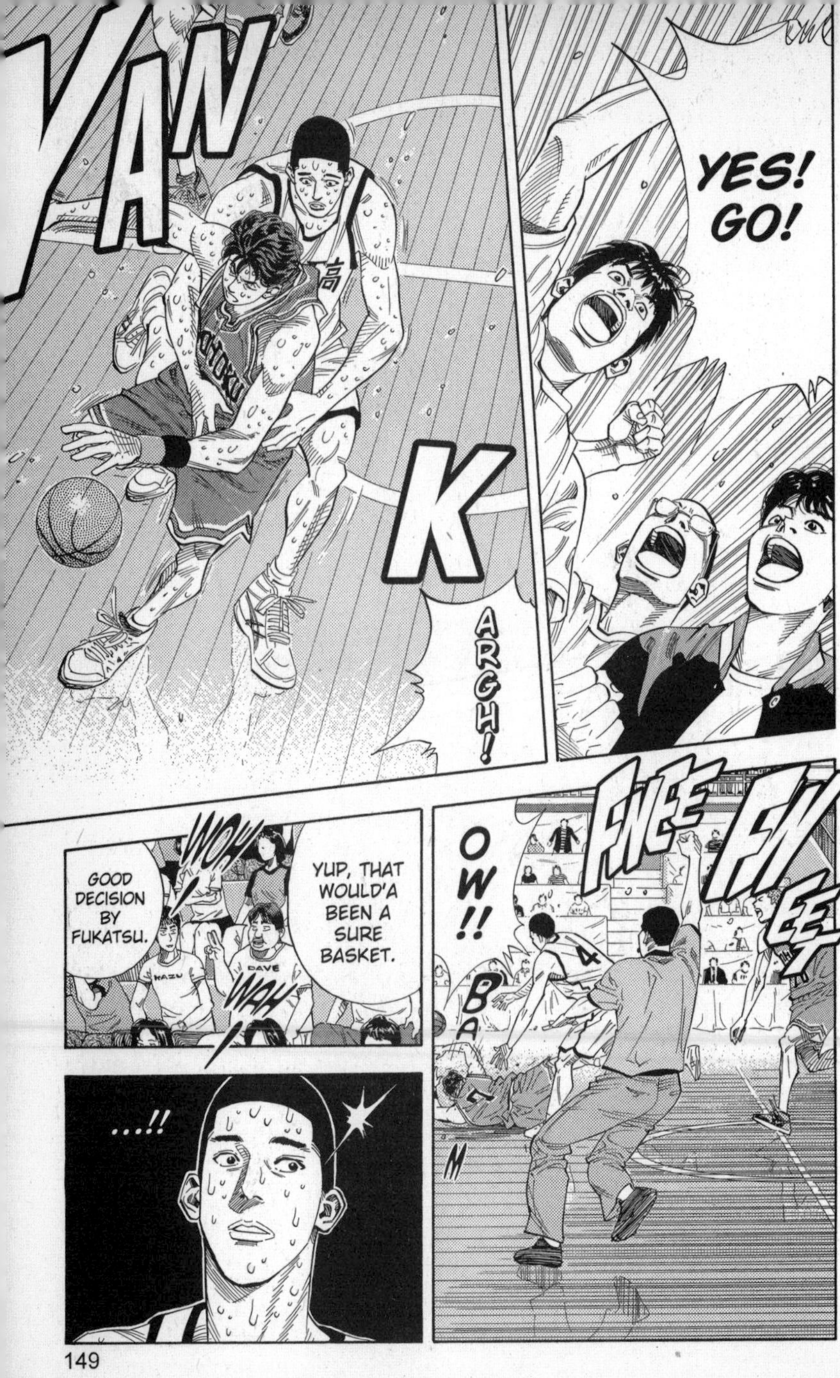
YES! GO!
K
ARGH!
FWEE
OW!!
BAM
YUP, THAT WOULD'A BEEN A SURE BASKET.
GOOD DECISION BY FUKATSU.
WAH
WAH
...!!

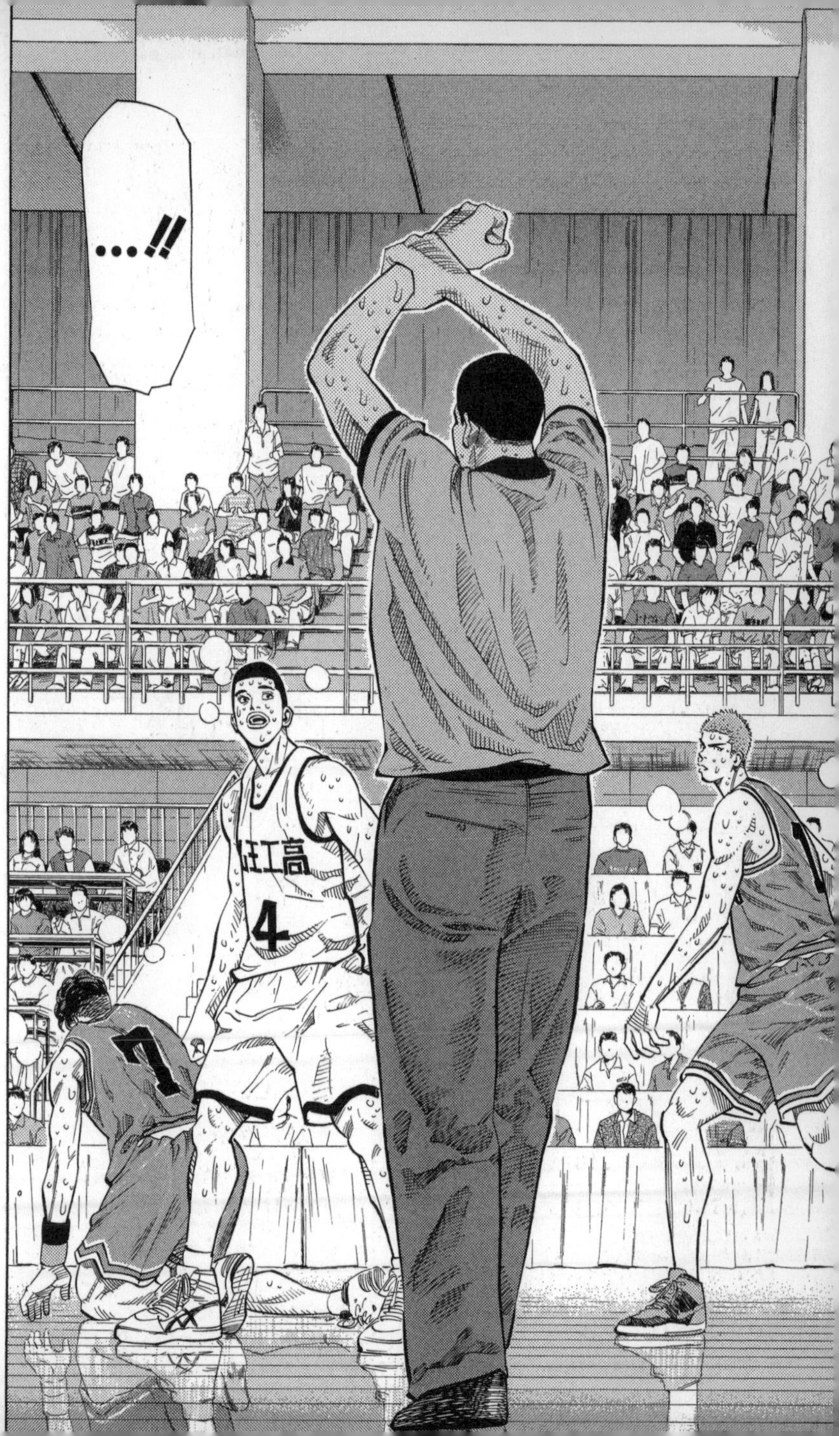
...!!

READ THIS WAY

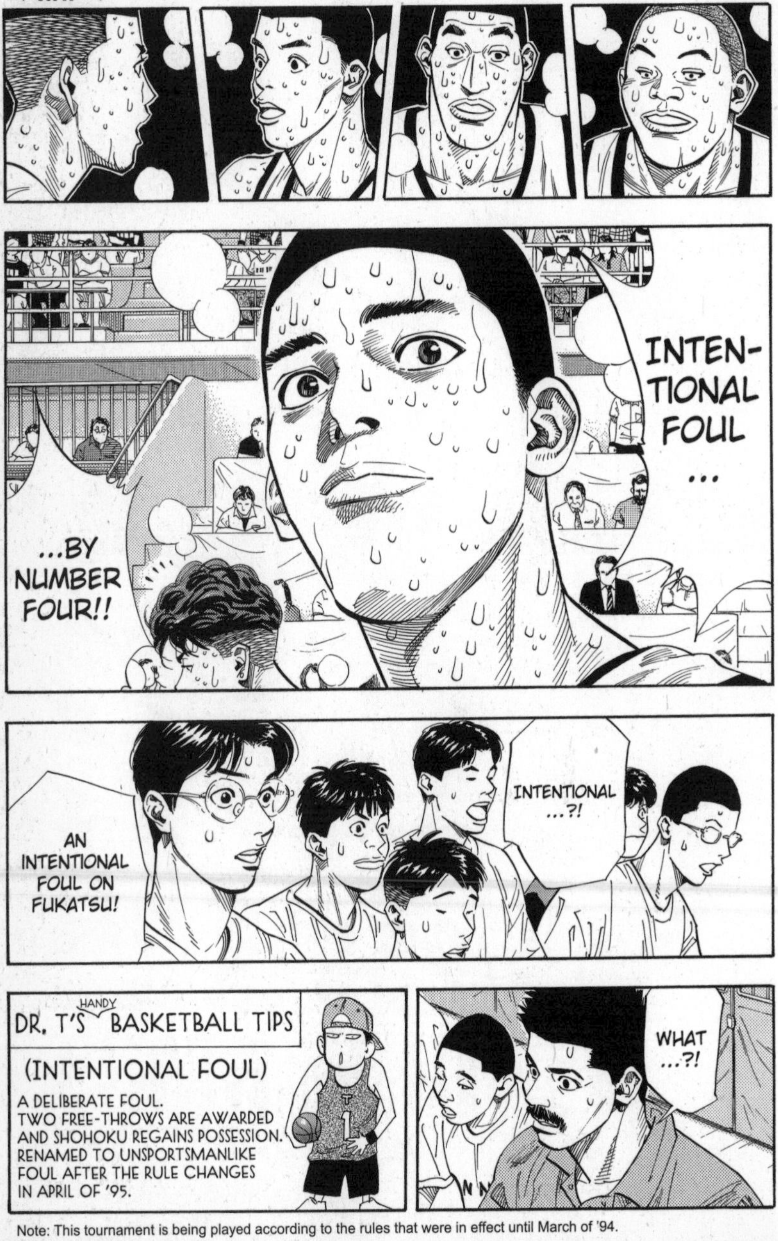
INTEN-TIONAL FOUL ...
...BY NUMBER FOUR!!
INTENTIONAL ...?!
AN INTENTIONAL FOUL ON FUKATSU!
WHAT ...?!
DR. T'S HANDY BASKETBALL TIPS
(INTENTIONAL FOUL)
A DELIBERATE FOUL. TWO FREE-THROWS ARE AWARDED AND SHOHOKU REGAINS POSSESSION. RENAMED TO UNSPORTSMANLIKE FOUL AFTER THE RULE CHANGES IN APRIL OF '95.

Note: This tournament is being played according to the rules that were in effect until March of '94.

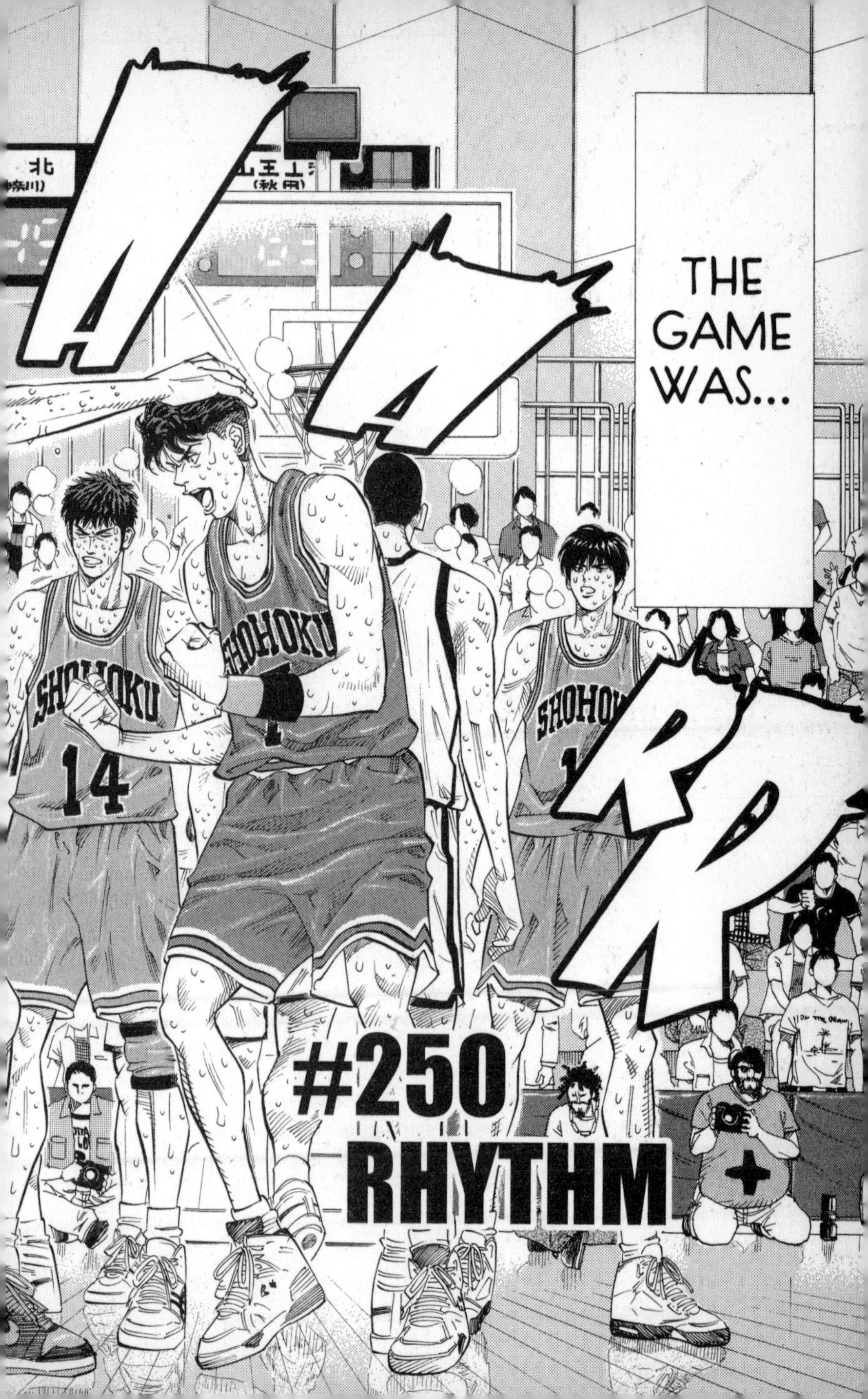
THE GAME WAS...
SHOHOKU
SHOHOKU
SHOHOKU
14
#250
RHYTHM

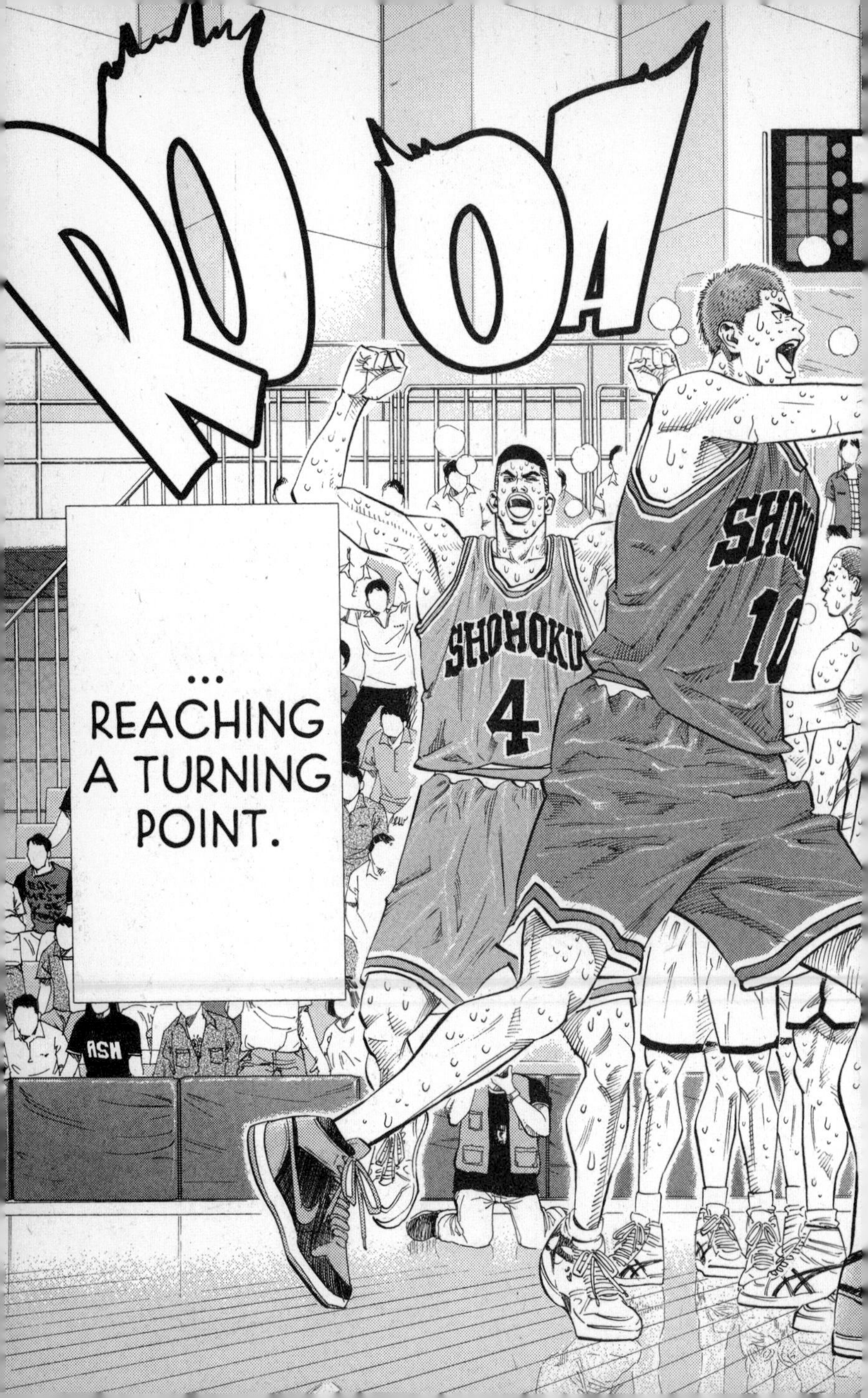
ROOA
... REACHING A TURNING POINT.
SHOHOKU
4

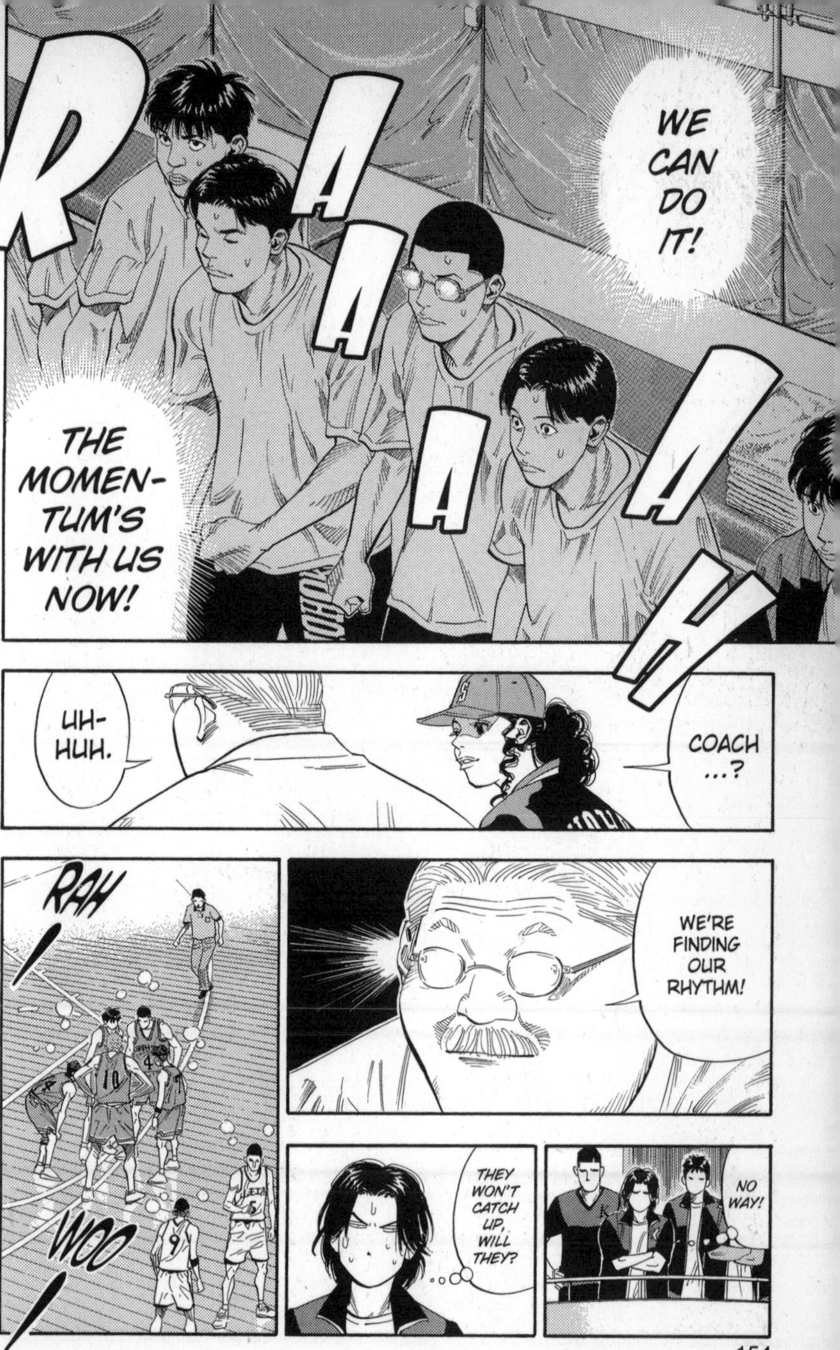
WE CAN DO IT!
RAAAAH
THE MOMENTUM'S WITH US NOW!
COACH ...?
UH-HUH.
WE'RE FINDING OUR RHYTHM!
RAH!
WOO!
NO WAY!
THEY WON'T CATCH UP, WILL THEY?

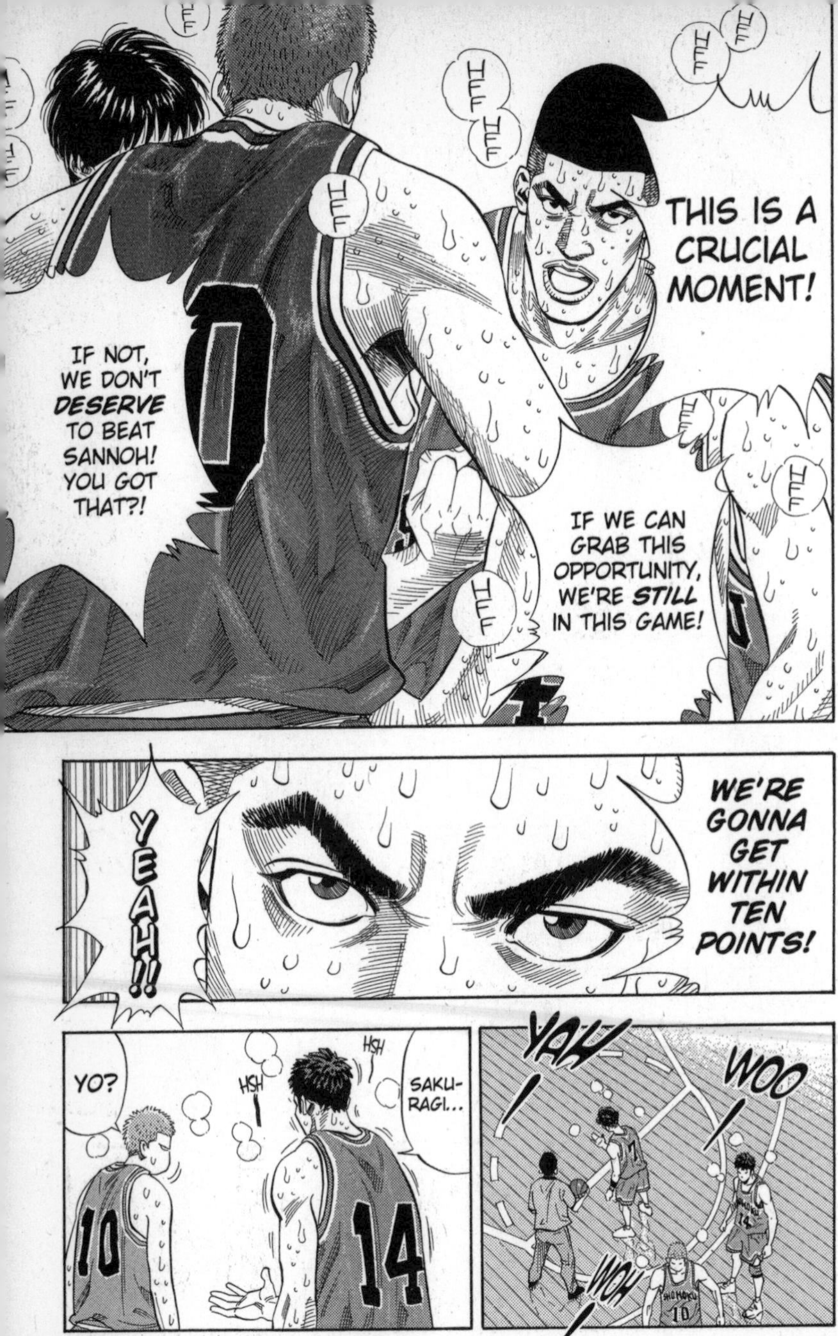
HEF HEF
THIS IS A CRUCIAL MOMENT!
HEF HEF
HEF
IF WE CAN GRAB THIS OPPORTUNITY, WE'RE *STILL* IN THIS GAME!
HEF
HEF
IF NOT, WE DON'T *DESERVE* TO BEAT SANNOH! YOU GOT THAT?!
WE'RE GONNA GET WITHIN TEN POINTS!
YEAH!!
WOO!
YAH!
WOH!
SAKU-RAGI...
HSH
HSH
YO?

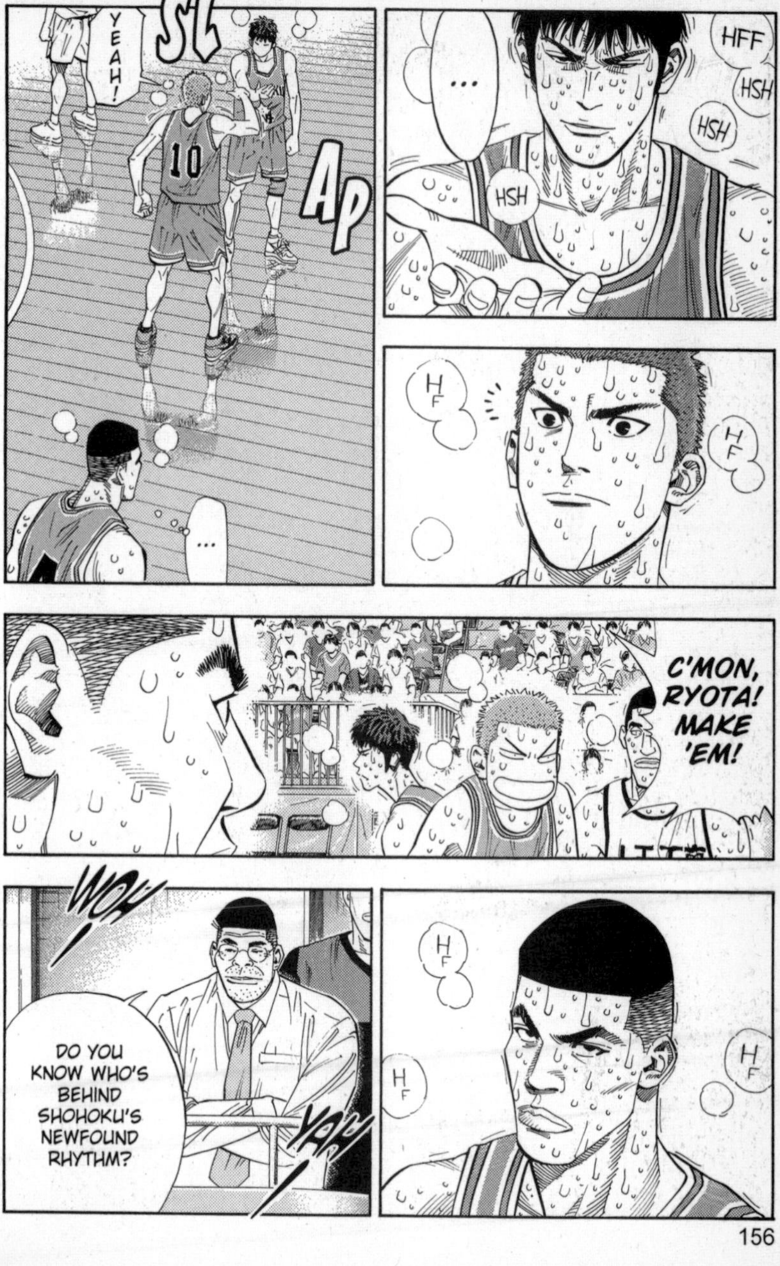
...
HFF
HSH
HSH
HSH
HF
HF
YEAH!
SL
AP
...
C'MON, RYOTA! MAKE 'EM!
HF
HF
HF
WOH
YAH
DO YOU KNOW WHO'S BEHIND SHOHOKU'S NEWFOUND RHYTHM?

READ THIS WAY

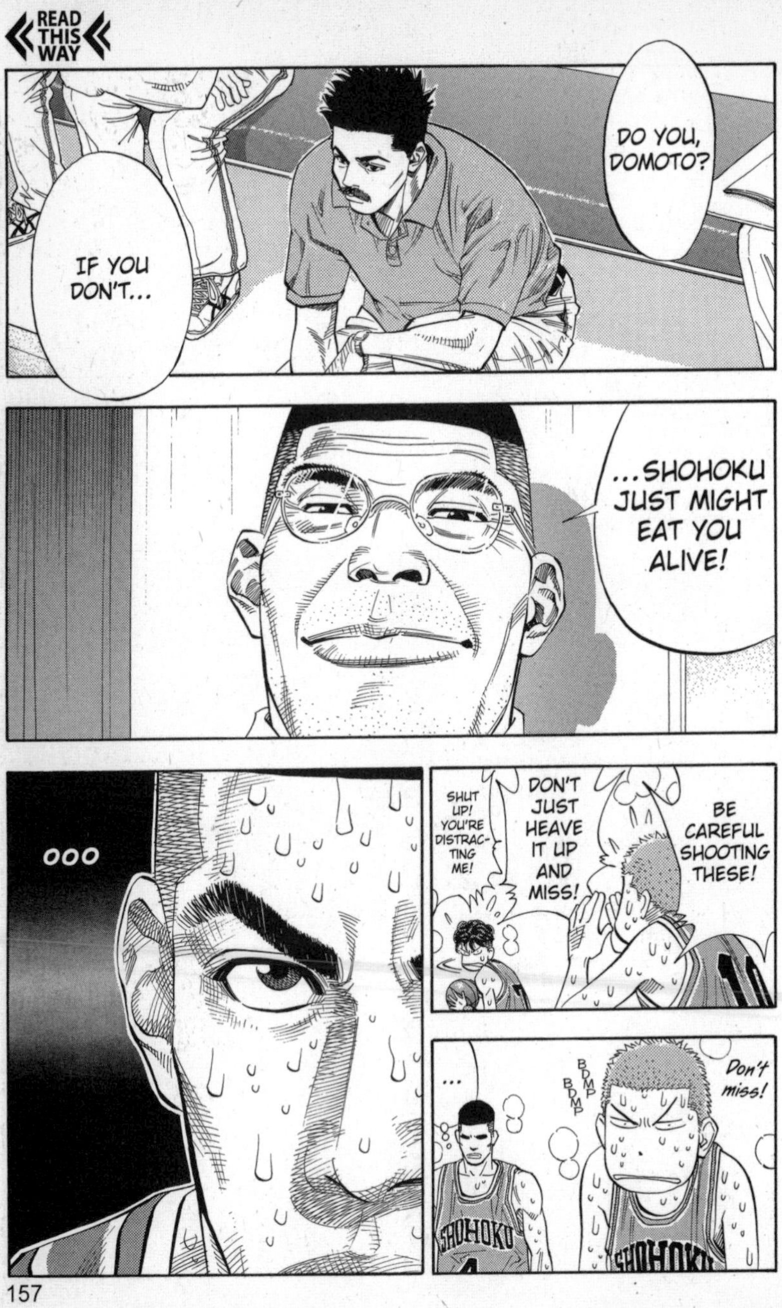

DO YOU, DOMOTO?
IF YOU DON'T...
...SHOHOKU JUST MIGHT EAT YOU ALIVE!
BE CAREFUL SHOOTING THESE!
DON'T JUST HEAVE IT UP AND MISS!
SHUT UP! YOU'RE DISTRAC-TING ME!
Don't miss!
BDMP BDMP
...
OOO

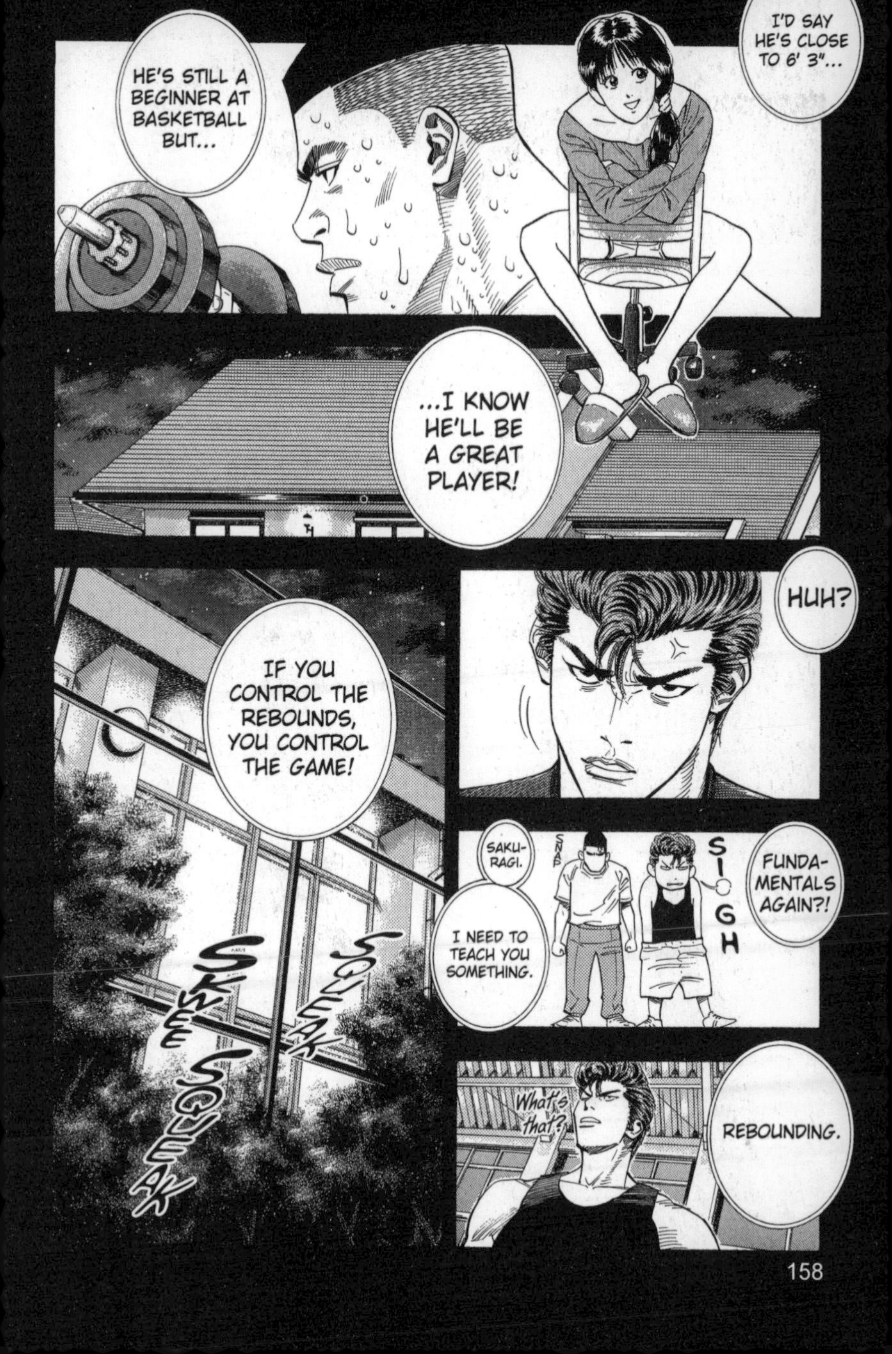
I'D SAY HE'S CLOSE TO 6' 3"...
HE'S STILL A BEGINNER AT BASKETBALL BUT...
...I KNOW HE'LL BE A GREAT PLAYER!
HUH?
FUNDA-MENTALS AGAIN?!
SIGH
SNAP
SAKU-RAGI.
I NEED TO TEACH YOU SOMETHING.
REBOUNDING.
What's that?
IF YOU CONTROL THE REBOUNDS, YOU CONTROL THE GAME!
SQUEAK
SKWEE
SQUEAK

READ THIS WAY

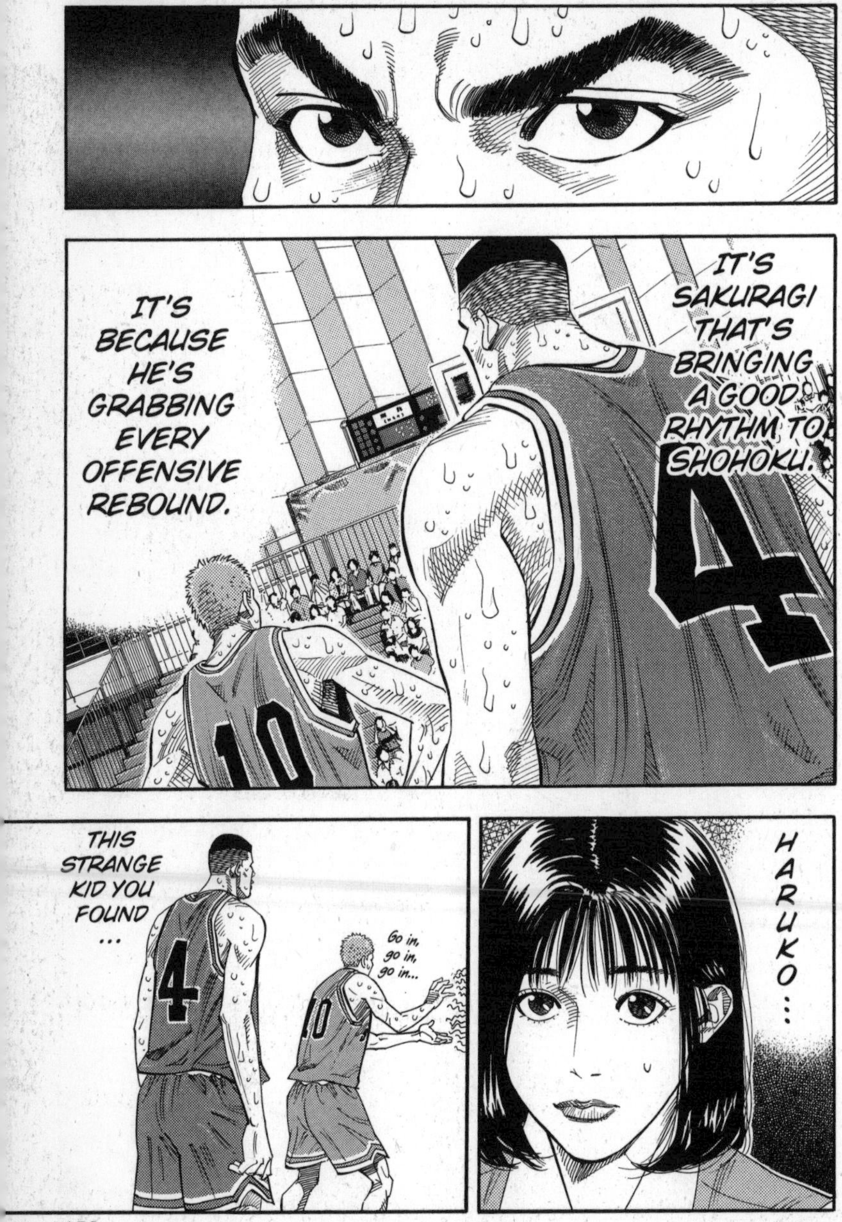

IT'S SAKURAGI THAT'S BRINGING A GOOD RHYTHM TO SHOHOKU.
IT'S BECAUSE HE'S GRABBING EVERY OFFENSIVE REBOUND.
HARUKO...
THIS STRANGE KID YOU FOUND...
Go in, go in, go in...

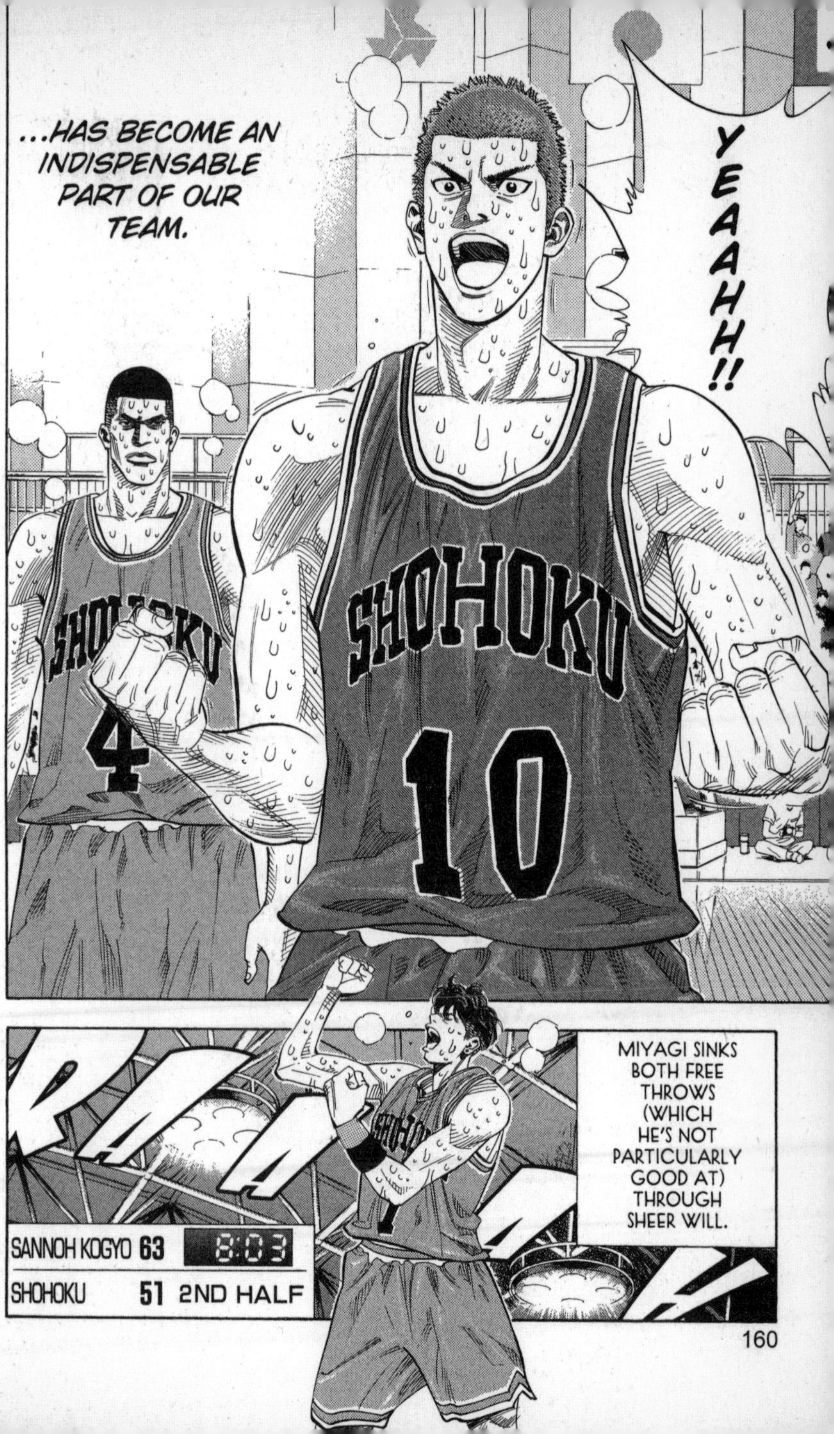
YEAAAHH!!
...HAS BECOME AN INDISPENSABLE PART OF OUR TEAM.
MIYAGI SINKS BOTH FREE THROWS (WHICH HE'S NOT PARTICULARLY GOOD AT) THROUGH SHEER WILL.
SANNOH KOGYO 63
8:03
SHOHOKU 51 2ND HALF

READ THIS WAY

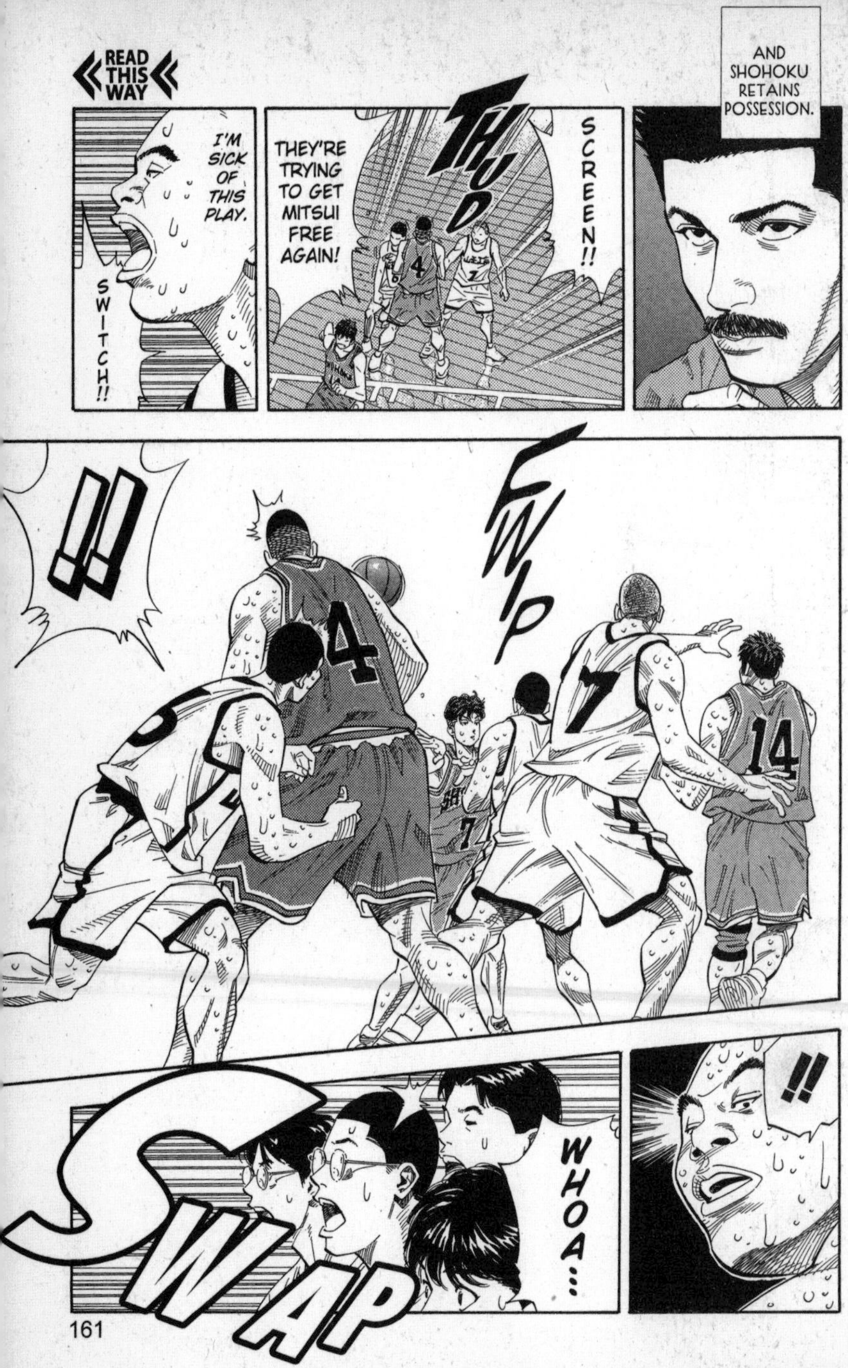
AND SHOHOKU RETAINS POSSESSION.
SCREEN!!
THUD
THEY'RE TRYING TO GET MITSUI FREE AGAIN!
I'M SICK OF THIS PLAY.
SWITCH!!
FWIP
!!
!!
WHOA...
SWAP

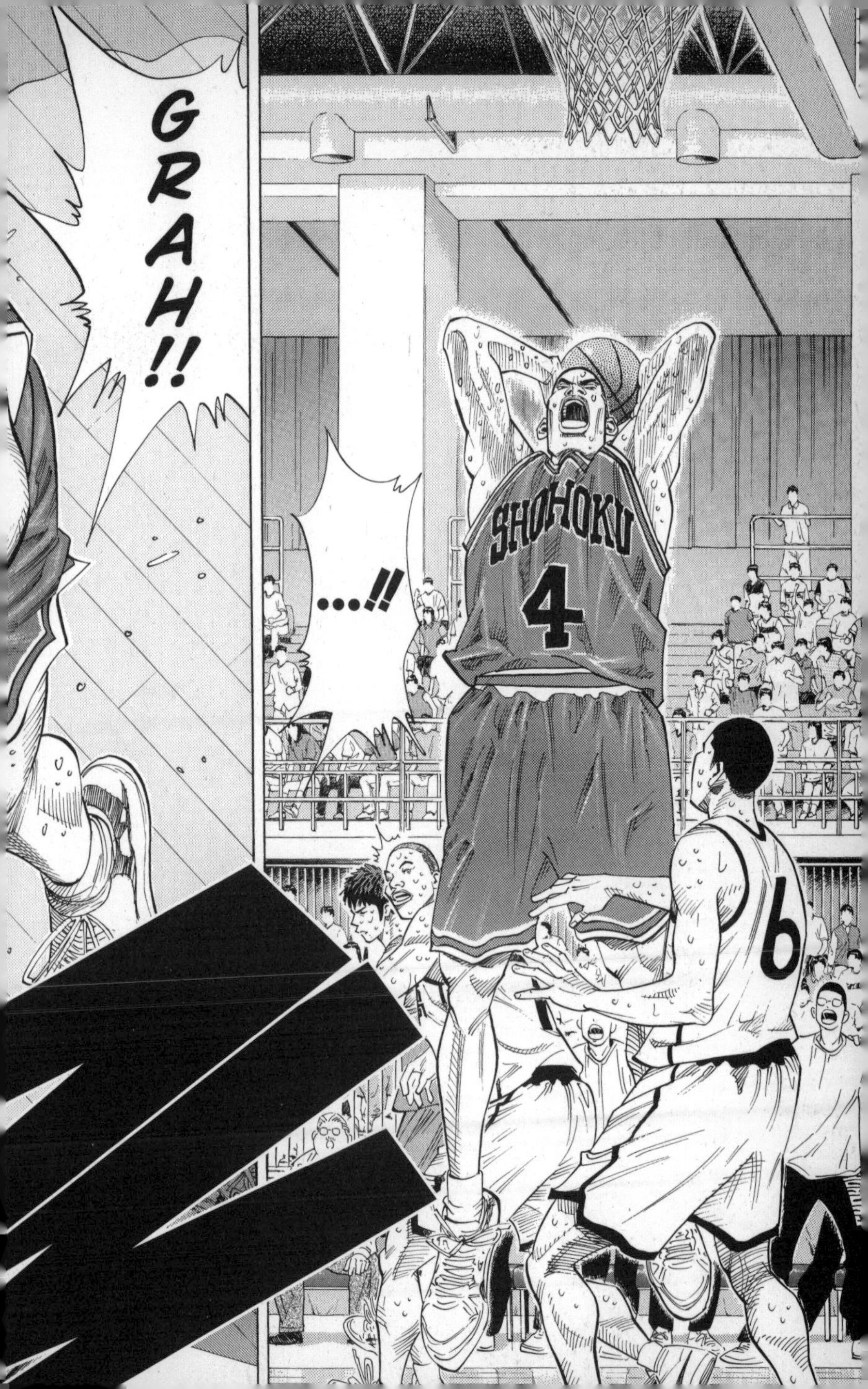
...!!
SHOHOKU
GRAH!!

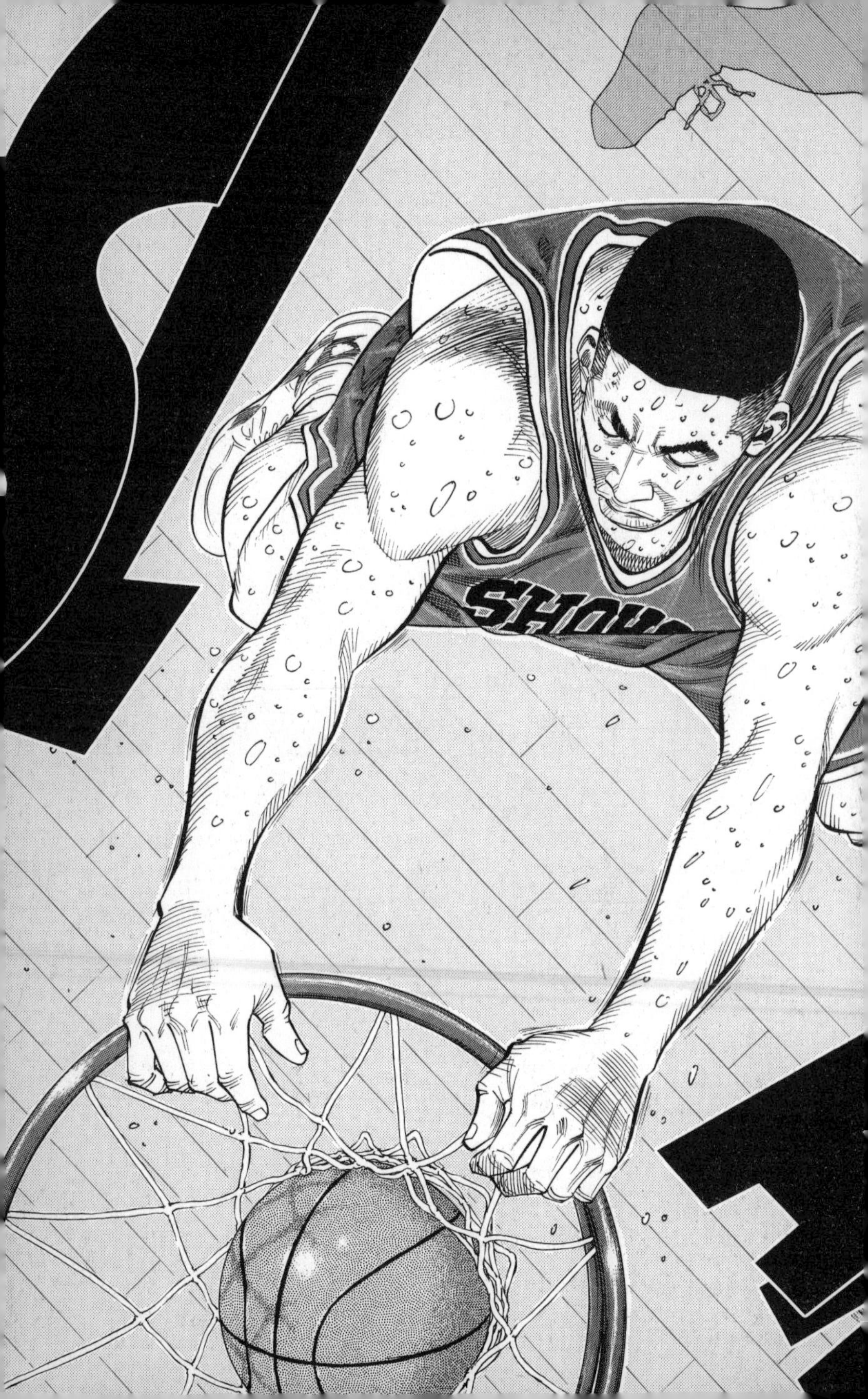

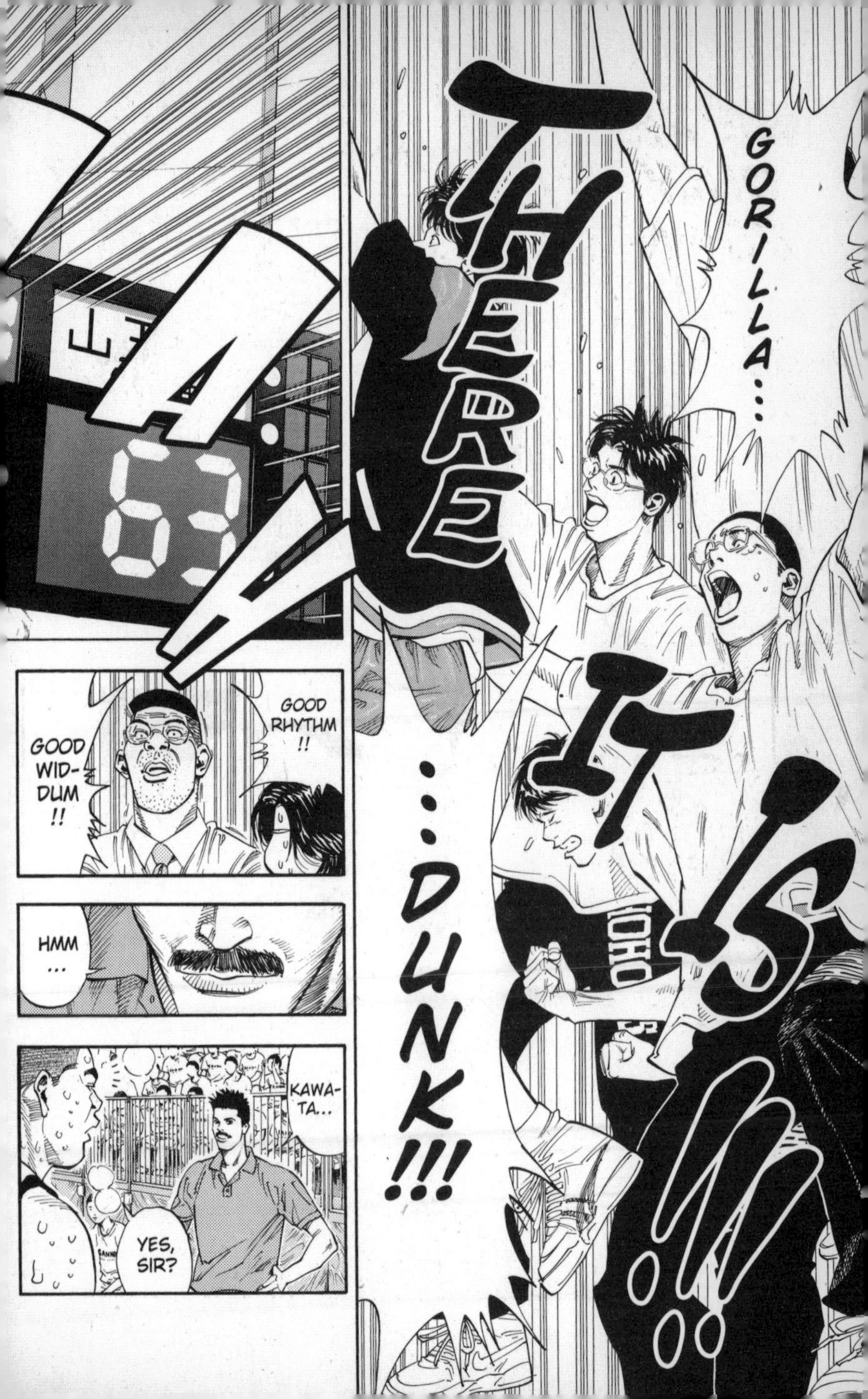
GORILLA...
THERE IT IS!!!
...DUNK!!!
A-!
63
GOOD RHYTHM !!
GOOD WID-DUM !!
HMM ...
KAWA-TA...
YES, SIR?

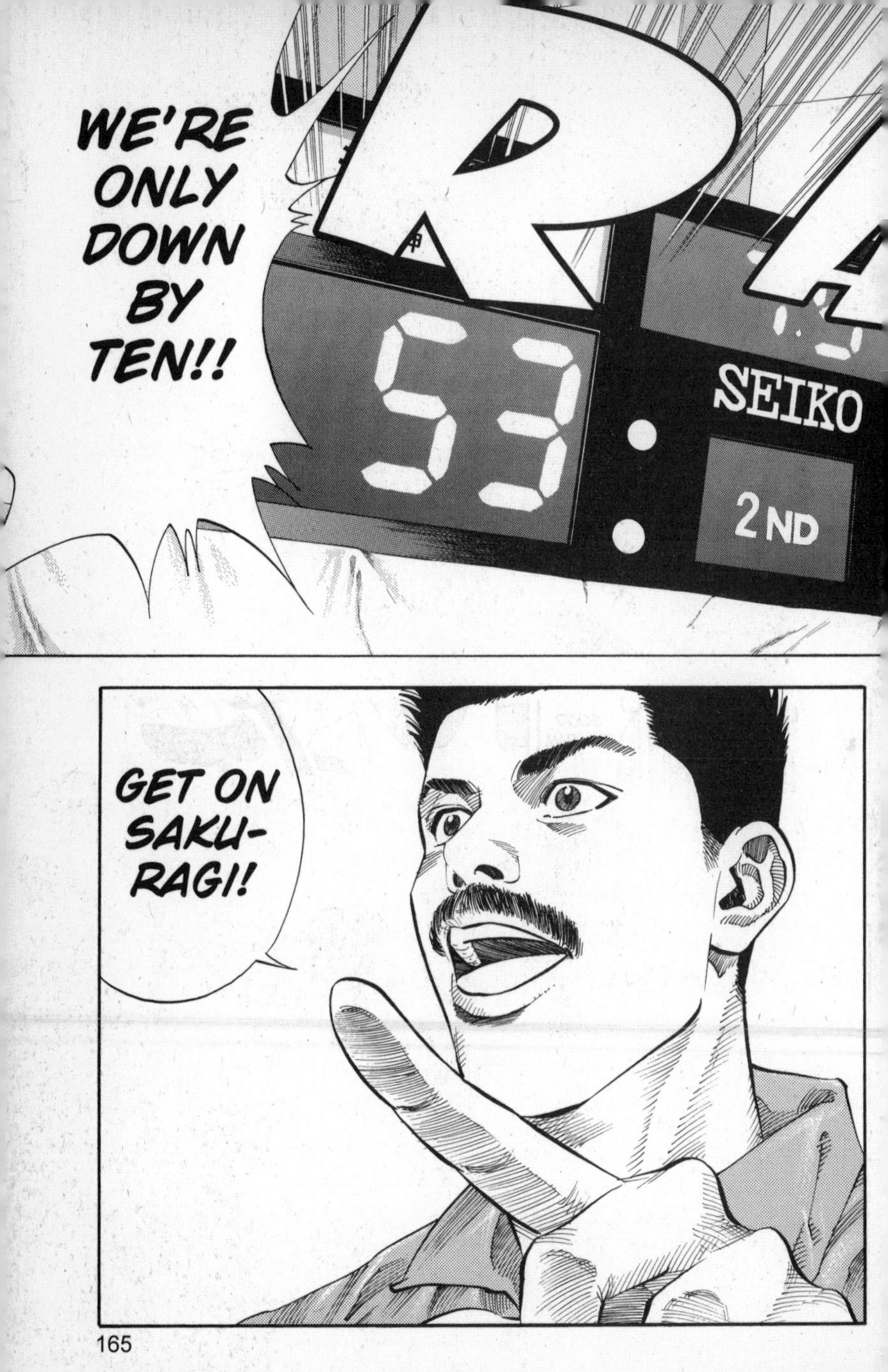
WE'RE ONLY DOWN BY TEN!!
53
SEIKO
2ND
GET ON SAKU-RAGI!

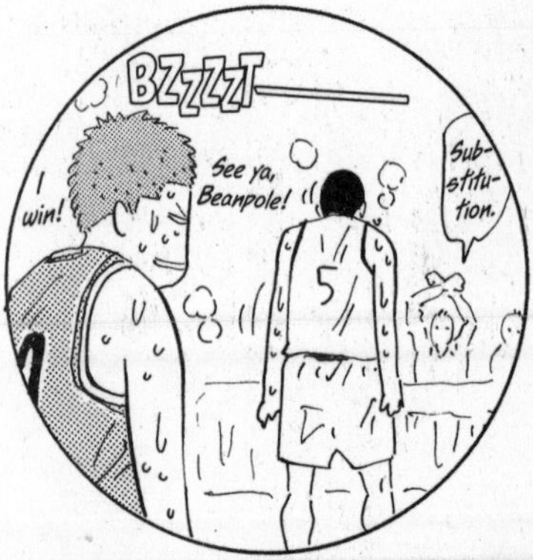
BZZZZT
Sub-stitu-tion.
See ya, Beanpole!
I win!

SLAM DUNK

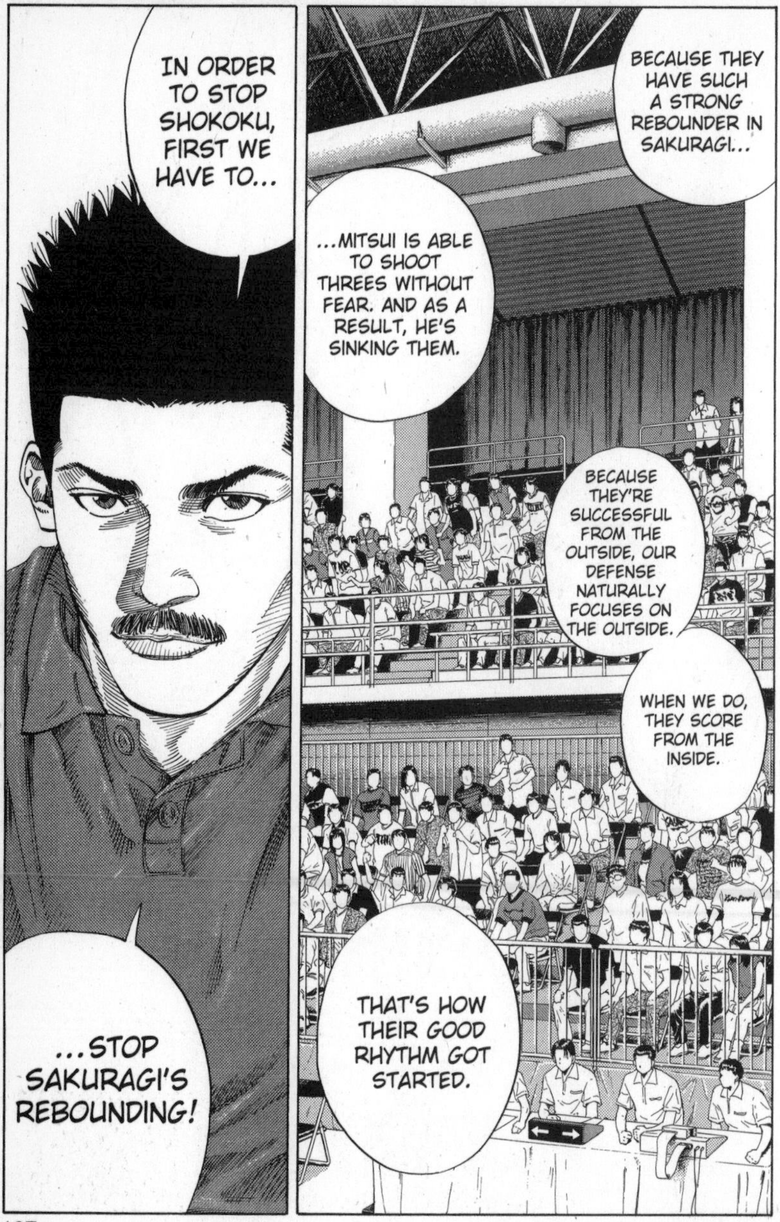
BECAUSE THEY HAVE SUCH A STRONG REBOUNDER IN SAKURAGI...
...MITSUI IS ABLE TO SHOOT THREES WITHOUT FEAR. AND AS A RESULT, HE'S SINKING THEM.
BECAUSE THEY'RE SUCCESSFUL FROM THE OUTSIDE, OUR DEFENSE NATURALLY FOCUSES ON THE OUTSIDE.
WHEN WE DO, THEY SCORE FROM THE INSIDE.
THAT'S HOW THEIR GOOD RHYTHM GOT STARTED.
IN ORDER TO STOP SHOKOKU, FIRST WE HAVE TO...
...STOP SAKURAGI'S REBOUNDING!

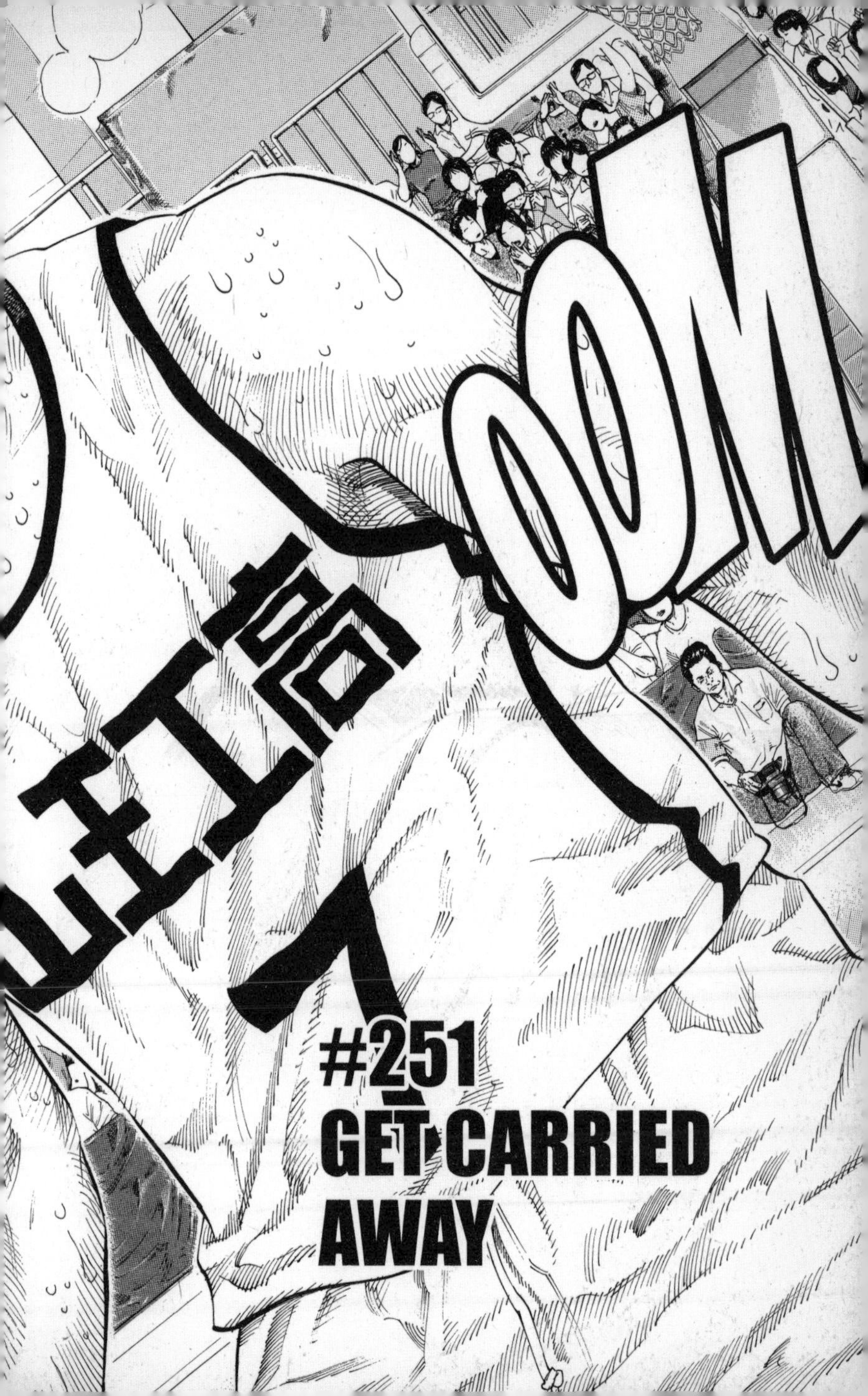
OOM

#251 GET CARRIED AWAY

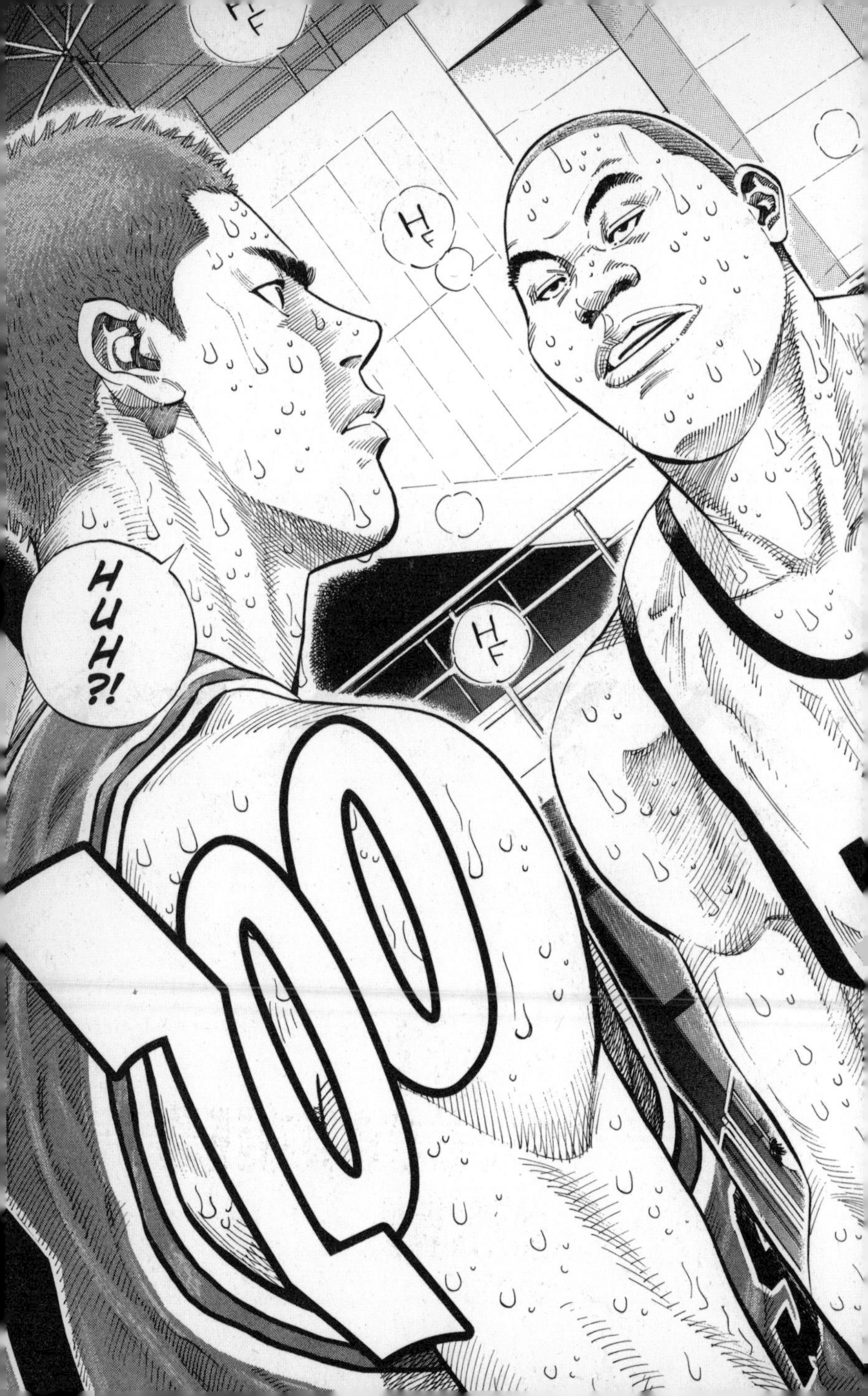
HF
HUH?!
HF

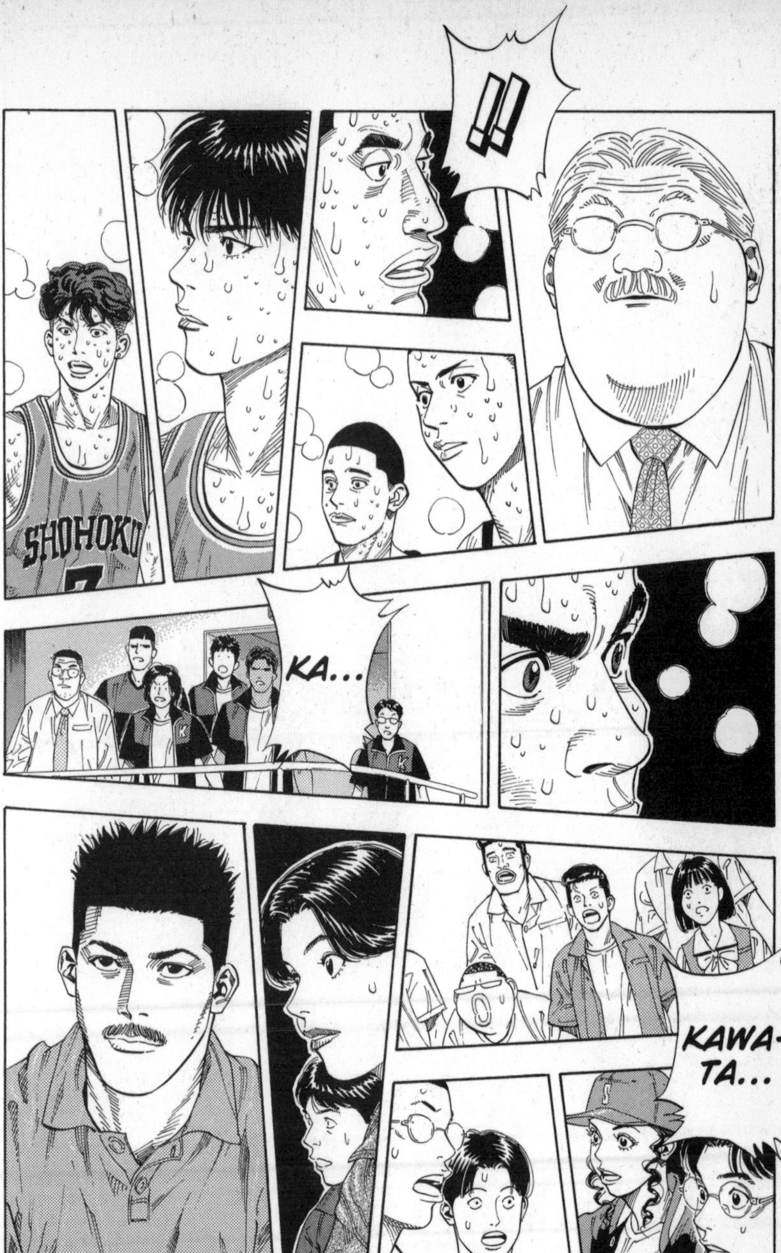
!!
SHOHOKU
KA...
KAWA-TA...

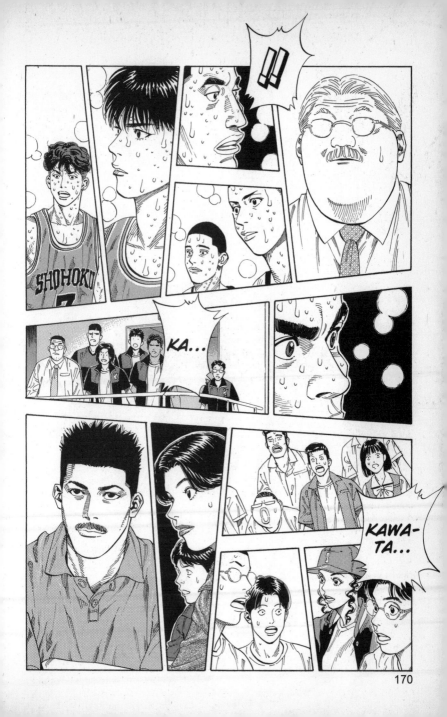

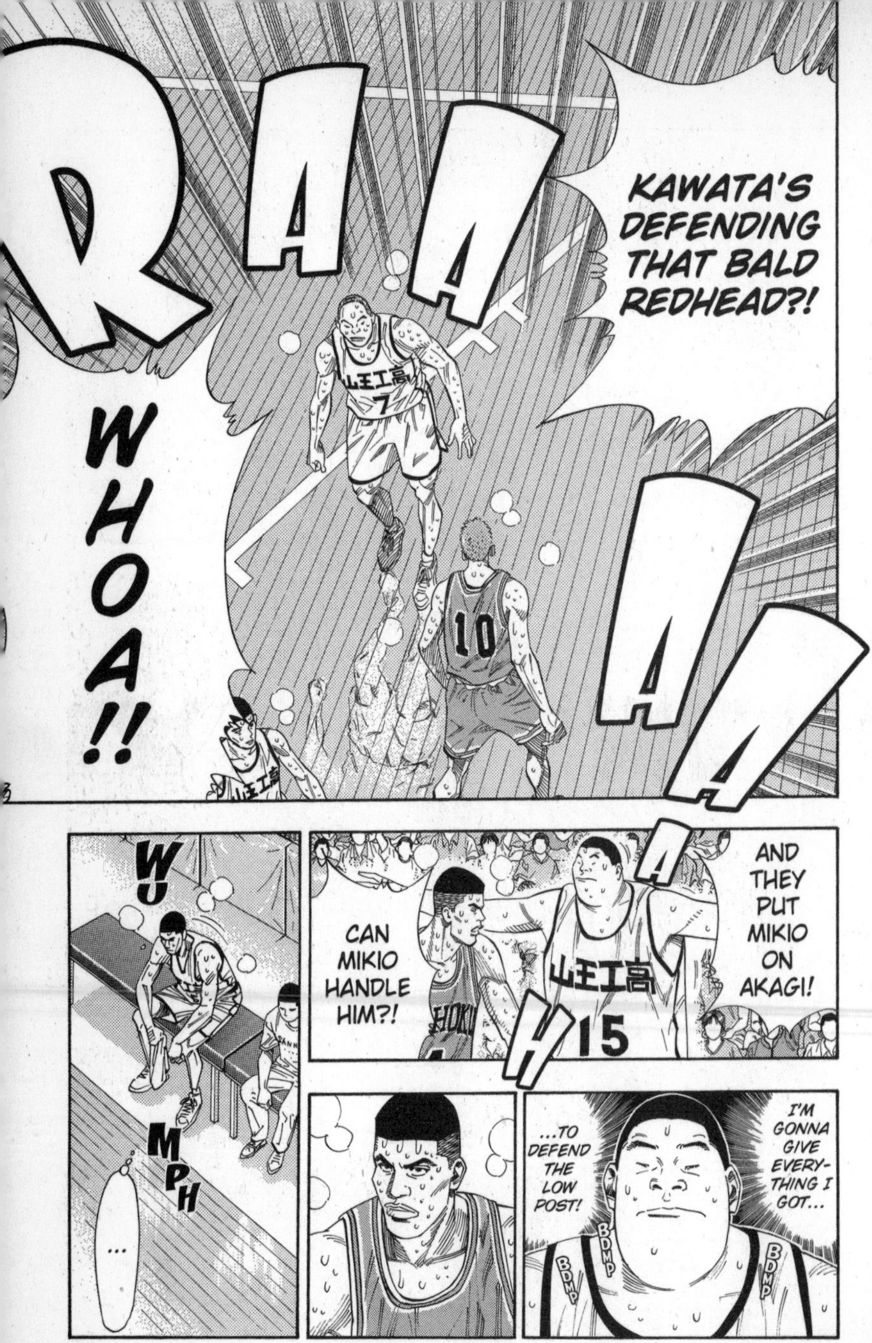
KAWATA'S DEFENDING THAT BALD REDHEAD?!
RAAAAAAAH
WHOA!!
AND THEY PUT MIKIO ON AKAGI!
CAN MIKIO HANDLE HIM?!
I'M GONNA GIVE EVERY-THING I GOT...
...TO DEFEND THE LOW POST!
BDMP
BDMP
BDMP
MPH
...

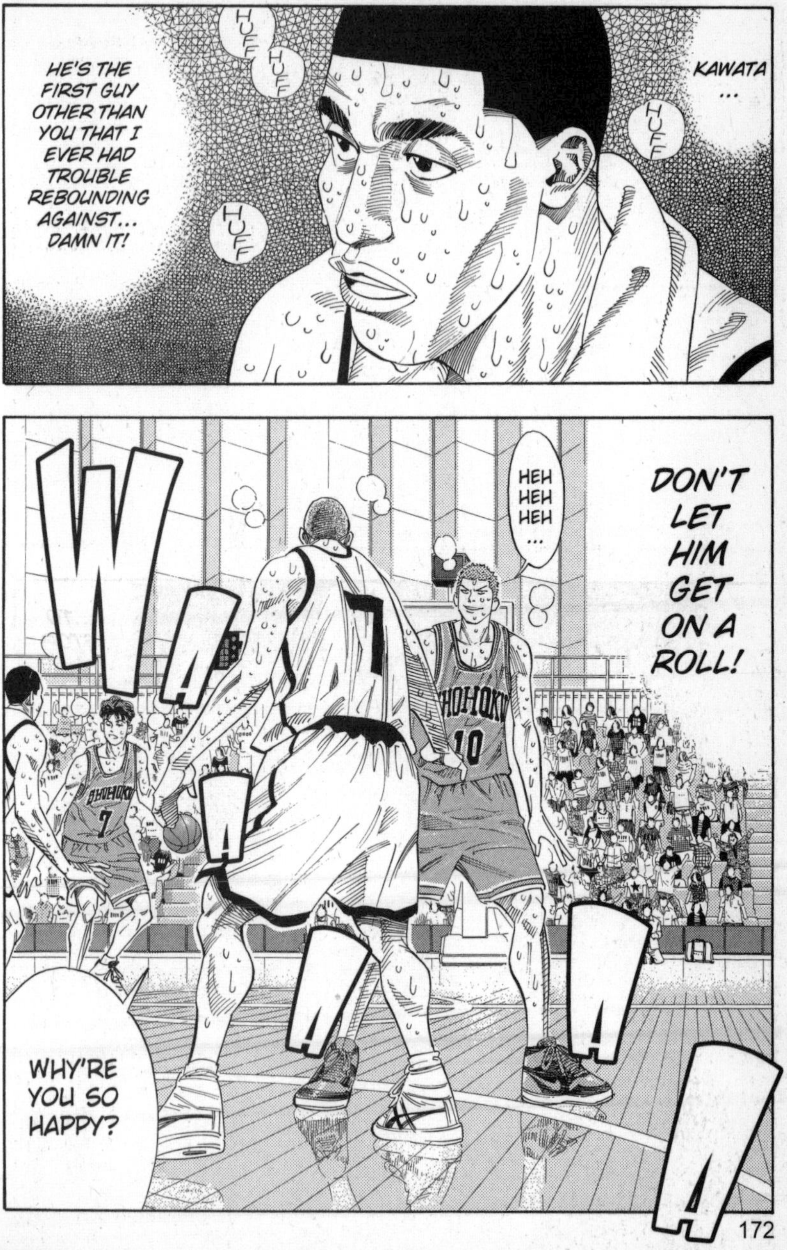
KAWATA ...
HUFF
HUFF HUFF
HUFF
HE'S THE FIRST GUY OTHER THAN YOU THAT I EVER HAD TROUBLE REBOUNDING AGAINST... DAMN IT!
DON'T LET HIM GET ON A ROLL!
HEH HEH HEH ...
WAAAAA
WHY'RE YOU SO HAPPY?

READ THIS WAY

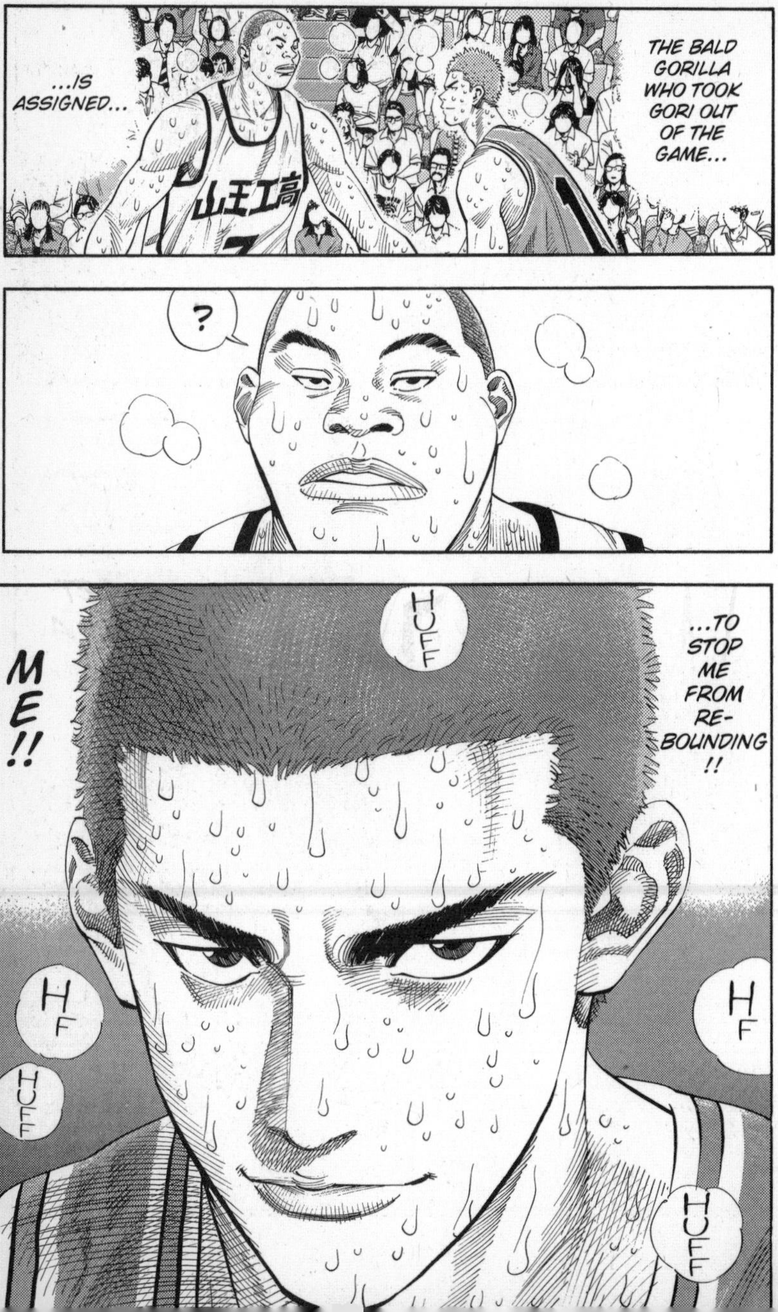
THE BALD GORILLA WHO TOOK GORI OUT OF THE GAME...
...IS ASSIGNED...
山王工高
?
...TO STOP ME FROM RE-BOUNDING!!
HUFF
ME!!
HF
HUFF
HF
HUFF

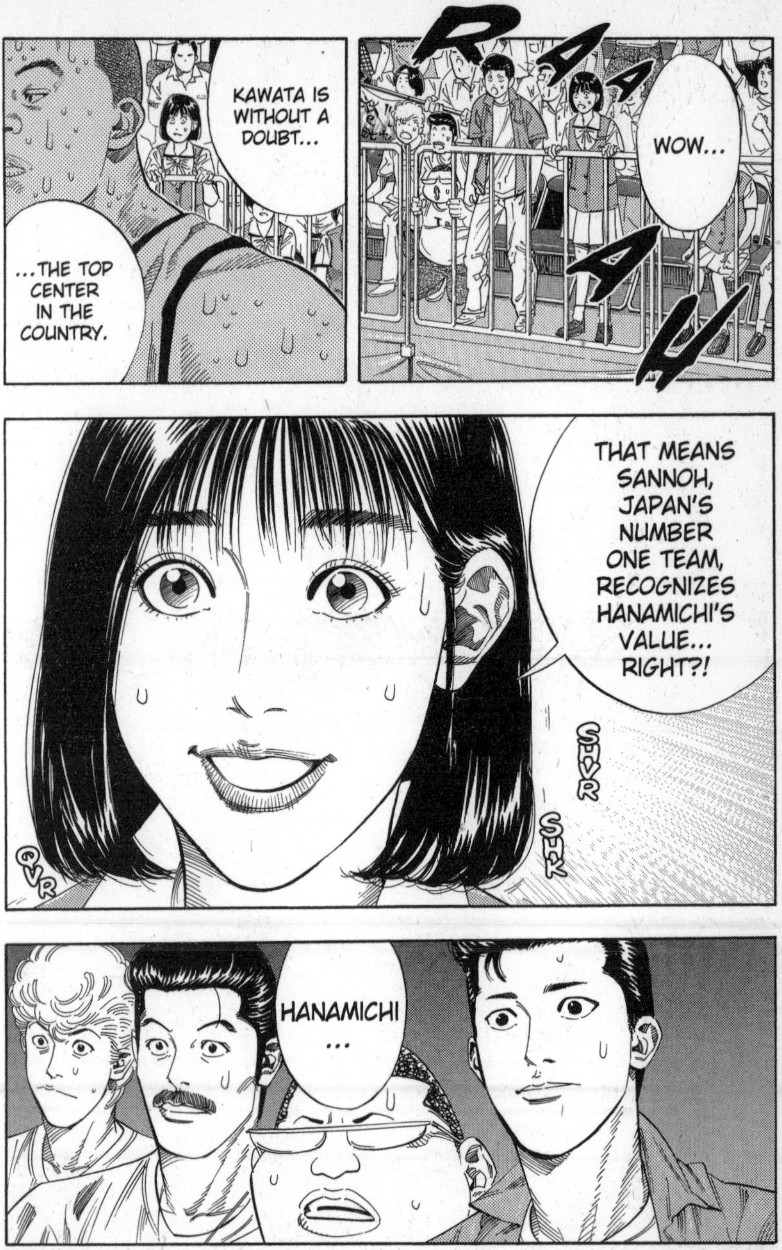
RAAAAH
WOW...
KAWATA IS WITHOUT A DOUBT...
...THE TOP CENTER IN THE COUNTRY.
THAT MEANS SANNOH, JAPAN'S NUMBER ONE TEAM, RECOGNIZES HANAMICHI'S VALUE... RIGHT?!
SHVR
SHK
QVR
HANAMICHI ...

READ THIS WAY

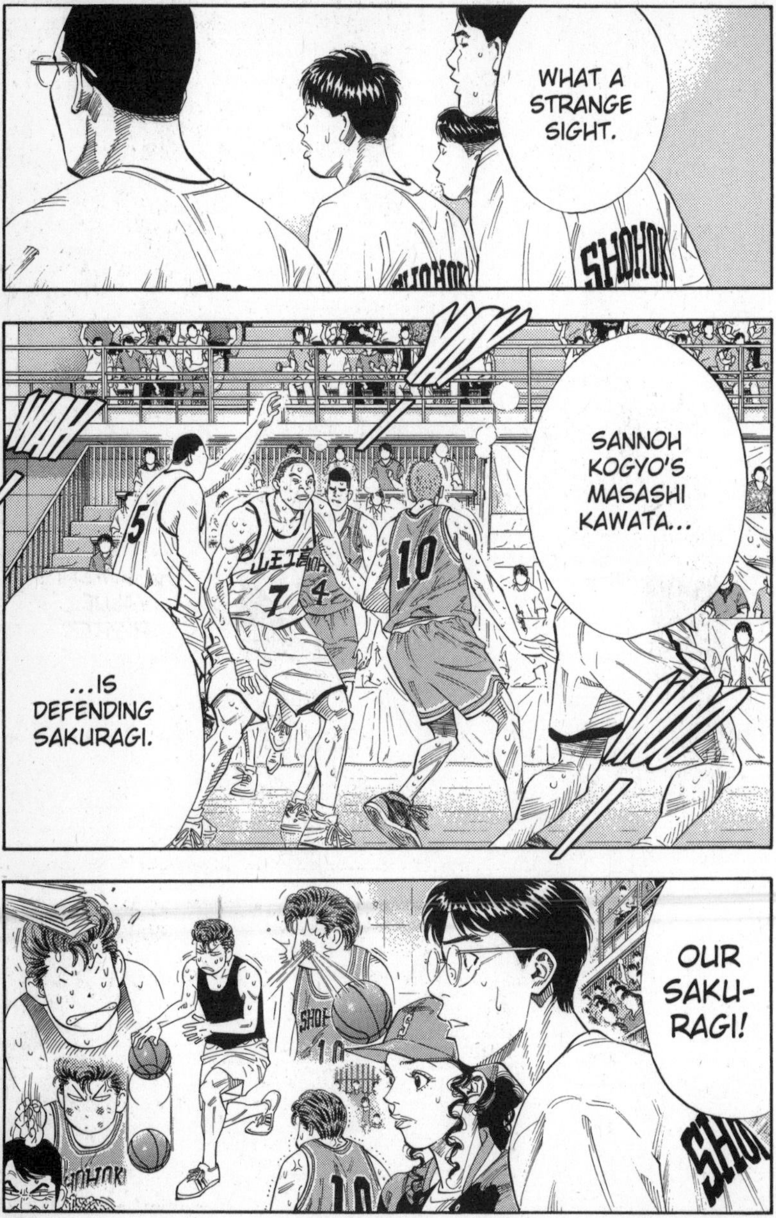
WHAT A STRANGE SIGHT.
WAH
SANNOH KOGYO'S MASASHI KAWATA...
WAH
...IS DEFENDING SAKURAGI.
OUR SAKU-RAGI!

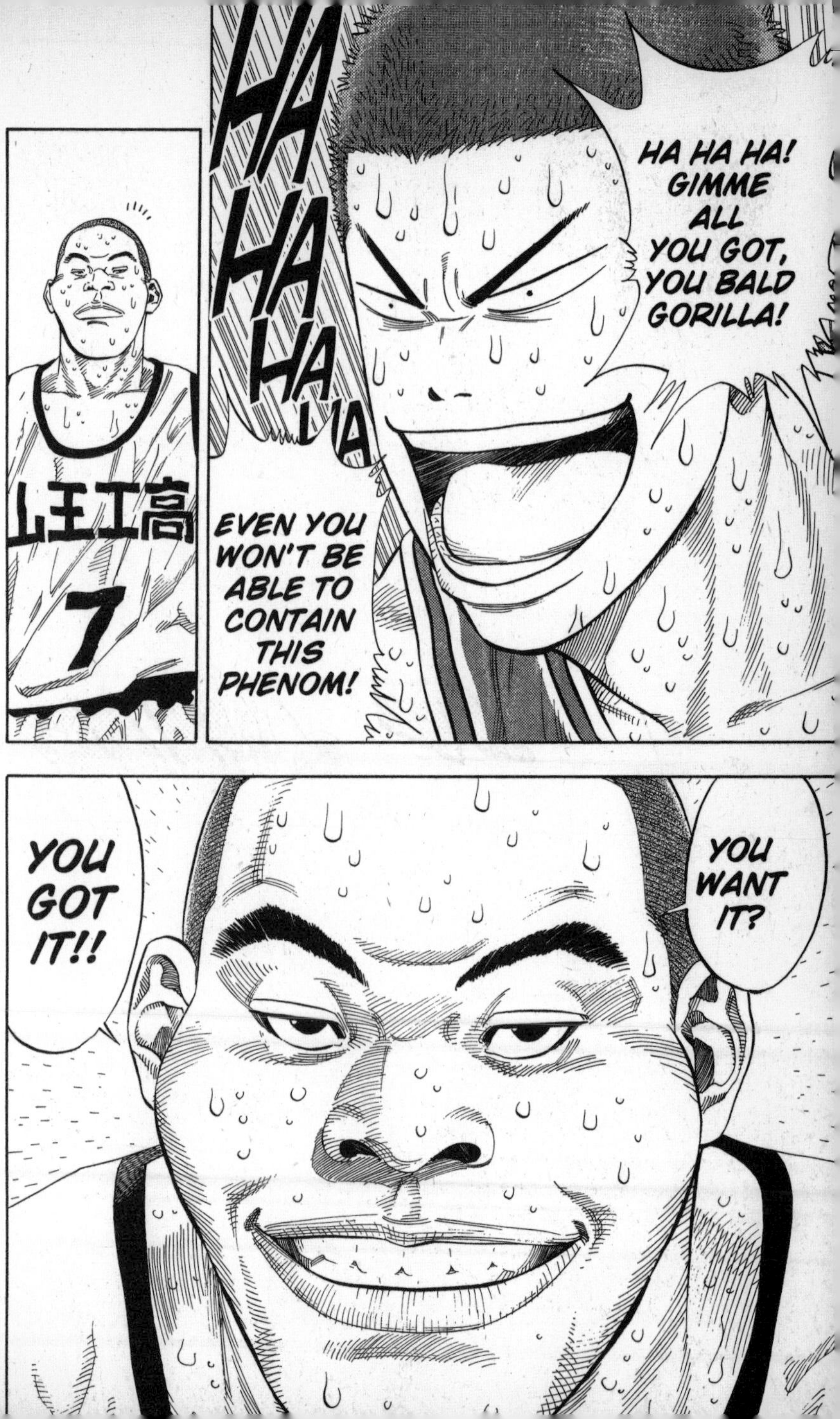
HA HA HA HA
HA HA HA! GIMME ALL YOU GOT, YOU BALD GORILLA!
EVEN YOU WON'T BE ABLE TO CONTAIN THIS PHENOM!
山王工高
7
YOU WANT IT?
YOU GOT IT!!

READ THIS WAY

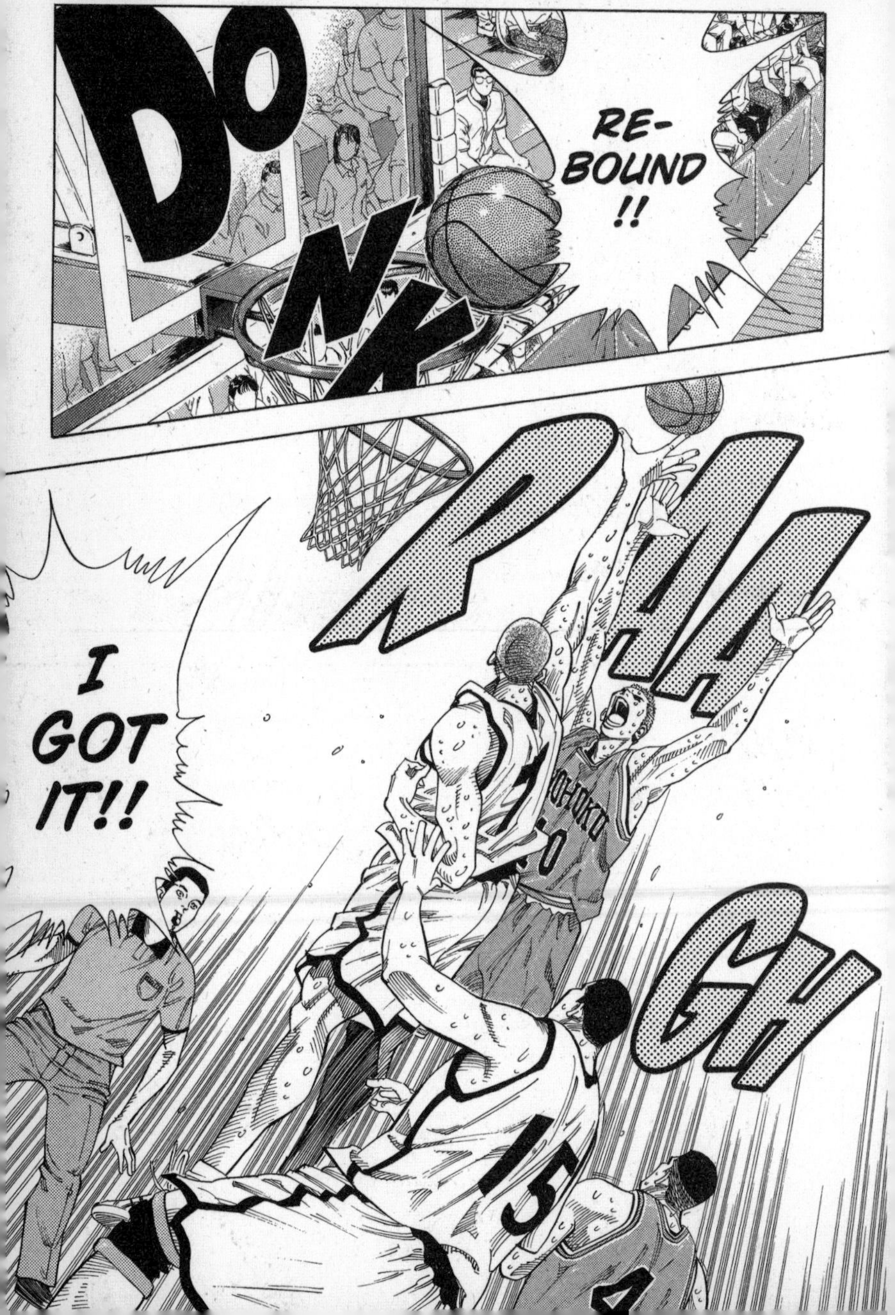

RE-BOUND!!
DONK
RAAGH
I GOT IT!!

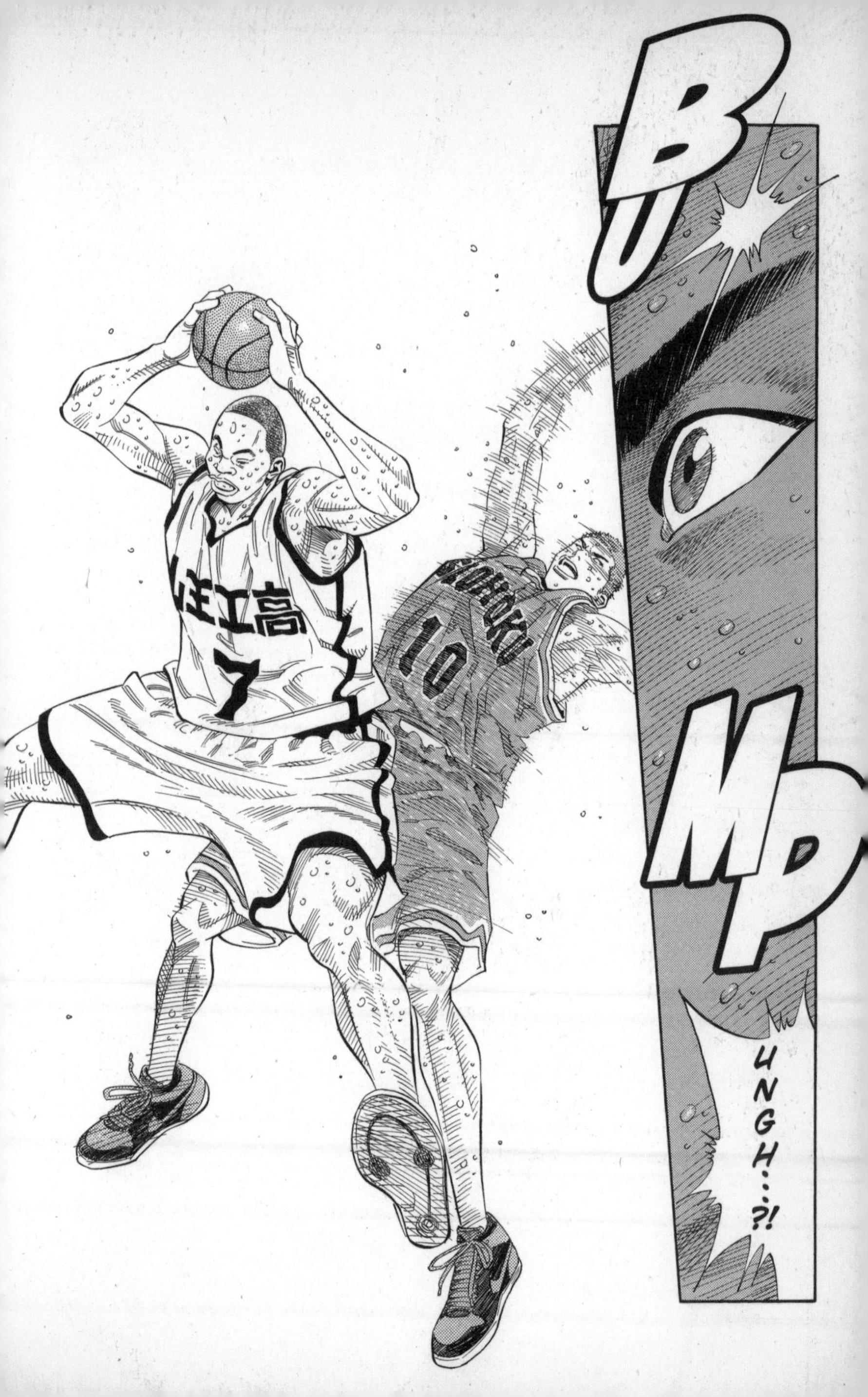
BUMP
UNGH...?!

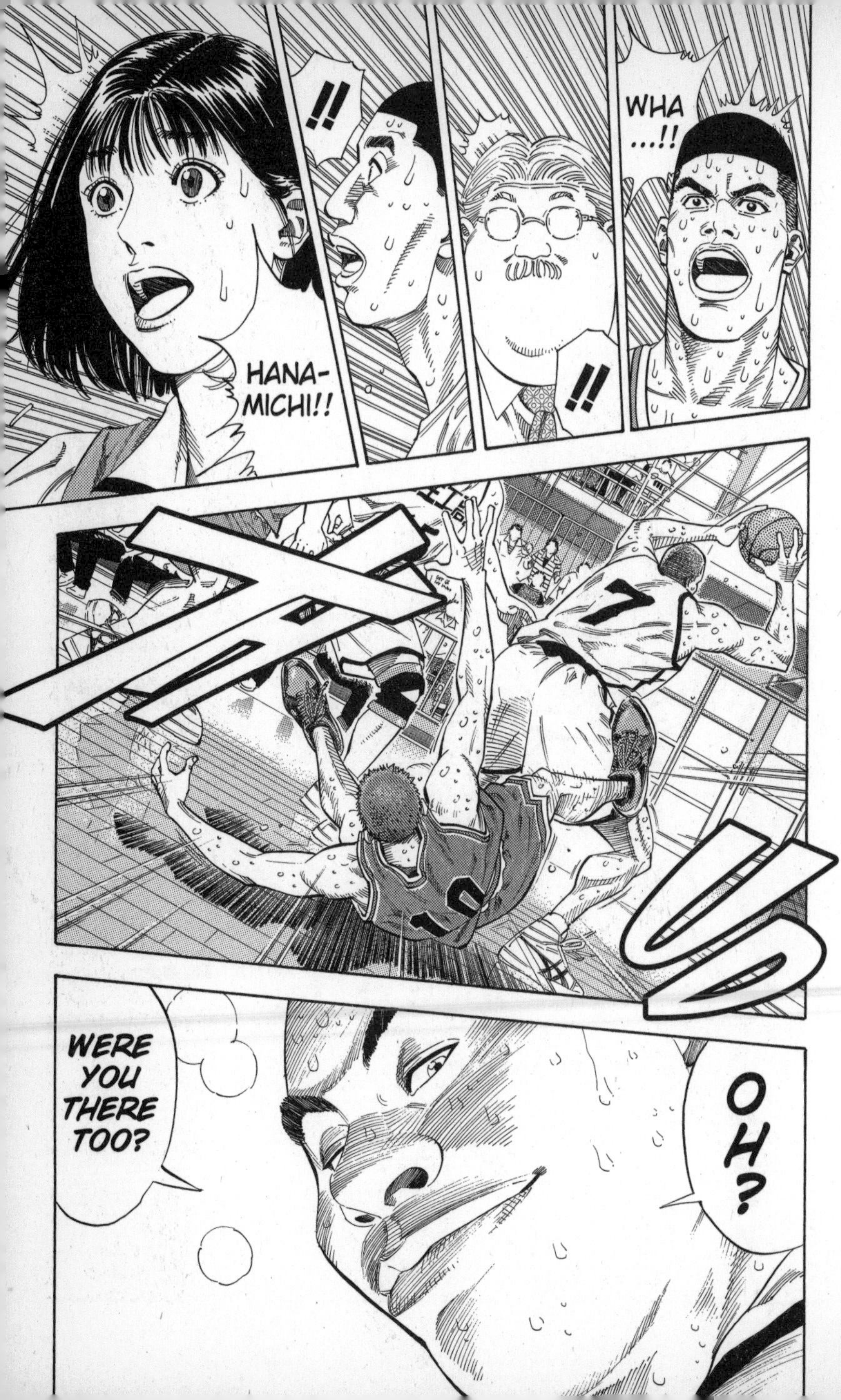
WHA ...!!
!!
!!
HANA-MICHI!!
OH?
WERE YOU THERE TOO?

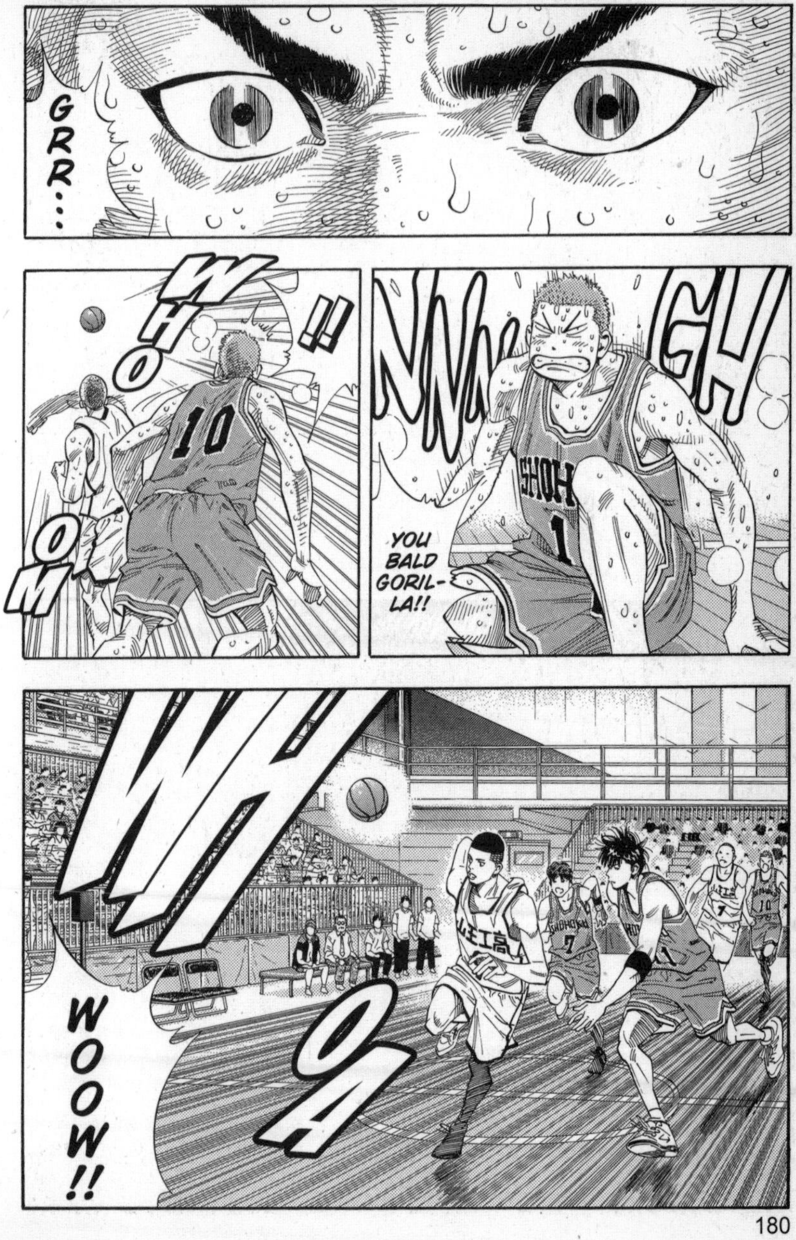
GRR...
NNNGH
YOU BALD GORIL-LA!!
WHOOM!!
WHOA
WOOOW!!

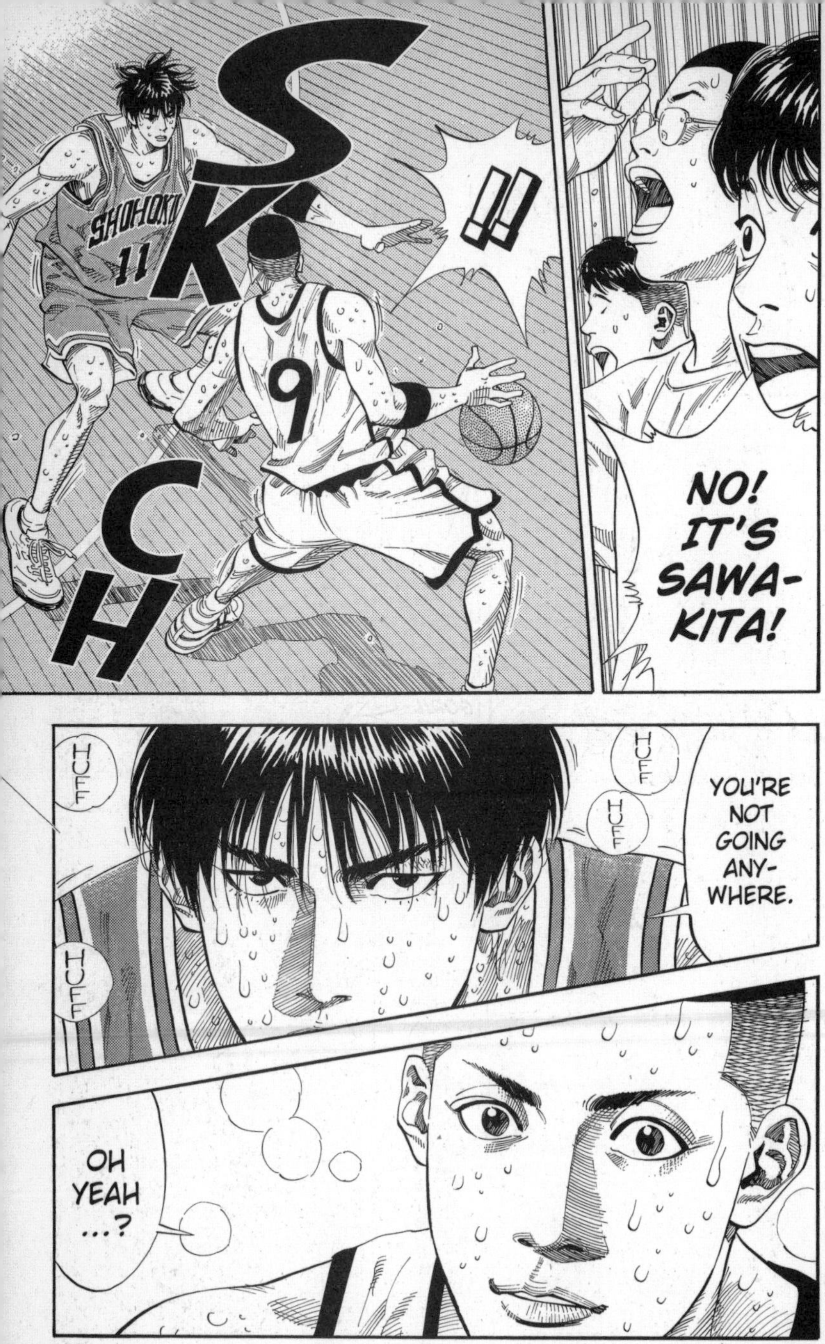
NO! IT'S SAWA-KITA!
SKKCH
!!
YOU'RE NOT GOING ANY-WHERE.
HUFF
HUFF
HUFF
HUFF
OH YEAH ...?

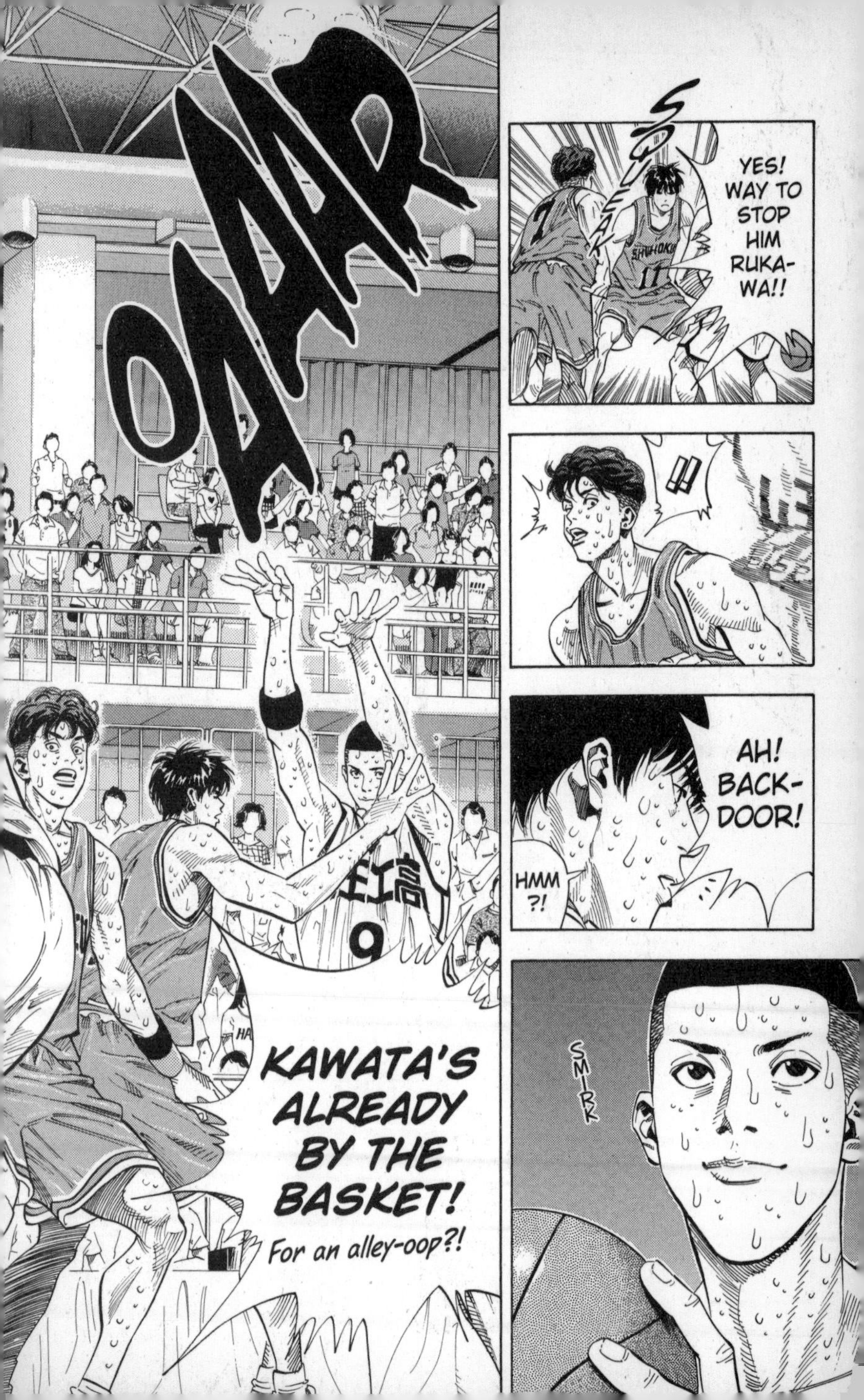
SQUEAK
YES! WAY TO STOP HIM RUKA-WA!!
!!
AH! BACK-DOOR!
HMM ?!
SMIRK
OAAR
KAWATA'S ALREADY BY THE BASKET!
For an alley-oop?!

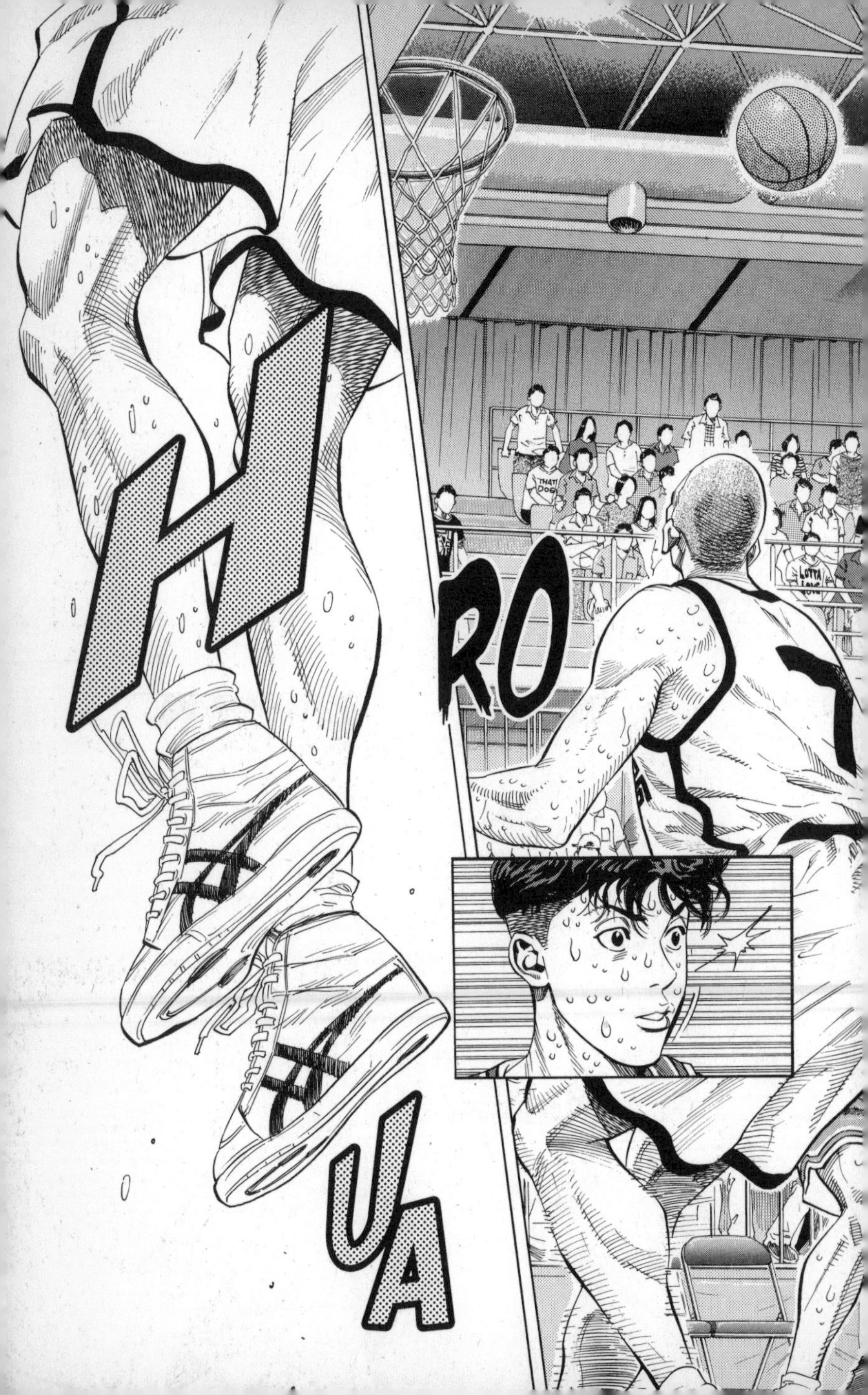
H
RO
UA

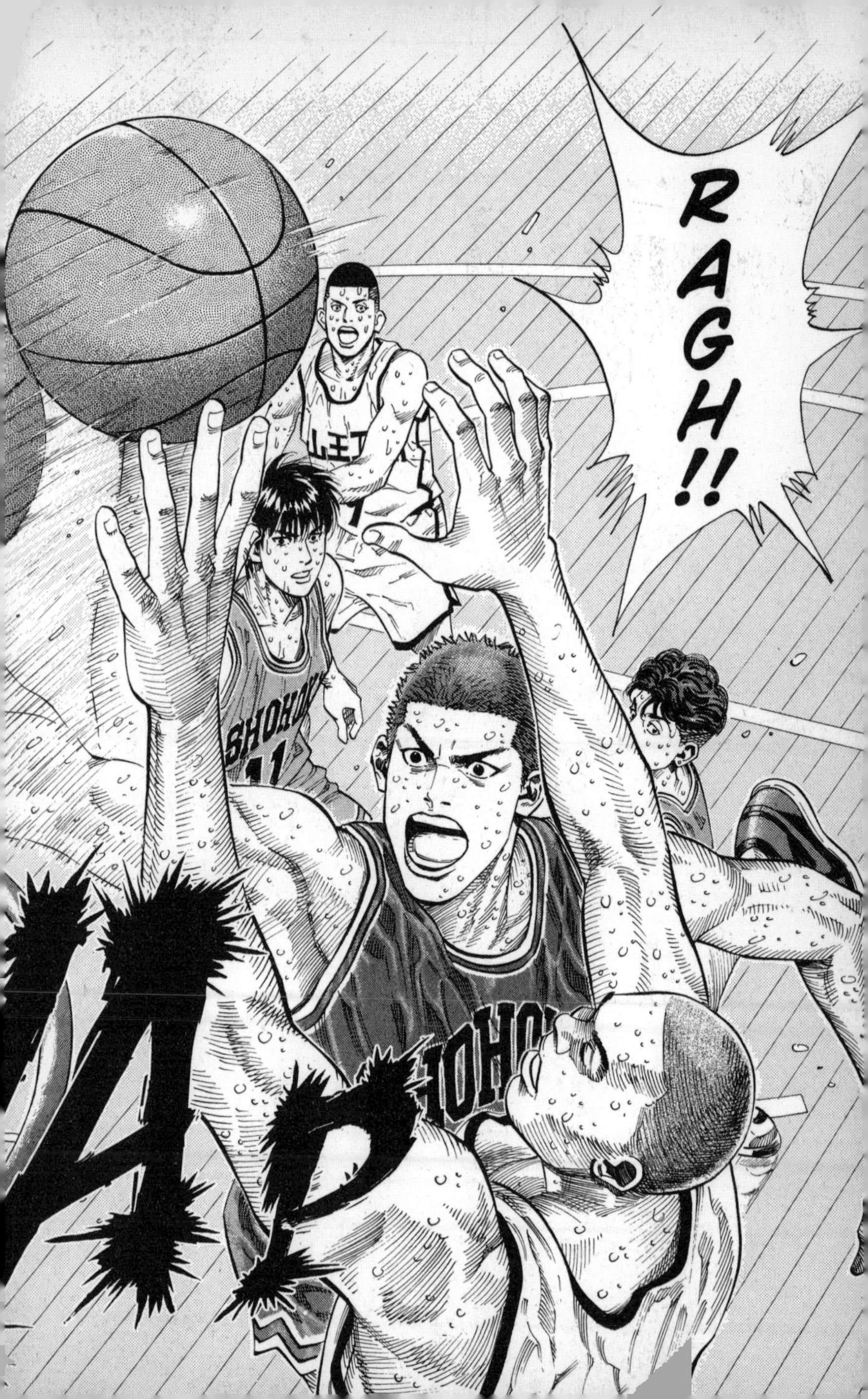
RAGH!!

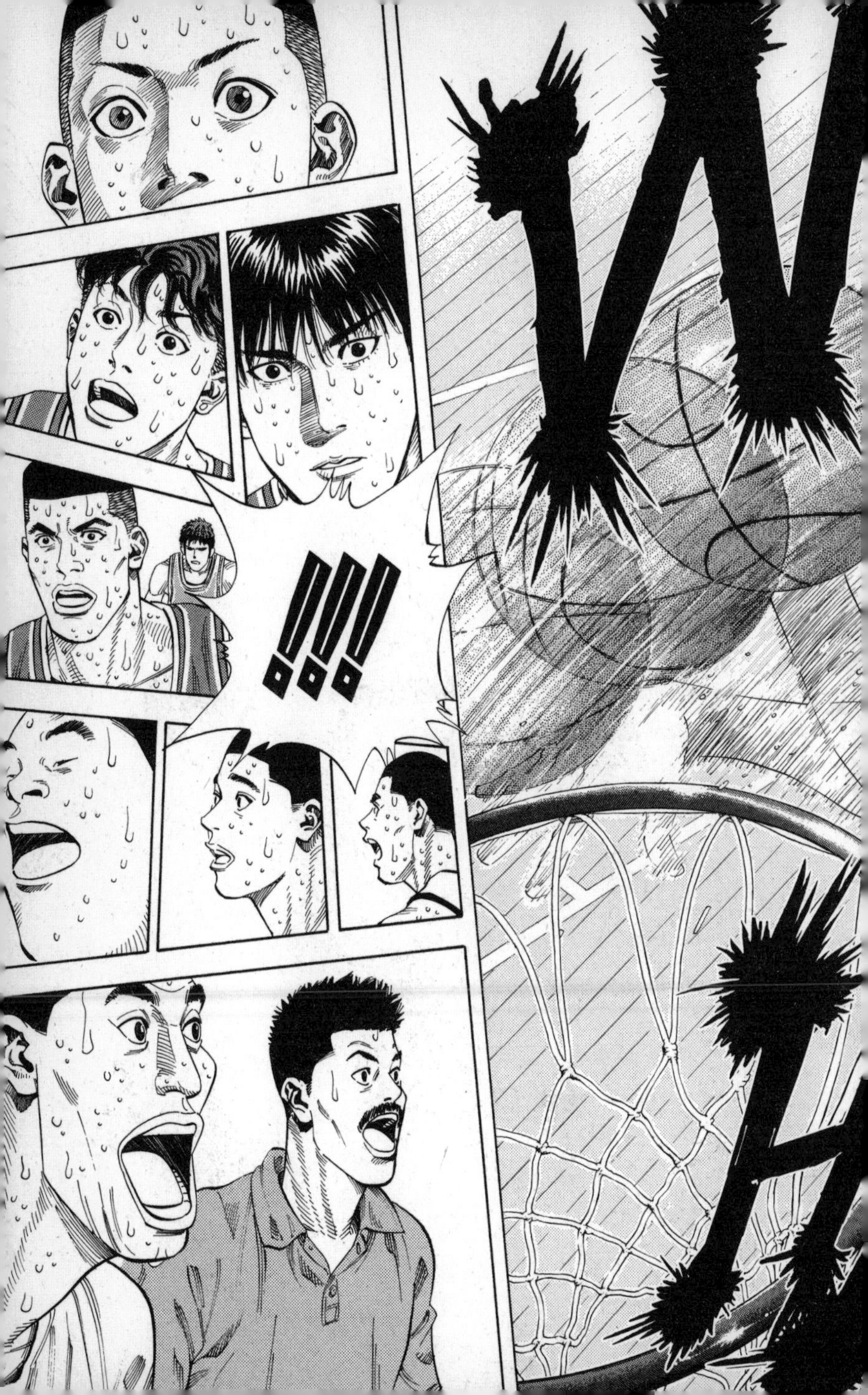
!!!

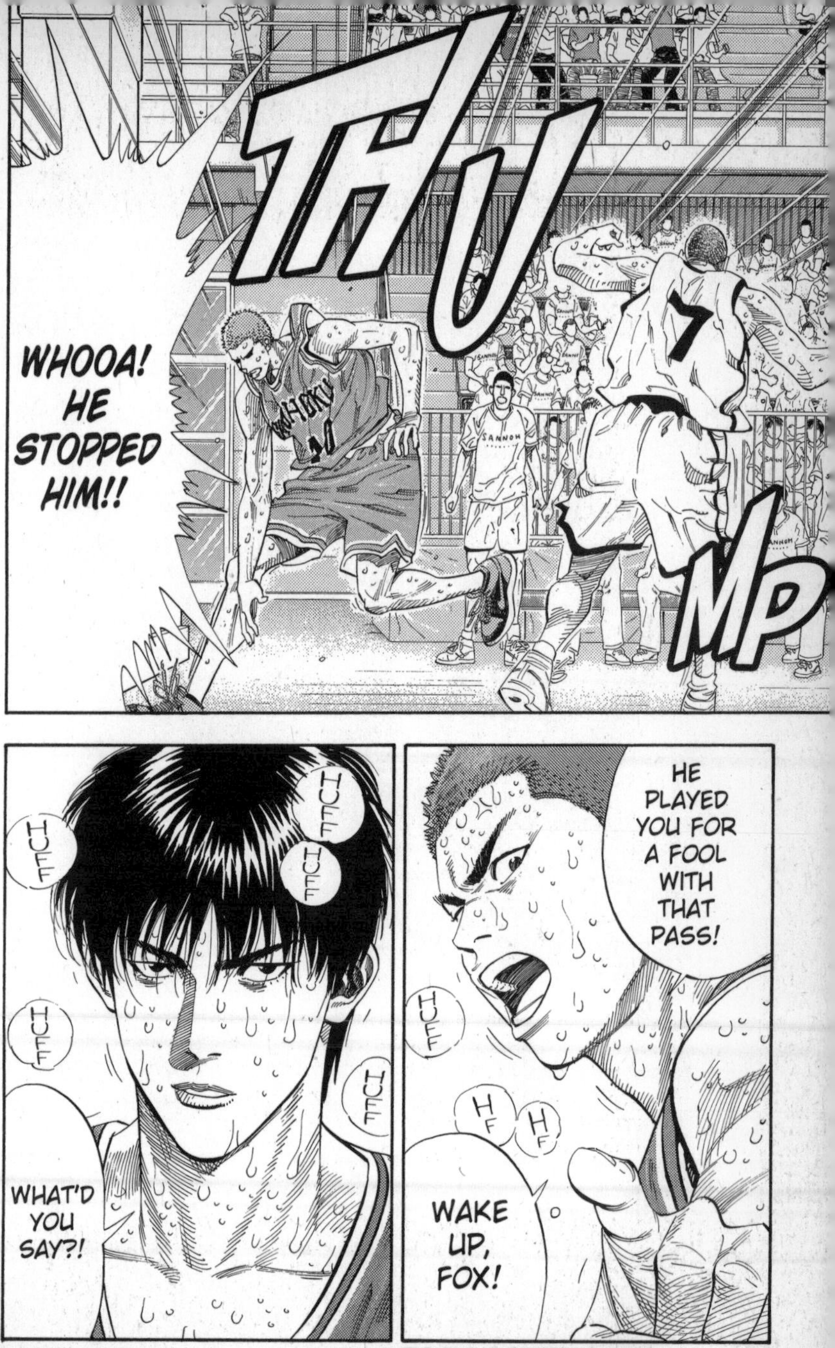
THU
MP
WHOOA! HE STOPPED HIM!!
HE PLAYED YOU FOR A FOOL WITH THAT PASS!
HUFF
HF
HF
WAKE UP, FOX!
HUFF
HUFF
HUFF
HUFF
HUFF
WHAT'D YOU SAY?!

TO BE CONTINUED!

Coming Next Volume

With seven minutes left in the second half, Shohoku slowly chips away at Sannoh's large lead thanks to Sakuragi's rebounds. But Sannoh's star player Sawakita isn't going to sit still for that! Faced with a seemingly unstoppable opponent, Rukawa and Sakuragi both have to dig deep to understand their own game and become the basketball players they were meant to be!

ON SALE AUGUST 2013

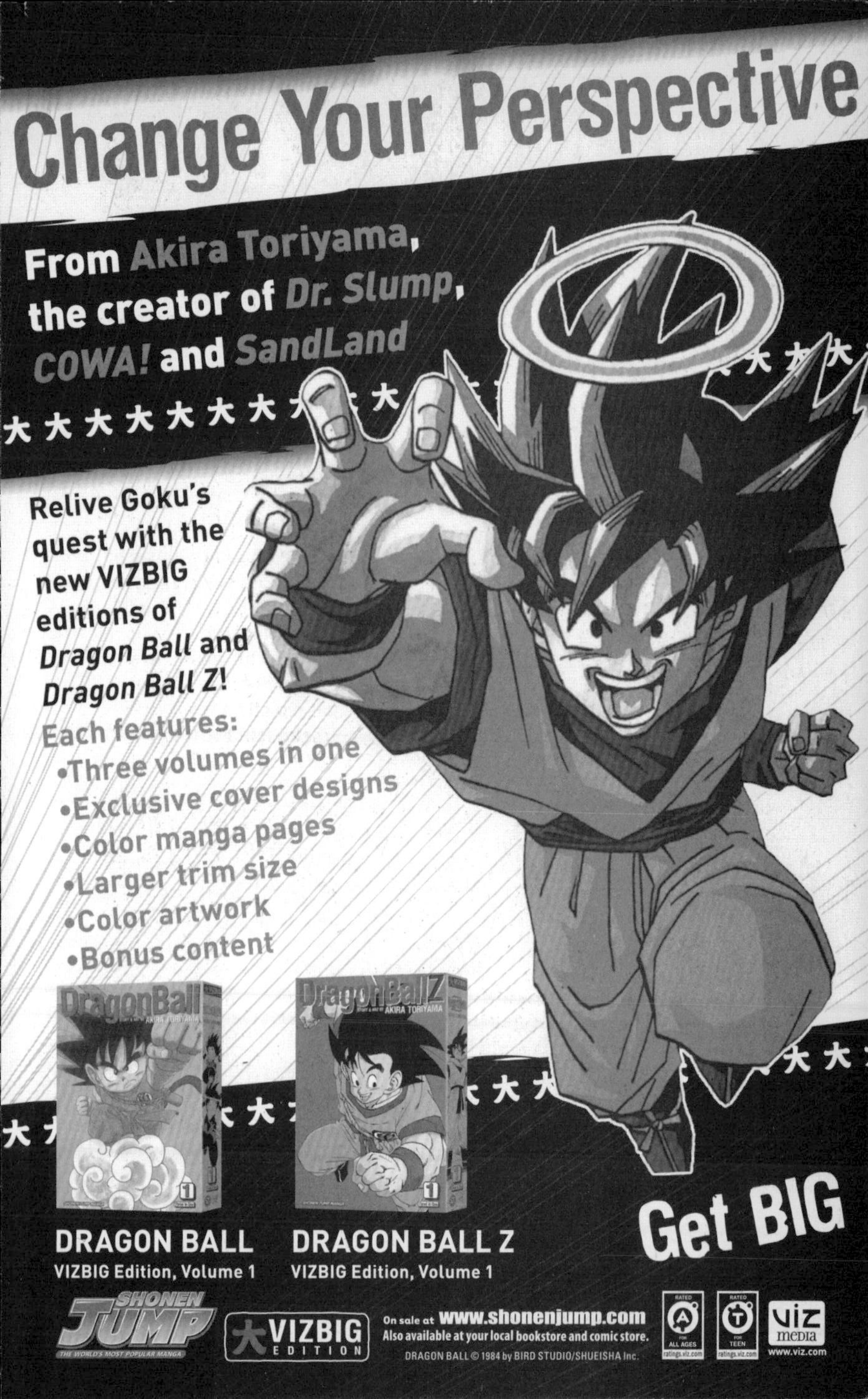
Change Your Perspective
From Akira Toriyama, the creator of Dr. Slump, COWA! and SandLand
Relive Goku's quest with the new VIZBIG editions of Dragon Ball and Dragon Ball Z!
Each features:
•Three volumes in one
•Exclusive cover designs
•Color manga pages
•Larger trim size
•Color artwork
•Bonus content
DRAGON BALL
VIZBIG Edition, Volume 1
DRAGON BALL Z
VIZBIG Edition, Volume 1
Get BIG
SHONEN JUMP
THE WORLD'S MOST POPULAR MANGA
VIZBIG EDITION
On sale at www.shonenjump.com
Also available at your local bookstore and comic store.
DRAGON BALL © 1984 by BIRD STUDIO/SHUEISHA Inc.
RATED A FOR ALL AGES ratings.viz.com
RATED T FOR TEEN ratings.viz.com
viz media
www.viz.com